The Moral Veto

Why have legislative initiatives occurred on such controversial issues as contraception and abortion at times when activist movements had demobilized and the public seemed indifferent? Why did the South – currently a region where antiabortion sentiment is stronger than in most of the country – liberalize its abortion laws in the 1960s at a faster pace than any other region? Why have abortion and contraception sometimes been framed as matters of medical practice, and at other times as matters of moral significance? These are some of the questions addressed in *The Moral Veto: Framing Contraception, Abortion, and Cultural Pluralism in the United States*. Based on archival and sociological research, and speaking to issues in the study of culture, social movements, and legal change, *The Moral Veto* examines what the history of controversies over such morally charged issues tells us about cultural pluralism in the United States.

Gene Burns is an award-winning teacher and associate professor of public affairs at James Madison College of Michigan State University. A sociologist by training, he is the author of *The Frontiers of Catholicism: The Politics of Ideology in a Liberal World*, a *New York Times* Notable Book of the Year in 1993. He has written articles on social movements, revolutions, and the politics of religion in the *American Journal of Sociology*, *Theory and Society*, *Sociology of Religion*, and other journals.

The Moral Veto

Framing Contraception, Abortion, and Cultural Pluralism in the United States

GENE BURNS
James Madison College
of Michigan State University

CAMBRIDGE
UNIVERSITY PRESS

CAMBRIDGE UNIVERSITY PRESS
Cambridge, New York, Melbourne, Madrid, Cape Town, Singapore, São Paulo

Cambridge University Press
40 West 20th Street, New York, NY 10011-4211, USA

www.cambridge.org
Information on this title: www.cambridge.org/9780521552097

First published 2005

Printed in the United States of America

A catalog record for this publication is available from the British Library.

Library of Congress Cataloging in Publication Data

Burns, Gene, 1958–
The moral veto : framing contraception, abortion, and cultural pluralism in the
United States / Gene Burns.
     p.   cm.
Includes bibliographical references and index.
ISBN 0-521-55209-5 (hardback) – ISBN 0-521-60984-4 (pbk.)
    1. Social values – United States.   2. Culture conflict – United States.   3. Pluralism
(Social sciences) – United States.   4. Abortion – Social aspects – United States.
5. Contraception – Social aspects – United States.   I. Title.
HN90.M6B87   2005
363.9′6′0973–dc22   2005000120

ISBN-13   978-0-521-55209-7 hardback
ISBN-10   0-521-55209-5 hardback

ISBN-13   978-0-521-60984-5 paperback
ISBN-10   0-521-60984-4 paperback

For Fred Block and Steve Warner, wonderful teachers

Contents

Acknowledgments   *page* ix

1   Introduction   1

2   Framing Contraception within Moral Worldviews:
    The Early, Radical Birth Control Movement   29

3   The Mainstreaming of Birth Control: A New Alliance
    with Eugenics and Medicine   69

4   Dennett's Moral Worldview and the Catholic Moral
    Veto: Unsuccessful Frames for Contraception   106

5   Abortion before Controversy: Quiet Reform within a
    Medical, Humanitarian Frame   150

6   Abortion and Legislative Stalemate: The Weakness and
    Strength of the Medical, Humanitarian Frame   207

7   Looking Back: Limiting Frames, Moral Vetoes, and
    Cultural Pluralism   244

Works Cited   315
Index   331

Acknowledgments

Although we academic authors often labor in a fair amount of obscurity, one advantage of writing a second book is that the author is not quite so obscure as during the writing of the first and so more easily connects with many helpful colleagues. Thus I had an opportunity to talk with many people about this project and fear that I may have lost track of a few names. One example is the very friendly and knowledgeable scholar from California whom I met over file drawers at the Library of Congress and who shared with me his impressive knowledge of Mary Ware Dennett and the suffrage movement; I never learned his name. More specifically, I would like to thank, first of all, the generosity of the Annenberg Scholars Program at the Annenberg School for Communication, University of Pennsylvania, where I spent the 1995–96 year on a fellowship. Elihu Katz, an impressively wide-ranging thinker, provided everything one could want in terms of intellectual stimulation and moral support. I also gained a great deal, both intellectually and personally, from my colleagues David Buckingham, Michael Griffin, and Dona Schwartz. I would like to extend special thanks to Barbara Grabias and Crispin Sartwell.

A number of scholars commented on parts of the project and led me to valuable scholarly literatures, including Nicola Beisel, Paul Burstein, Miguel Centeno, Michele Dillon, Paul DiMaggio, Frank Dobbin, John H. Evans, David Garrow, Stephen Hart, Ted Jelen, Carole Joffe, Beverly Lozano, Jon Christopher Pennington, Leslie Woodcock Tentler, Maureen R. Waller, Susan Watkins, and Mary C. Wright. Colleagues at Northwestern University, Loyola University of Chicago, the University of California at Davis, Wellesley College, Franklin and Marshall College, American University, and the University of Pittsburgh provided very helpful feedback to my presentations at their institutions. I also received generous assistance from archivists and librarians at the Schlesinger Library of Radcliffe College, the Sophia Smith Collection of Smith College, and, especially, the Library of Congress, whose collections are an invaluable resource. I am indebted also to Constance Chen, for sharing with me her deep knowledge of the life and career of Mary Ware Dennett. The most admirable and unusual college in which I teach now, James Madison College of Michigan State University, has also been a highly supportive environment. Special thanks to Katherine O'Sullivan See and Kenneth Waltzer for comments on the manuscript that became this book, and to Norm Graham and Sherm Garnett for being such supportive colleagues. I also thank the wonderful students of James Madison for pushing me to think and express myself more clearly, especially those in a senior seminar who read part of this work in manuscript form.

A number of other scholars have been important intellectual and personal influences. I have been very fortunate to know a number of good people, including Bill D'Antonio, Scott Appleby, Jim Davidson, Roger Finke, Jim Jasper, Ruth Wallace, and Mary Jo Weaver. Viviana Zelizer went beyond the call of duty in her professional support. John Noakes and Braulio Muñoz remain special friends and intellectual soul mates. And special thanks go to Kristin Luker.

My thanks also to Ed Parsons, Anoop Chaturvedi, Elizabeth Neal, Mary Child, and Malinda Barrett of Cambridge University Press, and the Press as a whole. It has been a delight to publish this book with Cambridge.

I cannot express enough the importance of my wife, Alison Hirschel, and our wonderful children, Danny, Timmy, and Nicky, for adding so much to life.

Finally, I would like to thank two scholars who are among the finest people I have ever known. Fred Block was my dissertation advisor back in graduate school and continues to provide friendship and unmatched insight. Fred inspires unusual devotion and affection from his students not because he seeks it, but because he does not.

I admire Steve Warner for multiple reasons, both professional and personal. He is an excellent illustration of someone who integrates depth of intellect with depth of character. Steve is one of those people who come into your life and are unusually supportive and helpful, for reasons we never fully understand.

In an academic world that is sometimes dominated by an overly professionalized atmosphere, both Fred and Steve are true models of personal generosity, intellectual vitality, and intellectual integrity. I dedicate this book to the two of them, with gratitude.

I

Introduction

In the early twentieth century, opponents of contraception often perceived the promotion of birth control as part of a radical socialist movement. There was also a strong moral argument against contraception,
which by the 1920s was led by Catholic prelates. Repeated attempts
to persuade federal and state legislatures to overturn anticontraception
laws failed, so the prelates appear, at least at first, to have been successful in their opposition. However, it is a bit strange that they would
be successful, since anti-Catholicism was rampant; arguably, associat-
ing any issue with the Catholic Church at that time was almost sure
to be an enormous political handicap. The failure to convince legislatures to overturn anticontraception laws is doubly puzzling given that
there is considerable evidence that many Americans found accessible
contraception an appealing prospect.

The history of the politics of abortion laws also has strange twists
and turns. Physicians were central in the movement to outlaw most
abortions in the mid– to late nineteenth century. Physicians were then
central in the movement favoring moderate liberalization of abortion
laws in the 1960s: These reformers and their allies convinced quite a
few state legislatures that they should institute abortion law reform
because abortion was *not* a moral issue. They had particular success
convincing Southern legislatures to liberalize abortion laws, though
today the South has a particularly strong pro-life movement.

The way that we think and talk about contraception and abortion
seems natural to us now. But the way we think about these issues

now may sound as odd half a century from now as does the idea that Southern states were particularly likely to liberalize their abortion laws in the 1960s, or that contraception was once a socialist cause. That past discussions of an issue appear strange, even inconceivable, to us suggests that a great deal of social change has taken place.[1]

The twists and turns of the debates over contraception and abortion initially seem confusing because we expect that the way that we ourselves define debates is the way that everyone else defines the same debates. This is often true, even when we look at contemporary debates: We can see our opponents as obviously wrong because we often define the issue for ourselves in a way that makes the opposing position contradictory and untenable. We do not see that our opponents define the issue quite differently and so refuse simply to adopt the mirror image of our own opinion. They maddeningly refuse to define the issue in our terms; from their perspective, it is we who hold an absurdly untenable position.

When we look to the past, we are even more likely to project our own definitions, our own understandings, of what a controversy is really about. But there are typically diverse ways that any given social and political debate can be framed. And, for debates important enough that they have a long history, the issues typically *are* framed in diverse ways over time. Consequently, groups that manage to ally at one point in time may find alliance impossible once the terms of debate have changed. Whole sets of controversial questions may define the debate at one time and then disappear at another.

This study asks why contraception and abortion have been issues of heated public controversy at some times and not others. The answer to that question, I will argue, is found by understanding how the participants in debates over contraception and abortion have collectively framed the debates over time. A number of historians and social scientists have noted the shifting nature of alliances and of the frames that informed these debates.[2] Their primary focus, however, has not been

---

[1] On the methodological approach of looking for what appears strange to us but did not appear strange to contemporaries, see Robert Darnton, *The Great Cat Massacre and Other Episodes in French Cultural History* (New York: Basic Books, 1984).

[2] Most notably Linda Gordon, James C. Mohr, Kristin Luker, Rosalind Pollack Petchesky, Faye D. Ginsburg, and Carole R. McCann. For an accomplished study of the changing public rhetoric used by different participants in discussion and debate

on explaining why these coalition shifts have ultimately affected how controversial the debates have been. But, because different coalitions produce different frames, a shifting coalition can dramatically redefine what an issue is about and thus dramatically change the salience of an issue and the level of controversy.

I do not think the issues of birth control and abortion are necessarily unique in this respect. But these dynamics may be easier to see in the debates over contraception and abortion than in other debates, partly because reproductive politics has been such a familiar presence in recent decades. We tend to think of abortion, especially, as inherently controversial. And yet abortion has, in other contexts, often been quite uncontroversial. In addition, in the early twentieth century contraception was remarkably divisive, and yet a gradual reframing of the issue defused much of the debate. Contraception involved many of the same issues that have affected abortion debates: sex roles, the value of children, sexual morality, and conflicting views of the family. A comparison of the path of contraception with the path of abortion is thus likely to provide insight into both.

Apparent Contradictions

The politics of abortion has received a great deal of attention from social scientists since the 1973 U.S. Supreme Court decisions in *Roe v. Wade*[3] and *Doe v. Bolton*.[4] To a lesser, but still significant, extent, the politics of contraception has also received considerable attention over the years, largely because the leader of the early-twentieth-century birth control movement, Margaret Sanger (1879–1966), has remained a compelling topic for biographers, historians, and polemicists. However, I would argue that there has not been a full attempt to explain the rhythms of political history and social movement history surrounding these issues, namely why these issues have been controversial some times and not others.

of abortion from the 1960s to the 1980s, see Celeste Michelle Condit, *Decoding Abortion Rhetoric: Communicating Social Change* (Urbana and Chicago: University of Illinois Press, 1990). Condit does not focus on the larger political dynamics but gives a good account of the type of images and ideas that have surrounded the issue.

[3] 410 U.S. 113 (1973).
[4] 410 U.S. 179 (1973).

The twentieth-century history of American reproductive politics is rife with apparent, though unexplained, contradictions, in addition to those I have already noted. Among the apparent contradictions are the timing of legal changes surrounding the issues, the context of those changes, and the immediate beneficiaries. In short, more often than not, legal changes took place not when there was a great deal of attention to the issues, but when there was little attention. The context of such changes is that they often occurred in places (e.g., courts rather than legislatures, or one region of the country rather than another) that make little obvious sense in hindsight – and indeed, are often quite opposite to our expectations – or in places that were not the primary focus of activists pursuing such changes. The immediate beneficiaries – usually physicians – were often not particularly interested in the issue at the time.

For example, the movement promoting birth control, associated with Margaret Sanger, tried to overturn the many legal restrictions on its dissemination. The movement was especially visible and vocal in the 1910s, but, as mentioned earlier, its activism resulted in little concrete success. The main victories in favor of legal, accessible contraception did not begin until the second half of the 1930s – a couple of decades after attention to that movement (and the movement itself) had mostly faded away.

By the early 1920s, in fact, advocacy for birth control was much less like the grassroots affair that it had been in the 1910s, and more of a lobbying effort by professionalized organizations. Birth control advocates spent the 1920s and 1930s pushing for *legislative* change, but the legal changes of the 1930s took the form of court decisions. Again, success did not come in the form that interested groups actually attempted to effect: Indeed, the most important substantive implication of those court decisions was that they greatly widened the right of physicians to dispense contraception as they saw fit. But, although some prominent advocates of contraception were physicians, there was hardly a broad medical movement that saw contraception as a burning issue. In fact, when activism in favor of accessible contraception was at its height in the 1910s, physicians were often seen as the enemy.

One would think abortion would be a more intrinsically controversial issue than contraception but, in fact, liberalization of abortion laws sailed through a number of state legislatures in the late 1960s. This was before there was much grassroots concern for, or even awareness of, abortion as a public issue; those who did talk about abortion did not generally speak of it in the pro-life vs. pro-choice terms familiar to us today. Small numbers of liberalizing physicians, lawyers, and clerics advocated new, more lenient laws, the goal of such laws being to allow unhindered the professional and humanitarian practice of medicine. Still, as with contraception earlier in the century, it was hardly the case that American physicians as a whole saw abortion as a central concern in their medical practice. But the argument that physicians should decide when abortion was appropriate was entirely convincing to a number of state legislatures, especially in the part of the country we would least expect, that is, the South.

Greater attention to the issue made it harder, rather than easier, to push legislatures into changing the law. That is, once there really were social movements heavily involved in debate over abortion – starting in about 1970 – it became nearly impossible to get any kind of abortion law through a legislature. That was not the only change: It was also the case that physicians were pushed to the side, and the grass roots took up the issue. And so, ultimately, did the courts, especially in the 1973 U.S. Supreme Court decisions, *Roe v. Wade* and *Doe v. Bolton*. Again, by 1973, the original handfuls of physicians attempting to change the laws were not important parts of the increasingly acrimonious public or legislative debate. But, mirroring the contraception court cases of the 1930s, the Supreme Court justified its 1973 decisions most explicitly and unambiguously in terms of physicians' right to practice medicine, not in terms of women's right to abortion. Relative to the previous legal status of abortion, the recognition of significant women's rights to choose abortion was arguably the most dramatic *innovation* of the 1973 decisions. Still, women's rights were not as unequivocally asserted as were physicians' rights; the recognition of the right of physicians to significant autonomy in making professional judgments about reproductive matters had a significant judicial history that was continued in the 1973 decisions. Once again, when it came to reproductive issues, courts seemed quite willing to hand physicians great victories, though physicians were not actually seeking such victories: that is, by 1973, the aura of physicians' professional autonomy remained quite influential in the courts, but physicians were no longer major players in the larger political battle over abortion.

Why do doctors have such success in the legislatures and the courts, even when they do not seek such "success"? Why has legal change in the status of contraception and abortion so often come when vocal social movements in favor of such change are *absent* from the scene? How could the South, of all places, have been particularly receptive to liberalizing its state abortion laws in the late 1960s (even though, again, groups we generally think of as favoring abortion rights were absent in the South)?

In asking these questions, we start to see that the debates over contraception and abortion have taken some apparently very odd twists and turns. Practices painted as moral outrages become major public controversies, then, over time, they disappear from public view. They sometimes reemerge as uncontroversial, respectable causes lacking very specific moral relevance. I will argue that we can understand these changes once we understand the dynamics of framing, as it affects social movements, legal change, and public policy debates.

I have attempted to organize this book so that it is interesting and accessible to a variety of readers – including those who could give a darn about sociological theory – while still making a worthwhile sociological argument that contributes to ongoing agendas of research within that discipline. In this introduction, then, I briefly sketch what I intend to argue, including how I use the concept of a "frame." Subsequent chapters follow the shifting coalitions and shifting frames in debates over contraception and abortion. The last couple of chapters, especially the concluding chapter, return to some of the theoretical concerns involved in studying these issues, which will be much easier (and less abstract) to address once the reader has encountered the history of the debates. Sociological analysis has a particular contribution to make in understanding moral conflict in American society. Thus there are particular sociological arguments – which necessarily have an important theoretical dimension – worth exploring in an extended discussion at the end of the book.

Most of the book's chapters focus on the historical development of these debates. I organize the discussion in a way that allows an easy transition into the sociological argument developed in greater detail in the final chapters. Through the first six chapters, I utilize primarily two central concepts, that of framing and the "moral veto." The closing chapter, again, will flesh out in further detail how we conceptualize certain other sociological phenomena of interest in this book.

In this first chapter, however, I will define what I mean by these central concepts of "frame" and "moral veto." Within this discussion I will also describe two important and distinct types of frames, that is, "limiting frames" and "moral worldviews."

Framing the Debates

By asking how people "frame" contraception or abortion, I mean to ask, what do they think the issue is *about*? For instance, is abortion primarily about "unborn children" (as the pro-life frame would insist) or is it about women's right to choose (as the pro-choice frame would insist)? All of us have encountered situations where the language we use is not neutral but implicitly legitimizes one way of framing a situation. For instance, to call the mid-nineteenth-century war between Union and Confederate forces the "Civil War" implies that the war took place within one country; thus many Southern whites long referred to it as the "War between the States," implying it was a multitude of states, not a single country, that were the primary actors in the conflict. To such Southerners, the war was *about* states pursuing their own choices and destiny, including the right to leave a country, that is, a union. Thus the war did not occur within one single country and cannot be called simply a "civil war"; implicitly, then, they frame the conflict to legitimate a particular view of the war.

If we look at the history of conflict over contraception and abortion, we find a variety of ways of framing contraception and abortion, a number of which seem obvious to us, others that do not. Within the contemporary discussion of abortion, for instance, there are two particularly visible frames, the pro-life frame and the pro-choice frame. Within the pro-life frame, abortion is a matter of whether one supports, or does not support, the right to life of an unborn child. Within the pro-choice frame, abortion is *not about* children; it is about preventing particular moral opinions from becoming enshrined in law, especially preventing laws that deny a woman's right to make her own reproductive choices. This is not to say that children are not important, only that the debate over abortion is not about children. Just as staunch Southern Confederates did not use the term "Civil War," pro-choice advocates would never use the term "unborn child." They would probably say "fetus" rather than "child," but, more to the point, they would talk about completely different issues from the start. They would want to avoid implying that the pro-life movement, in talking about "unborn children," has properly defined the terms of the debate.

At other times and in other places (e.g., in a number of state legislatures in the 1960s), what I call a medical, humanitarian frame has guided the discussion of abortion.[5] This frame portrays abortion as a regrettable tragedy, in which physicians provide assistance to women who deserve sympathy for being in a difficult situation. Physicians use their professional medical judgment to decide when abortion is appropriate; they do not make such a decision lightly, but (again, within this frame) medical judgment includes humanitarian sympathy for patients in unfortunate circumstances. Within the medical, humanitarian frame, then, abortion is not a matter of "life" or of rights. While pregnant women are the objects of sympathy, neither they nor fetuses are particularly visible subjects in the decision-making process. Abortion is not desirable but can be necessary, and moral absolutes or politicization are generally to be avoided.

Similarly, as we see in subsequent chapters, contraception has been framed in various ways. One frame in favor of accessible contraception was a feminist frame, in which the issue was a woman's right to control her reproduction. Another frame in favor of contraception, in contrast, saw it in socialist terms, as a means by which the working class could control their lives. With contraception, the working class could avoid producing large numbers of children whose parents could not afford to raise them, children who would grow up, like their parents, to provide labor that benefited wealthy capitalists.

It is often possible to express different opinions within a single frame. For example, if debates over foreign aid are framed in terms that assume that the goal of foreign aid is to extend the influence of the United States, one may be in favor of foreign aid because of an assumption that such aid does indeed make recipients more friendly to the United States. One could oppose foreign aid, within the same frame, with a claim that recipient nations ignore U.S. preferences. In either case, to ask whether foreign aid is valuable is to ask whether it influences the

---

[5] The medical component and the humanitarian component are sometimes separated from each other, with interesting consequences, as I develop in later chapters. However, for now, as the discussion here is primarily illustrative, I will consider the two components as part of a single frame.

policies of recipients, that is, to use the same frame. The issue of foreign aid is framed as a matter of international influence (within this frame): that is what foreign aid is about.

However, there exist distinct frames to the extent that different sides on an issue are in fact *not* directly negating the position of the other side, but rather that they think that the other side's position is a distraction from the *real* issue. For example, if one thinks that foreign aid is always good because it is a form of charity, that is, helping those less fortunate than ourselves, then the degree of influence the United States gains in a country that receives such aid is not the primary concern.

Framing is probably most effective in attracting support when it would be political suicide for opponents to take the opposite position within the same frame. Thus, opponents of foreign aid do not proclaim "we want to hurt people who are less fortunate than ourselves." Instead they use a different frame, as in the previous example: Discussing foreign aid as a matter of extending U.S. influence implicitly treats charity as a secondary or irrelevant concern in the debate over foreign aid. It does not directly deny that charity (in the proper context) is a good thing but instead avoids the issue.

The same is true of the contemporary debate over abortion: It is logically possible to take a position directly opposite that of the pro-life or pro-choice position, but generally no one does so. That is, we do not hear activists referring to themselves as "anti-life" or "anti-choice": They might so label their *opponents*, because to do so makes their opponents appear to take an unreasonable position. By using *different* frames, each side implies that the other side's concerns are secondary or irrelevant to the real issue, and each side denies the right of the other to define the terms of debate. Opponents of the pro-life movement do not argue that they think that killing children is a good thing: They instead say that killing children is not what is going on, or, perhaps more likely, they never specifically address the pro-life claim about fetal rights. They would describe the issue of abortion as a completely different matter: In their frame, different questions would be at stake. Usually they would cite the tragic circumstances that make abortion a reasonable choice, the right of individuals to make their own moral decisions in a pluralist society, the rights of women to control their reproduction, or some combination of these appeals. If pushed to answer "yes" or "no" to the question of whether fetuses have a right to life, they may say no, or they might argue that a developing life, or a potential human being, does not have the same rights as an already-born human being. But they would probably feel that that entire set of issues is at best secondary to other concerns involved in the legality and accessibility of abortion. They would rather not argue questions that matter primarily within the pro-life frame. When adversaries are using different frames, agreeing to debate within the opponent's frame is often strategic suicide.

Thus, pro-life forces do not directly negate the pro-choice position; they believe the pro-choice movement misstates what the issue is *about* (i.e., uses the wrong frame). Pro-life advocates do not generally claim to be against pluralism, against human sympathy in tragic situations, or against the equality and rights of women. Instead they would reject the relevance of the pro-choice frame entirely, as in the pro-life bumper sticker, "It's not a choice; it's a life." It's not *about* choice. It's about unborn babies. Many pro-life advocates would probably be willing to agree, at least in theory, that they're in favor of women's equality and the right of people to hold different opinions, although their position also in fact denies the existence of some of the rights pro-choice advocates would claim, especially the right to terminate a pregnancy.[6] But, in general, pro-life advocates do not want to discuss the issue in terms

---

[6] See Faye D. Ginsburg, *Contested Lives: The Abortion Debate in an American Community* (Berkeley: University of California Press, 1989). Although Ginsburg makes a reasonable case that some of the views of gender among pro-life and pro-choice proponents in (her ethnographic study of) Fargo, North Dakota, have similarities, I think she over-interprets in two ways. First, the abortion debate is very much nationalized, so that, for example, militant activists (especially within Operation Rescue and like-minded groups) may travel great distances to participate in protests. Thus the moderation that may arise in the case of opposing activists in the same small city may not generalize to the national debate well. (On the nationalization of the debate see, e.g., Jongho Roh and Donald P. Haider-Markel, "All Politics Is Not Local: National Forces in State Abortion Initiatives," *Social Science Quarterly* 84[2003]:15–31.) Second, Ginsburg's argument on the central point of what the two sides share is theoretically too ambiguous to be meaningful. That is, Ginsburg argues that what pro-life and pro-choice advocates have in common is an emphasis on "nurturance." But her definition of what constitutes nurturance includes nurturance of other people and of oneself. It is so conceptually broad that it obscures that for both sides of activists (but not necessarily for the general population), how one views the legal and moral status of abortion is an enormous divide. For instance, the pro-life side would condemn the value of "nurturance" that does not define fetuses as persons or that can emphasize self-nurturance to the point of justifying abortion.

of rights or women's equality: Those are pro-choice issues. It is not the case that the two sides simply have different opinions (within a frame); they use entirely different frames.

This book, then, examines how frames used to discuss contraception and abortion have changed over time, and why some of those frames have been more controversial than others. The discussion will focus on a few central components: First, who is involved in a debate at different times? Second, what kind of frame could or could not bridge the concerns of those participating in the discussion? And third, what assumptions were made about groups excluded from the discussion? To a significant extent, all three components of this discussion center around a single point: Because framing is a social and cultural process of sharing perspectives and attempting to privilege one frame over another, the question of who is involved in a debate (including who dominates it) at any given time is central.

The Political Cycle of Innovation, Frames, and Social Movements

This book deals with issues that, at times, have been highly contentious. Not until the 1910s did a real movement emerge that was daring enough to claim that contraception should not only be allowed and accessible but that it was fundamentally a good thing. That movement met with vociferous denunciations of contraception as immoral, unnatural, demeaning, and unpatriotic. And abortion has probably been the most perpetually divisive political issue of the last several decades.

Highly contentious issues, almost by definition, typically involve polarized social movements (i.e., the polarization has a mobilized quality), at least sporadically. This book includes, then, consideration of social movements that have surrounded the issues of contraception and abortion. In doing so, I explore an apparent paradox in the role of social movements: In short, the greatest substantive legal and policy changes concerning contraception and abortion have generally come at times when social movements were *not* particularly active. The greatest movement mobilization around contraception was in the 1910s, but the cause of making contraception legal and accessible achieved its greatest successes in the 1930s, and, to some extent, the 1960s. A series of court decisions starting in the 1930s undermined many of the previous restrictions on the distribution of contraceptives.

The largest number of legislative initiatives liberalizing abortion law came between 1966 and 1970, when movements for and against legal abortion were in their infancy. A greater change came once legislatures had stepped aside and the U.S. Supreme Court took over, with its 1973 decisions in *Roe v. Wade* and *Doe v. Bolton*. By that time social movements on both sides had picked up steam, but activism was considerably more extensive after the dramatic changes of *Roe* and *Doe* than it was before. (As a shorthand, I will at times simply use *"Roe"* to refer to the changes wrought by the two 1973 decisions together.) Even when further change would come with additional Supreme Court decisions modifying *Roe*, some of which could be attributed to pro-life mobilization, the decisions fell far short of pro-life activists' ultimate goals of overturning *Roe* and writing into law a fetus's right to life (and legal status as a person with the same rights as all other persons). The *legislative* changes after 1973 have had considerably less effect on the legal status of abortion than did *Roe* itself.

Is the best social movement strategy, then, *not* to start a movement? That is, do movements actually hamper their own goals? In an immediate sense, as will become clear, I argue that to some extent, yes, heavy mobilization around an issue often results in a polarization that can paralyze policy makers. The reason is that such mobilization typically requires policy makers to choose between two (or more) morally charged frames, in which any decision necessarily elicits condemnation by at least one side. Policy makers, especially legislators who depend on reelection, typically try to avoid such issues.[7]

However, that is not the whole story. First, ideas and innovations ultimately written into law often originate within earlier social

---

[7] Cf. Paul Burstein and April Linton, "The Impact of Political Parties, Interest Groups, and Social Movement Organizations on Public Policy," *Social Forces* 81(2002):380–408.

C. Thomas Dienes (*Law, Politics, and Birth Control* [Urbana: University of Illinois Press, 1972]) made related points (pp. 14, 106) but, just as frequently, lapsed into conflicting functionalist theoretical assumptions that legislatures are assigned a role of responding to social change and serving as a safety valve for social pressures, and so that is what they do (pp. 9, 19). His book included very good empirical analysis of cases where legislatures failed to respond to or defuse social pressures in the case of contraception, but, instead of attempting to account theoretically for such failures, he implied that legislatures and courts simply need to recognize their proper social functions and act accordingly (pp. 308–9). That is, the empirical reality is exogenous to his theoretical model.

movements, sometimes well after such movements have expired.[8] Though the idea often outlasts the social movement, victory might not have come without the movement's having raised the issue in the first place. More often than not, I would argue, controversial movement ideas cannot easily gain widespread acceptance until the history of division and anger that greeted the movement has faded into memory and the goal has been reframed to some extent. And movements will often frame a particular goal in a way that asks for more far-reaching changes than that movement is likely to achieve; when ultimately implemented, a single goal typically gains wider acceptance once it is somewhat whittled down (within an apparently less radical frame). Still, the idea for particular innovations, including the ultimate establishment of access to contraception as a legal right, often originates within social movements that are perceived, at first, as hopelessly radical. Without those movements, the innovative idea might never have arisen, or might have at least been delayed.

Second, there are some types of movement frames that succeed quite well, even while the movement remains vibrant, as I discuss in the next section.

Limiting Frames

What type of frames, then, allow societies to address moral disputes without fighting their moral battles to the death? In short, the answer is that the rhetoric of debate must isolate issues so that larger social and moral implications of concern to participants in the polity are minimally specified (whether those implications are real or imagined). Essentially, then, the more reduced and simplified discussion of an issue is – so that it is stripped even of the many specific moral implications that most people would, in other circumstances, attach to the issue – the more likely that groups with differing opinions can live with each other.[9]

---

[8] There is a similarity here to Goldstone's view of the legacy of ideological innovation among revolutionary movements: Jack A. Goldstone, "Ideology, Cultural Frameworks, and the Process of Revolution," *Theory and Society* 20(1991): 440–1, 443.

[9] Charles E. Lindblom, "The Science of Muddling through," *Public Administration Review* 14(1959):79–88, and John Kingdon (*Agendas, Alternatives, and Public Policies* [New York: Harper Collins, 1995], p. 84) suggested that detailing the implications of a particular policy, and thus detailing possible points of disagreement, generally

For some readers, an immediate objection comes to mind: Are not social movements, and indeed many innovations, persuasive to the extent that they have a certain moral power? I would argue that yes, that is often the case, but not all moral frames are of the same type, and one type of moral frame is strategically much more effective than another in building a large constituency. In most cases, the moral power of such movements succeeds strategically to the extent that those who need to be convinced perceive the movement's goal to be redress of a specific moral wrong, rather than implying an entire moral worldview. In such cases, the movement goal can typically be stated in a single sentence or phrase that addresses a matter considered an unambiguous moral wrong within diverse worldviews. A good example would be the goal of the early Civil Rights Movement, in the period between about 1954 and 1963. To most Americans, the movement raised the compelling moral point that segregation was wrong, or, a little more generally, that discriminating on the basis of race was wrong: In most minds, that was what the movement was about. The point was morally compelling, but to agree did not obviously require accepting a new, comprehensive worldview. Instead, opposition to segregation was compatible with a wide range of larger worldviews: For example, essentially every mainstream religious group could ultimately find the goal compatible with its theology, and most dominant perspectives on American law and American traditions could have little quarrel with the principle of equal justice before the law.[10]

---

derails policy initiatives. Such arguments converge theoretically with sociological arguments about political process and political culture, most notably that of Scott Sanders and James M. Jasper, "Civil Politics in the Animal Rights Conflict: God Terms versus Casuistry in Cambridge, Massachusetts," *Science, Technology, & Human Values* 19 (1994):169–88.

  However, we shall see later in this chapter that negative implications can be specified when those implications affect primarily groups whose participation in the polity is severely restricted, such as women in the nineteenth century.

[10] In the final chapter I address the question of whether a frame is perceived as limiting to the extent that it is not explicitly framed in worldview terms but is in fact compatible with a worldview that is so pervasive that it hardly occurs to anyone in the society to disagree. But for now, I refer to frames as "limiting frames" to the extent that a relevant audience does not *perceive* the frame to require a reorientation of its worldview, that is, does not seem to carry a great deal of moral baggage extraneous to the immediate issue at hand.

The integrationist goal could emerge only once African Americans had become a significant part of the polity, a group that could then build an alliance with other opponents of racism to voice that opposition. Thus the Civil Rights Movement emerged only once the African American vote mattered and African American voices could be heard, that is, once enough African Americans had emigrated away from the rural South to the urban South and the industrial North. They could then escape some of the exceedingly oppressive conditions that had made them nearly invisible to most Americans. But once the integrationist voice of the early Civil Rights Movement emerged, it became clear that the majority of Americans had no reason to support legally mandated segregation. Most Americans did not have to ingest an entirely new moral worldview to agree that legally mandated segregation should end: Almost any worldview within mainstream American society could find no quarrel with such a goal (with the significant regional exception of the Southern white view that glorified the Confederacy and favored segregation). While the substantive, mobilized opposition to integration was quite strong in the South for a number of years, the range of possible *moral* paths justifying such opposition was quite limited: Blatant racism was not acceptable within any mainstream political perspective, and even less blatantly racist claims about "states' rights," "separate but equal," and so forth elicited very little support outside the white South. While there were racists throughout the country, within public political appeals, the states' rights rhetoric required buying into too much of a worldview about what the South's history was about, what Southern society should be like, even what the Civil War had been about. From a framing point of view, at the national level the segregationist perspective was greatly handicapped relative to the integrationist perspective. Indeed, the ability of the Civil Rights Movement to focus on the moral imperative of that goal was central to its success, so that the violent opposition to integration in the South was ultimately no match.

I refer to frames such as the integrationist view of civil rights – that is, frames that invite agreement without appearing to require adoption of a new worldview – as "morally limiting" frames: They focus attention on a specific goal, but they do not invite numerous paths of opposition by appearing to require a wide-ranging moral reorientation. Morally limiting frames do not appear – to a given audience within a given context – to link explicitly to a web of larger moral commitments.

Morally limiting frames often elicit the same type of response as other limiting frames that have no explicit moral content at all. For example, successfully framing a legal change as a technical adjustment, so that public participation is unnecessary, keeps controversy to a minimum. We shall see in Chapter 5 that this type of frame is probably most likely when an idea or policy change is primarily an elite innovation, presented as a sensible reform rather than an imperative originating among the masses. Morally limiting frames and technocratic limiting frames are both instances of the more general concept of "limiting frames." A technocratic frame does not have the moral force of a morally limiting frame, but both are limiting in that they do not require, as a condition of agreement, explicit assent to an uncompromising moral worldview. They appear to isolate an issue rather than link it to a web of broader commitments.

Moral Worldviews

As is probably already obvious, then, I contrast limiting frames to a different type of frame, moral worldviews. "Moral worldviews" here refers to frames that are perceived by active participants within a debate to encompass many morally charged issues simultaneously, within a comprehensive and explicit worldview. For example, framing accessible contraception as a socialist issue invited assent only if the audience accepted socialism, as well as contraception. This type of frame, then, invited agreement with the goal of accessible contraception only within a package that accepted also that capitalism was a highly problematic, unjust system. Many early-twentieth-century Americans probably also rejected socialism (and thus, at the time, contraception) because they thought that accepting "socialism" implied rejecting democracy (though American socialists often were in fact quite committed to democracy) or that it at least was somehow anti-American. And so, the perception was that contraception as a socialist cause required accepting a very large ideological package, which elicited multiple objections. The implied worldview appeared quite encompassing. Strong disagreement with one component of the worldview colors perception of all the other components.

In a complex society of varying and cross-cutting allegiances and beliefs, then, explicitly stated moral worldviews encounter the strategic problem that they typically offer almost everyone something with which to disagree. And, since they are making sweeping moral claims, disagreements are likely to be passionate.

But *agreements* are passionate and comprehensive as well, at least among the minority of people willing to commit to that worldview. Thus there is the apparent paradox that social movements with strong allegiances among members often have to fade away before their central goals can be reframed in a way that is palatable to a large portion of the society. The moral passion and comprehensive worldview of many social movements (like that of many religious sects) provides a strong collective identity: Once someone decides to be an adherent, they have accepted a comprehensive theory of the world, with a strong component of moral passion. What such an identity does, however, is to erect a strong barrier between "us" and "them"; a decision whether to join approaches an all-or-nothing proposition. Thus movements with comprehensive worldviews can have a strong collective identity and retain the loyalty of members for long periods of time, and at the same time remaining small or finding themselves unable to expand influence beyond a core minority constituency.[11] Such was the case, for instance, of the American Communist Party for decades.

For a contemporary example of such a movement – one that is quite large, but unable to develop broad and consistent support within electoral politics – there is the Christian Right. (This political movement is also known as the Religious Right, but it consists almost entirely of Christians, and indeed most members are more specifically white evangelical Protestants.) Especially telling is the experience of the Christian Right in Republican presidential politics. The Christian Right became a significant force in the Republican Party during the first administration of President Ronald Reagan, in the early 1980s. The most notable organization at the time was Rev. Jerry Falwell's Moral Majority. There was a brief moment early in the 1988 campaign when it appeared the

---

[11] David S. Meyer makes a similar point in "Opportunities and Identities: Bridge-Building in the Study of Social Movements," pp. 3–21 in *Social Movements: Identity, Culture, and the State*, David S. Meyer, Nancy Whittier, and Belinda Robnett, eds. (Oxford and New York: Oxford University Press, 2002), p. 15.

religious broadcaster Rev. Pat Robertson, who was then becoming the most prominent force in the Christian Right, posed a threat to the Republican candidacy of then–Vice President George H. W. Bush. It turned out that Robertson's early success was limited primarily to the Iowa caucuses, the first major event of the nominating season. Caucuses involve gatherings of particularly committed party members and so draw the participation of highly committed partisans, even more so than do primaries. While primaries disproportionately elicit conservative participation among Republicans and liberal participation among Democrats, that is even more true in caucuses. Thus caucuses are especially susceptible to influence from passionate ideological minorities.

Patrick Buchanan, a conservative Roman Catholic who was the standard bearer of the Christian Right in the 1992 and 1996 presidential campaigns, did considerably better in the primaries than did Robertson in 1988, perhaps because he took Christian Right positions but was not himself the leader of a religious movement, had significant experience in politics and government, and included xenophobic and economically nationalist appeals that resonated both within and outside the Christian Right.[12] The dedication and commitment of time, energy, and money that Buchanan received from foot soldiers of the Christian Right were the envy of other politicians. In 1996, amid an initially crowded Republican field, the fervent loyalty and excitement within Buchanan's campaign made competing candidates look somewhat lackluster in the primaries. But in both cases Buchanan's support consisted of a fervent core that was unable to develop a broad coalition. In fact, Buchanan's nationally televised 1992 speech at the Republican convention contributed to then-President George H. W. Bush's failure to win reelection: Buchanan thrilled his loyalists with his call for a "culture war" against the Christian Right's opponents in a way that turned off millions of Americans worried that the Republican Party was narrow and intolerant. In a version of the speech a few months earlier, delivered at Jerry Falwell's Liberty University, Buchanan had instead referred to a "religious war."[13]

---

[12] See, for instance, Sara Diamond, *Not by Politics Alone: The Enduring Influence of the Christian Right* (New York and London: Guilford, 1998), pp. 90–2, 104–6.

[13] Diamond, ibid., pp. 92–5. Diamond quotes Buchanan's May 1992 reference to a "religious war" on p. 92.

Morally conservative views among a number of prominent Republicans easily gave the impression throughout 1992 that an uncompromising moral agenda from the

A call for a culture war attempts to broaden the moral agenda (to include uncompromising positions on abortion, homosexuality, and sex education and prayer in public schools, to name just a few). The flip side of having a passionate core in favor of such a broad, morally charged agenda is the problem of a broadly negative reputation: Such an apparently uncompromising agenda appears narrow-minded and intolerant to outsiders. It appears too threatening to too many people, for a variety of reasons (*because* it so explicitly addresses so many issues at once). Thus the Buchanan candidacy reached its limits because its passionate following seemed intolerant and extreme to too many outsiders. And thus a central goal of the Christian Right – that is, a constitutional amendment to outlaw abortion – remains a pipe dream, despite (indeed, partly because of) the movement's fervor. And yet, if anything, the Christian Right appears even more convinced that such an amendment is essential to the moral fabric of America.[14] The internal strength of the movement is inversely proportional to its ability to convince outsiders.

Thus the Christian Right generally influences others when it plays down its fervor a bit and gives up its all-or-nothing approach to fashioning an agenda. In the 1996 Republican presidential primaries, there were several candidates who made opposition to abortion a more central part of their candidacy than did Bob Dole. But Pat Robertson's Christian Coalition, the leading Christian Right organization in the 1990s, realized the limited appeal of the other candidates and initially avoided committing itself, until it ultimately threw in its lot with Dole, the eventual party nominee. The decision was that it was better to compromise with a victor than refuse to compromise and thus go down in

---

Christian Right had taken over the Republican Party. Vice President Dan Quayle, for instance, had condemned single motherhood in his comments over the TV character Murphy Brown (played by actress Candace Bergen), and a Republican convention speech by Marilyn Quayle seemed to condemn working mothers for neglecting their children. At the same convention Pat Robertson charged Democratic candidate Bill Clinton with "a radical plan to destroy the traditional family" (quoted in Diamond, p. 94).

[14] One indication, within the most militant wing of the religious pro-life movement, that passion intensifies as broader support evaporates is the fact that antiabortion bombings and assassination attempts increase with a drop in the political prospects of the movement. See especially Dallas A. Blanchard, *The Antiabortion Movement and the Rise of the Religious Right: From Polite to Fiery Protest* (New York: Twayne, 1994), and also Blanchard and Terry J. Prewitt, *Religious Violence and Abortion: The Gideon Project* (Gainesville: University Press of Florida, 1993).

defeat. A similar strategy emerged in the 2000 presidential election: The eventual nominee, George W. Bush, mostly avoided taking explicitly Christian Right positions. Candidates Alan Keyes and Gary Bauer had specifically Christian Right identities and platforms, but their fervent supporters remained small in number. For the most part, the Christian Right jumped on the Bush bandwagon, realizing strategically that a candidate explicitly identified with the Christian Right's views would never be elected. It is also the case that attempts to implement its agenda through legislatures face serious obstacles.[15]

Nevertheless, innovative social changes often originate among social movements that embed their advocacy of any one goal within a broader, moral mission to transform the society in which they live. They of course generally fail to transform their world, and most of their goals disappear without a trace. But many of the most far-reaching changes in American society – from the abolition of slavery, to voting rights for women, to legal and accessible contraception – originated within movements originally perceived as dangerously zealous, movements with a broad, morally charged agenda. Once reframed to eliminate the political baggage of a morally charged worldview, some of their individual goals at times leave a powerful legacy. And adoption of such limited, isolated goals often does not emerge until those movements

---

[15] Still, while the Christian Right agenda is not broadly popular, is politically disadvantageous in presidential elections, and faces severe uphill struggles when the subject of legislative debate, it is not without political influence. Arguably the 2000 strategy of downplaying that agenda resulted in the election of a president, George W. Bush, who is quite close to the Christian Right, though he never proclaimed so during the election campaign itself. And the preoccupation of the political process with international issues since the September 11, 2001, attack has probably deflected attention from Bush domestic policy initiatives that are friendly to the Christian Right.

It remains the case, then, when receiving specifically political attention, especially in general elections, that the Christian Right agenda is not popular. Not surprisingly, then, the Christian Right has found political success much more in influencing appointments than in influencing elections. One can find passionate support among the Christian Right for conservative judicial appointments that actually change the makeup of the federal bench, such as the appointment of Clarence Thomas to the U.S. Supreme Court (Diamond, *Not by Politics Alone*, p. 82). This success is ironic, since the Right often accuses liberals of depending too much on the courts. But the morally polarizing agenda of the Christian Right is strategically much better placed to influence a judicial appointment that does not directly require any elected official to vote on any specific part of the conservative moral agenda and does not require an election with an ideologically diverse voter pool.

have disintegrated, thus leaving no passionate constituency to object to reframing.

The contrasting strategic opportunities of limiting frames versus moral worldviews (which are also types of frames) have a number of interesting implications for our understanding of moral conflict within American society. Most centrally, it implies that understanding conflict, as well as legal and political innovation, involves a strong cultural component. When there exists the possibility of moral frames – and such a possibility certainly exists for any issue that touches on reproduction – one cannot simply tally up the number of supporters and opponents to predict whether a particular issue or innovation will meet with success. Even apparently popular movements can fail if they arouse too passionate an opposition: Framing helps determine what kinds of support and opposition emerge. Furthermore, innovation is most likely when an issue is framed so that there do not appear to be two sides of an issue at all, even though a different frame might evoke considerable opposition. Politics is not simply a matter of adding up the cumulative power of interest groups. Summing up the power of interest groups will explain best what happens when everyone involved in the discussion uses the same, limiting frame. But, for example, when explicit moral worldviews linger near the surface of a debate, even legislators who otherwise support a certain initiative may hesitate – they would often rather do nothing than to risk the moral wrath of one or another constituency, even when that constituency is a clear minority.

In addition, an understanding of why moral worldviews are more controversial than limiting frames helps us understand more generally how different groups, in a diverse society, manage to live with each other. Moral worldviews elicit opposition because there are, at any given time, diverse moral precepts coexisting within a complex society. There exist diverse moral worldviews, and there exist many moral commitments not explicitly tied to any comprehensive worldview. Moral pluralism is an empirical reality of complex societies, especially one in which different cultural traditions have contributed to the society. In the conclusion of this book, I argue that, within a complex society, attempts to forge a comprehensive moral consensus are generally self-defeating. Instead, political peace depends on framing controversies in a way that does not continually bring passionate moral divisions to the surface. In everyday politics, people cannot easily resolve their most passionate moral divisions, even though there may be fairly wide agreement on some issues that are uncontroversial to the point that people are not even particularly conscious that they agree. If this argument is correct, it has implications for how we understand American society and politics and how sociologists understand the bases of social solidarity and social order. In short, I conclude that Durkheimians, and others who assume that we must constantly work to eliminate moral disagreement, advocate a path that causes more conflict than it resolves. Multiculturalism, I argue, is not simply a nice goal; it is empirically the way that complex societies hold together. (Here I mean that there are diverse cultural values and beliefs, not just that there are different demographic groups within the same society.)

The Moral Veto

One of the central apparent paradoxes I want to explore in this book is the fact that what appears to be a strong movement with a moral passion in favor of a particular goal typically does not succeed in actually attaining its goal. That is, movements with great moral passion, which often are quite successful at mobilizing their forces, typically fail to get their central goals accepted within society. They have little positive mainstream success, and more specifically (as so many such movements want to change laws) their central goals are rarely written into law. The Christian Right's current commitment to a constitutional amendment to ban abortion is a clear example.[16]

But this does not mean that the movement is insignificant; in fact the movement often has considerable success *vetoing* the goals of its opponents. That is, it is very common that movements or groups that explicitly promote a moral worldview can serve very effectively as an opposition to the initiatives that it opposes, even when *its own* initiatives are not going anywhere. Its strategic success, then, is primarily negative rather than positive. In such a situation, for example, contestation over the legal status of something like contraception or

---

[16] For instance, prominent pro-life militant Randall Terry, leader of Operation Rescue, thought that pro-life social unrest would force passage of such an amendment (Michael Lienesch, *Redeeming America: Piety and Politics in the New Christian Right* [Chapel Hill, N.C., and London: University of North Carolina Press, 1993], p. 259). He could hardly have been more mistaken, as the 1980s and 1990s saw a gradual increase in the number of Americans who found such tactics extremist and unappealing.

abortion results in somewhat of a legislative freeze: Even if the legal situation does not draw much positive support, it is generally easier for legislators to leave in place the status quo. This can be true even when no one in particular is passionately in favor of the status quo. As we shall see in the history of battles over contraception and abortion, legislators would rather avoid dealing with an issue involving moral polarization, even if the group(s) exercising a moral veto are a definite minority. In such situations, change via the courts is much more likely.

It is, then, easy to overestimate the power of a group that manages to exercise a moral veto. At one level, it appears they are so powerful that legislators will never act against them. But it is more the case that the legislators simply will never *act*. Hence the apparent paradox that for decades the American Catholic hierarchy blocked legislative change on contraception, but in fact, as we shall see in Chapter 4, they had little ability to have their own preferences written into law, and support for their position was declining almost from the moment they entered the public debate. Thus when courts acted where legislatures would not, that is, to make contraception more accessible, there was no general outcry, as we would have expected if the Catholic hierarchy's power had been based on a general moral consensus against birth control. The Catholic Church's position on contraception could prevent legislatures from acting but did not elicit much support among the American population as a whole.

Groups that exercise moral vetoes do so because they tap into general cultural predispositions that may be somewhat inchoate but that nevertheless exist. For example, the potential to link contraception to unpopular images of sexual promiscuity was, I will argue, central to the veto that the Roman Catholic hierarchy exercised on numerous legislatures. This did not mean, however, that many people agreed with the particularly Catholic approach to contraception; surely most non-Catholics did not. Indeed, even many Catholics probably thought differently from their bishops and priests on the subject of contraception. Likewise, pro-life supporters – sometimes just a handful of elected officials in a particular state legislature – have had limited political success within legislatures, I would argue, ultimately due to the ability to conjure up unpleasant images of babies being killed. This does not mean that the pro-life worldview as a whole is popular: The pro-life movement can stifle new initiatives but never gets more than small parts of

its agenda written into law. It can mobilize opposition to the small proportion of abortions it calls "partial-birth abortions," but it has very
limited impact on the legality of abortion more generally. Even those
who do not accept that babies are killed during abortions know that,
politically, graphic images of fetuses that bring to mind babies are the
Achilles' heel of attempts to liberalize abortion laws. To the extent that
there is discomfort with abortion among the general population, concerns about the relationship of abortion to babies is clearly the reason.
But such discomfort does not translate into support for the pro-life
position as a whole: Thus, for instance, in the interest of electoral victory, the national Republican Party has in recent years toned down its
vocal opposition to abortion in general, an opposition that was more
prominent during the presidencies of Ronald Reagan and George Bush
Sr. (And even during those years, Republican administrations handed
the pro-life movement few concrete legislative victories.)

Limiting frames are successful to the extent that they divert attention away from any such cultural bases of moral discomfort or controversy. They limit attention to one particular component of an issue.
The defeat of one moral veto, then, is not via an opposing moral veto;
instead, it is via the institutionalization of a limiting frame. (How such
a frame is institutionalized will be addressed more directly in the final
chapter.)

The Exception: Framing and the Disenfranchised

Controversy over an issue can exist only if there are at least two sides
willing and able to stake out different positions. Linking a stand on
one issue to a moral worldview, which attempts to link various issues
together within a morally charged perspective, presents strategic difficulties because it typically invites many paths of opposition. Limiting
frames are typically more effective because they step on fewer toes.

It follows that frames that victimize groups who have little or no
voice in the polity (i.e., frames that step on the toes only of the disenfranchised) will not become publicly controversial. That is, specifying the implications of a social movement goal, or any goal, in a
way that assigns blame to disenfranchised groups (e.g., by referring
to nineteenth-century women who sought abortions as murderers) is
much less likely to engender resistance than specifying implications

that would alienate more privileged participants in the polity.[17] It is possible to link a social movement goal to stands on numerous other issues, as long as the only groups likely to object to those stands have no opportunity to voice their displeasure.

It was the case, for example, that in the early-twentieth-century debate over contraception, some activists in both the pro- and anti-contraception ranks included in their rhetoric derogatory portrayals of African Americans and recent immigrants. Assertions that the pro-creation of these groups in large numbers was undesirable often went unchallenged. As I mentioned earlier, central to understanding framing and moral conflict is a focus on who is involved in, and who is excluded from, the conversation.

The Organization of This Book

While this book delves a great deal into the history of the debates over contraception and abortion, it attempts not to sketch the entire history but instead to understand the pivotal moments in twentieth-century America in which controversy surrounding these issues arose or dissipated, as well as the political and cultural dynamics that led to change in the legal status of each. In doing so, this book addresses issues – for instance, the political outlook of Mary Ware Dennett and the history of state abortion laws in the 1960s – that have received little attention elsewhere, from either sociologists or historians.[18] But the

---

[17] See a related argument by Nancy Whittier, "Meaning and Structure in Social Movements," pp. 289–307 in *Social Movements*, pp. 295–6. Gamson also makes a related, but distinct, point: "As long as moral indignation is narrowly focused on human actors without regard to the broader structure in which they operate, injustice frames will be a poor tool for collective action, leading to ineffectiveness and frustration, perhaps creating new victims of injustice" (William A. Gamson, "Constructing Social Protest," pp. 85–106 in *Social Movements and Culture*, Hank Johnston and Bert Klandermans, eds. [Minneapolis: University of Minnesota Press, 1995], p. 92). I would add that placing blame for a social problem on "human actors" who are structurally disadvantaged – for instance, blaming nineteenth-century abortions on women who are supposedly morally ignorant or reckless – can unfortunately be a very strategically "effective" means of framing collective action goals. This does indeed involve unjust victimization.

[18] Attention to Dennett's historical significance was greatly enhanced by the first book-length biography of Dennett, by Constance M. Chen, *"The Sex Side of Life": Mary Ware Dennett's Pioneering Battle for Birth Control and Sex Education* (New York: New Press, 1996). Political scientists Christopher Z. Mooney and Mei-Hsien Lee try to

analysis here also benefits from the fact that the sociological and historical literatures on contraception and abortion are quite developed, and thus I can situate such issues within a well-researched context.

There are, then, a number of issues addressed in this book that have received extensive treatment elsewhere. For example, Margaret Sanger's relationship with socialist, feminist, and medical approaches to contraception has been the subject of a number of highly accomplished works by such authors as Linda Gordon, Ellen Chesler, David M. Kennedy, Carole R. McCann, and James Reed. While I have my own interpretation of these issues,[19] my central aim is not to offer a new interpretation of Sanger's biography, an endeavor accomplished by the authors just mentioned much more ably than I could do here. Instead, I focus on why certain frames within the contraception controversy – frames that Sanger influenced more than any other single person – emerged when they did, and why frames differed in their strategic effectiveness.

explain the pattern by which some states but not others passed new abortion laws, and they provide some good insights ("Legislative Morality in the American States: The Case of Pre-*Roe* Abortion Regulation Reform," *American Journal of Political Science* 39[1995]:599–627). However, I note some of the limitations of their analysis in footnotes in Chapter 5: they make important assumptions about the political processes involved that are disproved by a close look at the state-level evidence. Sociologist Jon Christopher Pennington has also recently collected a great deal of interesting information about the state-level process, independently of my own research. Some of his work appears in "The Role of Culture in Explaining the Failure of Social Movement Mobilization: Why Framing Is Not Enough," paper presented at the Annual Meeting of the American Sociological Association, Atlanta, August 2003. Also relevant is Rosemary Nossiff, *Before Roe: Abortion Policy in the States* (Philadelphia: Temple University Press, 2001): see note 59 in Chapter 5.

[19] For example, as will become clear in the discussion of Sanger's political effectiveness, I think some authors have based their interpretation of Sanger's relationship to eugenics too much on the earlier years (through the early 1920s) of her birth control career, and not enough on the 1930s. Ultimately, my view of Sanger's relationship to eugenics is probably closer to Gordon's (in *Woman's Body, Woman's Right* [New York: Penguin/Vintage, 1990]) than to that of the other authors named here. But, unlike Gordon and Rosalind Pollack Petchesky (*Abortion and Woman's Choice: The State, Sexuality, and Reproductive Freedom* [New York: Longman, 1984]), I would not argue that birth control advocates could have succeeded in remaining committed to a socialist and feminist approach to birth control that could have countered the medical model. I think Sanger could have dampened her eugenics rhetoric with little strategic cost, but gaining widespread acceptance of contraception outside of a medical model was, in my judgment, impossible in the first half of the twentieth century.

First, then, I examine in Chapter 2 the emergence of contraception as a matter of public debate. Controversy surrounding contraception emerged in the 1910s, as both opponents and advocates portrayed legal, accessible contraception as a radical initiative. Advocates argued that contraception was part of an egalitarian remaking of U.S. society. And yet, within a few decades, as Chapter 3 addresses, contraception had been stripped of its associations with radical movements and had been successfully reframed as a private matter between physicians and their patients. The imperative to put benefits for the poorer classes front and center dropped from the frame; indeed eugenic worries that the poorer classes were precisely the problem became more prominent. Organized opposition to contraception still existed, and liberalization of laws on contraception depended on the courts rather than legislatures skittish of controversy. Chapter 4 examines why, in the 1920s and 1930s, challenges to the medicalized mainstreaming of contraception were not strategically successful, including Mary Ware Dennett's misunderstood attempt to link contraception to a wider populist agenda, as well as the Catholic Church's attempt to condemn contraception as a moral outrage. In doing so, it examines the political dynamics that make moral vetoes effective.

Chapter 5 then turns to the issue of abortion. It begins by briefly summarizing the nineteenth-century history of abortion laws, which has been well documented by other scholars. It then examines the process by which abortion liberalization proposals passed in many states in the period from 1966 to 1970. These proposals gave physicians considerably wider discretion to allow legal abortion. As mentioned earlier, such legislative initiatives had particular success in the South, a rather surprising fact given the current strength of the pro-life Christian Right there. Finally, it examines the dynamics of debate in states in which attempts to pass such laws failed as the result of moral vetoes. Chapter 6 examines the brief moment in 1970 when one might have expected the beginning of a movement to push state laws even further in the direction of accessible abortion. That is, four states passed laws that removed all legal limits on access to abortion up until specified periods in pregnancy. Within those specified periods, such laws removed doctors from the role of gatekeepers of abortion decisions. But these four state laws turned out to be a flash rather than a trend; it took the Supreme Court to eliminate many of the previous restrictions on abortion, as the states' legislative reform processes ground to a halt. This chapter examines the fact that, nevertheless, the Supreme Court in 1973 justified its dramatic decision within a limiting frame, that is, the same medical, humanitarian frame that had inspired many of the state laws that the court overturned.

The final chapter looks back at the changing frames used in debating contraception and abortion, considering the implications for our understanding of the cultural dynamics of political controversy, social movements, and theories of social order. The discussion of this question at the end of the book considers the larger social context by which limiting frames are institutionalized, thus deflecting moral controversy but also at times reinforcing dominant cultural assumptions. It also challenges the common sociological assumption that a society must forge a moral consensus to avoid morally divisive conflicts. To the contrary, I conclude that the conscious pursuit of moral consensus is typically self-defeating. The history of contraception and abortion demonstrates that if one wants to avoid conflict in a diverse and democratic society, the surest path is the institutionalization of cultural pluralism. Still, many sociological arguments have too easily assumed that the avoidance of conflict is an unambiguous good. Thus, while I argue that limiting frames do empirically make democracy less conflictual, I recognize that for many groups, conflict over moral fundamentals is well worth the fight.

2

Framing Contraception within Moral Worldviews: The Early, Radical Birth Control Movement

Introduction[1]

There is clear evidence of widespread interest in birth control in nineteenth-century America, from the demand for public lecturers on the subject, to the widespread circulation of books on contraception, and to the fact that Americans dramatically reduced the size of their families by the end of the nineteenth century. But, in 1873, a federal law known as the "Comstock law," after its promoter Anthony Comstock, greatly restricted the circulation of information on, and sales of, contraceptives. The law treated contraception as a moral scandal. States

---

[1] Abbreviations to archival collections cited in this and subsequent chapters are

> MSP-LC: Margaret Sanger Papers, Library of Congress, Washington, D.C.
> MSP-SS: Margaret Sanger Papers, Sophia Smith Collection, Smith College.
> MWD: Mary Ware Dennett Papers, Schlesinger Library, Radcliffe College.

> I have cited materials in these collections (especially in MSP-LC and MWD) in a way that should allow future researchers to locate the cited documents fairly easily. That method has varied for each collection, depending on the exact organization of both microfilmed and original documents. Please note that the Sanger Papers at Smith College were in the process of being reorganized and microfilmed when I used them, so that it is pointless or impossible for me to cite specific locations of documents. But future researchers will apparently have access to a detailed index of documents.
> In referring to the location of documents from MSP-LC, "reel no." refers to the microfilm reels, as almost all of the papers are available on microfilm. The "volume" numbers, as indicated in the reels, are equivalent to the "container" numbers for the boxes that house the original papers. As some microfilm reels have materials from more than one container (=volume), I give numbers for both volumes and reels.

followed with Comstock laws of their own which, while often not very consistently enforced, greatly discouraged access to contraception. Though there were small groups who criticized these restrictions, for the most part, in mainstream American society sexual topics were enough of a taboo that, before the 1910s, there was only occasional and sporadic public opposition to the Comstock laws.

But the 1910s were a decade of considerable social-movement activity. Protests in favor of women's suffrage, as well as other feminist causes, were in full swing, and in 1912 Socialist Party candidate Eugene V. Debs polled almost 6% of the votes in the U.S. presidential election. Scores of Socialists were elected mayors, hundreds obtained office in city councils, and one was even elected to the U.S. House of Representatives. The Socialist movement remained strong through the decade, until opposition to World War I among many American Socialists led to breaks within the ranks and to strong political repression during and after the war.

Activism in favor of birth control emerged within the socialist movement in the 1910s. There were calls for working people to be able to take control of their lives, though exactly why birth control had to be a socialist cause was often unclear. Birth control activists did, however, argue very explicitly feminist principles, though women's organizations fighting such battles as suffrage (especially the National Woman Suffrage Association) or equal rights more broadly (especially the National Woman's Party) usually wanted to keep their distance from such a controversial topic as birth control.

Thus, early in the twentieth century, birth control was conceived as a very different sort of issue than it is today. Although most socialists and feminists did not make birth control a top priority, proponents of birth control used socialist and feminist rhetoric. Partly because of its sexual content, and partly because of its links to socialism and feminism, the birth control movement faced strong opposition: even the claim that married couples should have easy access to contraception was politically explosive.

Emma Goldman and Mary Ware Dennett, who had considerable ties to other social movements of the Left, were early prominent advocates of birth control, but Margaret Sanger quickly became its most celebrated and influential proponent. In the 1920s, Sanger moved away from the radical roots of birth control and emphasized more the need for birth control to be a decision between a physician and the patient. While Dennett denounced reframing birth control to portray it as a respectable, medical option, Sanger's turn to a medical frame for birth control was ultimately strategically effective. She lobbied the U.S. Congress to grant physicians an exemption from the Comstock laws, but her efforts achieved no legislative success. However, to a significant extent through a court case brought by Sanger and her supporters, judicial rulings in the mid-1930s began to undermine the Comstock laws, especially to the extent that the laws prevented doctors from providing contraceptive advice and devices to their patients. Making physicians the dispensers of legal contraception highly favored middle-class Americans who could afford private medical care. But in most states, contraception, including over-the-counter forms such as condoms, became more available over the next couple of decades. While enforcement of Comstock laws declined considerably after World War II, state legislatures were still slow to act to overturn Comstock statutes restricting access to contraception beyond physicians. Indeed, it was not until 1965, in *Griswold v. Connecticut*,[2] that the U.S. Supreme Court ruled definitively that married couples had a right to use contraception unencumbered by state regulation. In 1972, in *Eisenstadt v. Baird*,[3] the Court extended that right to unmarried adults.

In hindsight it is easy to see that making physicians the gatekeepers to the use of contraception was considerably less controversial than treating contraception as part of a socialist and feminist empowerment of poor women and working people. By the 1930s, only the Catholic Church hierarchy remained a consistently vocal opponent of contraception. Federal judicial rulings that gave physicians freedom to dispense contraception did not evoke widespread outcry but instead, as we shall see, emerged in a context in which most people, by the 1930s, seemed to find legal birth control a quite acceptable idea. Even before the 1930s, the evidence is that few prosecutors considered enforcement of the Comstock laws a high priority. A puzzle then arises: Given the lack of widespread outrage over the defanging of the Comstock laws, why were legislatures so unreceptive to attempts to make birth control legal and accessible? Why didn't legislatures, rather than courts, take

[2] 381 U.S. 479 (1965).
[3] 405 U.S. 438 (1972).

the initiative to change the legal status of contraception? Indeed why, even after courts took such action beginning in the 1930s, did it take additional *decades* until the Comstock laws were fully overturned (via the Supreme Court decisions of 1965 and 1972), ultimately nearly a century after they were passed?

To answer these questions, we must focus on the frames that were possible within the birth control movement by examining the social and political context of that movement. In this chapter and the next, we will see aspects of birth control politics that sound quite foreign today, including eugenic arguments that, first and foremost, birth control should be used to discourage reproduction by "inferior groups," often meaning that white, native-born Protestants should remain dominant, numerically and otherwise. Just as it is true that many Americans today want to treat abortion as a private decision, while many others do not, in the early twentieth century there were many Americans anxious for effective contraception for their own private use, but also many who thought that the decision to limit the population, and change the balance of racial and ethnic groups via birth control, was very much a matter of public policy and not simply a private decision.

The central aim of the current chapter is to examine the framing dynamics through which a new issue of debate, that of contraception, entered public consciousness through preexisting social movements that have a wider agenda. The discussion below aims to demonstrate that it is extremely difficult to focus attention on that new issue, as long as those preexisting movements (and thus their wider agendas) survive. Broad, morally charged agendas often elicit passionate commitment within social movements, so that mobilization of such movements is a barrier preventing narrowing the agenda to a limiting frame. The cause of accessible contraception emerged within preexisting movements, most directly socialism, and was associated in many minds with feminism. Though the main feminist social movement organizations kept their distance from the birth control controversy, the central advocates of contraception did indeed use feminist themes within their arguments. As a result, opposition to contraception often originated in opposition to socialism and feminism, and it was almost impossible to have a public, political discussion of contraception that could extract itself from controversy over socialism and feminism. Contraception became a more distinct concern only once feminism and, especially, socialism somewhat faded from the scene after World War I, for reasons that had nothing to do with contraception per se. Thus, to understand the fate of social movement causes, we must look beyond support for, or opposition to, that cause alone.

The next section of this chapter sets the context for the history of the debate over contraception for this chapter as well as Chapters 3 and 4.

The Political and Social Context of Twentieth-Century Debate over Contraception

Disenfranchisement: Race, Immigration, and Sex

Strong assumptions about sex roles, racial differences, and the influence of heredity on aptitude and behavior had an important impact on the American debate over contraception.

Contraception became a prominent social movement concern, and an explicit topic of public controversy, at a time when Americans were eager to make racial distinctions and feared that large waves of immigration would change American society for the worse. Establishment voices among white, native-born Protestants assumed that their dominance within American society was natural and proper. Other racial or ethnic groups, such as African Americans or immigrant Catholics of various ethnicities, were considered ignorant and culturally backward, and this supposed inferiority was commonly attributed to an inheritance passed from generation to generation. Contraception did not emerge as an issue *because* of racial and ethnic prejudices. But these preexisting prejudices affected the course of the debate: It was not uncommon to judge contraception in light of how it might affect the racial and ethnic balance in American society.

Let me briefly note the place of African Americans and immigrants in American society at the time, and then set the context of the discussion of women, sexuality, and reproduction in the early twentieth century.

African Americans were effectively disenfranchised in the late nineteenth century, preventing them from countering political discourse about their supposed inferiority. Following the Civil War (1861–1865) came Reconstruction (1865–1877), the period during which the Union Army occupied the South to protect newly freed slaves and made some progress assuring that the former Confederate states formally accepted the legal and political changes that came in the wake of the war. The white South's opposition to equal citizenship rights for blacks was such that, as soon as Reconstruction ended in 1877, Southern whites reversed what progress had been made. Through the use of political repression and terror (e.g., lynching and the threat of lynching), they deprived Southern blacks of land, economic independence, and legal equality. Southern blacks, economically impoverished and dependent, were also excluded from the political life of most of the South. Most African Americans lived in the rural South at this time, and they had thus essentially been excluded from participation in the national polity as well, despite the formal rights of equality they had gained as a result of the Civil War. In practice, for example, most Southern blacks were prohibited from voting, despite their legal right to do so. Not until the middle third of the twentieth century, after several decades of large-scale migration of Southern blacks to Northern and Southern cities, would African Americans become a significant political force in American society. (Even then, they were at first a voting force only in the North, until the 1960s, when the Civil Rights movement successfully pressured the federal government to enforce African American voting rights in the South. But migration to cities even in the South was an important factor in establishing black communities with some autonomy from white society.)[4]

African Americans would thus not be significant participants in the early-twentieth-century debate over contraception, nor in any other national debate during that period. Also disadvantaged, but not so much as African Americans, were immigrants, who came in such numbers that they dramatically changed the composition of American society in the late nineteenth and early twentieth centuries. Immigration into the United States picked up considerably in the 1880s, and the

[4] See, for instance, Frances Fox Piven and Richard A. Cloward, chapter 4, "The Civil Rights Movement," pp. 181–258 in *Poor People's Movements* (New York: Vintage, 1979); Aldon Morris, *The Origins of the Civil Rights Movement: Black Communities Organizing for Change* (New York: Free Press/Simon & Schuster, 1984), pp. 1–6, 78–80.

largest numbers (until the late twentieth century) came between 1900 and 1915. By 1920 one out of every three Americans was either an immigrant or the child of an immigrant.[5] Immigration supplied much of the industrial labor force in the Northern and Midwestern cities; industrialization was of course part of the context of the rise of the Socialist movement, discussed later in this chapter. And the health of immigrant women who experienced multiple pregnancies in impoverished conditions were a central focus of early birth control activists.

Immigration made Catholics, and to a lesser extent Jews, a much more significant presence in American society. There were calls for restrictions; nineteenth-century federal legislation had limited non-European immigration, and the new legislation of the late 1910s and 1920s limited further European immigration, especially from southern and eastern Europe.[6] At the time, it was common to refer to different ethnic groups as distinct "races." Assertions about the inferior biological inheritance of the southern and eastern European "races," like the black and Irish races before them, often went unchallenged. However, the term "race" was also used to apply to humanity more generally. In fact, the ambiguity of the term was such that, in a society dominated by whites, references to the future of the "race" sometimes did not distinguish between the human race and the white race. That is, the double meaning implied that the human race had a healthy future only as long as whites were dominant.

Relative to recent immigrants, and especially relative to African Americans, the political position of white, middle-class women had improved in the decades preceding the battles over contraception. Though women had by the early twentieth century failed to obtain even formal legal equality to men, let alone truly equal access to political or economic opportunities, they had at least become a presence within the American polity. Equal rights movements, including a demand for suffrage (i.e., the right for women to vote), had originated in the middle of the nineteenth century. In addition, women had been central to the

---

[5] Robert V. Wells, *Revolutions in Americans' Lives: A Demographic Perspective on the History of Americans, Their Families, and Their Society* (Westport, Conn.: Greenwood, 1982), p. 101.
[6] Wells, *Revolutions in Americans' Lives*, p. 110.

abolition movement before the Civil War, as well as temperance movements in the late nineteenth and early twentieth centuries. Women's movements met considerable resistance in the nineteenth century, but they did at least pave the way for acceptance of the idea that women had something to contribute to public life.[7]

Birth control was hardly a popular cause, nor even necessarily a respectable topic of conversation, in the early 1900s. But a few activists, most notably the socialist Emma Goldman, began to address the issue. By the early 1900s, women had enough of a voice in the American polity that there emerged explicit challenges to anticontraception rhetoric that birth control was a selfish, promiscuous practice subverting God's moral law and women's natural sex roles. This was a change, for example, from the time of the movement to outlaw abortion, led by physicians, which had its heyday between about the late 1850s and 1880 (discussed in Chapter 5).[8] At that time antiabortion physicians railed against supposedly selfish, immoral women who resorted to abortion for personal convenience. There was little organized response among women themselves. But a few decades later, that is, by the 1910s, women's voices were heard within political debates, even if their influence was limited. Suffrage was gaining respectability and became the law of the land with passage of the Nineteenth Amendment to the U.S. Constitution in 1920.

At times women's movements themselves adopted some of the racial and ethnic prejudices of the age. In 1894, for example, suffrage advocate Carrie Chapman Catt argued that the voting power of white women could counter the ignorant opinions that might otherwise prevail if blacks and immigrants voted in large numbers.[9] However, on balance, women's movements were one of the more egalitarian forces in American society, as their central concerns were legal equality between the sexes (including, e.g., the right of married women to serve on

---

[7] See, e.g., William H. Chafe, *The Paradox of Change: American Women in the 20th Century* (New York and Oxford: Oxford University Press, 1991), pp. 1–27.
   Formally the right to vote and other gains for women applied to all women, regardless of race or class, but in practice the race and class of African American and immigrant women was more important than gender in determining their (lack of) participation in the American polity.

[8] See James C. Mohr, *Abortion in America: The Origins and Evolution of National Policy* (New York: Oxford University Press, 1978).

[9] Chafe, *The Paradox of Change*, pp. 17–18.

juries or own property), access to democratic institutions, and social problems such as poverty and family stability.[10]

Still, most advocates within women's movements were not willing to make access to legal, accessible contraception a high priority – some wanted nothing to do with the issue. Expectations about women's propriety, and the taboo nature of public discussions of anything sexual in nature, were such that treating contraception as a women's issue was particularly controversial.

To understand, then, the obstacles faced by advocates of legal, accessible contraception, let us briefly examine the nineteenth-century heritage of birth control in American society.

The Emergence of the Comstock Laws

While this book's emphasis on framing processes focuses on the period when contraception became an important topic of public debate – the 1910s to the 1930s – I do not want to leave the impression that contraception was a new topic for twentieth-century America. Concern with the issue in the nineteenth century helped shape the contours of the twentieth-century contraception debate.

As a number of historians have chronicled, there is evidence of interest in contraception that goes back many centuries.[11] It appears both that interest in limiting pregnancy and childbirth was widespread and that public discussion of such matters in pre-twentieth-century America was taboo (thus, exactly how acceptable contraception and abortion were to Americans privately is difficult to determine).[12] Until about the 1930s, the practices and beliefs surrounding methods of preventing pregnancy were, by our standards, frighteningly inaccurate and unreliable. For example, advocacy of what we call the rhythm method – abstention from sexual intercourse during the fertile periods of a woman's monthly menstrual cycle – frequently suffered from

---

[10] See, e.g., Ellen Carol DuBois, *Woman Suffrage and Women's Rights* (New York and London: New York University Press, 1998), pp. 91–7; Steven M. Buechler, *Women's Movements in the United States* (New Brunswick, N.J., and London: Rutgers University Press, 1990), pp. 135–50.

[11] See, e.g., Linda Gordon, *Woman's Body, Woman's Right: Birth Control in America*, rev. ed. (New York and London: Penguin/Viking, 1990), chapter 2.

[12] See, e.g., Janet Farrell Brodie, *Contraception and Abortion in Nineteenth-Century America* (Ithaca and London: Cornell University Press, 1994), pp. 38–56.

misinformation about which part of the month was indeed the infertile period.[13] Considerable advances in knowledge about rhythm came into public view in the 1930s, but that was well after the movement to liberalize legal restrictions had begun.[14]

Until about the last half century, then, contraceptive knowledge and methods were unreliable enough that errors and tragedies abounded in the cases of many individual women and couples. Still, there was enough effective knowledge and advice in circulation – concerning the use of withdrawal, spermicides, condoms, and diaphragms, in addition to numerous ineffective methods – that American families, in the aggregate, were dramatically decreasing the size of their families by the middle of the nineteenth century. The average American woman in 1800 gave birth about seven times in her lifetime, but the rate was halved by 1900.[15]

Indeed, in the nineteenth century, various lecturers, medical writers, and self-help literature addressed the topic of contraception.[16] The slightest public allusion to sexuality scandalized many, so that these authors and lecturers found themselves, not infrequently, the subject of public condemnation or even criminal prosecution for obscenity and related offenses. Given the taboo nature of the subject, books and pamphlets addressing the prevention of conception often gave instruction about the actual methods using elliptical, indirect language and went by such nonobvious titles as *Moral Physiology*, *Fruits of Philosophy*, and *Esoteric Anthropology* (though subtitles sometimes referred to "the Population Question" or appealed to "Young Married People").[17]

---

[13] Ibid., pp. 79–86, 114–15.

[14] See the various materials in MSP-LC, vols. 114 and 115, reel 75, especially materials concerning Dr. Leo Latz, author of a book originally published in 1932 that claimed to demonstrate with scientific evidence the details and successful use of the rhythm method.

[15] James Reed, *The Birth Control Movement and American Society: From Private Vice to Public Virtue* (Princeton, N.J.: Princeton University Press, 1984), pp. 3–4; Gordon, *Woman's Body, Woman's Right*, pp. 48–9.

[16] A good source on such matters is Brodie, *Contraception and Abortion in Nineteenth-Century America*, especially chapters 4, 5, and 6; also Reed, ibid., pp. 4–18.

[17] Robert Dale Owen's *Moral Physiology* first appeared about 1831 with a subtitle referring to the "Population Question." Charles Knowlton first published *Fruits of Philosophy* in 1832, and most editions (through 1937) included subtitles designating the text "The Private Companion of Young Married People" or "A Treatise on the Population Question." Thomas Low Nichols was the author listed for *Esoteric Anthropology*, first published 1853, although Brodie, *Contraception and Abortion*, p. 127, believes that his wife, Mary Gove Nichols, a popular lecturer, wrote

But there was enough demand for birth control that even such obscurely titled works went through numerous editions over several decades, sometimes including pirated editions. The exact contraceptive advice, and how explicit it was, therefore could vary across editions, as the authors changed their minds about imperfectly understood methods, or texts were altered without the author's permission.

However, in the 1870s and 1880s, new federal and state laws specifically prohibited the circulation of contraceptive information, declaring it "obscene." These laws are collectively known as the Comstock laws, after Anthony Comstock (1844–1915), who was practically a one-man social movement to outlaw what he considered vice.

Comstock grew up in small-town Connecticut. While working at low-paying jobs in New York City as a young man, he was scandalized by the sale of erotic literature and contraceptive goods, abortion services, and prostitution. He made a number of formal legal complaints, attempted to spur the police to action, attracted the support of wealthy and influential men (e.g., the presidents of Amherst, Brown, Dartmouth, and Yale), and founded the New York Society for the Suppression of Vice. This support freed Comstock to devote his entire career to his moral passions. He became an effective lobbyist for the passage of the federal antiobscenity statute in 1873, which, in response to Comstock's insistence, specifically designated contraceptive information as "obscene." Upon passage of the law, he was appointed a special agent for the U.S. Post Office, empowered to investigate and arrest those who violated the statute. From that position he personally played a large role in enforcing the law, until his death in 1915.[18]

The Comstock laws most clearly prohibited the use of mails or published advertisements in promoting contraception. Because of the federal law's focus on the mails (which are under federal jurisdiction and thus a standard weapon when Washington wants to control commerce

parts. Its original subtitle was "A Comprehensive and Confidential Treatise on the Structure, Functions, Passionate Attractions and Perversions, True and False Physical and Social Conditions, and Most Intimate Relations of Men and Women."

There were also various other publications, not all of which went through different editions. For details see Brodie's book, especially Chapter 4 and the bibliography of nineteenth-century literature, pp. 357–65.

[18] See Brodie, ibid., chapter 8; Alvah W. Sulloway, *Birth Control and Catholic Doctrine* (Boston: Beacon, 1959), pp. 1–17; David J. Garrow, *Liberty and Sexuality: The Right to Privacy and the Making of <u>Roe v. Wade</u>* (New York: Macmillan/Lisa Drew, 1994), p. 15.

in particular kinds of goods or activities), supporters of contraception commonly had the most to fear from their encounters with the postal service, and, until his death in 1915, that sometimes meant encounters with Anthony Comstock.

The state Comstock laws varied, for example, in terms of whether physicians could provide contraceptive information in the privacy of their offices; in only one state, Connecticut, was the use of contraception itself specifically outlawed.[19] But for the most part the federal and state laws together effectively made dissemination of contraceptive information and materials illegal. Enforcement, however, was typically sporadic. And like people in many other societies, Americans still managed to practice some forms of birth control. Birth rates continued to decline. Indeed, women who married in the 1870s, and thus who experienced their child-bearing years as the Comstock laws were being passed, averaged 2.8 children across their lifetime, a dramatic contrast to the average of 4.9 children for women married between 1800 and 1849.[20] This was despite the fact that women often had to rely on uncertain methods, such as withdrawal. They often had little access to more reliable birth control technologies, such as spermicides, diaphragms, or condoms (though these technologies of the day were still often risky by today's standards).

The Comstock laws, then, had a chilling effect on the accessibility and discussion of contraception, but exactly how much, and in what ways, is complex. On the one hand, as one prominent birth control advocate, Mary Ware Dennett, noted in 1926, actual prosecutions for violating the contraception provisions of the Comstock laws were few.[21] Indeed, research by Amy Sarch indicates that, by the 1920s and 1930s, in at least some parts of the country, some contraceptive devices were widely available and appeared (with transparent euphemisms such as references to products for "feminine hygiene")

---

[19] Brodie reported (ibid., p. 257) that, because the Connecticut law was particularly extreme, it was in that state that lawyers brought the case that led to the 1965 U.S. Supreme Court ruling, in *Griswold v. Connecticut*, that cited a right to privacy in prohibiting states to regulate the use of contraception by married couples.

[20] Wells, *Revolutions in American's Lives*, p. 92.

[21] Dennett, *Birth Control Laws: Shall We Keep Them Change Them or Abolish Them* (New York: Frederick H. Hitchcock/The Grafton Press, 1926; reprinted New York: Da Capo Press, 1970), pp. 46–51, 279.

in mainstream advertising outlets.[22] Indeed, one of Dennett's central arguments against the laws was that they were rarely enforced and largely unenforceable. Anthony Comstock spent much more of his time battling pornography, which Nicola Beisel has convincingly argued reflected that his principal concern was prevention of what he saw as the moral corruption of youth, especially middle-class and upper-class, native-born, white youth.[23]

But publishing instructions for contraception could be risky. And for most people, access to reliable contraceptive information and technologies was difficult.[24] Such information traveled through informal networks and surreptitious media that, often enough, shared incomplete and inaccurate information. And, as Dennett herself noted, while enforcement in general was lax, it was used selectively,[25] especially against prominent activists (including Dennett herself).

Those activists emerged in the 1910s primarily because that decade saw a great deal of social movement activity surrounding the Socialist

---

[22] Amy Sarch, "Dirty Discourse: Birth Control Advertising in the 1920s and 1930s" (Ph.D. dissertation, Annenberg School for Communication, University of Pennsylvania, 1994). Sarch sees her interesting findings – including a contraceptive advertised (not very) surreptitiously in the Sears catalogue – as evidence that the strategy of placing contraceptives under medical control was primarily motivated by a desire among birth control advocates not to see sexuality and sexual messages commercially exploited. While there certainly may have been some birth control advocates who favored a medical framing of contraception in order to avoid contraception's being associated with crass commercialism, Sarch's interpretation is not tenable in light of the history of the birth control movement before the 1920s, and in light of the debate between Sanger and Dennett over medicalization, discussed in Chapters 3 and 4 in this book. That is, whether physicians would have control was simply not primarily about the problem of commercial advertising. Also relevant here is that some of the more desirable and effective contraceptive devices in practical and legal terms generally required assistance from medical professionals, for instance in fitting diaphragms.

[23] Nicola Beisel, *Imperiled Innocents: Anthony Comstock and Family Reproduction in Victorian America* (Princeton, N.J.: Princeton University Press, 1997), esp. pp. 58–75. More broadly, Beisel argued that Comstock's antivice campaign was a means of distinguishing the worth of native-born, upper-class culture from the perceived corrupting influence of immigrant, lower-class culture. See also Beisel, "Class, Culture, and Campaigns against Vice in Three American Cities, 1872–1892," *American Sociological Review* 55(1990):44–62.

[24] See, e.g., Brodie, *Contraception and Abortion*, pp. 281–6. The federal law also prohibited the importation of contraceptives, but enforcement was not always comprehensive or effective (Brodie, p. 208).

[25] Dennett, *Birth Control Laws*, p. 47.

Party and opposition to U.S. involvement in World War I. It is questionable that birth control would have become much of a cause in the 1910s if that decade had not been a time of heightened social activism in general (in favor of socialism and women's suffrage and against World War I). Given the circulation of activist ideas, activist organizations, and experience in protest in general the 1910s were a time propitious for left-wing activism. As social movement scholar Sidney Tarrow has noted, social movements for diverse causes generally clump together in time and space in "cycles of protest."[26]

Certainly, frequently cited social and economic changes that favored a new kind of family made birth control increasingly popular: Families living in the growing urban and industrial economy no longer found large families a source of useful labor, as had farm families. For both men and women working in growing manufacturing industries, large numbers of children were an economic handicap. Throughout society there was developing an increasing emphasis on the emotional strength of small families.[27] But the growing desire for small families, and even the use of methods (such as withdrawal and abortion) to control family size, was not enough to spark a birth control *movement*. As noted above, by the time of the passage of the Comstock laws, American families had effected a historical reduction in fertility, before sophisticated contraceptive devices were widely available. And the federal Comstock law was passed a good four decades before the birth control movement.

The birth control movement emerged, then, in a context in which it could borrow ideologically and organizationally from existing social movements. Activists emerged who challenged the Comstock laws, but through the 1910s, they framed their challenges by linking birth control to other causes, especially socialism and women's rights.

[26] Sidney Tarrow, *Power in Movement: Social Movements, Collective Action, and Politics* (Cambridge and New York: Cambridge University Press, 1994), pp. 153–69. It is important to note that Tarrow would also emphasize that such cycles begin with opportunity via weakened institutional authority when, for instance, geopolitical, economic, or other circumstances temporarily weakened a state's coercive power. In the 1910s, the major sources of protest – socialism and women's movements – had significant history previous to the decade, but the uncertainty and controversy over potential U.S. involvement in World War I heightened social movement activity.

[27] See, e.g., Edward Shorter, "Female Emancipation, Birth Control, and Fertility in European History," *American Historical Review* 78(1973):605–40; Reed, *The Birth Control Movement and American Society*, chapters 1 and 2.

The central activists in the movement to legalize accessible contraception – Margaret Sanger, Mary Ware Dennett, and Emma Goldman – all encountered prosecution for violation of Comstock laws. The difficulties the laws could present shaped the type of advocacy such activists were willing to risk. Attracting most attention were the various prosecutions of Sanger, beginning with her arrest in 1914.[28] After publishing the first issue of her revolutionary magazine, the *Woman Rebel*, in 1914, Sanger received a notice that the issue was unmailable (though copies had actually already been delivered), under the federal Comstock law. Sanger and her colleagues mailed subsequent issues in small bundles in various parts of town, so as to avoid detection. These issues did not contain specific information on how an individual could actually practice contraception, but Sanger later reported that within six months she received "over ten thousand letters" asking for such information. But she could not let "a single letter reach the wrong destination; therefore, I sent no contraceptive facts through the mails."[29]

William Sanger, Margaret's estranged husband, was arrested in 1915 for giving a copy of Margaret's pamphlet, *Family Limitation*, to a government agent posing as an ordinary citizen interested in birth control advice. Anthony Comstock became personally involved in the prosecution of William Sanger. William Sanger's defiant stance during his prosecution (including his choosing to spend 30 days in jail upon conviction, rather than take the easier route of paying a fine) helped rally publicity and support for the cause.[30] Margaret Sanger was arrested in 1914 for advocating both birth control and political violence and then again in 1916 for providing contraceptive information to women at her Brownsville, Brooklyn, clinic, the first birth control clinic in

[28] There were at the time, and remain to some extent, disputes about whether Sanger's first arrest resulted from advocacy, within articles in the *Woman Rebel*, for contraception or for political assassination. It appears the actual arrest was for the latter, but her advocacy of contraception also irked the authorities, and the public perception was that birth control was the central issue. David M. Kennedy, *Birth Control in America: The Career of Margaret Sanger* (New Haven, Conn., and London: Yale University Press, 1970), pp. 24, 78–9; Gordon, *Woman's Body, Woman's Right*, pp. 218–19; Ellen Chesler, *Woman of Valor: Margaret Sanger and the Birth Control Movement in America* (New York: Anchor/Doubleday, 1992), pp. 99, 102.

[29] Sanger, *An Autobiography* (New York: W. W. Norton & Company, 1938), p. 112.

[30] See, e.g., Kennedy, *Birth Control in America*, pp. 32–3, 72–3.

the country. Under New York state's Comstock law, providing such services was legal for the "cure or prevention of disease," under a physician's direction,[31] but not specifically for fertility control. With the prosecution of Sanger and her coworkers, the clinic closed completely after less than a month. Sanger spent a month in jail, and the harsh force-feeding of her coconspirator and sister, Ethel Byrne, during Byrne's prison hunger strike, elicited further sympathy for the cause.[32]

The U.S. Post Office banned Dennett's sex education pamphlet, *The Sex Side of Life*,[33] in 1922, declaring it unmailable. Dennett, however, continued to distribute it and was indicted in 1929 when she sent a copy, by mail, to a fictitious name that was used to catch her breaking the federal Comstock law.[34] Thus, like Sanger, Dennett found her efforts to promote the birth control cause greatly affected by the Comstock restrictions. In the 1920s, Dennett's Voluntary Parenthood League had a form letter to respond to inquiries for birth control information:

I have your inquiry of recent date and most regretfully must answer that we cannot send you the information you request. We get a great many inquiries like yours, many of them showing heart-breaking need for immediate help. But to all of them we must make the same reply. We are working to change the laws which prohibit the circulation of contraceptive information, and if we made a business of breaking the law in the meantime, we would subject ourselves to the possibility of heavy fine or imprisonment, and the stopping of all our work.

However, information can be secured by those who persistently inquire in different ways. Friends inform each other, etc.; many doctors will give instruction in spite of the laws. Have you asked one? In other words, the laws are neither enforced nor enforceable.[35]

---

[31] New York state statute quoted in Kennedy, *Birth Control in America*, p. 84.
[32] Gordon, *Woman's Body, Woman's Right*, pp. 227–8. It appears that Sanger's own account gives a slightly different chronology about how long the clinic was actually open, that is, whether just ten days or closer to a month: Compare Kennedy, ibid., pp. 82–4, esp. n.20, with Carole R. McCann, *Birth Control Politics in the United States, 1916–1945* (Ithaca and London: Cornell University Press, 1994), p. 24, and Reed, *The Birth Control Movement and American Society*, pp. 106–7.
[33] Reproduced as Appendix B of Constance M. Chen's biography of Dennett of the same title: *"The Sex Side of Life": Mary Ware Dennett's Pioneering Battle for Birth Control and Sex Education* (New York: New Press, 1996).
[34] On Dennett's legal wrangles over this pamphlet, see her book, *Who's Obscene?* (New York: Vanguard Press, 1930).
[35] MWD, folder 248. The form letter is not dated but placement with other materials would suggest a date of about 1925.

While a great deal of contraceptive information and materials – indeed, the great majority – made it safely through the mail and appeared under thin disguise in numerous advertisements,[36] the threat that there could be sanctions for sending "obscene" material through the mail was apparently in general an effective weapon for those opposed to contraception. Physicians, for example, did not generally need to fear prosecution for recommending contraception to a patient in the context of an office visit. But it appears physicians were cautious enough, and in general averse enough to public scandal, that most were hesitant to risk obtaining deliveries of contraceptive supplies through the mail, which might be construed as illegal. Thus they were not likely to be able to offer much assistance beyond recommending abstinence, withdrawal, or (perhaps ineffective instructions for) the rhythm method or homespun spermicides.

In most cases, advocates of accessible contraception could in practice freely champion the use of contraception and reform of the law, whether through public speaking or in print, even if their writings went through the mail. But they risked prosecution if they gave specific advice on how to *use* contraception, or directed others to pamphlets or other sources of such information, or even if their advocacy of contraception bothered to explain in any detail that contraception had to do with sex. Almost any explicit reference to sex could conceivably be construed as "obscene," given the vague, sweeping prohibitions of the Comstock laws.

Both Sanger and Dennett, the two most important figures in the ongoing movement to legalize accessible contraception, despaired of the sweeping power of postal censors. The censors could label materials "obscene" or otherwise unmailable without citing specific evidence or otherwise justifying their decisions.[37] Dennett and British sex reformer Marie Stopes suspected that their correspondence was being intercepted by American postal authorities, so that Stopes used pseudonyms and mailed correspondence via third parties in order to escape notice.[38] Thus, odd as it may seem today, birth control activists

---

[36] See, for instance, Sarch, "Dirty Discourse."

[37] Sanger, *An Autobiography*, pp. 110–11; Dennett, *Who's Obscene?* pp. 211, 228–9, 251–5.

[38] Marie C. Stopes to Robert L. Dickinson, May 24, 1929, in MWD, folder 430; Chen, *"The Sex Side of Life,"* p. 249

had the U.S. Post Office to fear most of all; they had to pay particular attention to what was available through the mail, and to whom. (If we wanted to find a contemporary public figure equivalent to Comstock, we would perhaps think of someone in the Christian Right. Maybe we would even look in the U.S. Congress. But we would probably not look in the U.S. Post Office.) Consequently, battles over the Post Office's authority to stamp out "obscenity" became a central rallying point for activists who supported contraception. Despite various interpersonal and strategic tensions that Sanger had with other activists, she rallied publicly to the cause when Emma Goldman faced prosecution, for example, and Dennett rallied to Sanger's defense when Sanger was indicted. When specifically threatened by a Comstock prosecution, sundry supporters of birth control set aside their differences and rallied to the cause.

Morality, Sexuality, and Motherhood in the Debate over the Comstock Laws

In order to examine how diverse sources of supporters of birth control framed the issue, and changed that frame over time, later in this chapter I consider some of the central ideas and movements involved in the issue in the early years of the birth control movement, especially socialism and feminism. First, however, in order to set the context for those more specific sources of support, I sketch here some of the more common, general ideas behind both support for, and opposition to, birth control.

A common complaint of opponents of the Comstock laws' provisions on contraception was that the 1873 federal law had been passed quickly, at the end of a congressional session, with little discussion or debate.[39] Quick passage can sometimes mean that an initiative could have come out differently if there had been further discussion.[40] But

---

[39] For example, Sulloway, *Birth Control and Catholic Doctrine*, p. 4.

[40] In general, it is common in American legislatures for the pressure of anticipated recess to result in passage of a flurry of bills at the end of a session. Sometimes such bills would indeed have been more controversial (and thus less likely to pass) if subject to extensive public discussion. That would probably have been the case for the state abortion reform laws in the period 1966–1970, discussed in Chapter 4. The laws were often passed at the end of a legislative session, often without extensive debate. But sometimes the bills are simply uncontroversial, period, and sometimes they have indeed been thoroughly discussed but it takes the time pressure of the end of a session to force a compromise. See, e.g., Robert S. Lorch, *State and Local Politics: The Great Entanglement*, 6th ed. (Upper Saddle River, N.J.: Prentice Hall, 2001), p. 146.

the quick passage may simply have meant that, at the time, there was indeed little opposition. That there was broad support for Comstock provisions is, moreover, suggested by the fact that many states subsequently passed similar laws.[41]

Although various clergy and public figures decried the evils of contraception, the sentiment in favor of Comstock laws may to a great extent best be described as a diffuse sexual puritanism, at least in polite society. Such antisensualism appeared in many contexts and saw birth control as a scandalous use of the body for debauched, purely selfish sexual pleasure, rather than for the sacred purpose of producing children.[42] (Antisensualist arguments were dominant in American public affairs in the nineteenth century, but, by the 1920s, had become predominantly associated with Catholicism.) It did not take massive, organized movements to convince late-nineteenth-century legislatures to define contraception as indecent and scandalous. It is true that the dramatic nineteenth-century drop in the size of American families, as well as the widespread (if sometimes underground) circulation of literature on contraception, indicates that the practice of birth control was hardly unusual. Still, in nineteenth-century mainstream America it was rare to hear public arguments in favor of contraception: The idea of separating sex from reproduction was scandalous. As noted above, contraceptive manuals – even while reaching enormous numbers of Americans – had an underground quality and were often illegal under the Comstock laws. There was scattered public opposition to the Comstock Laws, for instance from the freethinking National Liberal League, founded in 1876, which objected in general to restrictions on freedom of speech and freedom of the press.[43] But even progressive, feminist arguments in favor of "voluntary motherhood" – an idea radical for its time, in arguing that marriage did not give a man the right to force sex upon his wife, or force her to have children against her will – still found abstinence, rather than sex using contraception, to be

---

[41] Sulloway (*Birth Control and Catholic Doctrine*, p. 14) seems to have agreed that quick passage meant that opposition to contraception was so taken for granted that the 1873 Comstock law was not considered a pressing matter of concern, but there was no reason to oppose it once it was proposed.

[42] See, e.g., Rev. Mabel Irwin, "The True Birth Control," *The Arbitrator* 1, no. 3 (August 1918):8–11; copy in MWD, folder 273.

[43] Brodie, *Contraception and Abortion*, pp. 263, 278–9; Beisel, *Imperiled Innocents*, pp. 86–7.

the only acceptable means for women to control their reproduction. And the assumption was still that women's primary social role was in motherhood. Prudery about public discussion of sex was not simply an ideological whim; it was also the case that, given a lack of employment options for women to become economically independent, marriage and motherhood provided women security and stability. Thus even social reformers who focused on gender inequalities typically found contraception a dangerous threat to marriage, as it would allow men to engage in sex outside of marriage without having to worry about pregnancy and the resulting obligations.[44]

Once a pro–birth control movement emerged in the 1910s, the perspective of birth control advocates reflected the somewhat contradictory nature of the place of birth control in American society. That is, on the one hand advocates of birth control portrayed it pragmatically as a progressive and sensible practice for ordinary Americans, a message that in itself probably did not seem radical to the millions of Americans who were in fact doing something to control their fertility. It probably did not seem radical to the many Americans who may have been unaware of the exact nature of the Comstock laws, given how sporadically those laws were enforced. But the self-proclaimed radicalism of the birth control movement reflected that movement activists also perceived, not unreasonably, an entire social hierarchy arrayed against their cause, given that something many Americans practiced was legally restricted and morally condemned by religious and political institutions and elites. Within this context, it is not entirely surprising that proponents of birth control associated their cause with a wholesale assault on the system of power within American society. Many saw themselves as revolutionaries, and the socialist movement was a natural ally.

To a significant extent the arguments in favor of contraception shared the confidence in rationally conceived human progress that had informed Western liberalism generally, as well as contemporary movements such as American Progressivism, given its confidence in rationally organized politics. Thus the idea that it was sensible for people to control some aspects of nature, including their own reproduction. It

[44] Gordon, *Woman's Body, Woman's Right*, chapter 5; DuBois, *Woman Suffrage and Women's Rights*, pp. 147–51.

was important to emphasize moral and humanitarian ends rather than accept biology as a crude determinant of human action.[45] For example, a 1916 National Birth Control League publication argued,

The control of natural processes for human rather than for merely natural ends is now generally accepted as the mark of an enlightened humanity. We have left behind us the day when the use of anesthetics in child-birth could be condemned on the ground that the pains are divinely ordained. It seems to me that the outcry against birth-control is a survival of this discarded point of view; and that it stands, not for a higher morality, but only for primitive superstition, fortified by a biological view of life.[46]

Margaret Sanger, for instance, dismissed the Catholic argument that birth control was a violation of God's plan for the natural order by commenting that the pope frustrated nature every time he shaved.[47] While hardly addressing the nuances of Catholic natural law theology, such a comment did probably strike a chord with Sanger's allies.

The idea that it was sensible to allow people to separate sex from procreation implicitly rejected the antisensualism of many opponents of contraception and thus began to separate sex from reproduction, but not fully. Some of the early (1910s) advocacy of contraception,

---

[45] Sulloway, *Birth Control and Catholic Doctrine*, pp. 64–5; Chesler, *Woman of Valor*, p. 209.

[46] Warner Fite, *Birth-Control and Biological Ethics*, pamphlet published by National Birth Control League, p. 19 (in MWD, folder 173, reel 13). Fite is listed as a Princeton University professor, and the pamphlet indicates that it is a reprint from an article in *The International Journal of Ethics*, October 1916.

For another example of this view of nature and a rationalist view of humanity, see National Birth Control League, "An Endorsement of Birth Control" [1919?], in MWD, folder 273. Indications in Dennett's papers are that the National Birth Control League had many of its supporters sign this official endorsement, in the manner of a petition.

[47] Kennedy, *Birth Control in America*, p. 153. Here and throughout his book, Kennedy presents perceptive analyses of the politics of birth control mixed with highly questionable suppositions fueled by Kennedy's dislike of Sanger as a person. As Ellen Chesler has pointed out in her more recent biography of Sanger (*Woman of Valor*, p. 17; see also Reed, *The Birth Control Movement and American Society*, pp. xx–xxi), Kennedy's patronizing view of his subject sometimes leads him to attribute irrational and petty motivations to her with little evidence. Chesler and others agree that Sanger could be difficult and self-serving (indeed, as will probably become clear, but is not important in analyzing her significance, overall I personally do not find her very likeable), but there seems little reason to explain her career and politics as a whole as the result of some fundamental personality flaw of emotionalism, as Kennedy sometimes does.

most especially Sanger's, certainly stated or implied that women's freedom and sexual fulfillment were themselves sufficient reasons for the legitimacy of birth control.[48] However, even in the more radical, early years of the movement (1910s) only a small minority of birth control advocates openly argued that birth control was important in the pursuit of sexual fulfillment, or that such fulfillment was itself a valuable goal, independent of procreation. Arguments for the sexual liberation of women met with strong opposition, and there is no particular reason to think that commitment to such liberation was common even among birth control advocates. Instead, arguments for the need for birth control typically painted a sympathetic portrait of mothers whose health and families would best be served by the ability to limit the *number* of children, rather than avoid motherhood altogether. While Margaret Sanger herself had a much more liberal sex life in private than was considered proper for the time,[49] this was certainly not the type of lifestyle that birth control advocates publicly associated with their cause.

And so there were limits to the pro–birth control view that it was sensible for women to limit their reproduction: For the most part (though not always), the implication was that birth control was compatible with motherhood, rather than opposed to it. To give another example, opposition to the Comstock laws most emphatically did not include support for accessible abortion. Birth control advocates portrayed abortion as a scourge that widespread use of birth control would in fact diminish.[50] As historian Carole R. McCann has noted, in the early twentieth century "[l]egalized abortion was not supported by any groups within the American political spectrum."[51] The nineteenth-century physicians'

---

[48] See, e.g., Sulloway, *Birth Control and Catholic Doctrine*, p. 189n.14.

[49] Sanger had a number of partners outside of marriage and apparently lived in a somewhat open marriage during much of her time in public life. See throughout Chesler, *Woman of Valor*, especially discussions of Sanger's second marriage, to Noah Slee.

[50] Gordon, *Woman's Body, Woman's Right*, p. 106.

[51] McCann, *Birth Control Politics*, p. 43. For a possible nineteenth-century exception, see Gordon, ibid., p. 106.

The writings of birth control advocates very commonly promoted birth control as a counter to abortion. For example, Mary Ware Dennett, "The Case for Birth Control," *The Arbitrator* 1, no. 3 (August 1918):3–8, copy in MWD, folder 273; Henry Pratt Fairchild, "The Facts about Birth Control," photocopy of article from *The New Republic*, October 16, 1929, photocopy filed with Anna Lifshiz (Secretary to Mrs. Sanger) to Fairchild, January 8, 1929, MSP-SS; American Birth Control League, "Birth Control," undated pamphlet, MSP-LC, vol. 253, reel 144; Norman Carr, "Is

campaign to portray abortion as a moral outrage had been extremely successful. And advocacy of birth control was not portrayed in terms of a woman's right to sexual pleasure and any right to avoid motherhood altogether.

And so the arguments that it made sense to limit reproduction hardly seem radical from our vantage point nearly a century later. But they were so roundly and vociferously rejected within early-twentieth-century American public life that they could receive a hearing only within radical political circles. Still, the left had multiple factions, and arguments in favor of birth control came from a variety of perspectives.

Moral Worldviews in the Fight for Contraception: Socialism and Feminism in the Early Twentieth Century

Opposition to the Comstock laws was probably the only specific belief that united all advocates of contraception; these laws were a clear impetus and rallying cry for the pro–birth control movement. Indeed, in an otherwise divided movement, unity and mutual support was almost always apparent when a prominent activist encountered prosecution under the Comstock provisions. Given the problems that the Comstock laws presented for the cause of accessible contraception, and the laws' serving as a rallying point for opposition, one might think that the strategy of the pro–birth control movement would involve primarily an attempt to overturn those laws. In fact, we shall see in Chapter 3 that Mary Ware Dennett pursued that strategy (but not within a limiting frame), to little avail. But, even for Dennett, contraception did not enter early-twentieth-century public debate simply as a question of whether the law should declare that it was obscene for individual women and men to decide how many children they would like to have. No, the issue was much bigger than that.

The 1910s were an explosive time of social movement activity and social change, much like the 1960s. As noted earlier, there was a fairly strong Socialist Party, the suffrage movement to give women the vote was in full swing, and a vibrant peace movement attempted to prevent U.S. involvement in World War I. (A smaller contingent of that

Birth Control Right?" undated pamphlet [late 1930s?] published by The Eugenical Press, Chicago, in MSP-LC, vol. 253, reel 144.

movement would pursue its increasingly unpopular antiwar stance once the United States actually entered the war in 1917.) Some of the more prominent social activists of the time were passionately involved in a variety of causes; antiwar groups, for example, typically espoused a populist and/or socialist worldview. It was often difficult to see where one cause ended and another began. Under those conditions, it was almost impossible to discuss birth control, or any single issue, independently of the morally charged mélange of leftist causes.

Socialism

Social movements do not spring spontaneously out of social needs. They require mobilization, and they require a frame to conceptualize a problem or grievance. Socialist activist Emma Goldman first channeled social movement energy toward the problem of access to birth control, and Margaret Sanger did the most to cultivate the cause. Sanger's commitment to birth control clearly borrowed a great deal from Goldman, but ultimately Sanger gave the issue considerably more attention. For Goldman, birth control was one part of a much larger revolutionary agenda to free humanity from economic and social oppression. Because the issue of birth control began within a larger, highly morally charged worldview, it could not easily be extracted from the radical causes to which it was associated. That is true even though most Americans who used and wanted birth control were hardly revolutionaries. This was a clear case of a cause not having significant strategic success until it had been torn from its radical origins (which did not happen until the radical movements had largely faded from the scene). But it took radicals, in the first place, to plant the idea that birth control should be freely available, without shame and without legal restraints.

Goldman was instrumental in the uphill battle to get American radicals to consider sex and gender issues worthy of their attention; she had become committed to the cause of birth control by 1900. As an anarchist socialist (i.e., a socialist emphasizing decentralized authority rather than central planning), Goldman was attuned to individual levels of oppression and thus emphasized the need for women to have independence and options in life. Thus one of her causes was the elimination of antifeminist moralism. Much like Sanger after her, Goldman's experience as a nurse and midwife for poor women convinced her that contraception was an important cause. While it was ultimately a middle-class constituency for contraception that would be central in the 1920s and 1930s, in earlier years Goldman and Sanger had emphasized the desperate circumstances of immigrants and other poor women who could not control their fertility easily and who suffered severe health consequences from repeated, unwanted pregnancies.[52]

While the issue of "birth control" – a term that Sanger popularized[53] – became personally identified in the public eye with her, Sanger came to the issue through her association with socialist activists who were initially more prominent, especially Goldman.[54] Sanger was different in that she made birth control the central part of her radical agenda, more so even than Goldman, and concentrated on organizing support for birth control more effectively than Goldman.[55] But the support of socialist organizations was important in Sanger's early successes at publicizing the issue. For example, in 1914 locals of the International Workers of the World (known as the "Wobblies") were the primary distributors of her pamphlet, *Family Limitation*, which was much more explicit in actually giving contraceptive instructions than was anything that had yet appeared in the *Woman Rebel*.[56] Eugene V. Debs, leader of the Socialist Party, served on the editorial board of the *Birth Control Review* and offered moral support, especially during the trials of Sanger and her estranged husband, William, for breaking the Comstock laws.[57]

While birth control was not a central issue for the Socialist Party, and many socialists held quite conservative views of sex and gender,[58] in the first couple of decades of the twentieth century socialist circles were unusual in that they often and openly accepted birth control, and sexual

---

[52] Reed, *The Birth Control Movement and American Society*, pp. 48–53; Chesler, *Woman of Valor*, pp. 81–2, 85–8.

[53] Chesler, ibid., p. 97.

[54] Richard Drinnon, *Rebel in Paradise: A Biography of Emma Goldman* (Chicago: University of Chicago Press, 1961), pp. 169–71; Kennedy, *Birth Control in America*, pp. 10–17; Gordon, *Woman's Body, Woman's Right*, pp. 208–12, 222–3. Gordon's chapter 9, "Birth Control and Social Revolution," is an unequaled, especially thorough discussion of Sanger's and birth control's relationship to socialist activism.

[55] As noted by Gordon, ibid., p. 217.

[56] Gordon, ibid., pp. 219, 222–4; Kennedy, *Birth Control in America*, pp. 25–7.

[57] See the various correspondence with, and other materials concerning, Debs in MSP-LC, vol. 11, reel 8; also Chesler, *Woman of Valor*, p. 168.

[58] See, e.g., Gordon, *Woman's Body, Woman's Right*, pp. 238–9.

liberation, as legitimate causes. As a result, to be for contraception, for so many in the pre–World War I period, meant also to be against capitalism. Sanger couched her early support of birth control in terms of improving the lives of the working class, especially working-class women.[59] Through her own periodical, the *Woman Rebel*, Sanger publicized various socialist causes, especially her advocacy of contraception. Looking back at the first publication of the *Woman Rebel*, Sanger even later (in her 1938 autobiography) effortlessly connected her 1914 feminism with her 1914 socialism.

I defined a woman's duty, "To look the world in the face with a go-to-hell look in the eyes; to have an idea; to speak and act in defiance of convention." It was a marvelous time to say what we wished. All America was a Hyde Park corner as far as criticism and challenging thought were concerned. We advocated direct action and took up the burning questions of the day. With a fine sense of irony we put anti-capitalist soapbox oratory in print.[60]

(Hyde Park, in London, has a long "speakers' corner" tradition, in which anyone so moved stands up and makes political, religious, or other public appeals.)

However, there are limits to being a subsidiary cause within a supposedly larger movement: Supporters of the former enter into the controversies of the larger movement yet must necessarily defer to the movement's "larger" goals. Under such conditions, it is difficult for the subsidiary cause to develop its own core constituency or present a clear, well-defined message. Thus, as we shall see was also the case among feminists and eugenicists, socialists were divided over contraception, and none of these groups considered contraception a top priority.

Specifically, there was the recurring problem that many socialists were quite conservative on sex and gender issues, and even those who were supportive of the birth control cause easily jettisoned concern over birth control when issues that they saw as more central to the socialist cause were at stake. Thus the cause of overturning the Comstock laws was enmeshed in disputes and complex ideologies that most

---

[59] See, e.g., Drinnon, *Rebel in Paradise*, p. 147; Kennedy, *Birth Control in America*, pp. 10–11; Gordon, ibid., pp. 218–20; also Sanger's Hotel Brevoort speech, January 17, 1916; and her seven-page pamphlet, "Facts on Abortion and Legislation in Relation to Birth Control," 1921. Both in MSP-LC, vol. 200, reel no. 129.

[60] Sanger, *An Autobiography*, p. 110.

Americans would not find helpful in justifying the need for legal, accessible contraception.

Among socialists, for example, one possible fault line was a division between Marxists and other socialists, especially anarchists. Marxists emphasized a belief in laws of history which would result in a more rationally planned, interdependent society which would come about through a socialist revolution that overturned capitalism in a dramatic historical moment. In addition, while all socialists emphasized class oppression, the Marxist approach was particularly dismissive of claims of sexual or other oppression, distractions from the more "fundamental" system of class oppression. Anarchists (who did not simply favor chaos, as is often simplistically and incorrectly supposed) might be just as committed to socialist revolution but emphasized more the need to break up centralized power and so emphasized self-reliance and democratic autonomy instead of the need for an even more interdependent, planned society.[61]

In her introduction to the published record of a 1925 international conference of birth control advocates, Sanger herself took note that the second such international conference, in 1905, disintegrated into an "insoluble conflict" because Marxists advocated what is sometimes known as "the breakdown thesis." The Marxist argument was that revolutionaries should work to hasten a crisis within capitalism – despite short-term pain, even for the working class – in order to bring about such a social crisis that a revolution would emerge to destroy capitalism entirely. Thus, rather than advocate contraception, it was better to allow the working class to continue to procreate in large numbers and contribute to the surplus labor force that, Marxists believed, capitalism created (and depended on to keep wages low). As the labor force expanded, workers would become increasingly dissatisfied with their declining wages and would become an unstoppable revolutionary mass. In short, then, Marxists at the conference opposed contraception among the working class.[62]

---

[61] Kennedy, *Birth Control in America*, pp. 111–13.

[62] Margaret Sanger, "Introduction," pp. v–xii in *The Sixth International Neo-Malthusian and Birth Control Conference, Vol. 1: International Aspects of Birth Control*, Sanger, ed. (New York: American Birth Control League, 1925), at pp. vi–vii. Those familiar with the history of Marxism might be amused to learn that, perhaps due to a slip of the tongue, Sanger once referred to this Second International Neo-Malthusian Conference

But many non-Marxist socialists, on the other hand, generally saw contraception positively, as a method of self-determination in the lives of working-class people and a means of depriving the capitalist class of a surplus labor force. As odd as it may sound to the contemporary ear that support for birth control was entangled with debates internal to socialist revolutionary theory, it is important to remember that without a socialist movement, it is questionable whether contraception could have developed any significant social movement support before the 1920s.

Still, Linda Gordon has observed that socialists, weakened any-way through repression for their opposition to World War I, easily dropped birth control as a cause in the late 1910s. Most had always seen birth control as "a reform issue rather than a revolutionary de-mand" and thus of a lower priority than issues immediately connected to the economic structure and class relations in a capitalist society.[63] For proponents of contraception, strategically socialism also presented a "fellow traveler" problem: opposition to contraception could draw upon anti-Red hysteria. Contraception was sometimes lumped together with Bolshevism – that is, the communist ideology of the Russian Revolution – as a dangerous force; opponents took seriously the claim of Sanger and other birth control activists that contraception had rev-olutionary implications. Even as late as the 1930s, more than a decade since birth control proponents had used socialist rhetoric, a represen-tative of Sanger's National Committee on Federal Legislation for Birth Control felt it necessary to note in U.S. Senate hearings on a birth con-trol bill that believing in birth control does not put one "in league with the soviets."[64] (Noting the shift in frame by that time, she had however

as simply "the Second International" (p. vi), terminology typically used to refer to the international gathering of communists in Paris in 1889. This is the only instance in this Introduction where Sanger uses this abbreviated terminology to refer to an international Malthusian conference.

[63] Gordon, *Woman's Body, Woman's Right*, pp. 212–13, 246.

[64] Statement of Mrs. Thomas M. Hepburn (mother of the actress Katherine Hep-burn), in United States Senate, Committee on the Judiciary, Hearings on S. 4436, May 12, 19, and 20, 1932 (Washington, D.C.: Government Printing Office), p. 5.
    The National Committee on Federal Legislation for Birth Control was one of a number of different organizations that Sanger founded. Following the histories of all of them, and the relationships among them, requires detailed examination of Sanger's biography and so is not appropriate in this book. Suffice it to say that Sanger was the most powerful force in the pro–birth control movement, so that the particular organizations fall into the background. More than once Sanger left

begun her testimony emphasizing physicians' support for the work of Sanger's organization.)

The reframing of birth control away from socialism stemmed from the serious blow that befell the socialist movement, especially in the United States, as a result of World War I. Before the war started, internationally the socialist position was that any such war would be a war made by capitalists, and that workers from different countries should unite rather than mobilize to kill each other. However, once war broke out, socialist parties in many countries took a nationalist line and supported their government's war effort; the Socialist Party in the U.S. was a notable exception. As a result of the split in international socialist ranks, the war disoriented the movement. And as a result of its continued antiwar stand, the Socialist Party in the United States suffered considerable repression during and after the war. Other reform movements and elements of the Left, including the more mainstream wing of the suffrage movement, explicitly disassociated themselves from socialism.[65] A "Red Scare" just after the war helped repress what remaining vitality there was within the Socialist Party; the 1919 deportation of Emma Goldman, who was not a U.S. citizen, was just one of many attacks on the U.S. socialist movement. The 1920s were, in general, a much less active time for social movements than the 1910s had been, and the socialist foundations that linked various movement causes, including birth control, mostly disintegrated. But, while socialism was integral to the launching of contraception as a publicly visible cause, we shall see in the following chapter that the decline of the Socialist Party ultimately allowed for mainstream acceptance of contraception.

Feminism

Even if they had not themselves used feminist rhetoric, early-twentieth-century advocates of birth control would have had to counter

---

organizations she founded and/or in which she had been prominent once she became dissatisfied with some of the other leaders of the group. Often then (especially in the case of the American Birth Control League, which Sanger founded in 1921) the organizations continued and were publicly identified with Sanger's cause but were partly in competition with her. The bewildering history of Sanger's association with different organizations confused many people at the time, and a number of analysts since, about which organizations spoke for Sanger, and at what time.

[65] Nancy F. Cott, *The Grounding of Modern Feminism* (New Haven and London: Yale University Press, 1987), pp. 59–61, 66.

antifeminist arguments that had emerged before the birth control movement. In the nineteenth and early twentieth centuries, opponents of higher education for women, opponents of birth control, and proponents of tough antiabortion laws all railed against those women who were supposedly too interested in selfish and frivolous pursuits (sometimes, in shorthand fashion, referred to as too much concern for "fashion"). Such selfish women, the argument went, neglected their natural roles as mothers. Various antifeminist strands of argument merged, for instance, in charges that college education promoted selfishness in the form of low fertility.[66] A central target, then, was the elite women's college, whose students were mostly well-off white Protestants. (By this time, Bryn Mawr, Smith, Vassar, and other elite women's colleges were notable fixtures in American higher education.) While such institutions might appear to us to have been bastions of class privilege, and racial and ethnic dominance, they drew quite a bit of criticism from white Protestant male elites of the time.

Still, while birth control was undoubtedly a feminist cause ideologically, its links to the organized women's movements of the time were tenuous at best. To understand why, let us examine the trends within these movements, which will help us understand not only the framing challenges faced by birth control advocates, but also the framing dynamics of social movements in general.

While it is reasonable, within our contemporary sense of the term *feminism*, to date the emergence of such movements no later than about the middle of the nineteenth century, historian Nancy F. Cott notes that use of the term was "a rare quirk prior to 1910 ... [but] became frequent by 1913 and almost unremarkable a few years later."[67] Cott notes that proponents of the term *feminism* meant explicitly to distinguish their view of women's causes from the more limited goals of the suffrage movement[68] (though again, from today's perspective we would consider suffrage a feminist goal). It was in the 1910s that contraception became a prominent social movement concern, also a decade of

---

[66] Gordon, *Woman's Body, Woman's Right*, p. 128; Carl N. Degler, *In Search of Human Nature: The Decline and Revival of Darwinism in American Social Thought* (New York and Oxford: Oxford University Press, 1991), pp. 28–30; Reed, *The Birth Control Movement and American Society*, pp. 41–2.

[67] Cott, *Grounding of Modern Feminism*, p. 13.

[68] Ibid., p. 3.

particular strength of the suffrage movement, which obtained passage of a constitutional amendment to grant women the vote in 1920. And so one might have expected that the two causes – that is, suffrage and contraception – would naturally be part of a larger feminist agenda. But, in fact, while those who called themselves "feminists" did not necessarily reject these causes, it was nevertheless the case that they often did not identify these causes as their core agenda. Examining why that was the case tells us something about the social movement dynamics in which contraception found itself.

As Cott noted, by the 1910s, there was a partial split among feminists who focused on suffrage and those who focused on a broader goal of recognition of equal rights for women. The former were strident in their support of suffrage but avoided claims that suffrage would be a revolutionary change in sex roles. The latter were the precursors of the failed E.R.A. (Equal Rights Amendment) effort of the 1970s; indeed the National Woman's Party originally proposed that amendment in the 1920s. However, I describe the split as "partial" because equal rights feminists were not generally averse to mobilizing in favor of suffrage; it is more that they thought many suffrage advocates had too limited an agenda. And there was a difference of emphasis; rather than speaking of suffrage, or other causes, as facilitating women's special contribution to society, equal rights feminists talked of suffrage and other *rights* women had, and which should be legally recognized. Exactly what type of rights were emphasized – civil, economic, political, and so forth – varied. For example, many feminists argued that the emancipation of women would be built on more than the pillar of suffrage, that is, also through workers' rights in opposition to exploitative capitalism. Like contraception, early-twentieth-century equal rights feminism, building on a nineteenth-century heritage, had links to the socialist movement.[69] As is often true of the relationship between different causes at a time of strong social movement activity,[70] Cott noted that there was a certain "fuzziness" in this relationship of feminism to socialism[71]: Neither

---

[69] Ibid., pp. 34–7.

[70] See a related argument I make in "Ideology, Culture, and Ambiguity: The Revolutionary Process in Iran," *Theory and Society* 25(1996):349–88.

[71] Cott, *Grounding of Modern Feminism*, p. 60. But there were exceptions; for instance, Emma Goldman had a quite developed perspective on how the political and economic decentralization of anarchism went hand in hand with the liberation of women

feminists nor socialists typically felt a strong need to explain the exact relationship between the two causes.

There is no doubt that birth control activists such as Emma Goldman, Margaret Sanger, and Mary Ware Dennett were feminists. Sanger, after all, had launched her activism with a publication titled the *Woman Rebel*. And consider, for example, her 1928 book, *Motherhood in Bondage*.[72] The book is a collection of excerpts from letters that Sanger says she received from various women, in desperate circumstances, seeking contraceptive advice and supplies. The very title of the book appears an attempt to reframe the issue of women's sexuality as a social problem, given that previous American discussions of women's problems had generally implied that bondage was the opposite of motherhood. That is, "motherhood" was not always the solution to women's problems, because motherhood itself could be "in bondage." About twenty years before publication of the book, there was in the United States a moral panic about the "white-slave" trade, that is, the supposed abduction of white women into prostitution. Contemporary analysts have noted that this panic was part of a Victorian ideal which could partly explain away white women engaging in illicit sex by assuming that they did so only via direct, extreme coercion.[73] As Carole R. McCann noted, the Socialist Party view at the time (approximately 1907 to 1911) was instead that white slavery was evidence that the low wages and insecure position of working families under capitalism forced innocent women into a degrading and dangerous life.[74] Arguably, Sanger's discussion of slavery in *Motherhood in Bondage* was even a more radical assault on the moral validity of the status quo, although more from a feminist than a socialist direction. The very title of the book, of course, describes some women's

---

from oppressive social norms. Ideologically, anarchism is more obviously compatible with sexual radicalism than is Marxism. Goldman's perspective included the need for a liberatory view of sexuality, including homosexuality, more broadly (Reed, *The Birth Control Movement and American Society*, pp. 47–53; Gordon, *Woman's Body, Woman's Right*, pp. 214–17. But Gordon noted that this made for an ideological package that did not fit comfortably into either socialist or feminist organizations (p. 217).

[72] New York: Brentano's, 1928.

[73] For example, McCann, *Birth Control Politics*, p. 41; Kennedy, *Birth Control in America*, p. 58.

[74] McCann, ibid., p. 41.

experience of motherhood as a form of "bondage." In addition, Sanger spoke explicitly of "slave mothers"[75] and women's "slavery" in having to work like "beasts of burden" to care for large numbers of children.[76] Sanger, then, discussed slavery not in terms of prostitution but instead as the condition of married women forced to go without contraception and thus endure repeated pregnancies against their will, to the detriment of their family life, economic situation, and health.

Biographical accounts of Sanger note that she could often be self-promoting and fail to give credit to others where due; combined with her move away from her radical roots, these qualities of Sanger's have led to various charges of her being egotistical and unreliable. However, Ellen Chesler, Sanger's most recent biographer, makes a convincing case that one of the more constant aspects of her activist career was her goal of involving women in contraception, and her belief that doing so would give them greater control over their own lives. The routes she took to attaining that goal have been highly controversial, but it is quite clear that that is the goal she thought she was achieving, and toward which she devoted her life. While she did not obtain the support of feminist organizations, there was definitely informal support for Sanger's cause among many feminists.[77]

Mary Ware Dennett had especially broad feminist credentials: she was active in the National American Woman Suffrage Association, the feminist group Heterodoxy, feminist publications, and a group that promoted the use of anesthesia to allow painless but conscious childbirth.[78] But the birth control movement's relationship to the organized women's rights and suffrage movements was in some ways the worst of both worlds: long-standing opponents to feminism provided a ready-made opposition for the newer cause of birth control, and yet birth control did not benefit from any explicit support from established women's organizations. Indeed, suffrage groups and women's rights groups generally wanted to keep their distance from contraception's taint of scandal and controversy.

---

[75] Sanger, *Motherhood in Bondage*, p. 24.

[76] Ibid., p. 155.

[77] See, e.g., Chesler, *Woman of Valor*, p. 130, and a similar point in McCann, *Birth Control Politics*, p. 10.

[78] Chen, *"The Sex Side of Life,"* pp. 150, 203.

There seems to have been two central, mutually reinforcing reasons for this distance between contraception and feminist movements. First (the reason typically cited) is that contraception was simply too controversial, as would be any issue connected so explicitly to sexual issues.[79] The second reason, drawing from the argument of this book about social movement framing patterns, is that these various causes – contraception, suffrage, and equal rights – were at different stages of the political cycle of innovations and framing in social movements. It is worth examining this second reason at some length, by examining the battles over framing goals within women's movements.

As addressed earlier in this chapter, in the 1910s contraception was a new social movement cause, one embedded within social movement networks, in which the boundary between contraception and other causes (especially socialist causes) was sometimes difficult to identify. Women's movements (focusing on either suffrage or equal rights) had a much longer history and so were in a different stage of development, working through their own distinct and established organizations that were attempting to focus on core agendas. Thus established women's organizations were at this point narrowing rather than broadening their agendas, and even though there was a split among and within these organizations over how broad the agenda should be, those who held the opinion that contraception should be a core plank were very much in the minority. The basic tendency was to be suspicious of any new controversy as a potential distraction. Particularly disadvantaged was any new controversy that had little history of advocacy within feminist movements: For example, Sanger, a charismatic leader within an excellent intuitive sense of movement strategy, nevertheless had no personal history of participation in feminist organizations. She developed a public image as a personification of the cause of birth control quickly in the mid-1910s, before she had long been involved in any political activity at all: Sanger had a flair for portraying herself simultaneously as both a martyr sacrificed at Comstock's altar, as well as a victorious warrior against prudery and repression. She did not become known as a result of long-standing identification with women's movements, but instead through her publication *The Woman Rebel* and her

---

[79] Chesler, *Woman of Valor*, pp. 59–61.

subsequent legal battles. But, that meant that, as the established leader of the birth control movement, Sanger had little clout among women's organizations, whose leaders were, in any case, reluctant to venture too far into the terrain of sexual controversy.

But, more important than a particular person's connections was the fact that the women's movement had, by the 1910s, developed organizations whose leaders had learned the strategic value of avoiding fights on too many fronts at once. The National American Woman Suffrage Association emphasized in the early 1920s that women voters could and would disagree on many matters, and that supporting suffrage did not imply any particular, comprehensive political program.[80] The women's movement had, in effect, moved in the early twentieth century toward a strategy of developing limiting frames. This was particularly true of the suffrage movement; it follows, then, that suffrage had advantages achieving a legislative victory that the broader equal rights approach (e.g., of the National Woman's Party) did not. Indeed, the constitutional amendment giving women the vote required enormous legislative success, namely a two-thirds vote in each house of the U.S. Congress as well as legislative approval in three quarters of the states. Birth control never achieved anything remotely similar to that kind of legislative success.

Suffrage, over several decades, went from a cause that could not help but be radical to one that framed women's right to vote as a cause that was compatible with women's other existing roles in society. In the nineteenth century, suffrage had been one of the more prominent demands of women's rights activists, who more generally protested against women's legally sanctioned inequality. Other issues included the inability of married women to hold property. Within this framework, suffrage was one of several reforms necessary to change women's place in society.

But explicitly seeking a widespread change in sex roles implied to most men, and perhaps most nineteenth-century women, a moral worldview too radical to be acceptable. Many of the changes nineteenth-century women's rights' activists demanded ultimately did come about, but in a piecemeal fashion that generally rejected a frame

---

[80] Aileen S. Kraditor, *The Ideas of the Woman Suffrage Movement, 1890–1920* (New York and London: Columbia University Press, 1965), pp. 227–48.

implying radical social change. Suffrage was the most prominent example. Up through at least the first decade of the twentieth century, the very fact that women held open-air rallies in support of suffrage struck many Americans as a very unfeminine activity that debased the purity of domestic womanhood. And so in that sense, suffrage, like any feminist cause, was implicitly radical and far-reaching. A radical image can present strategic problems in gaining hearing for a social movement cause in mainstream circles; not surprisingly, then, the movement for the vote gradually turned away from linking suffrage to an explicit, wholesale indictment of gender-based injustice. Suffrage is generally portrayed as having cast its lot with a "separate spheres" notion of feminism, that is, a view that women's causes were not an attempt to erase all differences between men and women. Instead, social and legal changes should value, protect, and advance the distinctive contribution of women, typically presented as the defense of the moral health of society, especially through the proper socialization of children. Without women's voices, the moral health of the family and of society would be in danger. Nancy Cott has noted that, by the 1910s, "suffragists were as likely to argue that women deserved the vote *because* of their sex – because women as a group had relevant benefits to bring and interests to defend in the polity – as to argue that women deserved the vote *despite* their sex."[81]

Separate spheres movements typically attempted to retain the view that women were more morally pure than men but wanted to expand women's special moral mission to include the public sphere, not just the private world of the family. For example, women justified their involvement in the temperance movement by proclaiming a mission to prevent the disintegration of the family, and of the moral fabric of society more generally, that would otherwise result (it was assumed) from the widespread abuse of alcohol. While supporters of suffrage and temperance could take either conservative or liberal views of other gender issues, the separate spheres approach that dominated suffrage in the 1910s generally sanctioned Victorian family arrangements, in which there was little role for women who did center their lives on bearing and raising children.[82]

---

[81] Cott, *Grounding of Modern Feminism*, p. 29. Emphasis is Cott's.
[82] See Gordon's discussion, *Woman's Body, Woman's Right*, pp. 93–8, 139, 239.

The separate spheres approach to feminism, emphasizing the special needs and contributions of women, could not tolerate contraception. Contraception could raise the specter of female promiscuity, a violation of the notion of the special moral purity of women. More generally, it might imply fewer consequences for sex outside of marriage, not only for women but especially significantly, for men. The perception, then, was that contraception might ultimately weaken men's commitment to marriage, the central institutional source of stability upon which women could rely.[83]

The limiting frame that the suffrage movement came to adopt was undoubtedly a disappointment to those in the women's movement who pushed for a wider agenda. Indeed, as noted above, the very term *feminism* originated in an attempt to argue that a women's movement needed to be concerned with much more than merely suffrage.

I would argue, however, that there is a distinction to be made between the frame used to justify a social movement cause, and the ultimate implications of that cause. It is true that the cause of suffrage had separated from the movement for equal rights feminism as a whole. However, it can be the case that limiting the frame to argue that the cause implies (only) a circumscribed range of social change in fact leaves open the possibility of addressing wider causes in the future. An analogy could be made with legal test cases: A part of legal strategy, of civil rights and other social change organizations, is to judge when seeking legal redress on a broad principle is worth the risk of finality than can be involved in a high court's decision. That is, a poorly chosen or poorly timed test case can lead to a judicial decision that rules sweepingly *against* one's goals, so that it would have been better never to have brought the case at all, and thus not instigate such constraining legal precedents.[84]

Likewise, winning a cause via a limiting frame does not necessarily mean that a wider frame is forever excluded: One may instead be postponing final resolution to wait for a more propitious moment. Such a

---

[83] Linda Gordon, "Why Nineteenth-Century Feminists Did Not Support Birth Control and Twentieth-Century Feminists Do," pp. 40–53 in *Rethinking the Family: Some Feminist Questions*, Barrie Thorne and Marilyn Yalom, eds. (New York and London: Longman, 1982); Gordon, *Woman's Body, Woman's Right*, p. 233.

[84] Eva R. Rubin, *Abortion, Politics, and the Courts: Roe v. Wade and Its Aftermath* (New York and Westport, Conn.: Greenwood, 1987), p. 33.

victory may be much more favorable to a wider agenda than would
be an effort directly addressing that wider agenda, should that direct
effort lead to broad opposition to any social change that seems to be
part of the wider agenda.

Returning to suffrage, I would argue that more significant than any
positive endorsement of separate spheres was the avoidance of explicit
claims that suffrage would radically transform society. Once framed
as a specific, limited goal – suffrage, rather than a full overhaul of
women's social roles – advocates of suffrage did not need to defend
it explicitly in terms of a whole worldview. Some did so anyway, but
the limiting frame developed for suffrage in the 1910s was compatible
with a range of larger agendas, precisely because the frame for suffrage
itself did not primarily address larger agendas: it appeared to require a
single reform rather than a full reworking of society. Limiting frames
have the strategic advantage that they do not invite numerous paths
of opposition; instead, they can draw support on the basis of a wide
range of perspectives and worldviews. Cott noted, then:

[T]he suffrage movement of the 1910s encompassed the broadest spectrum of
ideas and participants in the history of the movement.

That was the only decade in which woman suffrage commanded a mass
movement, in which working-class women, black women, women on the radical left, the young, and the upper class joined in force; rich and poor, socialist
and capitalist, occasionally even black and white could be seen taking the same
platform.[85]

That is, the suffrage cause developed broad support less by *trumpet-
ing* that it was not associated with other causes than by providing a
limiting frame that did not include as a central component the explicit
championing of one worldview over another. Cott focused here on the
1910s, when the suffrage movement emphasized primarily a separate
spheres perspective, on the way to achieving, in 1920, the constitutional amendment giving women the right to vote. True, the separate
spheres worldview validated the social and sexual mores of the time,
but there was some political flexibility implied in not having to trumpet
that compatibility, but instead focusing on suffrage per se.

[85] Cott, *Grounding of Modern Feminism*, p. 30.

Exactly whether a limiting frame will contribute, or detract from, larger, long-term goals is often difficult to foresee. Central to the calculation is whether the larger goals have any reasonable chance of gaining wider acceptance – that is, wider than within a particular social movement – any time in the foreseeable future. In hindsight, it is quite clear that a complete acceptance of women's legal, economic, and social equality, all in one fell swoop, was not going to happen in the early 1900s. Even less strategically promising was an insistence that contraception was a woman's right that required rejection of the Victorian family, or that women's rights were a socialist cause.

The second element of any such calculation is whether the limiting frame actually does damage to the larger set of goals. That is, does it institutionalize some social change that actually makes it more difficult to attain the other goals? Those who oppose setting aside the larger goals in favor of a limiting frame will cite this problem as the greatest danger of a limiting frame. A standard source of tension within social movements are battles over whether limiting frames advance the cause in a realistic way or are, instead, sellouts.

In the case of suffrage, the argument would presumably be that justifying one change within a separate spheres framing undercut the legitimacy of appeals for equal rights. But, I would argue, one first has to meet the criteria that the other goals had a reasonable chance of progress before it is possible that focus on a single goal, within a limiting frame, could undermine that progress. None of the other components of early-twentieth-century feminist agenda made nearly the mainstream headway that suffrage made. It is not as if they were on the road to victory before suffrage started having success. It is at least as likely that suffrage helped carry other feminist goals while it thrived as a movement, as that its moderation undermined those goals.

Furthermore, it is not only the suffrage movement that was attempting to avoid too broad and controversial an agenda, as is clear when we consider the issue of birth control. While birth control certainly did not fit a separate spheres frame of women's causes, it was also the case that birth control emerged as a cause just as feminist equal rights organizations were very much learning the strategic value of limiting frames. That is true at least to the extent that these organizations did not want to designate the controversial cause of contraception as a central feminist goal. They were too concerned about the potential of division within their own ranks.

Ultimately the birth control movement, especially Sanger's wing, also narrowed its frame to achieve particular, circumscribed goals, as we shall see in the next chapter. Feminism and the birth control movement thus ultimately both followed the path of narrowing their frames. The goals they achieved within these more limited frames involved a more limited degree of social change than many of the initial movement supporters had originally thought acceptable (particularly in the case of birth control).

eugenics usually assumed that a great variety of traits that we would now consider to be at least partly shaped by upbringing, education, social class, and other environmental factors – such as intelligence, mental deficiencies, occupational achievement, criminality – were instead fixed at birth. For many adherents, an intrinsic component of eugenics was intervention to improve the quality of a given population, meaning promoting the fertility of desired groups and/or discouraging the fertility of groups considered undesirable. Eugenics had been influenced by evolutionary biology, especially after the considerable impact Charles Darwin (1809–1882) had on the scientific world with the 1859 publication of *On the Origin of Species by Means of Natural Selection*. However, eugenic ideas did not begin with Darwinism; perhaps more influential were the ideas of Thomas Malthus (1766–1834), another Englishman, whose *Essay on the Principle of Population* of 1798 argued that the human rate of reproduction naturally outstripped increase in the food supply. Eugenics was a precursor to the contemporary field of demography, that is, the study of changes in populations, for example, fertility rates, death rates, and immigration.

On the issue of contraception, eugenics, like socialism and feminism, could cut two ways. Some eugenicists opposed contraception because they thought middle-class, white Protestant women would be the most avid users of birth control[1] (and, on this point, they turned out to be right). Theodore Roosevelt was just the most prominent opponent of contraception who based his opposition on the fear of "race suicide" by white, native-born Protestants, pointing to declining birth rates.[2] And eugenicists tended to be more interested in reducing the numbers of those they considered undesirable than in promoting birth control as something to which every woman had a right.[3]

Birth control advocates took pains to deny the "race suicide" argument.[4] Through National Birth Control League publications, for

[1] David M. Kennedy, *Birth Control in America: The Career of Margaret Sanger* (New Haven, Conn., and London: Yale University Press, 1970), p. 120.
[2] Linda Gordon, *Woman's Body, Woman's Right: Birth Control in America*, rev. ed. (New York and London: Penguin/Viking, 1990), pp. 133–55; Ellen Chesler, *Woman of Valor: Margaret Sanger and the Birth Control Movement in America* (New York: Anchor/Doubleday, 1992), p. 215.
[3] Chesler, ibid., pp. 216–17.
[4] See, e.g., Mary Ware Dennett, "The Case for Birth Control," copy in MWD, folder 273.

example, Mary Ware Dennett argued that use of birth control helped reduce infant mortality and poverty among the groups and societies that used it.[5]

However, eugenicists were not always opposed to birth control and, in the 1920s and 1930s, increasingly became advocates. Indeed, because eugenics rhetoric pervaded most discussions of social reform, including that of birth control, it is important to understand what it meant to frame an issue within a eugenics perspective.

Within the study of biology and of society, there developed in the late nineteenth, and especially the early twentieth, century a view that social problems were linked to the heredity of particular groups. Growing concern about immigration probably helped fuel the leap that Darwin's influential ideas in biology made to discussion of social problems, and thus the emergence of eugenics. However, as the study of the quality of populations, eugenics did not always focus on immigration and was not always used simply to blame "inferior" peoples for social problems.

Eugenics, like most modes of thought, was more internally complex and diverse than it may appear to outsiders, such as ourselves. And its political implications were not unidimensional. To take an example, today we generally associate the rejection of the Darwinian approach to evolution with reactionary politics, such as a Creationist attempt to prevent children from encountering modern scientific theories as part of their education. But in the early part of the century, for some intellectuals, rejection of Darwinism was linked to a view of race and social justice that appears more modern and progressive than many of the alternatives extant during that period. According to historian Carl N. Degler,[6] for the first fifteen years of this century, discussions of race and population often resisted the Darwinian approach to evolution, which was still somewhat new and could only be fully convincing once

---

[5] All of the following National Birth Control League publications, from MWD, folder 273, have handwritten notes indicating Dennett was the author: "Race Conservation in War Time Makes Birth Control a Necessity" [handwritten notes indicating date of 1918]; "The Sixty-five Cities of Disgrace" [from *Birth Control Review*, with handwritten notes indicating date of 1919]; "An Eye Opener on Birth Control," pamphlet [1919?].

[6] Carl N. Degler, *In Search of Human Nature: The Decline and Revival of Darwinism in American Social Thought* (New York and Oxford: Oxford University Press, 1991), pp. 18–25.

there was widespread understanding of the science of genetics. (That is, Darwin focused on natural selection, the process by which survival is dependent upon fit with the environment, and adaptability to new environments. But the mechanism by which adaptations could be transmitted to later generations depended upon linking the theory of natural selection to an understanding of how genetic differences among organisms are passed to their offspring. In scientific circles, this link was developed in the late nineteenth century, but popular understanding and acceptance of genetics took another two or three decades.) Those who resisted Darwinism instead often opted for various versions of neo-Lamarckianism. French naturalist Jean Baptiste de Monet Lamarck (1744–1829) argued that animals develop acquired characteristics in an attempt to adapt to their environment, and these characteristics can be passed on to succeeding generations. One late-nineteenth and early-twentieth-century version argued that improving the education and economic conditions of disadvantaged peoples would raise their quality to that of dominant whites.

Such neo-Lamarckianism still was quite racist, typically assuming that the biological profile of Native Americans, blacks, and so forth was indeed inferior to that of whites at the time. But it ultimately implied that unequal, even unfair, social conditions were to blame. It could, then, be more supportive of social reform and racial equality than the harsh versions of social Darwinism.[7] The latter argued that white dominance demonstrated a biologically fixed, evolutionary superiority, so that social reform was pointless and racial equality was impossible.

Tracing out all the possible permutations linking social inequality to theories of heredity is less a process of following different branches than an attempt to hack through hopelessly tangled and multiple vines. For example, neo-Lamarckianism could become considerably less supportive of social reform if one argued that environment affected

---

[7] There were, for instance, elements of this rejection of Darwinism in William Jennings Bryan's populist view of social justice (which, however, did not include a focus on racial equality). Bryan was one of the best-known U.S. public figures of the late nineteenth and early twentieth centuries and three-time Democratic presidential nominee. Stephen Jay Gould, "William Jennings Bryan's Last Campaign," *Nebraska History* 77, nos. 3–4 (1996):177–83; Willard H. Smith, "William Jennings Bryan and the Social Gospel," *Journal of American History* 53(1966):41–60.

heredity over the very long term, not the short term, so that reversing evolutionary adaptation once it has actually occurred was generally beyond human control.[8]

The central point here is that the internal logic of an ideology fashioned in one context – for example, eugenics, fashioned as an attempt to understand the quality of populations – will not usually be enough in itself to predict the nuances that will develop once the ideology encounters a new issue, such as birth control. One must take into account the political and other agendas involved in those attempting to frame particular issues.

For example, many people, including Margaret Sanger, used the language of eugenics but did not greatly distinguish between inherited and acquired traits.[9] Further, Sanger focused primarily on the "quality" not of whole groups of people but of individuals, so that generalizations about ethnic and racial groups were not, for example, a central concern. Eugenics was diverse enough that it was invoked for a range of political purposes.

Contraception was just one of many issues that caught the attention of eugenicists. However, the link with ideas about large-scale population dynamics was close enough that, in Britain, advocacy of birth control was typically labeled "Malthusianism" or "neo-Malthusianism." In the United States, eugenicists approached the issue typically from the point of view that the birthrates of the working class, immigrants, and/or African Americans were too high, especially when compared to native-born white Protestants. Although racist and right-wing Malthusianism (i.e., the belief that the inferior "races" of immigrants and African Americans were particularly guilty of irresponsible reproduction) fueled such concerns, it was nevertheless the case that neo-Malthusian and eugenic thinking pervaded the American Left. The American, anarchist version of socialism of the Wobblies and that of Emma Goldman had absorbed the Malthusian concern with overpopulation as a cause of poverty. For strict Malthusians of the Right,

---

[8] Degler, *In Search of Human Nature*, pp. 11, 22.

[9] See, e.g., Sanger, "A Plan for Peace," *Birth Control Review*, April 1932, pp. 107–8, where at times she seems to imply that criminals and prostitutes have hereditary problems that required they be barred from immigrating, to protect "the stamina of the race" (p. 107). On the next page she suggests they could, after a period of social segregation and training, be morally transformed.

overpopulation was *the* cause of poverty, and doing anything to help the living standards of the poor would only exacerbate overpopulation and make matters worst.[10] For anarchists, overpopulation was a powerful tool in the bourgeois arsenal but was only a proximate cause of poverty; capitalism was the fundamental problem.

The support for eugenics involved, for some, a vague sense that it was possible to develop a healthy, genetically well-endowed stock that would take advantage of the best that nature and society offered. As with so many ideas whose exact assumptions or implications are left underspecified in most minds, exactly what this mix would entail could mean very different things.

Flexibility in considering inherited versus acquired traits was just one of the ambiguities of eugenic rhetoric that allowed different people to fill the rhetoric with different assumptions and goals. Eugenics could, for example, be interpreted to mean that most people, once they learned and had available the means (i.e., birth control) to make rational reproductive decisions, would naturally make decisions that benefited both themselves and society. Ellen Chesler set the context of early-twentieth-century eugenic thinking well and is worth quoting at length:

> Though its darker potential was always clear to some skeptics, eugenicism enjoyed a surprisingly large intellectual following well into the 1930s among liberals and progressives in the United States and Europe, who simply assumed that hereditarian principles were compatible with a commitment to egalitarianism and to social welfare initiatives in education, health, and labor....
>
> Knowing of the reactionary and inhuman objectives that scientific theories of human improvement have since served, it is difficult to recapture this naive confidence.... The ugly and tragic link of eugenicism with the intolerance and prejudice that produced Naziism has undermined its earlier association with scientific progress meant to promote the welfare of the individual and the public. Also lost is the fact that eugenicists were largely responsible for having

---

[10] It is not difficult to see similarity to the American Right today, especially if one substitutes the word "welfare" for "overpopulation." In both cases, it is counterproductive to try to help the poor, as Charles Murray and conservative Republicans have argued since the Reagan Administration (Murray, *Losing Ground: American Social Policy, 1950–1980* [New York: Basic Books, 1984]; Richard J. Herrnstein and Murray, *The Bell Curve: Intelligence and Class Structure in American Life* [New York and London: Free Press, 1994]).

introduced explicitly sexual topics into the boundaries of acceptable scientific discourse.[11]

Chesler goes on to note that Margaret Sanger's English mentor, Havelock Ellis always considered himself both a eugenicist and a Socialist and convinced Margaret of the coherence of this viewpoint. A pioneering advocate for the socialization of medicine as a public responsibility, he never tackled difficult moral or practical considerations about the implementation of eugenic policy, instead assuming, as she also would, that its benefits would be universally understood, because all human beings desire self-improvement. Medical and scientific advances would be available to all and welcomed by all; they would never need to be imposed. As the naïveté of this viewpoint became apparent with the rise of Fascism, Ellis shied away from the subject altogether, claiming to be bewildered, and refusing to hold himself in any way responsible for what he believed was a total perversion of eugenic theory.[12]

Again, suggesting that eugenic sympathies did not automatically imply the level of bigotry we might expect, Chesler noted that Ellis went on to assist in the relocation of German Jewish refugees as Nazism's violence increased in the late 1930s.[13]

Much more often than not, Sanger's use of eugenics rhetoric was so flexible that it did not have most of the negative connotations that we today associate with eugenics. An example of the loose way that Sanger used eugenic terminology appears in her 1928 collection of letters from women who wanted access to contraception. I mentioned this collection, titled *Motherhood in Bondage*,[14] earlier in the discussion of Sanger's feminism. The chapters in this book contain brief introductions by Sanger, then a number of excerpts on different types of problems associated with an inability to control fertility, such as

---

[11] Chesler, *Woman of Valor*, pp. 122–3. I should note, however, that I would agree with Chesler that the "link of eugenicism with the intolerance and prejudice that produced Naziism" was indeed "ugly," but disagree with the possible implication, through the use of the word "tragic," that eugenics was an otherwise progressive ideology linked to a more sinister force through historical accident. I would, however, agree that the word "tragic" is appropriate if taken in its stricter, literary meaning of disaster resulting from an inherent flaw. As will become clear later in this chapter, the hierarchical view of society implied in the logic of eugenics is far from accidental and has, in the case of Sanger's rhetoric, been underestimated by Chesler and others.

[12] Ibid., p. 123.

[13] Ibid., p. 496n.34.

[14] New York: Brentano's, 1928.

"The Pinch of Poverty" and "Methods That Fail." One of the chapters is titled "The Struggle of the Unfit." At the time, "unfit" referred, in many minds, to those who were genetically inferior. However, judging by the letters included in the chapter, by "unfit" Sanger refers to those whose health has been damaged by unwanted, repeated pregnancies. The usage is closer to the way we would today talk about health and "fitness" than it is to social Darwinist versions of eugenics. Sanger's introduction to the chapter talks of "the frightful toll" on women unfit to bear children "by physical defect, by psychic abnormality or defective heredity. . . . "[15] But the main point of the chapter is simply that the health of many women was seriously injured by repeated, unwanted pregnancies. Thus, far from considering these women inferior, Sanger states,

My unshaken conviction is that most women of the type represented in the following records, women who have been disciplined by suffering and educated by sorrow, and who possess the native intelligence to express themselves as clearly and accurately as these letters indicate, are fully competent – and more than willing – to be instructed in hygienic methods of contraception.[16]

I argue later that in this chapter that Sanger's eugenics was less flexible, and more distasteful, in the 1930s. However, in the first few decades of the twentieth century the association birth control had with eugenics depended upon a very ambiguous, loose conception of what eugenics was all about. More often that not, eugenics included assumptions about the inferiority of particular groups, especially immigrants and African Americans. But that was not necessarily the case.

It is interesting to compare the effect eugenics had on the discussion of birth control with the effect of socialism and feminism. We have seen that contraception's association with political debates over socialism and feminism did initially allow for a motley alliance in favor of contraception. But there were two problems as well: First, as we have seen, for activists whose top priority was contraception, there was the problem that debates internal to socialism and feminism could distract from support for contraception. Second, these same associations made it unlikely that the cause of accessible contraception could ever be widely acceptable within American society. As we have seen, opposition

[15] Ibid., p. 60.
[16] Ibid., p. 62.

to contraception could draw on many themes within American political culture.[17] As long as contraception was intertwined with debates over socialism and feminism, the opposition to birth control was considerably more fierce and durable than anything its supporters could produce. Attacks on contraception could draw upon anti-Red hysteria and the same misogynist themes that appeared in the physicians' crusade against abortion a half century earlier. For example, like Dr. Horatio Storer (who led the nineteenth-century physicians' crusade against abortion), Anthony Comstock's view of contraception was no doubt informed by his view that it was scandalous and irresponsible for women to step outside the roles of homebound wife and mother.[18]

In contrast to socialism and feminism, eugenics offered the first problem but not necessarily the second. That is, a link with eugenics meant that the cause of contraception could be submerged to the larger priorities of eugenicists, but, within early-twentieth-century America, eugenics did not elicit the level of opposition experienced by socialists and feminists. Chesler's view was that, "Indeed, there is no evidence that the birth control cause suffered politically because of the expressly classbound, or even racist, viewpoints of some of its advocates...."[19] To the contrary, strategically, the scientific status of eugenics at the time actually provided to the birth control cause "a patina of respectability."[20] I would modify Chesler's view, as I argue later in this chapter that the appeal to eugenics was a mixed bag of strategic advantages and disadvantages. Social movements do not adopt positions only based on what is strategically effective: More important is what groups are involved in the movement. And so, in understanding the prominence of eugenics in the later 1920s and 1930s, more significant than strategic calculation is that the explicit socialist and feminist elements of the birth control movement had faded away, so that egalitarian restraints

[17] Gordon, *Woman's Body, Woman's Right*; Donald K. Pickens, *Eugenics and the Progressives* (Nashville: Vanderbilt University Press, 1968), p. 72.

[18] Janet Farrell Brodie, *Contraception and Abortion in Nineteenth-Century America* (Ithaca and London: Cornell University Press, 1994), pp. 272–4. I am skeptical, however, that one has to resort to psychodynamic explanations (as Brodie does, p. 274) to explain this misogyny.

[19] Chesler, *Woman of Valor*, p. 345.

[20] Quotation from ibid., p. 196. Carole R. McCann makes a similar point in *Birth Control Politics in the United States, 1916–1945* (Ithaca and London: Cornell University Press, 1994), pp. 122–7.

on the use of eugenic rhetoric had weakened considerably. But it also is the case that eugenics was less controversial than socialism or feminism because limiting frames only need to be narrowed to the extent that they become uncontroversial to active participants in the polity. Strategically effective frames, unfortunately, can still take shape in a way that victimizes those who hold merely a tangential position in the polity, which in the early twentieth century could include African Americans and recent immigrants. Even economic egalitarians resorted occasionally to racist language when referring to those deemed inferior by birth.

Eugenic rhetoric certainly reinforced the loss of feminism as a strong influence on the birth control movement: As Carole R. McCann noted,

Within the dominant culture of the 1916–45 period, the declining fertility of the white, native-born middle class relative to that of the ethnic immigrant poor provoked great concern about both the nation's future in general and the advisability of contraception in particular. These nativist concerns, as they referred to women, separated birth control and feminist politics on the issue of women's sexuality and, in turn, stymied the feminist impulses of the birth control movement. Thus, contraception was legalized in terms of the need for society to protect maternal and infant health, the need of families to limit their size to their incomes, and the need of the nation to control the size and ethnic character of its population. The needs of women, as sexual beings, to control their fertility to their own ends were muted by these other rationales.[21]

McCann is overly optimistic in thinking that there ever was much of a chance, in the political culture of pre–World War II America, to legitimate any social change in terms of the needs of women as "sexual beings." Still, McCann points to an interesting component of the framing of birth control in the 1920s and 1930s: Ultimately birth control was to be of use to plan and regulate procreation, not to avoid it (and thus not to engage in sex independently of the planning of procreation). Also, the comparison of feminist and eugenic impulses brings into relief the sinister strength of a eugenics frame: Unlike feminism, it victimized people who did not have much opportunity to voice objections. That victimization was really quite vague into the early 1920s, given how flexibly eugenic ideas were applied across the political spectrum. But the victimization was implicit, and available to justify more explicit

[21] McCann, ibid., p. 3.

bigotry once the egalitarian, leftist movements that occasionally used eugenic rhetoric weakened in the late 1910s and early 1920s, as we shall see later in this chapter.

Medicalization of the Issue

Again, frames are likely to succeed (strategically) in a liberal polity to the extent that they do not elicit broad opposition. Thus frames that do not appear to challenge powerful groups within the polity are more likely to succeed than those that do. One of the ways frames limit their agendas – and thus become what I have called "limiting frames" – is to define an issue in a way that, to participants in the polity, it appears to separate the issue from larger moral agendas. Explicit links to broad moral agendas will tend to elicit opposition from diverse corners, because they touch on a wide set of issues and thus invite many different paths of opposition.

In the case of contraception, from our contemporary perspective, eugenics most obviously victimized those excluded from the polity. Medicalization also did so; making contraception available only through physicians favored those who were in economic or social circumstances in which professional medical care was accessible. However, I argue below that medicalization was so strategically successful because it appeared to sanitize the issue and to separate it from larger moral agendas.

It was, then, only after contraception had been separated from debates over socialism and feminism, and made somewhat antiseptic,[22] that opposition withered away. There was of course a significant price to pay for such a reframing: From a position that poor women must have direct control over their own reproduction, without the intervention of anyone else, Sanger had come to make promotion of medical gatekeeping over access to contraception perhaps her highest priority.

Sanger, perhaps largely as a result of her experiences with European advocates of birth control, moved toward medical control over access to contraception by the early 1920s, even as she continued to advocate

---

[22] To say that contraception had been framed in an antiseptic, depoliticized way is not to say that such a view of contraception was indeed "less political" by some absolute standard. The point is that both proponents and opponents ultimately perceived such an approach to contraception as divorced from heated political and ideological debates of the day.

a very egalitarian view of the benefits of birth control.[23] As early as 1918 and 1919, Sanger and the *Birth Control Review* moved away from socialist rhetoric and came to a focus, as in the June 1919 official statement of the magazine's purpose, on "Birth Control pure and simple. No other propaganda work of any kind."[24] This was the period that Linda Gordon called the professionalization of birth control, following the weakening of the organized Left.[25] This less obviously politicized approach, then, involved advocacy of a doctors' exemption from the Comstock laws, so that doctors could prescribe contraception according to their medical judgment.

Mary Ware Dennett, Sanger's principal rival for leadership of the birth control movement, denounced such a "medical monopoly." Dennett, however, lost support among medical proponents of birth control.[26] Sanger cultivated that support in the 1920s and 1930s, not because physicians as a group were passionate advocates (indeed, they were remarkably cautious and typically held patronizing or even misogynist views of women's use of birth control), but because having some acceptance within the medical community gave the issue of birth control a certain legitimacy. Thus it is interesting to note that Sanger's approach to physicians remained primarily strategic at least into the 1930s, a significant decade for her cause. She did not blindly trust medical experts, even as she allowed physicians to set the pace for public discussion of the issue. Just after acceding to prominent physicians' insistence on cancellation of a conference on birth control, scheduled for 1935, she lamented privately:

[O]f course, we all want to do everything in our power to...get the A.M.A. leading the B.C. [birth control] movement. My own action must be based on

---

[23] McCann, *Birth Control Politics*, p. 11, asserted that the very name *birth control* "embraced the values of rational, scientific management." Perhaps the word itself has such implications in the minds of those who heard it, but Chesler reported (*Woman of Valor*, p. 97) that the word emerged among a discussion of radical friends in 1914. Although radical groups of the time often included a strong rationalism in their ideology, the group and the timing suggest that this was not an attempt to make the issue less radical and more acceptable among scientific professionals.

[24] Chesler, ibid., pp. 168–9.

[25] Gordon, *Woman's Body, Woman's Right*, pp. 245–6.

[26] Kennedy, *Birth Control in America*, pp. 220–3. For a summary of Dennett's position, see her book, *Birth Control Laws: Shall We Keep Them Change Them or Abolish Them* (New York: Frederick H. Hitchcock/The Grafton Press, 1926; reprinted New York: Da Capo Press, 1970), esp. pp. 200–61.

my own experience in the past.... The American Medical Association will act when public opinion forces them to do so. When the well-to-do patients of the distinguished specialists put them on the spot every time they meet them, they will soon act not only in their private capacity but voice a public opinion as well.[27]

Thus, well over a decade after Sanger had turned toward a medical framing of contraception, she still was skeptical of the medical profession's commitment to the issue. She did not accept physicians' worldview but did see them as strategically crucial allies.

Still, she felt that success would have been achieved more quickly if physicians had taken the initiative themselves, as indicated in comments the following year. (Here she speaks of sixty-four advocacy meetings during a recent trip to India.)

Thirty-two of all these meetings were before medical groups. In this way it was possible to reach the doctors and carry on a medical campaign first. This is, I believe, preferable to the way the movement developed in America, where the public was appealed to first and the medical campaign followed.[28]

Sanger, contrary to Dennett, often stated that placing contraception in the hands of the medical profession was not "a matter of class legislation but in order to maintain the highest standards and to ensure the best and most reliable information going to those who seek it."[29]

[27] [Sanger] to Mrs. Francis N. Bangs, November 15, 1934. On cancellation of the conference, see also Catherine C. Bangs [=Mrs. Francis N. Bangs] telegram to Margaret Sanger, October 11, 1934; Secretary to Mrs. Margaret Sanger [Adelaide Pearson] to Mrs. C. C. Bangs, October 18, 1934; Catherine C. Bangs to Mrs. Margaret Sanger, November 8, 1934. All of these materials are in vol. 62, reel 41, MSP-LC.
    I would agree with Carol R. McCann, then, that Sanger did not simply adopt the perspective of medical professionals. McCann, *Birth Control Politics*, p. 4fn.
[28] This 1936 address was at an American Eugenics Society gathering. "Birth Control in India," address by Margaret Sanger, vol. 63, reel 41, MSP-LC. The address appears in Sanger's papers in two forms (with the same words), as typescript attached to a letter from Stella Hanau to Dr. Ellsworth Huntington, June 1, 1936; and in a pamphlet, "Proceedings at the Annual Meeting and Round Table Conferences of the American Eugenics Society, New York City, May 7, 1936." The correspondence indicates that this version of the address had been revised, to be less informal than Sanger's actual comments.
[29] This is from a letter marked "Not used," from Sanger to Myra Plaut Gallert (President, Voluntary Parenthood League), June 8, 1932. This was apparently a draft for a letter that was sent to persons associated with the Voluntary Parenthood League, dated September 6, 1932, which did not refer to the "class legislation" issue but

But at times her logic was primarily strategic. Though Sanger criticized Dennett's legislative stance because it would not allow proper medical supervision – and analysts generally agree that she had become convinced that the most effective methods of contraception required a physician – she did not always stick to the "physicians only" position. In 1938 Sanger still argued that in some settings in which trained physicians were not available, such as poor rural areas, it was better to provide methods that did not require a doctor's examination but which would be at least somewhat effective.[30] She did not specify methods but presumably was distinguishing diaphragms from methods that did not require fitting, such as condoms and spermicides.

Former allies of Margaret Sanger criticized her depoliticization of birth control, which rejected radical support in favor of a frame that treated contraception as a sensible, pragmatic option for families (and, implicitly, especially middle-class families). However, critics a decade earlier had criticized her arguments that accessible contraception would solve a myriad of other social problems, saying Sanger claimed too much for birth control. And it certainly was the case that mainstreaming the cause of contraception not only broadened its support but was part of Sanger's considerable ability to elicit contributions for the cause from wealthy patrons,[31] whose support for birth control was certainly more compatible with noblesse oblige than with radicalism.

Mary Ware Dennett's consistent opposition, on egalitarian grounds, to a medical monopoly over access to contraception showed signs of being impractical. Because having physicians as gatekeepers was much more socially and politically acceptable, and legally less risky, than open access to contraception, Dennett herself forwarded requests for contraceptive information to Robert L. Dickinson,[32] leader of the physicians' group working to legalize contraception under medical

---

rebutted the VPL's position on the "open bill" vs. Sanger's bill. Both letters in MSP-LC, vol. 77, reel 50.

[30] Sanger, "Human Conservation and Birth Control," address delivered at Conference on Conservation and Development of Human Resources, Washington, D.C., March 3, 1938, MSP-SS, p. 16.

[31] See, e.g., Chesler, *Woman of Valor*, p. 394.

[32] Evangeline Wilson Young, M. D., to Dennett, November 13, 1927; Louise Stevens Bryant to Young, November 21, 1927; both in MWD, folder 56.

supervision. She had little choice to develop such alliances given that lay circulation of contraceptive information was illegal. Indeed, she and Dickinson, at least in the late 1920s, developed friendly relations and Dickinson apparently recommended Dennett's *The Sex Side of Life* to his patients.[33] Further, the prosecution Dennett faced for violating the Comstock laws, by mailing *The Sex Side of Life*, forced her to use medical, scientific expertise as legitimation for her activities. Dickinson aided Dennett's defense, including gathering testimonials from other physicians. Dennett, in mapping part of her legal strategy with Dickinson, noted that, "if we can show that there is scientific authority behind us, the Court can not then conclude that scientific truth is 'filth'."[34]

Dennett's argument that a doctors only bill would still greatly limit access to contraception seemed to have been confirmed by Dickinson's own experience that even the free circulation of medical publications about contraception faced considerable opposition within the medical profession itself.[35] There are those who would argue that the failure of the radical movements in favor of contraception – some would even say Sanger's personal strategy to extract the issue from broader, radical ideologies – resulted in only a limited acceptance of the legitimacy of birth control in the United States. It was, after all, not until 1965 that the Supreme Court (in *Griswold v. Connecticut*) placed the decision of couples to contracept within the realm of the right to privacy.[36] And it certainly is the case that the larger agendas of many supporters of birth control fell by the wayside.

But the evidence suggests that the radical strategy, that is, linking birth control explicitly to broader issues of social and economic justice,

---

[33] Dr. Louise Stevens Bryant (Executive Secretary, Committee on Maternal Health) to Mrs. Mary Ware Dennett, December 6, 1928, and other materials in MWD, folder 56.

[34] This quotation, from Dennett to Dickinson, January 20, 1929, in MWD, folder 430, referred specifically to showing that Dennett's discussion of masturbation was supported by scientific research. On Dickinson's (and other physicians') role in Dennett's defense, see folder 430 as a whole.

[35] See, e.g., Robert L. Dickinson to Mr. George H. Engelhard (of Voluntary Parenthood League), May 13, 1925, in MWD, folder 252.

[36] That decision nullified any state attempts to limit married couples' right to contraception, and in 1972, in *Eisenstadt v. Baird*, the Court declared that it was legal for any adult to purchase and use contraception, whether or not that adult was married.

could not have worked.[37] The prominent American social movements of the early twentieth century hardly went on to win many of their battles; among the few successes were birth control and suffrage. And while a commitment to women's rights ultimately fueled the suffrage movement, it was a separate spheres feminism that ultimately prevailed in the suffrage campaign.[38] As I mentioned earlier, the term *feminism* emerged to make the point that suffrage should not be isolated from a larger women's project on the Left; however, it was indeed those who attempted to justify suffrage independently of that larger agenda who had the greatest strategic success. (The contrast of Dennett's vs. Sanger's approach to birth control, developed further in the following chapter, demonstrates further why framings of the birth control issue that attempted to widen the moral agenda faced strategic obstacles.) Also, despite the restrictions in many areas, birth control was, in relative terms, much more socially acceptable, and accessible, by the middle decades of the century than it was in the first few decades.

Even with the considerably more mainstream framing of contraception that Sanger pushed in the 1920s and 1930s (compared to her more radical days of the 1910s), the topic carried enough controversial baggage that most legislators preferred to avoid it. Her bills had trouble attracting influential sponsors and rarely went much beyond legislative hearings.[39] In 1934 one such bill passed the U.S. Senate at first, at the end of a session, with no debate (much like the passage of the federal Comstock law in 1873, as Kennedy notes), and by voice vote, thus leaving no record of the votes of individual legislators. But a senator asked for reconsideration, routinely granted as a standard Senate courtesy, and perhaps reflecting expectation that the bill would never pass the House, in any case. The bill then died.[40] This episode,

---

[37] Despite her occasionally strong criticisms of Sanger's turn away from her 1910s radical approach in favor of 1920s moderation and compromise, Gordon's analysis basically agrees with this assessment. See *Woman's Body, Woman's Right*, pp. 255, 354.

[38] See, e.g., William H. Chafe, *The Paradox of Change: American Women in the 20th Century* (New York and Oxford: Oxford University Press, 1991), pp. 3–21.

[39] See, e.g., Chesler, *Woman of Valor*, pp. 326–30. Alvah W. Sulloway, *Birth Control and Catholic Doctrine* (Boston: Beacon, 1959), pp. 190–1 (note 20) gives a brief account of the fate of federal birth control bills introduced between 1923 and 1938.

[40] Furthermore, the Senate sponsor of the bill thought it had no chance in the House, and after 1934 Sanger's National Committee on Federal Legislation never managed to get a new bill even to the hearing stage. Chesler, ibid., pp. 347–8; Kennedy, *Birth Control in America*, pp. 239–40.

considered in light of the fact that such a bill never became law and rarely made it very far through the legislative process, suggests that it was not that many senators themselves (or, most likely, even a majority of the public[41]) strongly and personally opposed birth control, or even considered it a particularly important issue. With an essentially anonymous vote, the bill at first passed quickly, but once anyone, including a single senator, was willing to make moral objections, most senators preferred simply to avoid the issue.[42] The history of contraception (like abortion, as we shall see later) is an example of an issue very vulnerable to moral vetoes: explicit moral controversy typically paralyzes elected legislators. Such politicians are sensitive to the pressure of elections and would rather avoid action on a topic in which there are at least two opposed, morally committed constituencies. Under such conditions, any action will deeply offend at least one side. Sanger seemed to be aware of this problem.[43]

However, in the history of reproductive politics, courts have sometimes been willing to act when legislatures have not. The general pattern has been that, once moral division is explicit, the courts are faced with legal cases initiated by those unable to find legislative redress. But in twentieth-century America, when the courts decide the cases, they have relied heavily on assumptions that medicine is an ideologically neutral, socially beneficial practice that works best when doctors have authority to make medical judgments autonomously. Thus courts take an issue that has the potential of moral controversy, but the court decision is made within a limiting frame.

Thus, while Sanger's fight for legal birth control never won the legislative approval for which she worked (through the National Committee for Federal Legislation on Birth Control), a series of federal court decisions in the mid-1930s essentially nullified the Comstock

---

[41] Chesler, ibid., pp. 371–2; Sulloway, *Birth Control and Catholic Doctrine*, p. 31.

[42] I should note, however, that the U.S. Tariff Act of 1930 included a provision similar to the 1873 Comstock law, that is, prohibiting the importation of contraception (Sulloway, ibid., p. 30; John J. Noonan, Jr., *Contraception: A History of Its Treatment by the Catholic Theologians and Canonists* [Cambridge, Mass.: Harvard University Press/Belknap Press, 1966], pp. 412–13.) However, I suspect that provision of the act was simply a routine codification of the statute to reconcile it with existing law, not a measure specifically meant to reaffirm the Comstock law.

[43] Sulloway, ibid., pp. 24–5.

prohibitions and thus allowed the provision of information on birth control, or contraceptive materials themselves, *in a medical context.*[44]

These court decisions did not evoke the controversy that would meet the Supreme Court's 1973 decision, greatly expanding legal abortion. That is, within mainstream society and politics, contraception within a medicalized context had become fairly uncontroversial, certainly by the Second World War. Indeed, most likely by some time in the 1930s, Sanger and her allies were gradually winning the battle over public opinion. Even as they had such little success in the U.S. Congress, birth control advocates were acknowledging that by the mid-1930s it was almost unheard of for a physician to be prosecuted for a Comstock violation.[45] In practice, access to contraception through a doctor was achieved even before the court decisions officially recognizing physicians' rights to decide on contraception for their patients.

Why then were legislatures unwilling to approve what had come to be a generally accepted practice? The earlier attempts to reverse Comstock laws, apparently started in 1917 in the New York state legislature,[46] are easily understandable, given the radical frames used to promote contraception at the time. But why still in the mid-1930s? Because legislators do not simply add up public opinion, or interest group opinion, and pass any measure that comes out with more support than opposition. The possibility of morally charged opposition, even among a minority, will usually translate into a veto over legislative initiative.

And again, even courts have shown a history of favoring limiting frames in deciding cases about reproductive rights. While judges can be bolder than elected legislators, their usual inclination is to appear

---

[44] Chesler, *Woman of Valor*, pp. 372–4; Kennedy, *Birth Control in America*, chapt. 8; Garrow, *Liberty and Sexuality*, pp. 41–6. The decisive, federal decisions started in 1936, but a medical framing of contraception achieved court victory as early as 1918, in New York state. The prosecution of Margaret Sanger under the state Comstock law resulted in a conviction but also in a judicial decision that allowed licensed physicians to give contraceptive advice for the cure or prevention of disease, an exemption that the legislature had not included in its Comstock law (Sulloway, *Birth Control and Catholic Doctrine*, pp. 28–30; C. Thomas Dienes, *Law, Politics and Birth Control* [Urbana: University of Illinois Press, 1972], pp. 85–7). The then–relatively liberal New York state law permitted Sanger's New York City birth control clinic to operate, as those involved could officially claim to be preventing disease.

[45] Kennedy, ibid., pp. 240–1.

[46] Sulloway, *Birth Control and Catholic Doctrine*, p. 22.

to decide upon solid, carefully drawn legal foundations, not sweeping, explicitly morally charged arguments. Thus the 1930s court decisions did not proclaim a clear right of individuals to birth control but instead agreed that physicians should be able to use their medical judgment and thus should be free of Comstock restrictions. It would be another three decades until the really decisive judicial attack on Comstock laws, the 1965 U.S. Supreme Court decision in *Griswold v. Connecticut*. With the *Griswold* decision, legal access to contraception no longer relied on medical justifications. However, by emphasizing married couples' right of privacy in making reproductive decisions (and extending the logic to unmarried persons in a 1972 decision), the Court still used a limiting frame, that is, one which emphasized privacy rather than a specific set of positive, moral commitments. There was in *Griswold* of course implicit rejection of the legitimacy of sex outside of marriage, but in the context of American public life in the mid-1960s, this was not at all a controversial position. No significant force within the American polity was offering a moral worldview advocating the legitimacy of extramarital sex, and so there was no manifest moral division around the issue of marriage.[47]

Significant for this study, then, conflict over birth control died down once support for accessible birth control was no longer presented as a drastic social change, favoring the downtrodden and overturning traditional sex roles. People could favor birth control without having to favor larger programs of social reform, and thus opponents could not attack the legitimacy of birth control from quite so many avenues.

The Implications of a Strategic Frame

The Durability of Eugenics

As I have noted, eugenics was a powerful component of the frame that came to dominate the pro–birth control movement. Initially, the eugenics rhetoric involved had an egalitarian orientation, odd as that may sound to the contemporary ear.

---

[47] Unmarried pregnancy and unwed motherhood became more frequent, not just in the United States but throughout the Western world, in subsequent decades. See the thorough account in Kristin Luker, *Dubious Conceptions: The Politics of Teenage Pregnancy* (Cambridge, Mass.: Harvard University Press, 1996).

As Ellen Chesler and others have noted,[48] Sanger herself seems mainly to have idealistically and naïvely expected that eugenics could be progressive and nondiscriminatory. Earlier in her career, she was mostly consistent that one can speak only of "unfit" individuals, not whole groups or ethnicities. Thus eugenic decisions, she believed, should and could only be made by individuals planning their own families.[49]

In her use of eugenics rhetoric, Sanger, much as she personally shaped the pro–birth control movement, was not alone. For example, the American Birth Control League (ABCL) stated in a pamphlet that its aim was to "promote eugenic birth selection throughout the United States so that there may be more well-born and fewer ill-born children – a stronger, healthier and more intelligent race."[50] Though the pamphlet as a whole was not primarily a discussion of eugenics, this statement of aim implied that birth control was the means, while eugenic birth selection was the central goal. Sanger had founded the ABCL in 1921 but left it in 1928; the pamphlet was published after Sanger was no longer associated with the organization and instead occasionally feuded with it.

Eugenics had a certain appeal to birth control advocates because, for example, one could hold out the promise that contraception would rid society of social undesirables. Such an appeal could then avoid controversial rhetoric about women's rights to control her sexuality, or even just her fertility. And the supposed undesirables were generally not in a position to object. An example arises in the 1932 U.S. Senate hearings on Sanger's bill, which would allow doctors to prescribe contraceptives for their patients freely. The sponsor, Senator Henry D. Hatfield of West Virginia, a physician, mentioned concerns for the health, financial, and family situation of the mother. But he spent more time noting the need to arrest "the universal growth in number of our idiotic, imbecilic and

---

[48] Chesler, *Woman of Valor*, p. 196. See also Pickens, *Eugenics and the Progressives*, p. 84.

[49] For an example of her push for an egalitarian and empowering eugenics (odd as that sounds to the late-twentieth-century ear), see a four-page typescript that Sanger submitted for a 1921 eugenics conference, "Eugenic Value of Birth Control Propaganda," vol. 200, reel 129, MSP-LC.

[50] American Birth Control League, "Birth Control" (undated pamphlet), MSP-LC, vol. 253, reel 144. My best guess would be that this pamphlet was published about 1932.

epileptic wards to be found in our State institutions." Indeed, while governor of West Virginia, Hatfield had approved a eugenically motivated, coercive sterilization law.[51]

It may also have been the case that an alliance with eugenics was at times useful financially. Through the 1920s, Sanger's activism was probably well funded via her second marriage to millionaire Noah Slee in 1922.[52] But once Slee lost money in the stock market crash of 1929, Sanger had to depend more on lecture fees and writing income to continue to fund her lobbying and organizations.[53] It is possible that she then needed not to alienate allies in the pro-eugenics community in order to get lobbying support and to keep getting profitable speaking invitations.

However, though there may have been some strategic advantages to an alliance with eugenicists, there were also some significant drawbacks. In the 1920s, eugenics was respected and certainly did have strategic value. During that decade, in Ellen Chesler's words, Sanger "had pandered to a eugenically minded audience"[54] but had generally kept her distance from explicitly bigoted versions of eugenics. Indeed, in 1928, Sanger fought against a proposal to merge the American Birth Control League's *Birth Control Review* and an American Eugenics Society publication.[55] One might initially suspect, for example, that wealthy elites who could provide funding would favor a eugenic approach to birth control, and Sanger had to pander to such a bigoted mindset. But if anything, the evidence would suggest the opposite: the Rockefellers, one of Sanger's primary funding sources, apparently objected to overly harsh, elitist eugenics.[56]

Even more difficult to explain is why relations between the birth control movement and eugenicists grew even stronger in the 1930s.[57]

---

[51] Statement of Senator Henry D. Hatfield in United States Senate, Committee on the Judiciary, Hearings on S. 4436, May 12, 19, and 20, 1932 (Washington, D.C.: Government Printing Office), p. 2, see also p. 3. Concerning Hatfield's eugenics, including approval of coercive sterilization, see also Chesler, *Woman of Valor*, pp. 331–2.

[52] Chesler, ibid., pp. 242–7.

[53] Ibid., pp. 337–8.

[54] Ibid., p. 240.

[55] McCann, *Birth Control Politics*, p. 122.

[56] Chesler, *Woman of Valor*, pp. 240–2.

[57] McCann, *Birth Control Politics*, pp. 180–2; Gordon, *Woman's Body, Woman's Right*, pp. 300–1, 343.

Sanger's use of eugenics rhetoric grew harsher as the 1930s progressed (as I demonstrate below), even though eugenics as a movement was generally weakening in the 1930s, especially once Naziism developed. Its decline in influence may have begun as early as the late 1920s.[58] Indeed, if Sanger had simply used eugenics rhetoric because it was the fashionable language of the day, that rhetoric should not have been so durable. It appears that by 1934 Catholic critics of contraception at least at times pointed to eugenics arguments (apparently relying on statements by the American Birth Control League, not Sanger) when publicly criticizing the birth control cause.[59] That is, apparently they felt that eugenics could be persuasively portrayed as negative. And so why did Sanger and the ABCL (even more than Sanger) find themselves drawn to harsher versions of eugenics in the 1930s?

It became more harsh, I would argue, because the more egalitarian sentiments of socialism and feminism had largely disappeared from pro–birth control rhetoric, in turn because socialism and feminism had considerably weakened as social movements. So there was little left to temper the harshness of a eugenic endorsement of social hierarchy: The voices that, in the 1910s, would have objected most strongly to antiegalitarian versions of eugenics had by the early 1920s greatly weakened and lost any connection to the birth control cause.[60] Indeed, even eugenics as a whole lost most connections to the Left, given that the Left itself weakened in the late 1910s and early 1920s.

The persistence of eugenics rhetoric in the birth control movement has something interesting to tell us about the durability of different kinds of frames. Frames develop in a direction compatible with the nature of social solidarity in a movement. Movements with a strong internal identity as outsiders fighting the status quo do not automatically develop the frame best placed to gain political acceptance. This should not be surprising, since most social movement agendas fail to sway the larger society. It is true that movements that are very professionally

---

[58] Gordon, ibid., p. 299; Kennedy, *Birth Control in America*, pp. 118–19; Pickens, *Eugenics and the Progressives*, pp. 203–6; Chesler, *Woman of Valor*, p. 217.

[59] McCann, *Birth Control Politics*, p. 184.

[60] See, e.g., Kennedy, *Birth Control in America*, pp. 117–19, 121; Chesler, *Woman of Valor*, pp. 344–5, 379.

organized – more like formal organizations than the messy and perhaps raucous kind of activism we usually think of as a "social movement" – can strategically try out and change different frames very rapidly. But that is because the more that the movement is organized like a business, the less likely that there is a strong cultural solidarity within the movement. The birth control cause could not dramatically change its frame while surrounded by socialist and feminist movement rhetoric with which it felt a kinship.[61]

Furthermore, while Franklin Delano Roosevelt's "New Deal" pushed government social policy moderately to the left, and helped revive the American secular Left, it also left birth control out in the cold. Before her husband Franklin was elected governor of New York in 1928, Eleanor Roosevelt had served on the board of the American Birth Control League. Once Franklin Roosevelt took office as president in 1933, Sanger led a delegation to the president, aiming to promote their cause. But Chesler reports that one by one, "members of the Roosevelt circle who had previously supported birth control formally severed their ties and refused to speak out on the issue."[62] Sanger initially tried to ally birth control with the social reform goals of the New Deal, but she quickly came to feel frozen out. Birth control remained controversial enough that New Dealers probably did not want to distract from the goal of economic recovery, which undoubtedly to them was of a much higher priority than contraception. In addition, Catholic support for the New Deal was surely relevant. One of Roosevelt's central political accomplishments was (building upon support for previous Democratic presidential candidate Al Smith) to integrate Catholics into the Democratic Party. Given that most Catholics were no more than a generation or two removed from immigration, and were among the working class and poor, Roosevelt's economic recovery policies garnered strong Catholic support. And he developed close political alliances with some prominent Catholic clerics. Thus, promoting birth control – anathema to the Catholic hierarchy – could fracture the New Deal coalition. Not surprisingly,

---

[61] A similar point is made in the very interesting analysis by Francesca Polletta, *Freedom is an Endless Meeting: Democracy in American Social Movements* (Chicago and London: University of Chicago Press, 2002).

[62] Chesler, *Woman of Valor*, quotation p. 339; see also p. 340.

this turn of events fed Sanger's paranoia about the sinister power of the Catholic Church.[63]

In general, then, it seems there was a turn toward the right in the most visible pro–birth control rhetoric (coming from both Sanger and from the American Birth Control League, which Sanger left in 1928). Before the early to mid-1930s, especially in the case of Sanger's own politics, the birth control movement included sympathy for the problems of poor people – who could benefit from birth control by gaining better control over their lives. But by the 1930s the dominant birth control rhetoric explicitly or implicitly blamed poverty on the over-breeding of the unfit. In some circles it did not take alienation from the New Deal to produce such rhetoric, but that seems to have been important in Sanger's case.

Social reform circles on the left, in the 1910s, included among their causes birth control (though that was usually not a top priority) and a high degree of egalitarianism. In the 1920s, the egalitarianism of socialist and feminist movements largely dropped from the scene, while eugenics was popular and edged closer to the birth control cause. By the late 1920s and early 1930s, eugenicists – many of whom had initially been skittish about birth control – were openly supportive. And in the 1930s, birth control could rely on that support from eugenics but, in great contrast to the 1910s, lay outside the causes of social reform circles of the Left, given the New Deal alliance with Catholics. In contrast to the New Deal, in the 1930s birth control did not sound very egalitarian.

Thus Sanger continued links to the eugenics movement even after some of its more negative possibilities – or probabilities, we should say – should have been very clear, through both the European and an American experience with eugenics. Even as she achieved judicial and public-relations victories for birth control in the mid-1930s, she remained a member of, and participant in, the American Eugenics Society,[64] which formally endorsed contraception in 1933, years after its

---

[63] Ibid., pp. 340–6.

[64] Concerning membership in 1936, see Rudolf Bertheau (Assistant Secretary, American Eugenics Society) to Mrs. Margaret Sanger, September 29, 1936; concerning her speaking at a 1936 Society luncheon, see Ellsworth Huntington (President, American Eugenics Society) to Mrs. Margaret Sanger, April 11, 1936; Stella Hanau (of National Committee for Federal Legislation on Birth Control) telegram to

inegalitarian and bigoted outlook should have been clear.[65] Medicalization had clearly been the strategically most successful part of the framing of birth control, but eugenics also survived.

The evidence suggests, then, that the justification of class privilege that was an essential part of eugenics became more dominant in Sanger's rhetoric (and thus in the rhetoric that was most likely to reach the newspapers, the Congress, and the courts) as the 1930s, and the Depression, progressed. Indeed, I would also argue that the association with eugenics ultimately had a more reactionary effect on Sanger's thought than a number of analysts (including David M. Kennedy, who was more critical of Sanger than was Chesler) have allowed. The evidence better supports Linda Gordon's more harsh judgment of the role of eugenics in 1930s birth control politics.[66]

Alienation from the New Deal contributed to this trend but was not the only cause. As I noted, among some pro–birth control groups a harsh eugenics was visible in the late 1920s. And in 1932, months

---

Professor Ellsworth Huntington, April 22, 1936; Stella Hanau to Dr. Ellsworth Huntington, April 22, 1936; Mrs. Walter Timme to Mrs. Alexander C. Dick, April 29, 1936; Ellsworth Huntington to Mrs. Margaret Sanger, May 15, 1936. All in vol. 63, reel 41, MSP-LC.

The connection to the American Eugenics Society, and to eugenics in general of course, was not sudden. See, e.g., the friendly interchanges about collaboration on lobbying for federal birth control legislation: Leon F. Whitney [Executive Secretary, American Eugenics Society] to Mrs. Margaret Sanger, January 26, 1931 (there are two such letters, with the same date); [Sanger] to Leon F. Whitney, January 29, 1931; Leon F. Whitney to Mrs. Margaret Sanger, January 30, 1931 and January 31, 1931; [Sanger] to Mr. Leon F. Whitney, January 31, 1931; Roswell H. Johnson telegram to Margaret Sanger, February 3, 1931; [Adelaide Pearson,] Secretary to Mrs. Margaret Sanger to Mr. Leon F. Whitney, February 9, 1931; Roswell H. Johnson to Mrs. Adelaide Pearson, February 10, 1931; Margaret Sanger to Mr. Leon F. Whitney, March 15, 1932. All in vol. 63, reel 41, MSP-LC.

Sanger's correspondent Leon F. Whitney, as part of this same lobbying effort, wrote the following in a confidential letter to a U.S. representative:

[O]bviously we are breeding from the bottom as a nation. All the figures show that the stupid people are having large families while the intelligent people are cutting down the size of their families....

[Leon F. Whitney,] Secretary [of the American Eugenics Society] to Hon. Albert Johnson, January 26, 1931, vol. 63, reel 41, MSP-LC. On views within the American Eugenics Society, see also Chesler, *Woman of Valor*, p. 343.

[65] Chesler, ibid., p. 343.

[66] Gordon, *Woman's Body, Woman's Right*, e.g., pp. 299–309.

before Roosevelt was elected, Sanger advocated that Congress appoint a "Parliament of Population" whose goals would include

to apply a stern and rigid policy of sterilization and segregation to that grade of population whose progeny is already tainted, or whose inheritance is such that objectionable traits may be transmitted.[67]

That was to be one of the seven central goals. Just in case anyone missed the point, stated as a separate goal (of the seven total) was the synonymous aim "to give certain dysgenic groups in our population their choice of segregation or sterilization."[68]

Still, Sanger's particular turn away from sympathy for the poor was more pronounced later in the 1930s. In her 1934 congressional testimony on birth control legislation, she still supported government relief (and birth control) for those suffering economically from the Depression.[69] But in hindsight, it appears that she was also somewhat making a transition in her arguments, as her 1934 testimony advocating such relief also pointed to high birth rates of the unemployed as the central cause of high relief costs, and thus a burden on taxpayers.[70]

In 1938, this former socialist, in the same year she published an autobiography that described in very positive terms her earlier days of "anticapitalist" oratory,[71] delivered an address in which she decried the evils of providing relief to the poor and unemployed. The justification for her position was the dysgenic consequences of providing such relief, which worked against the "conservation of the race."

Relief, by its very nature is not conservation [of the race]. It may serve a destructive purpose, first by keeping alive the most unfit and encouraging them by federal, state and local aid, to multiply their kind.[72]

---

[67] Sanger, "A Plan for Peace," *Birth Control Review* (April 1932), pp. 107–8, quotation p. 107. The article is labeled as a summary of an address given in New York in January of that year.

[68] Ibid., p. 108.

[69] Chesler, *Woman of Valor*, p. 342.

[70] Ibid., p. 310; Kennedy, *Birth Control in America*, pp. 235–6.

[71] Sanger, *An Autobiography* (New York: W. W. Norton and Company, 1938), p. 110.

[72] Sanger, "Human Conservation and Birth Control," address delivered at Conference on Conservation and Development of Human Resources, Washington, D.C., March 3, 1938, MSP-SS, p. 5.

Now it remains the case that Sanger's somewhat vague use of eugenics did not explicitly state that there were whole ethnic or racial groups who needed to be segregated or who would be better off being allowed to die. In fact, there is considerable evidence during approximately the same time period that she was ahead of most white Americans of her time in opposing discrimination against African Americans.[73] The eugenic problem, she believed, was that relief led people to lose pride in themselves and "assume the responsibility carelessly, knowing that some one else will carry the burden for them. . . ."[74] The problem, ultimately, then, was one of motivation of individuals. But again, in contrast to the egalitarian rhetoric of her earlier days, she argued in 1938 the social Darwinist view that particular individuals were in circumstances of poverty because they were the least fit, and providing them relief was doomed to fail because it attempted to counter the laws of nature. In this 1938 speech she was much more concerned about the tax burden on the "fit" that funded relief than the misery experienced by the impoverished (i.e., the "unfit").

As Ellen Chesler has noted, Sanger was always "eager to incorporate the most current intellectual fads into her argument" for birth control.[75] In general her single-minded focus on birth control meant that she would support anything that seemed at the time to help the cause. In any case, Sanger's tunnel-vision approach to the benefits of contraception, combined with a commitment to eugenics, led her to argue at this time that, while pensions might be good for those with hereditary diseases who agree to sterilization, for the most part government relief should be provided to the educated (and thus generally the wealthier part of the populace) and not to the poor. If given to the

---

[73] See her explicit statements opposing racial discrimination in the armed services and medical services during World War II, and in society at large, in Sanger, "Suggested Plan for American Health Service," six-page typescript, April and May 1940; Sanger, one-page statement "Discrimination in National Defense Employment," September 1941; Sanger, "Children of Tomorrow's World," seven pp., typed, March 1944 (apparently intended for publication in *Magazine Digest*). All these documents in MSP-SS.

[74] Sanger, "Human Conservation and Birth Control," address delivered at Conference on Conservation and Development of Human Resources, Washington, D.C., March 3, 1938, MSP-SS, p. 6.

[75] Chesler, *Woman of Valor*, p. 342.

poor, aid would simply encourage the breeding of the unfit; instead aid should go to

those healthy, intelligent young men and women skilled artisans, profession-als, agriculturalists, who wish to marry and would welcome a family, if only there were some provision to tide them through possible emergencies in the first few years until they could become entirely self-supporting. Money spent here . . . must inevitably promote and insure individual and national welfare.[76]

Most troubling of all, however, here in 1938, five years after Hitler first came to power, Sanger argued that

we must stress the fact that in a national program for human conservation institutional and voluntary sterilization are not enough; they do not reach those elements at large in the population whose children are a menace to the national health and well-being.

Reports in medical journals state that the indications laid down in the German law are being carefully observed. These are congenital feeble-mindedness; schizophrenia; circular insanity; hereditary epilepsy; hereditary chorea (Huntington's); hereditary blindness or deafness; grave hereditary bod-ily deformity and chronic alcoholism.

. . . There are 1,700 special courts and 27 higher courts in Germany to review the cases certified for sterilization there. The rights of the individual could be equally well safe-guarded here, but in no case should the rights of society, of which he or she is a member, be disregarded.[77]

Now, there was in early 1938 still a general (if naïve) hope that Hitler, who had come to power early in 1933, was not really so bad. World War II and the widespread murder of the Holocaust had not yet begun; indeed, it was still six months later, in September 1938, that British Prime Minister Neville Chamberlain agreed to allow Hitler to an-nex part of Czechoslovakia in order to achieve "peace in our time." Much as Chamberlain's actions have since come to symbolize the self-defeating appeasement of dictators, at the time many Europeans and

---

[76] "Statement from Mrs. Margaret Sanger, Director, Birth Control Clinical Research Bureau," November 12, 1938, on completion of Southern States tour, four pages, typed, MSP-SS.

[77] Sanger, "Human Conservation and Birth Control," address delivered at Conference on Conservation and Development of Human Resources, Washington, D.C., March 3, 1938, MSP-SS, pp. 17–18. I find it odd that Sanger's biographers and other analysts have apparently not cited this speech.

Americans were willing to hope and believe that grave danger did not lay just around the corner. And so we must remember that when Sanger made these remarks, reasonable people would have been unaware of the extent of horror that Naziism would bring. Even those willing to turn a blind eye were not therefore justifying anywhere near the extent of evil that we know, from today's vantage point, did indeed develop.

Still, Sanger's advocacy of forced sterilization in the late 1930s included the view that "in no case should the rights of society" be subordinated to individual rights, while expressing the hope that the rights of individuals in the United States could be "equally well safe-guarded" as they were in Nazi Germany. Such a trajectory in her rhetoric must lead us to be very suspicious of the potential that lay in the eugenics rhetoric used to support birth control. And, considering Sanger herself, it is clear that her eugenics rhetoric was not so benign as many analysts have claimed. Her position on forced segregation and/or sterilization, noted above, was the same policy endorsed by the American Eugenics Society.[78]

A defender of Sanger has argued that Sanger was not a eugenicist and cites statements from Sanger, primarily from 1919 and 1922, that criticize eugenics language and the class bias of eugenicists.[79] There

---

[78] See American Eugenics Society pamphlet, "Aims and Objectives of the American Eugenics Society," attached to a letter of January 7, 1937, from the Assistant Secretary of the Society to Sanger's National Committee on Federal Legislation (though the address was actually that of the Western regional office of her Birth Control Clinical Research Bureau); MSP-LC, vol. 56, reel 36.

[79] Charles Valenza, "Was Margaret Sanger a Racist?," *Family Planning Perspectives* 17, no. 1 (January–February 1985):44–5. Valenza cited especially *The Pivot of Civilization*, published in 1922 (New York: Brentano's). In 1939 quotations Valenza cites (p. 45), it is not entirely clear whether it is really eugenics per se that Sanger is criticizing. For example, he cited a 1939 letter in which she criticized the view that the "fit" should have more babies, but it seems quite possible that Sanger was criticizing the promotion of births among anyone, as she had always favored promoting birth control for *everyone*. As Chesler noted, Sanger always opposed promoting fertility, that is, she opposed "positive" eugenics but approved of "negative" eugenics, the weeding out of the unfit (*Woman of Valor*, p. 195). Her counter to the view that birth control would be dysgenic, because the fit would be more likely to use it, was always that the effective use of contraception among the wealthier and more educated simply demonstrated that it needed to be promoted more widely. Also, Valenza seemed to imply that Sanger was disassociating herself from Hitler-inspired racist eugenics, when, in a letter on the same topic a few days later, she spoke of the need of the birth control movement to avoid "sliding backward or into the Hitler and Stalin and Mussolini phobia." But the reference to a "phobia" may indicate that she thought it was the

are two problems here: First, eugenics rhetoric in general was flexible enough in application, and common enough in Sanger's rhetoric, that to say that Sanger was not a eugenicist is not as meaningful as it may initially appear. Yes, she was not employed as a eugenicist, as were some academics of the time, but she used a popular rhetoric that was applied flexibly. Second, the reactionary potential of Sanger's eugenics was stronger in later years, so that it is easier to defend Sanger by focusing on 1922 than it is if we include the late 1930s.

This defender, Charles Valenza, himself stated that among eugenicists, "the more bigoted believed the difference was evident in class or ethnic distinctions."[80] Sanger's statements of the late 1930s very much meet the criterion of making class distinctions. Sanger's eugenics developed more reactionary tones as her more egalitarian commitments fell to the wayside, while the eugenicism that had begun in a vague and socialist fashion came to stand more on its own. And this despite the fact the eugenics movement as a whole was probably weaker in the late 1930s than when Sanger first became involved with birth control. What remained was actually more logically consistent and more virulent: because there was less diversity left among those who used eugenic language (as the feminist and especially socialist movements were weaker in the 1930s than they had been before World War I), it was by this time easier to identify a core to the eugenic perspective. And that core opposed egalitarian views of society, or attempts to intervene in society to help those who were most disadvantaged. Eugenics became less vague, less flexible, more class-biased, and thus nastier.

As I noted, in my view a number of analysts of Sanger's career have been too forgiving of her eugenics. Chesler stated that Sanger "always carefully distinguished between voluntary and coercive application of her ideas,"[81] noting that Sanger approved of enforced contraception only for "the physically or mentally incompetent, who could

---

controversy surrounding these dictators, rather than the dictators themselves, that was problematic. (Valenza did not cite the location of the letter and so I have not been able to examine the larger context of the passages he quoted.)

[80] Ibid., p. 44.

[81] Chesler, *Woman of Valor*, p. 15. However, we should not lose sight of the fact that Chesler's biography is thorough and impressive overall and is particularly good at documenting other sources of racist eugenics used to support birth control: *Woman of Valor*, pp. 343–5, 379.

not themselves understand the benefits of smaller families."[82] Chesler's discussion here seems to refer to the period of about 1920 or so; like Valenza, when it comes to eugenics, she focused on the earlier years of Sanger's career. Chesler saw Sanger as making occasional lapses, using language that could be open to more racist and coercive interpretations than she generally intended. I would agree with that interpretation as applied to the early- and mid-1920s examples that Chesler cited,[83] but those examples do not compare with Sanger's unambiguous language of 1938. Still, even Sanger's more distasteful eugenics of the late 1930s was not a consistent stand; she seemed to go back and forth between accepting the more elitist forms of eugenics and criticizing them. For example, Carole R. McCann cited a 1939 statement of Sanger's that rejected the view that the most educated sector of the population is necessarily more fit than other sectors.[84] Nevertheless, McCann's defense of Sanger's eugenics is stronger than deserved. McCann's view that Sanger's eugenics was meant to be voluntary except for "the undeniably feebleminded, insane, and syphilitic" and was critical of the class-bound assumptions of eugenics focuses primarily on the early 1920s, especially Sanger's 1922 book, *The Pivot of Civilization*, on which Valenza also concentrated.

McCann also stated that Sanger had been improperly associated with the desire of the American Birth Control League – during the period that Sanger had split with it – "to limit the higher fertility of the socially inadequate."[85] It is true that the ABCL was more consistent and harsh in its eugenics than was Sanger. But we have seen Sanger did more than once endorse forced sterilization and social segregation if necessary for eugenic purposes. One of the arguments that Sanger used against Pope Pius XI's 1931 encyclical on contraception used precisely that logic:

Assuming that God does want an increasing number of worshipers of the Catholic faith, does he also want an increasing number of feeble-minded,

---

[82] Ibid., p. 195.
[83] Ibid., p. 216.
[84] McCann, *Birth Control Politics*, p. 118.
[85] Ibid., p. 184; Valenza made a similar point; "Was Margaret Sanger a Racist?," p. 45. McCann did note, however (p. 184), that "Sanger did link birth control and relief babies," presumably referring to the reproduction of poor people whose babies add to the relief rolls.

insane, criminal, and diseased worshipers? That is unavoidable if the Pope is obeyed, because, as we shall see, he forbids every single method of birth control except continence, a method which the feeble-minded, insane, and criminal will not use.[86]

Chesler, McCann, and Kennedy have accurately characterized the main thrust of Sanger's personal use of eugenics, for example, the fact that she was in general much less biologically deterministic than were credentialed eugenicists. Through the early 1920s it was the case that Sanger, if anything, pushed eugenic approaches to birth control in a more egalitarian, less bigoted direction. But such authors do not emphasize enough the dangerous applications that even Sanger herself occasionally endorsed. If we focus on the way that frames can leave an opening for, and sometimes positively endorse, beliefs that victimize those excluded from participation in the polity, this danger is easy to understand. Because the door to eugenic interpretations of birth control was very much open, there were all kinds of bigoted and coercive eugenic beliefs that could walk through at various times. Sanger's own single-minded focus on birth control, and the audiences to which she played, were not particularly attuned to the problem of victimizing immigrants and poor people. Thus, as Linda Gordon pointed out, Sanger could easily slide into a designation of the poor as the "unfit,"[87] particularly after the more egalitarian movements that used eugenic rhetoric had fallen by the wayside.

In one sense, the peculiarities of the beliefs of one person, Margaret Sanger, are not the central issue. But because the cause of birth control was so personally identified with Sanger, her own public orations, and the company she kept, are the best indicators of what kind of issues framed concern with birth control. Plus there is ample evidence that other prominent supporters of birth control aimed for government support of contraception in order to limit the reproduction of those they saw as inferior and unfit.[88] That is, there was an audience for a bigoted, eugenic approach to birth control, and unfortunately the

---

[86] Sanger, "My Answer to the Pope on Birth Control," 3-page reprint, published by the [National] Committee on Federal Legislation for Birth Control, of "The Pope's Position on Birth Control," *The Nation*, January 27, 1932. Both in MSP-SS.

[87] Gordon, *Woman's Body, Woman's Right*, pp. 282–3.

[88] In addition to the evidence already cited, see, e.g., Chesler, *Woman of Valor*, pp. 343–4.

alliance of birth control with the more egalitarian strands of American politics had, for complex reasons, weakened in the 1920s and was almost entirely lost in the 1930s.

Among the audiences that may have been receptive to this inegalitarian, eugenic approach to birth were Southern white racists. In the pre–World War II period, whites of course politically controlled Southern states, as blacks were effectively disenfranchised, subject to blatant discrimination and, in the extreme, at risk of lynchings and other brutal methods of enforced submission. And it appears that Southern states were particularly receptive to establishing birth control clinics in the 1930s,[89] with the evidence suggesting a goal of reducing black fertility.[90] Sanger did not support such racism, but racists found eugenic birth control compatible.

While it is difficult to cite definite evidence either way, the type of rhetoric in which Sanger was one of many parties almost certainly was an enormous influence on public consideration of the issue, at the national level. For example, a *Ladies' Home Journal* survey of 1938 showed opinions on birth control that demonstrated support for birth control, limiting family size, and "decreasing the number of feeble-minded and physically unfit. . . . "[91] Methodologically, this survey's validity is questionable (e.g., there was no attempt to gather a representative sample). But the more basic point is that the *Ladies' Home Journal*, not just obscure academic journals, could, in 1938, imply that eugenics was a central facet of birth control.

---

[89] Sulloway, *Birth Control and Catholic Doctrine*, p. 33.

[90] Lincoln Pashute, "Economic versus Racial Discrimination in the Provision of Birth-Control Services in the United States," pp. 189–96 in *Research in Population Economics*, vol. 1, Julian L. Simon, ed. (Greenwich, Conn.: JAI, 1978); Chesler, *Woman of Valor*, pp. 344, 378–9.

[91] "What Do the Women of America Think about Birth Control?: A Nation-wide Survey Conducted by the Ladies' Home Journal," reprint from *Ladies Home Journal*, March 1938, in MSP-SS. The survey found that seventy-nine percent of respondents favored birth control and that the ideal number of children was considered to be four. The reasons cited for use of birth control were, first, that "parents should not have more children than they can care for properly," and second, to decrease "the number of feeble-minded and physically unfit. (Specific percentages are not given.) The survey claimed to use the "science of statistics," but the methods used in popular magazine surveys (still today, but even more so) at that time are generally highly questionable.

Eugenics: Not a Necessary Part of Birth Control

The central point of this discussion of eugenics is not that birth control was or is primarily a eugenic endeavor. I do not believe that is true: Most supporters of birth control were interested primarily in the ability of families to make their own decision about the number of children they would have. But that was not the only component of arguments in favor of birth control. I urge readers not to misinterpret the fact that I devoted considerable space, above, to documenting the most unpleasant aspects of the politics of birth control. I did so because I believe that previous authors, whose research in general is highly accomplished, have neglected the particular aspects of Sanger's eugenics in the 1930s. And so I needed to document that turn convincingly. But eugenics was definitely *not* the reason that birth control was a popular cause: It was popular because there was clear demand for contraception by individuals and couples wanting to control their own fertility. Birth control, in fact, was *not* forced on enormous numbers of people, even though some eugenicists would have preferred such a situation.

The point about eugenics, then, is that, given who participated in the polity at the time, early-twentieth-century framing of contraception could negatively characterize African Americans and recent immigrants at little cost. Central to understanding the framing of birth control advocacy is understanding who participated in the conversation, both within pro–birth control circles, and within American society as a whole. Most African Americans remained effectively disenfranchised through the period discussed in this chapter, and recent immigrants were commonly and openly denigrated, especially in the first couple of decades of the twentieth century. So bigotry was common even in otherwise egalitarian movements like socialism and feminism; still, these movements were more likely than was mainstream opinion to sympathize with the plight of the economically downtrodden. And so the vague, ambiguous eugenics that appeared in these movements was not as persistent or virulently bigoted as was eugenics in other circles. But once the socialist and feminist movements had faded, and especially after the birth control cause was alienated from the New Deal, the eugenic argument in favor of birth control became more specifically bigoted and elitist.

One might easily conclude that medicalization and eugenics went hand in hand. Most obviously supporting such a conclusion would be the fact that both had a middle-class, white bias: Medical care from physicians was most available to those who could pay, meaning middle-class whites. And eugenicists generally assumed that middle-class whites were superior to other Americans.

However, I would argue that medicalization did not require eugenics as a partner in the mainstreaming of the cause of accessible contraception. One piece of evidence is that, within U.S. courts, the legitimacy of contraception continued to depend upon the role of physicians as gatekeepers, even after eugenics had dropped from the scene and even though in practice, after World War II, most Americans did not need physicians to obtain contraception easily. Also relevant as a comparative piece of evidence is that, as we shall see in Chapter 5, physicians' role as gatekeepers of the abortion decision was central to the legitimacy of abortion law, even though eugenic advocacy of abortion has always been taboo in the United States. That is, medicalization has been important in legitimating reproductive policy independently of eugenics. After the war with Nazi Germany, of course, it was impossible to argue for just about anything from an explicitly eugenic viewpoint.

Eugenics did serve as a catalyst to ease the mainstream acceptability of Sanger's cause, especially in the 1920s. She allied with eugenicists at a time that they had scientific respectability, so that her cause could come across less as a radical challenge to society and more as a sensible policy with elite support. But it was ultimately court decisions that assumed that medical practice, and ultimately marital privacy, should remain outside the realm of politics that paved the way for more accessible birth control.

Furthermore, with the emergence of the New Deal coalition, the birth control movement's eugenics indirectly expressed its alienation from the center of political power, rather than an expression of dominant viewpoints. It is not tenable to argue that eugenics was a politically strategic necessity for the mainstream acceptance of birth control, when birth control's most virulent eugenics reflected its alienation from the political mainstream. By the 1930s, medicalization was more broadly acceptable than was eugenics.

The concern of this book is the pivotal periods during which American approaches to contraception and abortion were reframed in this century. For contraception, the pivotal period is the 1910s to 1930s, and for abortion, the 1960s and 1970s. However, relevant to the discussion of the ultimate place of eugenics, I would argue that contraception lost most of its connections to eugenics with the Second World War. There have been critics of what is sometimes called "the family planning establishment" – that is, established groups such as Planned Parenthood, and government agencies that have at times promoted funding of birth control. Especially stinging has been the criticism that elite foundations and government agencies have sometimes been particularly motivated to push birth control in Third World countries, in an implicitly eugenic strategy.[92] It certainly is the case that implicitly eugenic strategies appear in the discussion of contraception; for example, a proposal in the mid-1990s to coerce women receiving welfare into using Norplant (a small drug delivery device implanted under the skin, rendering a woman infertile for several years at a time) suggests an implicit attempt to treat poverty by coercively controlling the reproduction of the poor. But it simply is not the case that eugenics – in the sense of designating some groups who are to remain dominant via selective reproduction – is an essential part of American contraceptive practice today. Contraception is too widely available; it is hard to imagine contraception primarily as a matter of eugenic planning, when it is available for purchase at most drugstores.

However, it is the case that contraception became widely available via a gradual establishment of a limiting frame that managed to convince Americans that contraception was a sensible option for sensible people, not a radical social initiative.

---

[92] For example, Rosalind Pollack Petchesky, *Abortion and Woman's Choice: The State, Sexuality, and Reproductive Freedom* (New York: Longman, 1984), pp. 118–19; Gordon, *Woman's Body, Woman's Right*, pp. 387–9. As noted above, Gordon's harsher view of the influence of eugenics in the 1930s birth control movement seems to me better supported by the evidence than the more apologetic views of that decade; however, her discussion of the post–World War II population control movement loses the impressive subtlety, through most of the book, of her analysis of the diverse historical meanings of "eugenics." Given that the term "eugenics" by that time was of course associated with the Nazi version, and Gordon does not clarify her use of the term in that context, her discussion of post–World War II population control too easily implies a continuity that is unfair and obscures more than it explains.

See also note 51 in Chapter 4.

4

Dennett's Moral Worldview and the Catholic Moral Veto: Unsuccessful Frames for Contraception

Introduction

Mary Ware Dennett (1872–1947), generally described as Margaret Sanger's chief rival for leadership of the birth control movement, had many of the qualities Sanger's critics have found lacking in Sanger: Dennett never abandoned her commitment to a broad-ranging social justice agenda, and Dennett never accepted that physicians, rather than women themselves, should have control over access to contraception. She framed contraception as a social justice cause in the interest of a democratic, egalitarian society that respected the right of free speech. An admirer of Dennett would say that, unlike Sanger, Dennett never sold out. And yet Dennett, despite persistent efforts, never really came very close to dominating the framing of contraception. A critic of Dennett, then, would say that she was ineffective.

The hierarchy of the Roman Catholic Church, on the other hand, is often credited with *too much* success in opposing Sanger. Sanger herself saw Catholic opposition as a monolith, and Catholic resistance is often enough portrayed as the chief obstacle in the path toward legal, accessible contraception. But, contrary to many analyses, this Catholic opposition does not, on its face, appear to have been particularly successful. In general, Catholic social and political influence in this country grew as the twentieth century progressed; nevertheless, acceptance of contraception also grew during the same period. So contraception seems to be one issue over which Catholic influence was of questionable effectiveness. I argue below that the apparent success of Catholic opposition was, first, less than it seemed. There is suggestive evidence that the U.S. Catholic hierarchy, far from setting a national agenda opposed to birth control, did not feel confident that even Catholics could be counted on to resist the appeal of birth control. Second, to the extent that Catholic opposition did succeed, for the most part the success had little to do with the fact that it was the Catholic Church specifically that provided the opposition. Instead, Catholic opposition managed to tap into a general discomfort with anything suggesting sexual immorality, so that legislators generally avoided the issue of contraception where possible. When Catholics entered the public sphere to oppose contraception, their public arguments were often not very specifically Catholic but instead drew upon other arguments common within the American debate, including moral, gendered, and vaguely eugenic arguments. Catholic opposition translated into a moral veto: It could prevent legislative initiatives but could not rally support for a specifically Catholic agenda. There is little evidence that a specifically Catholic view of contraception was particularly popular. Indeed, at the same time that Catholic opposition appeared effective, Sanger's medical framing of contraception was gradually changing the legal and practical status of contraception, ultimately paving the way for a gradual mainstreaming of support for contraception.

Although historians and social scientists who examine Sanger's career and the birth control movement always note the opposition of the Catholic Church, sometimes repeatedly, neither Dennett's approach nor the Catholic approach typically receive much detailed consideration in their own right.[1] Sanger was indeed extraordinarily influential

---

[1] I can only speculate why both Dennett and the Catholic Church have received such limited attention. The latter case, that of Catholicism, is probably easier to explain. As we shall see, there have been a number of works looking at Catholic doctrinal and other objections to birth control, but the historical literature on the birth control movement says very little in detail about Catholic opposition. The reason would seem to be that historians of the Catholic Church and historians of the birth control movement are two very different sets of people. The former have mainly been associated with the church in some form or other (sometimes as dissidents), while historians of the birth control movement have approached it primarily from the point of view of attempting to understand a movement that was primarily secular.   - .

An excellent, recent historical treatment of the Catholic Church's involvement in the birth control debate is Leslie Woodcock Tentler, "'The Abominable Crime of Onan':

and ultimately quite successful (in her promotion of a medical frame), and so she deserves extended consideration, but not to the point of neglecting her rivals and opponents. Indeed, since both Dennett and the Catholic hierarchy did not simply attempt to negate Sanger's views, but instead to reframe the issue entirely, they are worthy of a fresh examination. We can fully understand to what extent, and why, Sanger succeeded only by also understanding to what extent, and why, the alternatives failed.

The point of this chapter, then, is to develop further our understanding of the framing battles over contraception by examining the two most persistent attempts to counter Margaret Sanger's approach to the issue. One of those attempts came from within the forces that favored legal, accessible birth control. The other came from Sanger's most implacable opponents. The previous two chapters did include consideration of some failed alternatives, including those that Sanger herself promoted in the early years of her public career. The current chapter hopes to add to our understanding of why framing battles over contraception took the path they did. In sum, this chapter aims to demonstrate that Dennett's broader social justice agenda – though in many ways more appealing than Sanger's approach to birth control – had the problem that it explicitly broadened the moral agenda. That is, it did not easily allow for strategic alliances. Second, I aim to demonstrate that the history of Catholic opposition to birth control indicates that a strong moral objection to a particular policy – as long as that moral objection can speak to a number of constituencies without itself insisting on radical social change – has veto power over policy initiatives. That veto power was quite strong for several decades; given strong opposition from Catholic prelates, a number of state legislatures

Catholic Pastoral Practice and Family Limitation, 1875–1919," *Church History* 71 (2002):307–40.

Again, the neglect of Dennett is more puzzling. Sanger was indeed ultimately much more influential and politically effective, but the relative emphasis on Sanger over Dennett is greatly out of proportion to their importance. This is especially the case since Dennett's values and politics include precisely many of the qualities and content that critics have found wanting in Sanger. Perhaps Sanger's noted public relations success, and her tendency to downplay the contributions of others, was such that it outlasted her by several decades. The best source on Dennett is Constance M. Chen, *"The Sex Side of Life": Mary Ware Dennett's Pioneering Battle for Birth Control and Sex Education* (New York: New Press, 1996). I am indebted to Connie Chen for a long discussion that aided my understanding of Dennett's politics and career.

were hesitant to act on contraception, preferring simply to avoid such a tinder box. But such veto power should not be confused with the ability actually to control the frame; outside of a couple of New England states where Catholics were particularly numerous and well connected to local politicians, there is little evidence that the Catholic Church actually changed any minds about the legitimacy of contraception or had much success injecting specifically Catholic perspectives into the debate as a whole. The negative power of a moral veto should not be confused with the positive ability to have initiatives written into law.

Finally, in both cases – the case of Dennett and that of the Catholic hierarchy – failure to control the framing of contraception demonstrates the power of limiting frames, specifically the power of a medical framing of contraception.

Opposing Medicalization: Mary Ware Dennett and the Birth Control Movement

Mary Ware Dennett: Principles and the Law

In discussing the birth control movement, the previous chapter, like most analyses, has focused primarily on Sanger's role. To a great extent, this emphasis is justified; the birth control movement was to a large degree shaped by this single personality, much more so than is true for most social movements.

But there has been neglect of the frame for birth control offered by the second most prominent wing of the pro–birth control movement, a very different frame, also dominated primarily by one activist, Mary Ware Dennett.

The central strategic distinction between Dennett's approach and Sanger's was that Dennett could not accept the legitimacy of a medical framing of contraception. That is, she opposed Sanger's willingness to revise the Comstock laws to allow physicians to be the gatekeepers for access to contraception. In contrast to the "doctors only" legislation for which Sanger lobbied, Dennett staked her name on what she called an "open bill," that is, one which would entirely eliminate mention of contraception from the Comstock obscenity provisions. As I mentioned in the previous chapter, from our contemporary vantage point, Dennett's strategy may seem the more obvious one, given the importance of the Comstock laws for the birth control movement. Given that opposition to Comstock was the most unifying plank of the diverse forces that supported accessible contraception – so that unity among the different groups and dominant personalities was strongest when any one of them was indicted under the Comstock laws – why did Dennett not have greater success?

Existing historical work has to a great extent oversimplified and neglected Dennett's role in the struggle to legalize contraception. Dennett has generally elicited only brief mention in histories of the birth control movement and in the numerous biographies of Margaret Sanger. Nancy Cott's history of early-twentieth-century feminism mentioned Dennett only in passing,[2] noting (quite accurately) that within the birth control movement, Sanger's "leadership was more compelling. . . ."[3] James Reed's history of the birth control movement[4] also mentioned Dennett only in passing. Sanger has been the subject of numerous biographies, but the first biography of Dennett appeared only within the last decade and thus nearly half a century after her death.[5] However, given that Dennett and Sanger were the central ideological rivals within the birth control movement, we cannot fully understand Sanger's achievements without understanding Dennett's inability to control the framing of birth control.

Sanger's legacy is so much better known at least in part because she was strategically more effective and because she was more self-promoting.[6] On the one hand, Sanger's self-promotion was a byproduct of her dogged determination to keep birth control on the agenda and to win legislators, physicians, and other influential persons over to her side. Indeed, Dennett's lack of stomach for the nitty gritty, give-and-take of lobbying and publicity was an integral part of her strategic weakness. On the other hand, the current emphasis on Sanger's dominance of the birth control movement[7] plays into Sanger's own

---

[2] Nancy F. Cott, *The Grounding of Modern Feminism* (New Haven and London: Yale University Press, 1987), pp. 68, 90–1.

[3] Ibid., p. 91.

[4] Reed, *The Birth Control Movement and American Society: From Private Vice to Public Virtue* (Princeton, N.J.: Princeton University Press, 1983). Originally published (except for the 1983 preface) as *From Private Vice to Public Virtue: The Birth Control Movement and American Society since 1830* (Basic Books, 1978).

[5] Chen, *"The Sex Side of Life."*

[6] See, e.g., Ellen Chesler, *Woman of Valor: Margaret Sanger and the Birth Control Movement in America* (New York: Simon & Schuster, 1992), pp. 314–5.

[7] In addition to the works noted in the text, see also, e.g., Lawrence Lader, *Abortion II: Making the Revolution* (Boston: Beacon, 1973), p. 35.

unpleasant tendency to denigrate and downplay the contributions of others to the cause. It is often difficult to entangle who was more responsible for tension within a particular relationship, especially in a context of the threat or reality of arrest and the struggle of a long movement that necessarily includes many disappointments. But there was a pattern that, once she achieved prominence, Sanger tended to downplay those who had preceded her in promoting the cause, and she broke with anyone who showed any potential for threatening her preeminence. Characteristically, her later writings would omit or diminish the contributions of such persons. For the early years of the movement, the prime example was Emma Goldman. In later years, examples included Dennett and Eleanor Dwight Jones (president of the American Birth Control League after Sanger split with the organization; she generally went by the name Mrs. F. Robertson Jones).[8]

Dennett, on the other hand, while perhaps obstinate in pushing her own particular view of what the birth control movement should do, was not as interested in personally receiving credit.[9] As she described

[8] Concerning Goldman and Sanger, see Chesler, *Woman of Valor*, pp. 85–8. For an example of the tension between Jones and Sanger after Sanger split with the ABCL, and an example of Sanger's sensitivity to perceived slights, see Margaret Sanger, "Fifth News Letter from National Committee on Federal Legislation for Birth Control," December 11, 1930; and Mrs. F. Robertson Jones [President, American Birth Control League] to members of the ABCL, January 2, 1931. Both in MWD, folder 322.

Dennett's relations with the ABCL under Jones were considerably more cordial. See, e.g., Eleanor Dwight Jones [a.k.a. Mrs. F. Robertson Jones] to Mary Ware Dennett, October 16, 1930, MWD, folder 322; Dennett to Jones, October 19, 1930, MWD, folder 322; Jones to Dennett, February 5, 1931, MWD, folder 322; Mary Ware Dennett to Mrs. F. Robertson Jones, March 25, 1936, MWD, folder 323; and Mrs. Louis de B. Moore (with signature by Allison Pierce Moore) to Mary Ware Dennett, April 25, 1936, MWD, folder 323.

[9] Note, for example, Dennett's communications with a group that, in 1938, espoused the same positions Dennett had taken all her life. The group, the National Committee for Revision of the "Comstock" Law, published a pamphlet stating: "In 1876 the National Liberal League worked for repeal of the [Comstock] statute and failed. Since then there has been no united effort." While the pamphlet noted the injustice of the prosecution of Dennett about a decade before, they seemed to be unaware of the previous existence of Dennett's Voluntary Parenthood League. Yet it appears that Dennett wrote to the group, made a $5 contribution, but failed to inform them of her previous efforts (though apparently she did notify the group's Executive Secretary about some of her writings later that year). It is impossible to imagine Sanger not taking the first opportunity to indicate vociferously that she felt she deserved more credit for an initiative.

See the materials in MWD, folder 712, especially "What Shall We Do with the 'Comstock' Law and the Post Office Censorship Power?" (1938, 44-page pamphlet)

the difference herself in a 1931 letter to Sanger, in which she urged Sanger to use her great leadership abilities to push for a bill to eliminate all restrictions on contraception (i.e., as opposed to a "doctors only" bill):

Forget please, that you have not liked me any too well. Forget about everything except your big opportunity as a leader. You and I are in totally different positions. I have never had any ambition or bent toward being a public character. You are that, by force of personality and the course of events. I shall be only too glad to help you if you will rise to your present chance to be both big and true, and my help will be quiet in proportion as your stand is steadfast.[10]

Neglect is not the only problem that has emerged in historical assessments of Dennett's role. There has also been an oversimplified, and ultimately untenable, claim that Dennett was more conservative than Sanger. Sanger has been criticized from the Left for discarding her socialism and explicit feminism of the 1910s, in favor of a middle-class bias and an alliance with the medical profession. A puzzle then emerges why Dennett, whose opposition to Sanger mainly took the form of denouncing the biased "class legislation" of Sanger's "doctors only" approach, has sometimes been portrayed as more conservative. Margaret Sanger's most recent biographer, Ellen Chesler, described Dennett as a "Boston Brahmin"[11] who led the group "more conservative than Margaret by temperament"[12] that founded the National Birth Control League during Sanger's stay in Europe. And she implied that Dennett

by Elton Raymond Shaw; Elton R. Shaw to Dennett, April 5, 1938; Dennett to Linn A. E. Gale, December 21, 1938; Shaw to Dennett, January 17, 1939.

It is also worth noting that despite their interpersonal tensions and disagreements, in her 1926 book *Birth Control Laws: Shall We Keep Them Change Them or Abolish Them* (New York: Frederick H. Hitchcock/The Grafton Press, 1926; reprinted New York: Da Capo Press, 1970), Dennett spoke highly of Sanger's "generous impulse" (p. 66), "gallant zeal" (p. 67), and leading role in the pro–birth control movement. It is true that Dennett was also highly critical of Sanger's "doctors only" bill, stating that Sanger had undergone an "extraordinary swing of the pendulum from revolutionary defiance of all law to advocacy of special-privilege class legislation" (p. 201). But she did not then denigrate Sanger's earlier role, which was more typically Sanger's approach to those with whom she later broke.

[10] Dennett to Sanger, February 28, 1931; this letter is in both MSP-LC, vol. 77, reel 50, and MWD, folder 329.

[11] Chesler, *Woman of Valor*, p. 130.

[12] Ibid., p. 131.

was less feminist.[13] Noting that Dennett's position in favor of total repeal was ultimately less compromising, Chesler finds this difference paradoxical, but it seems paradoxical only because Chesler still held on to the view that Dennett was more conservative.[14] Linda Gordon's view of Dennett is more complex. Gordon argued that Sanger's focus on clinics was "more visible, more confrontational, and more capable of stimulating and absorbing local reform energies" than was Dennett's more purely legislative approach.[15] But she also noted that the difference between Sanger and Dennett was ideologically complex and not simply a question of Dennett being more conservative. Still, Gordon also made the incorrect assertion that "Dennett, always a liberal, had never even flirted with radicalism."[16] As we shall see, Dennett had been deeply involved with radical movements in the 1910s; her involvement with feminist and peace causes (through, for example, the National American Woman Suffrage Association and the Women's Peace Party) during that decade were clearly deeper than Sanger's.[17] Sanger's personal lifestyle, especially her love life, was considerably less orthodox than Dennett's.[18] But that lifestyle was mostly sheltered from public view and not a reason used to justify the dubious claim that Dennett was more conservative than Sanger.

Though the characterization of Dennett as conservative is rarely detailed enough to distinguish between strategy and ideology, there is a case to be made that, in the 1910s especially, Dennett preferred less radical strategies. Dennett's position focused on the pragmatics of legal change rather than symbolic statements against the status quo. Thus Dennett opposed what she considered extreme rhetoric that would send the wrong message. For example, she opposed a "birth strike"

---

[13] Ibid., pp. 169–170.

[14] Ibid., p. 145.

[15] Linda Gordon, *Woman's Body, Woman's Right: Birth Control in America*, rev. ed. (New York and London: Penguin/Viking, 1990), p. 287.

[16] Ibid.

[17] Chen, *"The Sex Side of Life,"* pp. 168–9, 188–9, 195–204.

[18] See Chen, ibid., and Chesler, *Woman of Valor*. Sanger had a number of lovers, essentially practicing open marriage during her second marriage to Noah Slee. The couple often lived apart. Dennett's love life did not completely match the circumscribed options allowed to women of the time (see Chen, pp. 155–6). But she consistently opposed promiscuity and had seen her own marriage disintegrate due to her husband's slide into open marriage, while she recovered from illness.

by which women would refuse to bear children for five years, giving the rationale that this would incorrectly imply that birth control and motherhood were incompatible.[19] And she opposed Sanger's initiatives deliberately to break the law, as a movement strategy. But so did the Socialist Party.[20] While it is the case that the Socialist Party in the United States was not as radical as in some European countries, it was at the core of the American Left at this time. And, while Dennett remained consistent across time, Sanger's own later legislative approach included repeated criticism of Dennett for not being enough oriented toward (and thus as willing to compromise because of) the pragmatics of legislative lobbying. Even if one based the "conservative" label only on strategy, it would apply better to Dennett only in the 1910s; in later years, it was comparatively more applicable to Sanger.

Carole R. McCann did provide an accurate description of some of the ideological and strategic differences between Sanger and Dennett on the issue of birth control.[21] And though historian Linda Gordon gave scant attention to Dennett when compared to Sanger, Gordon did note that "Dennett's NBCL, with its more respectable image, was nevertheless fighting for a more thoroughgoing legislative reform – a bill simply removing birth control from any definition of obscenity."[22] Finally, Chen's recent biography of Dennett examines the full depth and history of her political commitments.[23]

Indeed, to understand Dennett we must move beyond the issue of birth control: There is little doubt that Dennett's involvement with the birth control cause was part of a larger commitment to radical social change. Dennett's ideal model of politics was somewhat anarchist: She favored a political model that Frank Stephens, another activist and fellow follower of Henry George's "single tax" ideas,[24] attempted to implement in Arden, Delaware. Within that

---

[19] Dennett to Board of Directors of the New York Woman's Publishing Company, January 20, 1920, in MSP-LC, vol. 15, reel 10; Alvah W. Sulloway, *Birth Control and Catholic Doctrine* (Boston: Beacon, 1959), p. 190n.16.

[20] Carole R. McCann, *Birth Control Politics in the United States, 1916–1945* (Ithaca and London: Cornell University Press, 1994), p. 42.

[21] Ibid., pp. 68–73.

[22] Gordon, *Woman's Body, Woman's Right*, p. 254.

[23] Chen, *"The Sex Side of Life."*

[24] George (1839–1897) was an influential egalitarian economist and reformer who believed that profits from land unfairly benefited the few, and that land should be a

model, government representatives would serve as long as a designated number of citizens gave them their proxy; citizens could with-
draw that proxy and designate a new representative at any time.
Once any elected official fell below the threshold number of proxies,
that official ceased to hold office. Dennett, then, opposed bureaucratic models of politics and argued for a view in which citizens
could act upon their evaluation of the government whenever they
wished. Throughout her public career, Dennett tried to publicize
this approach to government. Her endorsement of the early period
of the Russian Revolution of 1917 was based on her belief that it
would implement some version of this antibureaucratic, democratic
populism.[25]

More generally, Dennett was strongly committed to decentralized
power within the rule of law; her opposition to the concentration and
repressive use of power was quite clear in her antiwar activities and
the political philosophy she espoused throughout her public career.
Note, for example, that Dennett was a founder of the National Birth
Control League in 1915[26] and a participant in 1917 in the People's
Council of America, a group with populist and socialist sympathies
(and strong support for the Russian Revolution) that opposed restrictions on free speech undertaken by the American government during
World War I.[27]

The central difference between Dennett and Sanger was that Dennett
never discarded her political and ideological commitments of the
1910s. She remained remarkably consistent in her political worldview,
perhaps because she was more deeply involved in various movement
organizations than was Sanger during that decade. Indeed, Dennett's

---

community resource belonging to all. Thus he proposed funding government entirely
from a high tax on earnings from land rentals that would eliminate the tax burden
on labor and capital.

[25] See the various versions of the article-length manuscript that Dennett attempted to
publish in the 1920s and 1930s, in folders 716 and 717 of MWD. Among the titles Dennett used at various times for this article were "Modernizing Government,"
"100% Democracy," and "Is Democracy Workable?" Note how consistent the ideas
in the 1930s versions are with Dennett's 1918 manuscript, "Pragmatic Politics," in
MWD, folder 714.

[26] Chen, *"The Sex Side of Life,"* pp. 181–4.

[27] See, e.g., ibid., pp. 200–3 and *The Bulletin of the People's Council of America*, vol. 1,
no. 5, dated September 13, 1917, and other materials in MWD, folder 660.

involvement in suffrage preceded that decade[28]; by 1910, Dennett had already developed a considerable reputation within suffrage circles.[29] Sanger's support for accessible birth control developed within a socialist movement. But Sanger did not have a long history of involvement with political causes independently of her advocacy of birth control; her primary cause was always birth control, not socialism. Dennett was more deeply involved in movement causes at the time, including the National American Woman Suffrage Association, the feminist group Heterodoxy, various antiwar groups, and, as noted above, the movement for Henry George's "single tax."[30] As James Reed observed, in contrast to suffrage leader Carrie Chapman Catt, Dennett "provided an example of continuity between the suffrage and birth control movements, a continuity that is somewhat obscured by Catt's indifference to Sanger's cause and by Sanger's frequently voiced contempt for suffrage, which she considered a superficial reform."[31]

Throughout her career, Dennett consistently distrusted professionalism and was suspicious about the compromise of principles. She was a purist: It was always more important to remain faithful to a populist principle than to any particular movement or bureaucratic organization.[32] She herself thought this was a sensible strategy, as people would be convinced by clear, simple principles; but if we examine her career as a whole, there is a distinct pattern that she always thought more in terms of principle than strategy. Dennett was deeply opposed to Sanger's attempts to exempt only doctors from Comstock provisions against contraception for two principal reasons, the first reflecting Dennett's position on birth control, the second reflecting her more general political philosophy, especially as it related to her view of the function of law.

---

[28] Reed, *The Birth Control Movement and American Society*, pp. 336–7. The earlier history of Dennett's political involvement may initially seem to be a matter of age, as Dennett was born in 1874, Sanger in 1879. However, Sanger did not rush into activism: She lived a conventional suburban life before becoming politically involved in her thirties.

[29] Chen, *"The Sex Side of Life,"* pp. 105–6.

[30] Ibid., pp. 105–6, 132–49, 151, 157–60, 162–3.

[31] Reed, *The Birth Control Movement and American Society*, p. 337.

[32] See, e.g., "Pragmatic Politics," a short (5 1/4 pages) manuscript from 1918 that was apparently never published, MWD, Folder 714.

The first reason, that such an approach gave a special privilege to doctors and thus was an antiegalitarian "class legislation," was probably fairly clear to Sanger and others involved in the debates, as Dennett repeated it again and again. Sanger countered with strategic reasoning, arguing that there was no possibility of having any legislature accept the "open bill" that Dennett favored (i.e., a bill making contraceptive information and supplies open to anyone, not just physicians).[33] Indeed, in Sanger's view, the very existence of Dennett's proposals was strategically problematic. In a 1932 letter to supporters of Dennett's organization, the Voluntary Parenthood League, Sanger noted, referring to Congressional hearings,

At both our Hearings the opposition spent all of their arguments on discussing the "open bill" and the dangers of "promiscuity"; the effect on "young people" and "opening the mails to all kinds of literature." No one spoke against the Bill we are trying to put through. No one tried to deny the right of the physicians to give or receive scientific information. We are constantly forced to explain the difference between the two Bills and to clear away the prejudice and confusion that the "open bill" has created.[34]

Sanger was right in asserting that no legislature would accept the open bill, and she apparently used the open bill as a foil against which to demonstrate the merits of medicalization of access. (She had success in pursuing a medical frame, as we saw in the previous chapter, though no legislature was willing to pass her bill either. Still, because of the medical frame, more legislators were willing at least to discuss Sanger's proposals.)[35]

However, it seems that Sanger's more practical, strategic mindset could not really absorb the second reason for Dennett's opposition to the "doctors only" bill, that is, that Dennett in principle was opposed to what she perceived as bad law. Dennett believed that the injustice of the Comstock law should be attacked directly, so that removal of any

---

[33] For a rebuttal by Sanger of Dennett's arguments about the relative merits of the two legislative strategies, see Sanger to Dennett, March 4, 1930, in MWD, folder 329.

[34] Letter, on stationery for (Sanger's) National Committee on Federal Legislation for Birth Control, sent to "names taken from Voluntary Parenthood League Stationery," September 6, 1932, in MSP-LC, vol. 77, reel 50.

[35] See, e.g., David J. Garrow, *Liberty and Sexuality: The Right to Privacy and the Making of Roe v. Wade* (New York: Macmillan/Lisa Drew, 1994), p. 15.

reference to contraception as obscenity was the only legitimate, acceptable reform.[36] Dennett, the purist with faith in populist democracy, was opposed in principle to any law that was unenforceable and/or involved a cynical approach to law in general: laws should do what they say and say what they mean.

In an October 1925 memorandum Dennett's organization, the Voluntary Parenthood League, sent out a position paper that included a list of fourteen points (presumably modeled on Woodrow Wilson's fourteen points for a just peace following World War I) that should be the basis of the birth control movement. Dennett's organization had originally included these points as a supposed basis of discussion with Sanger's group (as well as a physicians' group in favor of legal contraception under medical control). The attempt led only to further acrimony, as Sanger accused Dennett of making a proposal that Dennett knew Sanger would not accept and then attempt to blame Sanger for division among the procontraception forces. One interesting aspect of these fourteen points is that the first does not even mention birth control; it implies instead a particular view of the function of law: "*Proposed legislation should be tested* for its *soundness* as law, its *enforcability*, and its *adequacy* to meet the people's need."[37] Logically prior to a position on birth control, then, was a position on the function of law.

Further, Dennett's position on birth control was always linked logically to a specifically pluralist conception of law and of society that she thought was both principled and strategically effective. Dennett was a civil libertarian[38] and was convinced that inclusive pluralism was beneficial to all groups. She was very hesitant to vilify anyone. For example, she made a number of attempts, through Voluntary Parenthood

---

[36] On Dennett's view of the two legal strategies and the principles behind them, see, e.g., Dennett, "Birth Control and the Law," address to National Birth Control Conference (sponsored by American Birth Control League), November 18–20, 1929, New York City, in MWD, folder 325; Dennett to Sanger, July 16, 1931, in MWD, folder 329.

[37] Myra P. Gallert (President, Voluntary Parenthood League), memo to the League's Legislative Committee, October 26, 1925, MWD, folder 248, reel 13.

[38] For example, in her support of the right of nudist groups and nudist camps to exist, though she apparently did not take them seriously and saw them as an inevitable offshoot of more serious causes. Linn A. E. Gale to Dennett, November 19, 1938; Dennett to Gale, December 31, 1938; Dennett to Elton R. Shaw, December 31, 1938; all materials in MWD, folder 712.

League pamphlets and letters to Congressmen, to convince Catholics that legal birth control was compatible with a freedom of religion that would benefit Catholics.[39] Indeed, she argued that her "open bill" particularly was something Catholics could accept, in contrast to Sanger's "doctors only" bill, as an open bill would take the religious division over birth control out of the legal arena entirely. Thus Catholics would not be accepting a law that specifically legitimated something they opposed, but everyone would be free to follow their consciences if the law made no mention of the topic whatsoever. And Catholics are better off, she argued, if religious differences over morality are not settled by law, as many such laws would then be used against the right of Catholics to proclaim and teach their beliefs. For example, she specifically supported the right of Catholics to have their own schools, unfettered by legal restrictions (a timely issue in the 1920s, given, e.g., a revival of the Ku Klux Klan, an attempt to outlaw Catholic schools in Oregon, and controversy over Catholic views of religious freedom, discussed below[40]). Freedom of religion and the removal of religiously inspired restrictions from the law, she argued, would benefit Catholic schools and Catholics in general, and would imply the lifting of legal restrictions on individual decisions over the morality of birth control.

There were some indications at the time that Catholic worries about Protestant religious hegemony would make the U.S. Catholic hierarchy at least partly receptive to Dennett's view of religious freedom, which was close to what would become the Roman Catholic doctrine on religious freedom in the 1960s. In the later decades of the twentieth century, the U.S. Catholic hierarchy even largely abandoned its attempt to prevent Catholics from using birth control, though the doctrinal ban on birth control very much remains.[41] But in the first half of the twentieth

---

[39] See Voluntary Parenthood League, four-page undated pamphlet, "A Friendly Word with Catholics Concerning Birth Control," MWD, folder 280; the Voluntary Parenthood League letter of January 16, 1925, from Dennett to every Catholic member of Congress, reproduced in Dennett, *Birth Control Laws*, pp. 307–9; and Dennett, "Birth Control and the Law" (p. 15), address to National Birth Control Conference (sponsored by American Birth Control League), November 18–20, 1929, New York City, in MWD, folder 325.

[40] Gene Burns, *The Frontiers of Catholicism: The Politics of Ideology in a Liberal World* (Berkeley: University of California Press, 1992), pp. 78, 89–90.

[41] See, e.g., William V. D'Antonio, "Autocracy and Democracy in an Autocratic Organization: The Case of the Roman Catholic Church," *Sociology of Religion*

century, there was simply no way that prominent Catholic clerics or politicians were going to take a public position accepting the legalization of birth control. According to the Catholic hierarchy, its natural law doctrine then, and still today, would not accept such a position, as Roman Catholic doctrine would assert that secular law is supposed to uphold central moral tenets of natural law.[42] Before Pope Pius XI's 1931 encyclical addressing birth control, it was the case that the official doctrine had some ambiguities on the fine points of exactly under what conditions Catholics can try to avoid having children (including the legitimacy of the rhythm method), and some prominent church officials felt both European and American Catholics were quite ignorant of the doctrine.[43] But it was nevertheless clear that the hierarchy considered birth control (and any position on sexuality suggesting the least bit of permissive liberalism) an outrage.

Like Sanger, and apparently feminist and suffrage organizations,[44] Dennett was quite aware of Catholic opposition to birth control and the effect it could have on politicians,[45] but she did not hold Sanger's conspiratorial view of the Catholic hierarchy and Catholic politicians and did not simply give up on influencing Catholic opinion. Whereas Dennett was fairly pluralist in allowing that different groups could make their own moral choices about birth control, Sanger instead asserted directly that "Catholic doctrine is illogical, not in accord with

55[1994]:379–96. The American Catholic Church historically was much more receptive to arguments in favor of religious pluralism than was the papacy, given that the minority status of Catholicism in the United States meant that separation of church and state was a significant check on Protestant hegemony. See Burns, *The Frontiers of Catholicism*.

[42] And, in fact, it appears that the Catholic hierarchy could more easily accept a medicalization of the issue–because it could be taken to imply an effort to control, rather than promote, the spread of birth control – rather than the complete lifting of any restrictions. See the clipping from *Our Sunday Visitor* (a Catholic publication, Huntington, Indiana), May 1, 1938, attached to a confidential memo Sanger sent to clinics associated with her Clinical Research Bureau, June 2, 1938, in MSP-LC, vol. 56, reel 36. Also Kennedy, *Birth Control in America*, p. 236fn.31.

[43] John T. Noonan, Jr., *Contraception: A History of Its Treatment by Catholic Theologians and Canonists* (Cambridge, Mass.: Harvard/Belknap, 1966), pp. 414–26, 438–47.

[44] McCann, *Birth Control Politics*, p. 51.

[45] Dennett, "Birth Control and the Law" (pp. 14–15), address to National Birth Control Conference (sponsored by American Birth Control League), November 18–20, 1929, New York City, in MWD, folder 325; Dennett to Elton R. Shaw, August 24, 1941, in MWD, folder 712.

science, and definitely against social welfare and race improvement."[46]
Dennett's position was partly indicative of her poorer strategic sense,
compared to Sanger's: The Catholic Church remained the central organized opponent of birth control for the rest of Dennett's lifetime.
But her approach toward Catholics also indicated a more principled
consideration of the nature of pluralist society.

The Complexities of Framing: Principles, Laws, and Social Movements

It is the case that Dennett's organization, the Voluntary Parenthood
League, reflected her own viewpoint, much as Sanger defined the positions of the various organizations she headed. However, these were, at
least at times, very active organizations; for example, both engaged in
legislative lobbying to attempt to overturn the federal Comstock law.
These two figures were personally responsible for most of the central
ideas in the birth control debate: These were the ideas that were discussed within the movement. For example, other leaders (e.g., Mrs. F.
Robertson Jones of the American Birth Control League) were at times
drawn to Dennett's less compromising strategy.[47] Dennett's ideas, then,
are of interest here not simply as a matter of intellectual biography.

It is true that some other proponents of birth control were perplexed
by the assumption by Sanger and Dennett, especially the former, that
support for one involved opposition to the other.[48] Supporters – who
typically focused on the particular question of fighting restrictions
on access to contraception, rather than underlying philosophies –

---

[46] Sanger, "The Pope's Position on Birth Control," *The Nation*, January 27, 1932 (copy in MSP-SS), which Sanger's Committee on Federal Legislation distributed as a reprint under the title, "My Answer to the Pope on Birth Control" (also in MSP-SS).

[47] In 1930, when Jones was the President of the ABCL and after Sanger split from the organization due at least partly to her resentment of Jones' prominence, Jones stated privately to Dennett her view that Dennett's "open bill" was preferable to Sanger's "doctors only" bill. Jones stated that Dennett's defense of the open bill in letters to Sanger seemed "absolutely unanswerable." However, Jones felt she could not publicly commit to the Dennett bill given that the ABCL board of directors had officially committed itself to Sanger's bill. Eleanor Dwight Jones to Mary Ware Dennett, October 16, 1930, MWD, folder 322; see also other correspondence between the two, in the same folder.

[48] Examples include Marie C. Stopes: Stopes to Mrs. [Juliet] Rublee, October 28, 1921; Stopes to Sanger, October 28, 1921. Both in MWD, folder 326.

sometimes had trouble distinguishing the two positions, failing to see any essential difference.[49] But we have seen that their ideological differences were quite profound. And, I would argue, Dennett's approach to birth control tells us a great deal about how birth control fit into the political and ideological web of the 1910s, and the legacy of that decade for later stages of the debate. In addition, the fate of Dennett's approach, an approach that remained consistent across the decades, helps us understand why Sanger's ideological repositioning of the issue in the 1920s and 1930s was strategically more effective.[50]

Dennett's approach tells us something, first of all, about the social and political uses of birth control. That her position was the second most dominant within the movement provides considerable evidence that birth control is not inevitably a eugenic or class-bound issue. A popular history of Planned Parenthood from a Christian Right perspective claims that eugenic thinking was intrinsic to the cause of birth control; Dennett's different path indicates that such a claim is clearly incorrect.[51] While she did use eugenic language

---

[49] See, e.g., Kate Crane-Gartz to Sanger, September 13, 1932, in MSP-LC, vol. 77, reel 50. Crane-Gartz notes, in addition to her confusion, "It is just too bad that there should be a split between you two people working so faithfully for the same cause."

[50] Dennett apparently held to her position that contraception should be removed from the obscenity laws, and that laws should be sensible and enforceable in principle, until her death. See Dennett to Arthur Kallet (of Consumer's Union), June 12, 1943, in MWD, folder 711; this was just four years before Dennett died.

[51] George Grant, *Grand Illusions: The Legacy of Planned Parenthood*, 4th rev. ed. (Nashville: Cumberland/Highland, 2000.) The first edition was published in 1988 (Brentwood, Tenn.: Wolgemuth & Hyatt). Some of Grant's portrayal of Sanger's eugenics is accurate and based on Linda Gordon's *Woman's History, Woman's Right*, but Grant greatly oversimplifies Gordon's subtle historical and cultural analysis and adds to it many erroneous claims. Grant quotes Sanger out of context and sometimes in error, and makes sweeping claims about the sin of racist eugenics being the "bad seed" that gave birth to the cause of birth control, a guilt by association it can never leave behind. By that absurd logic, the fact that evangelical Christianity mostly accepted or even endorsed racial segregation in Sanger's time, and that some evangelicals supplied supposedly divine sanction for racism, makes it impossible for evangelicals to escape that legacy.

An example of misrepresentation comes from p. 82 (all page citations here are from Grant's 2000 edition), where Grant takes an inaccurate quotation from another author (that author in turn drawing from p. 67 of Sanger, *Woman and the New Race* [New York: Truth Publishing, 1920]). Grant states that Sanger saw abortion as justified killing of children in large families, but any reasonable reading of Sanger's sarcasm in context is inconsistent with Grant's interpretation. Sanger is lamenting

occasionally,[52] and her National Birth Control League was responsible for some publicity which implied that immigrants were dirty and stupid overbreeders,[53] eugenics was simply not a dominant theme or preoccupation of Dennett's. And thus she never came to treat "poor" as synonymous with "unfit."

Dennett's position also tells us something about why the framing of social movement causes and legal strategies can become so complex, specifically why it is difficult to achieve a limiting frame at a time of great social movement activity.

Different laws will have different kinds of social effects, depending upon the letter of the law and the way executive powers choose to enforce it. In the early twentieth century, birth control was taboo enough a subject that most people, including most physicians, were not about to openly challenge the Comstock laws. As mentioned in the previous chapter, prosecutions for violations of the contraception provisions of Comstock laws were not common. But they were effective in limiting access to contraception, primarily by encouraging self-censorship. That is, physicians and others avoided the issue entirely, so as not to risk prosecution.

The most obvious targets of prosecution, then, were activists who loudly proclaimed their opposition to (and sometimes defiance of) the

---

the plight of children born into large, poor families with serious health problems; for obvious dramatic, rhetorical effect she suggests that such children might be better off dead. Sanger, in fact, generally opposed abortion but did sometimes argue that it is understandable why desperate women resort to abortion. To cite one other error, of many: on p. 116, Grant makes the bizarre, inaccurate statement that in "most African American communities today abortions outstrip births by as much as three-to-one." This wildly accusatory, error-ridden book would be worth ignoring except that it is no obscure work – as noted, it is in its fourth edition, and it has been endorsed by such prominent conservatives as Ralph Reed, Howard Phillips, James Robison, and Marvin Olasky (see pp. iii–xiv). It is a good example of how badly historical writing can turn out if the author is set on unambiguously supporting a contemporary ideological agenda. Even while, for instance, Linda Gordon had a clear socialist–feminist agenda in writing *Woman's Body, Woman's Right*, the book is a classic because it is a model of subtlety and explication of the multiple political and cultural possibilities present in social movements and ideologies.

[52] For example, in mention of a need to stop the reproduction of "morons"; "One Hundred Percent Democracy" (text of speech), in MWD, folder 717. (A version of this speech labeled "1st Draft" is not dated, but another draft – with the same reference to "morons" – is dated April 5, 1938.)

[53] National Birth Control League (pamphlet), "An Eye Opener on Birth Control" [1919?; handwritten notes indicate Dennett was the author], in MWD, folder 273.

law. Activists were among the relatively few actually indicted for violating the Comstock provisions on contraception. And activists are
commonly involved in what sociologists John McCarthy and Mayer
Zald dubbed the "social movement sector," that is, networks of social
movement activists and organizations that, collectively, address more
than one cause.[54] As is often true of activists and opinion makers, the
activists willing to challenge the Comstock law publicly were already
involved in other movements and causes. Their pool of legal, financial,
and moral supporters, likewise, were typically engaged in activist circles, linking complex networks of persons involved in various causes.
Perhaps, especially once activists were actually arrested for violating
the Comstock laws, birth control was not about to become simply an
isolated issue in their lives. Thus the most prominent targets of Comstock prosecutions for birth control advocacy – Sanger, Dennett, and
Goldman – encountered such prosecutions at a time that they also had
made commitments to other causes as well, especially socialist and
peace movements.

When a new cause develops within the context of already existing social movements, its framing will reflect its source of support:
Diverse, politically committed groups cannot suddenly give up their
larger worldview in the interest of strategic success. Thus, even though
opposition to (at least some provisions of) the Comstock laws was a
central plank of all promoters of accessible contraception, the various
frames linked to support for birth control included more than just opposition to Comstock. Existing movements grafted contraception onto
their existing agendas. For example, when an avowed socialist encountered prosecution for violation of the Comstock laws, fellow socialists
naturally saw opposition to Comstock as a socialist cause, whether or
not they bothered to articulate any logical connection.

It was only once some of those other movements weakened that
birth control came to be framed in a more limiting, less controversial
way. And it was ultimately Sanger – who had a shorter history of
involvement in such movements than did Dennett or Goldman – who

---

[54] John D. McCarthy and Mayer N. Zald, "Resource Mobilization: A Partial Theory,"
American Journal of Sociology 82(1977):1212–41; McCarthy and Zald, "Social Move-
ment Industries: Competition and Cooperation among Movement Organizations,"
Research in Social Movements, Conflicts and Change 3(1980):1–20.

most easily separated birth control from these other causes. The most discouraging aspect of that process was that the person who led the reframing process, Margaret Sanger, was willing to take the path of least resistance, that is, one that continued to rely on eugenics rhetoric. But again, the willingness to take such a path appears to be related to the fact that she had more shallow roots in the egalitarian movements which, for Goldman and Dennett, had always strongly informed their positions on birth control.

It is true that Sanger's approach to birth control was often perceived as quite radical at the time, that is, even into the 1930s and beyond. Still, I would argue that by the 1930s the topic was more *controversial* than *radical*; that is, as noted in the previous chapter, most likely many legislators would have supported contraception if there had been no electoral consequences for doing so.[55] They avoided the issue not because of strong personal convictions against it, but because constituencies exercised what I have called a moral veto. Thus, as noted in the previous chapter, the U.S. Senate could in 1934 approve one of Sanger's bills on a voice vote precisely because there was no debate on the bill and no roll call record of the vote (and perhaps because there was little chance of passage in the House). But once a single senator exercised his procedural prerogative to have the bill reconsidered, it became clear that support was shallow: This was not high enough a priority for the issue to receive further hearing, when there would be time for moral objections to arise. Legislators generally prefer simply to avoid issues over which there is evidence of morally charged polarization within the mainstream polity.

But Sanger's acceptance of a medical frame for contraception – that is, treating access to contraception as a matter appropriate for a doctor's judgment in treating patients – ultimately paved the way for mainstream acceptance. Ultimately it took a series of court decisions to exempt physicians from the Comstock restrictions on contraception. And so by 1920, if not before, Sanger had charted a path that would frame contraception in a way that made practical change possible. And she was fairly effective at pursuing that path, despite the considerable opposition she garnered and her continued reputation as

---

[55] Sulloway, *Birth Control and Catholic Doctrine*, pp. 25–6.

a sexual radical. Sanger, who thought very strategically, was, perhaps understandably, irritated and bewildered by Dennett's advocacy of a strategy that Sanger thought was naïve and impractical. Indeed, after about the mid-1920s, when Dennett greatly reduced her public presence, Sanger considered Dennett a nuisance out of touch with real-life battles.[56]

Dennett, indeed, is not the kind of leader likely to win a long-term battle, as she was unable to compromise on principle. Although Dennett was less prone to inegalitarian compromises, she was also considerably less effective in shaping the public agenda. Ultimately, Dennett's frame was strategically disadvantaged, because it explicitly attempted to broaden rather than narrow the social and moral agenda involved in challenging the Comstock laws. To support Sanger's cause, the only change one had to accept is that the law needed to recognize that physicians should have the medical autonomy to prescribe contraception when they see fit. One also then accepted implicitly many assumptions about the status quo (e.g., that it is fine to change the law on contraception without challenging the class system, and without acknowledging that access to medicine partly depended on one's class standing, and perhaps that inferior racial and ethnic groups were inappropriately breeding like rabbits). But the point is precisely that one did not have to advocate a broad reshaping of the social order in order to agree with Sanger's framing. Dennett refused to make such a narrow claim: For her, access to contraception was possible only in a fair society in which the law did not sanction social privilege, and in which the law both expresses the popular will and is fully in accord with the right of free speech (i.e., not just for doctors). Sanger's frame, then, was perceived as isolating contraception away from questions about the larger social order, because, to a significant extent, it implicitly

---

[56] As noted, Sanger was more singularly devoted to birth control and had stronger financial backing (through marriage and through effective fund-raising). Dennett found public life tiring and frustrating and seemed to be more physically present in her children's lives than was Sanger. Dennett's Voluntary Parenthood League continually ran into financial problems. Dennett, however, did continue to support publicity of opposition to the Comstock laws throughout her life, for example, through support for the Consumers Union's opposition to remaining legal restrictions on contraception and publication of a 1943 pamphlet providing information on, and evaluation of the effectiveness of, various contraceptives. This was just four years before Dennett died. See the materials in MWD, folder 711.

accepted that social order. The one way that Sanger's frame involved explicitly broader claims than Dennett's was in its use of eugenics, which did *not* elicit much opposition, because it victimized groups who were weak within the polity.

It is true that Sanger thought that accessible contraception would in itself revolutionize society. At various times, she claimed that it would emancipate women and/or the working class, that it would end war (which she thought resulted from population pressures), and that it would greatly reduce economic inequality. But she thought these wonderful consequences would more or less follow automatically from the use of contraception. Thus she could justify a single-issue focus on birth control, which, for her, was in itself the single most important issue of the age: One did not have to *first* achieve these other goals. Indeed, if one believed that birth control would in itself lead to so many other social improvements, the issue would take on paramount importance.

Strategically, then, Sanger required of her audiences only that they accept birth control itself; oddly, her naïveté (in believing that birth control itself would lead to a broad range of revolutionary social changes) was strategically effective because it meant that acceptance of birth control did not depend on first making broader commitments within an explicit moral worldview. Within Sanger's perspective, these other changes were indeed *consequences*, not prerequisites, of the use of birth control.

Within Dennett's frame, however, change of the law on contraception was embedded within a broader conception of society and politics. For Dennett, free speech should be protected, laws should be enforceable and should not be regarded cynically, issues on which there is moral division should not be settled by law, and, *therefore*, the Comstock laws should be repealed. Without each of these logical steps, her position on contraception is not really understandable.

Dennett's position on contraception was thus asking more of her audiences than was Sanger's. Dennett's more sophisticated position only made sense if one accepted political and cultural notions of freedom and privacy that were threatening to a great many constituencies at the time. While Dennett's frame anticipated late-twentieth-century law on privacy and sexuality much more than did Sanger's, Dennett's approach was entirely too controversial to succeed in the early twentieth century.

Sanger's success at lobbying and fund-raising was undoubtedly the result at least partly of particular personal qualities; she was expert at
obtaining sympathy through media coverage in publicizing her cause.
But Dennett's strategic disadvantages extended beyond a lack of such
personal charisma. It is also the case that Dennett could never even
take the first step toward such strategic success: She could not accept –
indeed, she could not bring herself even to pursue – a partial victory.

Sanger's framing of the issue, then, was strategically much more effective at the time. That does not mean that Sanger's position was somehow morally or politically preferable – indeed, even if some of Dennett's
views on direct democracy were utopian, I personally find Dennett's
position ultimately more thoughtful and her long-term commitment to
egalitarianism and pluralism considerably more compelling. As is clear
in the concluding chapter in this book, I myself lean toward Dennett's
position that issues on which there empirically exists polarizing moral
division should usually be free from legal restraint. But this simply was
not a politically viable position in the early twentieth century. It quickly
became entangled in conceptions about sex roles, the role of religion
in society, and the worth of different cultural and moral traditions
among diverse ethnic groups, many of whose values were considered
thoroughly disreputable among dominant cultural circles of the time.

Nevertheless, the existence of Dennett's frame suggests there may
have been a third viable framing alternative (i.e., alternative to both
Sanger's and Dennett's), one that unfortunately did not emerge at that
time. It is conceivable that an effective frame would have accepted
medicalization – a compromise on the original motivations for birth
control, obviously, but a compromise that was probably necessary at
the time – without cozying up to eugenics. Even Dennett, facing prosecution for violating the federal Comstock law, was forced to defend
her actions by appealing to the legitimacy of medical authority. That
is, given the legal and political climate of the time, medicalization
was probably unavoidable; justifying contraception by appealing to
women's sexual and reproductive autonomy, or broad social justice
concerns, was highly unlikely to gain widespread acceptance and be
translated into law. As I noted in the previous chapter, even advocates for accessible contraception generally emphasized birth control
as compatible with, rather than opposed to, women's roles as mothers.
Medicalization was, on the other hand, strategically very effective.

Perhaps, then, strategic success would still have been possible had either Dennett or Sanger been willing to accept medicalization as a necessary strategic first step, while still keeping very alive the long-term aim of making access to birth control part of an egalitarian agenda. That is, perhaps such an approach to contraception would have been compatible with the path of medicalization that ultimately allowed for Sanger's success, but would have led to affirmations in the 1930s that poor people needed to be able to *choose* birth control to prevent unwanted pregnancies and thus exert greater control over their futures. Then Sanger's position at the very outset of the New Deal – that access to contraception should be paired with economic relief – could have remained part of the birth control frame throughout the 1930s and beyond. In such a case, perhaps the cause of birth control could have gradually won back some of the New Dealers. Even if not, at least the voice of birth control would not have been also a voice that reinforced widespread prejudices that poor people, immigrants, and African Americans were inferior beings, incapable of full participation in American society.

A Moral Veto: The Catholic Church and Birth Control

Catholic Perspectives: A Moral Veto While Failing to Convince

Catholic arguments against contraception shared moral assumptions about sexuality and reproduction with other parts of American society. There were specifically Catholic theological arguments about why contraception was morally unacceptable, but a moral veto could work even when few accepted the specifically Catholic arguments. The moral veto of Catholics worked in some state legislative debates simply because Catholics were a significant portion of the population, legislators did not want to alienate them, and Catholics were raising moral controversies that resonated beyond Catholics themselves. As noted thirty years ago by C. Thomas Dienes, one of the few authors of a work that considered both the larger politics of birth control and, in any detail, specifically Catholic involvement:

Even though the numerical membership of associations declaring for change in the law [i.e., for liberalization of Comstock restrictions] exceeded the Catholic opposition, . . . legislators could not be certain of the political repercussions of a pro-birth control vote. The obvious answer was to take no chances; as long as a bill never left committee, most legislators could avoid responsibility.[57]

With such a political dynamic, the reasoning behind Catholic objections was not particularly relevant. In any group's initial involvement in a cause, in general, I would indeed expect that the frame would reflect the group's internal agenda and not be shaped to appeal to outsiders. Such was the case among initial advocates of birth control, and such seems to have been the case with the Catholic Church's occasionally fumbling attempts to influence public opinion in opposition to birth control.[58] However, Catholics did ultimately attempt to frame their objections in a way that would appeal to non-Catholics, indicating that specifically Catholic arguments had made little headway. Still, they were always swimming against the tide. The quotation from Dienes above refers to the early to mid-1930s, just a few years before federal courts decisively, and mostly uncontroversially, began to implement the liberalization to which legislators were unwilling to commit.

Catholics may have helped delay that liberalization, but they never controlled the national agenda on contraception: They became players in the debate several decades after the outlines of the conflict had already been established. Catholics had little or nothing to do with passage of the Comstock laws, as Catholics were hardly even on the political map of the United States in 1873. A number of analysts have pointed out that before the Catholic Church became the most visible of Sanger's opponents in about the late 1910s, the central opposition was rooted in conservative Protestantism. Anthony Comstock and his supporters were the prime example.[59] The American Catholic bishops did not issue their first formal statement on contraception until 1919.[60]

Through the 1910s, at least, Catholic opposition to contraception included strange bedfellows. There was no grand strategic alliance against contraception, as different elements of the opposition used such different frames. Among the opponents, for example, were those

---

[57] C. Thomas Dienes, *Law, Politics, and Birth Control* (Urbana: University of Illinois Press, 1972), p. 106.

[58] See, for instance, Garrow, *Liberty and Sexuality*, p. 17.

[59] Chesler, *Woman of Valor*, pp. 209–10; Emily Taft Douglas, *Margaret Sanger: Pioneer of the Future* (New York: Holt, Rinehart and Winston, 1970), p. 97; Sulloway, *Birth Control and Catholic Doctrine*, p. 45.

[60] Tentler, "'The Abominable Crime of Onan,'" pp. 338–9.

eugenicists who thought access to contraception would lead native-born white Protestants to commit "race suicide," thus tipping the population balance in favor of African Americans, Catholics, and other supposed undesirables. Less significant politically, but at least present on the scene, were Marxists who thought working-class use of contraception would in fact aid capitalism by preventing the growth of a mass of disaffected proletarians. Orthodox Marxists thought the growth of a proletarian revolutionary consciousness depended upon the polarization between an increasingly small and wealthy capitalist class and an increasingly large and immiserated proletariat.

Like many issues, then, contraception in fact did not have just two sides: knowing that two groups were both on the "same side," for example, in opposition, may not tell us much about their actual position on the issue. And outside of contraception, Catholic prelates and theologians had many more differences of opinions with eugenicists and Marxists than they had agreements.

Catholics had a long history of doctrinal opposition to birth control, but through most of the nineteenth century the Vatican noticed the topic, at most, sporadically.[61] In an encyclical on Christian marriage in 1880, Pope Leo XIII did not even mention the Catholic Church's long-standing opposition to birth control.[62] The Anglican church spoke of the "awful heresy" of contraception by the late 1880s, reflecting the fact that explicit, politicized advocacy of contraception in England preceded such a movement in the United States by a few decades.[63] (As noted in the previous chapter, nineteenth-century American lecturers advocated contraception – again, following the lead of the English[64] – but such advocacy was framed more as advice and self-help for young persons than as a political cause.) But some Europeans and Americans, in the late nineteenth century, grew concerned that birth rates were declining in Europe and the United States quickly enough to indicate that birth control was clearly a widespread practice. Birth control became an increasing concern, and the subject of public statements,

---

[61] Sulloway, *Birth Control and Catholic Doctrine*, pp. 198–9; Noonan, *Contraception*, pp. 400–6.

[62] Sulloway, ibid., p. 44; Noonan, ibid., pp. 415–16.

[63] Noonan, ibid., pp. 406–7. J.A. Banks and Olive Banks, *Feminism and Family Planning in Victorian England* (New York: Schocken, 1964), pp. 98–101.

[64] Banks and Banks, ibid., pp. 20–1.

for European Catholic bishops starting in the last decade of the nineteenth century.[65] The concern was mainly at the level of the hierarchy: Historian Leslie Woodcock Tentler noted that typical Catholics rarely heard much emphasis on birth control before the 1920s, and most likely a significant number of Catholics were using contraceptives by the end of the 1800s.[66]

American Catholic concern with birth control may have been quite significant within the church itself by the first decade of the twentieth century,[67] but real alarm about the issue seems to have been in response to Sanger's making the issue a more explicit social movement cause. It is noteworthy, for example, that a 1916 article about birth control by Rev. John Ryan had the title "Family Limitation,"[68] the same title as a pivotal 1914 pamphlet by Sanger, which was distributed by locals of the International Workers of the World and resulted in Comstock prosecutions. (Ryan was a priest who worked for the American Catholic bishops' conference and was the prime Catholic point man for opposition to contraception,[69] as well as a very visible supporter of economic justice and, later, of the New Deal.) One of the most frequently cited examples of Catholic opposition to birth control occurred in 1921, when representatives of New York's Catholic archbishop convinced police to break up forcibly a pro–birth control gathering, organized by Sanger, at the city's Town Hall.[70]

Catholic theologians based their opposition to birth control on natural law doctrine, that is, the idea that there are certain God-given processes that are intrinsically meant to be used only for their natural purpose. From this perspective, the sexual act, of great importance with the holy state of matrimony, was meant for reproduction.[71] Every

---

[65] Noonan, *Contraception*, pp. 418–22; Sulloway, *Birth Control and Catholic Doctrine*, pp. 37–41.

[66] Tentler, "'The Abominable Crime of Onan," pp. 307–8, 310–11.

[67] Sulloway, *Birth Control and Catholic Doctrine*, pp. 38–9.

[68] Noonan, *Contraception*, p. 423.

[69] Chesler, *Woman of Valor*, pp. 209–13, 332–4.

[70] Chesler, ibid., pp. 203–4. Sulloway, *Birth Control and Catholic Doctrine*, p. 46; Kennedy, *Birth Control in America*, pp. 95–6.

[71] Even during the prime period of Catholic opposition to Sanger, there were hints of a secondary purpose of sex, that is, the expression of love within marriage. This purpose became increasingly important among many theologians over the course of the twentieth century, so that Catholic support for contraception within marriage grew. Indeed, the objection of many Catholics to Pope Paul VI's reaffirmation of the

sexual act had to be open to the possibility of conception. However, abstract discussions of natural law would hardly be effective lobbying tools, not least because they would certainly imply to many listeners that the Catholic Church was trying to have its doctrine written into law.

Catholic testimony against state and federal bills that would weaken Comstock provisions on contraception, then, focused on the moral decay they thought contraception would introduce. The argument was that, first, there were some immediate immoral and debased consequences, such as the transformation of marriage relations into little more than the type of selfish pleasure involved in prostitution. In addition, contraception would result in a slippery slope of consequent degradation of public morals. If, for example, married couples feel childbearing is inconvenient, why should not unmarried couples also take advantage of the convenience of contraception? A widespread lack of respect for moral standards would ensue, replaced by selfish pursuit of desire.[72] In general, Catholic discussions of sexuality implicitly assumed that sexual urges (especially of males) needed to be controlled and restrained. The implication was that sexual desire always stood on the verge of danger and scandal, if not for its legitimate outlet within marriage.[73]

Citing the danger to public morals was probably the most common argument used by Catholics in public forums. But Sulloway and Kennedy noted the interesting way that Rev. John Ryan, representing the Catholic bishops in opposition to pro–birth control legislation at congressional hearings in the 1930s, linked that opposition with New Deal arguments about economic recovery. That is, a central liberal argument within the New Deal was that the Depression was the result of underconsumption: Within the economy there was

---

doctrinal prohibition of contraception, in 1968, was perhaps the most important sign of dissent within the Catholic Church in the second half of the twentieth century. (See Gene Burns, "Abandoning Suspicion: The Catholic Left and Sexuality," pp. 67–87 in *What's Left? Progressive Catholics in America*, Mary Jo Weaver, ed. [Bloomington: Indiana University Press, 1999]). But that matter is beyond the scope of this book's focus.

[72] Sulloway, *Birth Control and Catholic Doctrine*, pp. 79–84, 99; Kennedy, *Birth Control in America*, pp. 145–6; Chesler, *Woman of Valor*, pp. 211–12.

[73] See, e.g., Sulloway, ibid., p. 80. For a larger discussion of this conservative Catholic view of sexuality, see Burns, "Abandoning Suspicion."

inadequate purchasing power, so that there was an insufficient market for the goods of a productive economy. Furthermore, the argument went, this problem resulted from a distribution of income skewed too much to the wealthy, who did not spend as high a proportion of their income as did the average person. If income were spread more equitably more people would be able to purchase goods, thus increasing the demand for production, to get the economy going. Using the arguments of a prominent statistician who predicted at the time (but later changed his mind) that American birth rates were changing to the point that population would eventually decrease, Ryan argued that birth control would exacerbate this decrease in population. And lower population would mean even less consumption, so that birth control ultimately worked against economic recovery.[74]

One might think that, because eugenic opposition to birth control was, to a great extent, aimed at keeping Protestants dominant over Catholics, Catholics would have no use for eugenic arguments. Indeed, part of the Catholic attempt to discredit birth control was to criticize eugenic implications of birth control.[75] However, the Catholic relationship to eugenics is not quite as neat as one might expect. Sulloway cites a number of Catholics writers, between about 1923 and 1930, who did resort to arguments about the health of the race, using arguments similar to those used by eugenicists worried about Protestant "race suicide." That is, such writers argued that the better educated and better off portion of the population would use contraception more than the poorer groups, leading to overall deterioration of the quality of population.[76] It is odd that Catholics used the arguments of eugenicists, many of whom were interested precisely in keeping Protestants dominant over Catholics. In the 1920s, after all, the less educated and

---

[74] Sulloway, ibid., pp. 94–6; Kennedy, *Birth Control in America*, pp. 236–8.
[75] McCann, *Birth Control Politics*, p. 184.
[76] Sulloway, *Birth Control and Catholic Doctrine*, pp. 98–9. Particularly bigoted eugenic arguments were made by Father Charles Coughlin on his popular radio show, but Coughlin's rantings were certainly not typical of Catholic arguments about birth control. This anti-Semitic fascist sympathizer used a race suicide argument, arguing that with birth control use by the "Anglo-Saxon and Celtic majority," blacks and Poles would ultimately become dominant. Presumably the reference to "Celtic" people as part of the majority implied Irish were superior to Poles (both predominantly Catholic). See the newspaper clippings dated January 19, 1934, in MSP-LC, vol. 115, reel 75; also Kennedy, *Birth Control in America*, pp. 148–9.

poorer portions of the population included a lot of Catholics. But it appears to be the case that indeed some Catholics did use such arguments, demonstrating how Catholic arguments about birth control were often far from specifically Catholic in origin. Notes that Sanger took after meeting with a French cardinal several decades later (in 1951) indicate that the cardinal's objections to birth control included racist, eugenic references. According to Sanger's notes, the cardinal argued that Sanger's work in the United States led to lower fertility of the more intelligent, and of whites, relative to the less intelligent and blacks.[77]

As we survey the arguments that Catholic prelates and theologians used against birth control through the 1930s, the most important pattern is that the arguments were not specifically Catholic. That is, while Catholic natural law doctrine provided specifically Catholic reasons to see birth control as intrinsically immoral, an appeal to broader moral distaste for contraception, and to presumed deleterious consequences of its use, was the mainstay of Catholic rhetoric. One did not have to be Catholic to think that contraception posed moral dangers for marriage or for society as a whole, or that liberal attitudes toward sexuality were wrong, that high fertility among the poorer members of society was undesirable, or even that declines in population would have bad economic consequences. While long-standing Catholic belief and theology provided the original motivation to oppose birth control, once Catholics took their opposition to the public stage they partook of the mélange of morally charged arguments against contraception then extant in the United States. Many of the same arguments had been made by Protestants and other opponents of contraception, often before Catholics were particularly prominent in the debate. Particularly telling here is the use of eugenic arguments that, while not exactly the same as "race suicide" arguments, used similar logic. Such arguments were a useful rhetorical tool against contraception, but they were of course not Catholic in origin. In fact, they had been

---

77 "Historical Interview" (with Cardinal Eugene Tisserant, apparently in Paris), September 18, 1951, typescript, MSP-SS. Michele Dillon provides interesting evidence that even on abortion, in recent years Catholic Church opposition has appealed more to prevalent cultural themes than to specific Catholic doctrine: "Cultural Differences in the Abortion Discourse of the Catholic Church: Evidence from Four Countries," *Sociology of Religion* 57 (1996):25–28.

used against Catholics. They were not a particularly prominent part of Catholic rhetoric against birth control, but that they appeared at all is striking.

This is not to say that Catholic arguments were not innovative; it is quite possible to take arguments that originated with another group but to combine or promote them in new ways. Such was the case with the underconsumption argument: New Dealers developed this argument to justify government innovation to promote more equitable distribution of wealth. Ryan himself actively supported the economic policies of the New Deal anyway, and his innovative use of the underconsumption argument to support the Catholic position on birth control made a great deal of sense in the context of Catholic support for the New Deal.[78] The contrast with Sanger's arguments, in the later 1930s, demonstrates the alienation of Sanger from the New Deal alliance. Ryan argued for New Deal social programs to counter the Depression, and against contraception, for economic and moral reasons. Sanger took to portraying those receiving government relief as an overbreeding burden who needed contraception to keep their numbers down, and she argued that government relief should target the educated middle class. This is not to say that Sanger ever abandoned her belief that birth control would make life better, especially for women. Sanger still believed that birth control would have egalitarian consequences, but in the 1930s she was also drawn to formulations of the need for contraception that smacked of inegalitarian blaming of the poor for their condition. Had the Roosevelt administration been more amenable to the cause of birth control, Sanger would probably have argued a more economically egalitarian view of contraception. However, it was the administration's susceptibility to a Catholic moral veto that made it avoid initiating any change in the Comstock laws. The administration did not actively promote the Catholic view of birth control but simply avoided the issue.

Even, then, among their "supporters" outside the church itself, the Catholic hierarchy benefited from a lack of opposition rather than

---

[78] And by doing so, he made use of Catholic social doctrine, which could be interpreted to favor more economically equitable policies. Ryan was a particular promoter of this use of Pope Leo XIV's 1891 encyclical, *Rerum Novarum*, which initiated contemporary Catholic social doctrine but, before Ryan, was little known among American Catholics. See Burns, *The Frontiers of Catholicism*, pp. 88–9.

active support. Opposing the mainstreaming of contraception, as re-framed by Sanger in the 1920s, was so difficult that Catholic opposition was itself forced to backpedal. Dienes noted that enforcement of anticontraception laws was rare by the 1930s, so that Catholic opposition served "as a symbolic expression" of moral opposition, with little practical effect.[79] Kennedy noted that as the 1930s progressed, Catholic opposition aimed for smaller and smaller goals, for instance, focusing on limiting contraceptive access in public health programs once they began to lose the larger legal battle.[80]

Indeed, the Catholic hierarchy came indirectly to legitimize the desire for birth control, by accepting and even promoting the rhythm method. In a very accomplished 1959 study that seems in recent years to have been forgotten, Alvah W. Sulloway argued that support for rhythm helped undermine opposition to contraception.[81]

The idea that there was a sterile period in the menstrual cycle preceded the twentieth century and even the nineteenth, although it was in the 1840s that the idea first circulated widely in Europe and North America. But there were differences of opinion over exactly when in the menstrual cycle conception was unlikely.[82] Rhythm could work for those who happened to get it right, but, especially by contemporary standards, the uncertainty made for an unreliable method of birth control. Nineteenth-century Vatican opinion on the use of such a method generally approved it, quietly and cautiously, but this was not a burning concern until the 1930s. One reason for the low level of Catholic concern may have been that it was unclear exactly how the method worked, and thus whether it worked very well. So it was conceivable to think of the method as less than true, effective birth control.[83]

It was not until about the early 1930s that medical studies in Germany and Japan established the rhythm method essentially as we understand it today. Although the excitement about the rhythm method in the early 1930s overestimated its reliability as contraception, at the time there was a definite advance in knowledge of the menstrual

---

[79] Dienes, *Law, Politics, and Birth Control*, p. 107.
[80] Kennedy, *Birth Control in America*, pp. 149–50.
[81] *Birth Control and Catholic Doctrine*.
[82] Janet Farrell Brodie, *Contraception and Abortion in Nineteenth-Century America* (Ithaca, N.Y., and London: Cornell University Press, 1994), pp. 58–9, 79–86.
[83] Noonan, *Contraception*, pp. 438–43.

cycle, as well as a great deal of publicity and excitement.[84] A 1932 book, *The Rhythm of Sterility and Fertility in Women*, sold widely, along with many calendars designed to help women keep track of their fertile and infertile periods. The author, Dr. Leo J. Latz, was a Catholic physician at Loyola University Medical School in Chicago, a Catholic institution.

An encyclical published just a year before, Pope Pius XI's *Casti Connubii* ("On Christian Marriage"), added a great deal to the discussion.[85] The pope directed the encyclical against liberal views of sexuality, contraception, gender roles, and divorce; one of its central points was that God had decreed that the primary purpose of marriage was the bearing and raising of children.[86] It referred to artificial contraception as a "horrible crime."[87] But many American Catholics also interpreted it as an endorsement of the rhythm method; in fact, as a number of observers have noted, the encyclical does not address the rhythm method in any direct fashion. It does state that sexual intercourse is natural and proper for married persons even when they are unable to conceive children. And, in addition to producing children, sex within marriage does have "secondary ends, such as mutual aid, the cultivating of mutual love, and the quieting of concupiscence" (i.e., of sexual desire) as long as there is no artificial attempt to prevent conception.[88] It was not until 1951 that the Vatican officially accepted rhythm (Pius XI's successor, Pope Pius XII, approved rhythm via interpretation of a cryptic passage in *Casti Connubii*[89]). But Sulloway's research indicated that Pius XII's action simply ratified the fact that many Catholics, including a significant number of prelates, had by the early 1930s seized the opportunity to discuss and put into practice what appeared to be a church-endorsed form of contraception. Many Catholic priests and bishops endorsed

---

[84] From clippings in MSP-LC, vol. 114, reel 75 (in a folder marked "Rhythm Method, Dec. 1931 – May 1933"), it appears that it was just about January 1933 that public attention to the rhythm method greatly increased.

[85] Some authors date *Casti Connubii* as a 1930 encyclical, some 1931, the confusion probably resulting from the fact that the Vatican officially pronounced the encyclical December 31, 1930. For the English text, see *The Papal Encyclicals. Vol. 3: 1903–1939*, Claudia Carlen, ed. (Raleigh, N.C.: McGrath/Consortium, 1981), pp. 391–414.

[86] Ibid., pp. 393–4, §11–18.

[87] Ibid., p. 399, §55.

[88] Ibid., p. 400, §59.

[89] Sulloway, *Birth Control and Catholic Doctrine*, pp. 108–9.

Latz's book and vigorously promoted the rhythm method. And with that excitement, and despite how limited we think of rhythm as a contraceptive option today, some aspects of the Catholic view of sexuality and contraception had begun to change.[90]

The central change was in emphasis; secondary purposes of sex, that is, the expression of love within marriage, took on increased importance. Arguments that any regulation of conception at all was harmful to marriage – which American Catholic writers had occasionally made before 1932 – disappeared.[91] My point is not to address which position exactly is doctrinally correct (I am not competent to do so), but that there was a difference in the public face of Catholic opposition to contraception before and after the early 1930s.

With the enthusiastic Catholic acceptance of rhythm in the 1930s, the distinction between "natural" birth control (i.e., rhythm) and "artificial" birth control became increasingly important to Catholic arguments.[92] Interestingly, in 1934, U.S. customs and postal officials applied such a distinction themselves, approving importation or mailing of Latz's book, *The Rhythm*, but not writings on "artificial" methods of contraception.[93]

Catholic theologians stressed that the rhythm method should be used only for serious reasons, such as dangers to health from pregnancy, economic privation, or moral dangers (namely, strong temptations to use artificial contraception).[94] Even these notes of caution, though, suggested a change in emphasis; for example, the allowance that there were valid economic reasons for a family to limit its size was, at the least, a change of emphasis from some of the pre-rhythm Catholic arguments made publicly against contraception. And, arguably, there was a downright contradiction, as the earlier arguments were that decreased fecundity produces economic decline, and that expecting working-class families to limit the size of their families is an undeserved punishment.[95]

With arguments that emphasized the sexual expression of love at a time that conception was unlikely, and the economic benefits that

90 Ibid., pp. 110–16; Chesler, *Woman of Valor*, pp. 321–4.
91 Sulloway, ibid., pp. 92, 100, 116–19, 125.
92 Ibid., pp. 125–6.
93 Ibid., pp. 28–9, 108, 134.
94 Ibid., pp. 132–8.
95 Ibid., pp. 95–6, 142–6.

might result from limiting family size, Catholic arguments appear to have become more compatible with the reasoning that birth control advocates had long used. Doctrinally, the Catholic hierarchy insisted in the 1930s, and insists today, that sexual relations (permitted only for married couples) must always be open to the possibility of conception – thus artificial contraception is unacceptable. But, while there is no way to know how the typical Catholic couple thought of rhythm in the 1930s, I would suspect the acceptance of rhythm made it much easier to make the leap to accepting contraception in general. For example, Sanger's standard critique of the Catholic position was that it accepted the legitimacy of birth control by allowing the rhythm method, and that therefore there was no point emphasizing the relatively minor issue of what method exactly one used.[96] While not allowing for the doctrinal distinctions important to Catholic prelates, Sanger's reasoning probably mirrored that of the average American, including most American Catholics, much more than did the hierarchy's prohibition of contraception.

It is, indeed, difficult not to conclude that rhythm was accepted partly because upholding the Catholic position against any kind of control of one's fertility was increasingly difficult, not least because Catholic prelates and theologians were anxious about the definite possibility that Catholics themselves frequently resorted to contraception. Noonan reported that the fear that priests were not enforcing the prohibition of birth control contributed to Pope Pius XI's decision to issue *Casti Connubii*.[97] As noted earlier, Sanger frequently claimed that Catholics were a large proportion of her clinic's clients; some Catholic writers apparently feared as much. The enthusiastic promotion of rhythm suggests that Catholic priests and bishops were relieved that they could abandon an unwinnable struggle, that is, offering only continence as a legitimate way to limit family size. In fact, many had probably been avoiding the issue when dealing with individual Catholics, amid evidence that Catholics were almost certainly using birth control in large numbers, probably as early as the nineteenth century.[98] Although both proponents and opponents of contraception saw advocacy

---

[96] In addition to Sanger's writings cited earlier, see also ibid., p. 35.
[97] Noonan, *Contraception*, p. 424.
[98] Ibid., pp. 409–10, 504–5; Chesler, *Woman of Valor*, p. 29.

of rhythm as a form of opposition to "artificial" contraception,[99] ultimately rhythm probably was the beginning of the end of American Catholic commitment to the birth control cause. Catholic opposition continued to remain important in some state legislatures into the 1950s, and the Catholic hierarchy continued for decades to oppose groups like Planned Parenthood, as well as government support for population control programs abroad. But in the 1950s and 1960s, especially, Catholic theologians increasingly argued for permitting contraception within the context of a loving marriage. And American Catholics came more and more to ignore the official prohibition of contraception; today, while in the Vatican's view, the doctrine has not changed, American Catholic bishops do not even bother trying to make an issue of it.

Oddly, then, the Catholic hierarchy helped delay the legal recognition of physicians' autonomy in prescribing contraception, but they could not stem the tide as a whole, either in American society or even within their church. Their ability to exert a moral veto – which did indeed prevent legislatures from acting on the issue – did not reflect a corresponding ability to control opinion or to take anything but a defensive posture. An apparent exception – Massachusetts in the 1940s – turns out to be the exception that proves the rule. In 1942 anti-Comstock activists gathered enough signatures to force a referendum on the state's Comstock law, a matter which by Massachusetts law then mandated that there first be hearings and a roll-call vote in the state legislature. The Catholic hierarchy became very involved in the matter, and, in a very divisive process, the Comstock law was upheld in both the legislature and the referendum. A similar process repeated itself in 1948.[100] Highly relevant here is that, at the time, Massachusetts, along with Connecticut, had the highest proportion of Catholics in the country. It is also relevant that the legislative vote and referenda affirmed existing law rather than institute new law, and that the referenda did not allow for the option of revising the state law so that physicians could provide contraceptives to married women.

---

[99] Sanger, e.g., strongly proclaimed that Latz's book simply repackaged a method proven ineffective already, although it is also clear that she felt the claims about rhythm were threatening to her cause. She closely followed claims about its scientific evidence. See the materials in MSP-LC, vols. 114 and 115, reel 75.

[100] Dienes, *Law, Politics, and Birth Control*, pp. 123–37.

Dienes noted that public opinion evidence suggested that such a provision would have had the support of a large majority of Massachusetts residents.[101] Dienes also implied that, because in fact contraception was fairly available in practice and the law resulted in few prosecutions, the anti-Comstock forces had trouble convincing the public that the law really caused that much harm.[102]

It is interesting to note that in Connecticut, a 1940 challenge to the state Comstock law's prohibition against physicians prescribing contraception survived being challenged in federal court only because the state dropped prosecutions of alleged violators just before a federal appeal could take place.[103] Anti-Comstock activists then had trouble making further progress because the state courts thought the legislature should decide the matter – not recognizing, as Dienes noted, that the legislature simply did not want to deal with the topic – and because it was so difficult to bring a test case against the most restrictive provision, the prohibition even of the use of contraception (as opposed to dissemination of information about contraception). That is, without an actual prosecution, there was no court case to be appealed to the federal level. In 1961, it took Planned Parenthood of Connecticut quite a bit of work and publicity to get a reluctant state to make a Comstock arrest. The arrest would ultimately lead to the U.S. Supreme Court's landmark 1965 decision, in *Griswold v. Connecticut*, that state attempts to restrict married couples' use of contraceptives violated a constitutionally implied right to privacy.[104]

Even in the states where the Catholic hierarchy had the greatest political influence, then, the best that the Catholic hierarchy could get from a state legislature was symbolic affirmation of the existing Comstock laws, and only when the legislature had no choice but to vote on the matter. For the most part, even in Massachusetts and Connecticut, state legislatures were content to avoid addressing the matter, and even symbolic affirmation was possible only because the state governments themselves were not committed to enforcing the Comstock laws.[105]

---

[101] Ibid., p. 132.
[102] Ibid., pp. 133–5, 137.
[103] Ibid., pp. 139–40.
[104] Ibid., pp. 138–41, 162, 186–8.
[105] In addition to the passages from Dienes already cited, see Garrow, *Liberty and Sexuality*, pp. 39, 201–12.

The Significance of Catholic Opposition

There has never been any serious scholarly claim that Mary Ware Dennett was as strategically effective as Margaret Sanger. However Sanger, other advocates of birth control, and some scholarly analysts of the birth control movement have seen the Catholic Church, on the other hand, as quite effective in its battle against contraception.

It is, for example, common for historians sympathetic to the birth control movement to state that the Catholic Church was the central opposition to Sanger and her allies.[106] And there is indeed no doubt that the Catholic hierarchy strongly opposed Sanger, considering her cause scandalous, even murderous.[107] The most explicit, organized opposition to legal, accessible contraception from about the late 1910s through at least the 1950s was Catholic in origin, though it took various forms: It might come directly from bishops' pronouncements, through Catholic legislators, or among non-Catholic legislators who perceived a risk of alienating Catholic constituents. In Sanger's mind, the central enemy – sometimes she claimed "the only enemy" – was always the Catholic Church,[108] though she frequently claimed that ordinary,

---

[106] See, e.g., Dienes, *Law, Politics, and Birth Control*, pp. 5, 106; McCann, *Birth Control Politics*, p. 123; Douglas, *Margaret Sanger*, p. 97. As will become clear, I agree more with McCann's statement elsewhere (p. 187) that, while church officials were the "most vocal opponents," more significant was that "the tenor of their moral opposition resonated with moral anxieties of the dominant culture." It is also worth noting that Kennedy's discussion of the role of the Catholic Church in the politics of contraception, while not extensive, is more nuanced than most (*Birth Control in America*, pp. 98, 141).

[107] McCann, ibid., p. 45fn.75.

[108] Sanger called the Catholic Church "the only enemy the birth control movement has in any country" in "Message from Mrs. Sanger to Annual Meeting [of the Birth Control Federation of America], Hotel Roosevelt, 1940," written from Mexico, in MSP-SS. There are numerous other examples of her views of the Catholic Church, including Sanger, "Human Conservation and Birth Control," address delivered at Conference on Conservation and Development of Human Resources, Washington, D.C., March 3, 1938, MSP-SS, p. 14; Sanger to Dr. C. C. Little (and various other correspondents, with the same text, but each letter individually addressed), June 7, 1949, MSP-SS, upon her receipt of an honorary degree from Smith College; "Historical Interview" (with Cardinal Tisserant, apparently in Paris), September 18, 1951, 1-page typescript, MSP-SS.

There are also numerous examples in Sanger's published writings, e.g., *My Fight for Birth Control*, pp. 352–3. See also Kennedy, *Birth Control in America*, p. 97.

working-class Catholic women visited her birth control clinics in large numbers.[109]

The evidence noted in this chapter, however, indicates that the Catholic Church's role in the American debate over contraception has been misunderstood. Statements that Catholic opposition posed an obstacle to the birth control movement are not exactly wrong; it is more that they are incomplete and thus easily misinterpreted. In short, I would argue that the opposition worked, for a while, because it was morally charged and because sexual conservatism was a definite presence in U.S. society (even while such morally conservative opposition to contraception was a minority position), not because the Catholic Church itself had any particular power to have its views written into law. The central opposition to legal, accessible contraception was not any particular social or political group, but more the moral and political climate as a whole. Within that climate, accusations of sexual immorality could be very effective, even when they originated from a group as unpopular as Catholic bishops.

Indeed, the problem with the implication that the Catholic Church was the central obstacle to the birth control movement is that the Catholic hierarchy was generally quite unpopular within American politics.[110] For the first few decades of the twentieth century, it is not too much of an exaggeration to say that, in most of the country, if you were going to have a visible political opponent, you could not ask for a much better opponent than the Catholic bishops. Having them as enemies would surely make you some friends. And, for a group whose opposition was supposedly so central, there is the puzzle that, as Catholics became more accepted within American society and politics (in fits and starts) as the century progressed, at the same time contraception was becoming more acceptable (again, in fits and starts). Note, for example, that advocates of accessible contraception met much more resistance in the 1910s than they did in the 1940s. Yet, the Catholic hierarchy was much more of a player on the public, political stage in the 1940s than it was in the 1910s.

---

[109] Sanger, *My Fight for Birth Control*, p. 354; Sanger, "My Answer to the Pope on Birth Control," 3-page reprint, reprinted from *The Nation* of January 27, 1932, in MSP-SS, Box 30, Folder 236.

[110] The discussion here of the relationship of Catholicism to American society and politics draws upon the more detailed discussion in Burns, *The Frontiers of Catholicism*, chapters 4 and 5.

In the early nineteenth century, Catholics were a tiny proportion of the American population. As European Catholic immigrants began to arrive in substantial numbers, they met accusations that their loyalty to an authoritarian, foreign pope meant that they could not be loyal to American democracy. Anti-Catholic sentiment was quite pronounced in the nineteenth century; while less virulent in the twentieth century, it was quite significant through at least the first half of the 1900s. Among large, nationally visible sectors of the population, through much of the late nineteenth and early twentieth centuries, after African Americans and women, Catholics were probably the least politically favored group in the country.[111] Catholics faced employment discrimination as well as continued accusations that they could not be loyal Americans. In response, nineteenth-century Catholic bishops usually attempted to avoid any appearance of political meddling, save for a few issues that they felt were especially important to their church. They put particular energy into defending the establishment of Catholic schools, which many Protestants opposed.

By the 1910s, the Catholic hierarchy had developed a bit more of a public presence, for example, by strongly supporting the American effort in World War I (to prove that Catholics were indeed loyal Americans) and, increasingly, via opposition to birth control. Still, they could not have been considered influential in American politics as a whole. Accusations of the incompatibility of Catholicism with democracy were made often and openly. For example, there was furor over a 1922 book by Rev. John Ryan. In the book *The State and the Church*,[112] Ryan addressed Catholic doctrine which at the time (it has since been dramatically revised) implied that if Catholics ever became a majority in a country, they would be obliged to suppress other religions. Ryan also noted that the possibility that Catholics would ever dominate the United States was so remote it was not even worth considering. He actually seemed to think that the central message of the book was the assurance that, in actual fact, this doctrine was not relevant in the United States.[113] In practice such doctrines were indeed irrelevant to

---

[111] I would emphasize that this would be true among large, visible groups and thus do not intend any comparison, e.g., with American Jews, Chinese immigrants, or a number of other groups that were much smaller than American Catholics.

[112] John A. Ryan and Moorhouse F. X. Millar, *The State and the Church* (New York: Macmillan, 1922).

[113] See Burns, *The Frontiers of Catholicism*, pp. 89–90.

most American Catholics; American Catholic support for the U.S. separation of church and state had in fact gotten U.S. bishops into trouble with the Vatican.[114] (And even the papacy's view on such issues has since been dramatically revised in favor of church–state separation.) But, not surprisingly, Ryan's 1922 book helped fuel suspicions that the Catholic Church was an enemy of American democracy, suspicions that were already quite common, leading, for example, to Catholics being a target of conspiracy theories of bigoted groups like the Ku Klux Klan.

Again, change came in fits and starts. Even as Ryan's book caused such an uproar, by the 1920s Catholics were becoming more important in American politics. They had become integrated into some urban political machines, and in 1928 a Catholic (Democrat Al Smith) was for the first time a major party's nominee for president. But suspicions about the political loyalties of Smith, as a Catholic, were openly voiced; Smith lost the election, to Republican Herbert Hoover, at least partly because of his Catholicism. And note that even Smith did not arouse quite as much suspicion as would a priest or bishop pronouncing on political issues. It was prominent prelates who led the Catholic attack on birth control, and they elicited particular hostility and suspicion.

Catholic opposition to birth control worked as a moral veto because it was not a specifically Catholic power. Any extended, public attempt to promote contraception was morally controversial (even when it was a minority that was actually opposed), reflecting that legislators acted within a social context of sex being a controversial topic for explicit, public discussion and policy debate. The accusation that legislators were encouraging moral laxity, sexual promiscuity, and the weakening of marriage was, through much of the twentieth century, enough to make the issue a hot potato most legislators would just as soon avoid entirely.

If the organized opposition had instead been led by some large but minority group of Protestants, or by just about any group included in the polity, politicians would have done the same thing. And if Comstock restrictions had not already been in place, the Catholic Church could not have had them written into law in the 1920s or 1930s: Again,

---

[114] Ibid., pp. 80–3, 90; Margaret Mary Reher, "Leo XIII and Americanism," *Theological Studies* 34(1973):679–80; Thomas T. McAvoy, *The Great Crisis in American Catholic History, 1895–1900* (Chicago: Regnery, 1957).

politicians preferred simply not to act on the matter, because sexual morality was an explosive topic.

Interest group theories of politics, prominent especially among political scientists and economists, generally assume that political outcomes are the result of different groups pushing their particular views: Greater interest-group power means more impact on political outcomes. Within an interest group theory of politics, other things being equal, the power of an interest group on any given issue should increase as its power across a range of issues increases. But the Catholic Church was clearly becoming more powerful in U.S. society as it was *losing* the battle over Comstock and contraception.

By the 1940s, the hierarchy had benefited from its visible support for the American effort in World Wars I and II and gained some degree of respectability through the support, by many prominent Catholics, of Franklin D. Roosevelt (first elected president in 1932). But even in the 1930s and 1940s, when Catholics were an important part of the New Deal coalition and a few prominent prelates had become political confidantes of Roosevelt, Catholics hardly could dictate their political wishes to the American populace. Catholic involvement in controversial issues was almost certain to draw accusations that Catholics were attempting to impose their religion on others and were violating the boundary between church and state. Indeed, Catholic involvement in the politics of contraception and abortion remains today a lightening rod for such criticisms.[115]

Suspicions of the loyalties of Catholics lingered long enough that John F. Kennedy's victory in the 1960 U.S. presidential election is generally credited in part to his effectiveness at assuring non-Catholics

---

[115] One of the more prominent authors and activists in favor of legal abortion wrote a book portraying the institutional church as endangering American pluralism and church–state separation: Lawrence Lader, *Politics, Power, and the Church: The Catholic Crisis and Its Challenge to American Pluralism* (New York: Macmillan, 1987), esp. pp. 2–4, 9–10, 56–60. Fear that the Catholic Church was a central threat to church – state separation has a long history, some of which has been genuinely liberal and pluralist in nature and some of which has been part of a rabid anti-Catholicism. Lader's book, while highly critical, does not have the paranoid and mean-spirited style of some such works.

The Catholic hierarchy does indeed explicitly assert that it should condemn government allowance of legal abortion; see Burns, *The Frontiers of Catholicism*, pp. 54–5, 120–2, 125–7.

that his Catholicism was a private matter, separate from his obligations and commitments as a public official. But by the 1960s the Catholic hierarchy had lost much of its fear of accusations of disloyalty and violating the boundary between church and state. In the decades following World War II, Catholics made a dramatic ascent into the middle class and, through such symbolically important accomplishments as the election of a Catholic to the presidency, they entered the mainstream of American political life.

Without consideration of the dynamics of a moral veto, it is impossible to explain *both* of the following simultaneously: First, why did birth control become more acceptable across the same period of time that Catholic influence in American society and politics increased? Especially relevant here is that Catholic Church was, across much of the century (roughly, the 1920s to 1960s) the only large, organized force that consistently and strongly opposed contraception. Second, why did Catholic opposition matter at all, and (related) why did most of the legal advance in the accessibility of contraception come via court decisions?

That is, it is the case that the Catholic Church could stymie efforts to pass anti-Comstock legislation, but only because passing such legislation involved a majority within a legislature actively going on record with a vote to make contraception more available. Had the legal situation instead been that there were no Comstock laws on the books in early- or mid-twentieth-century America, for example, the Catholic Church could not itself have effectively pressured legislatures to pass such laws. But, given the Comstock laws did exist, the church could itself exercise a moral veto, given residual discomfort of potential controversy of dealing with matters of sex and reproduction in a legislative context. Again, there is a difference between exercising a moral veto and actively having one's positions written into law. Analyses of politics that see power as the sum of interest group positions would be mistaken not to make such a distinction.

But the medical framing of contraception defused much of the non-Catholic opposition to birth control, starting in the 1920s. The opposition to contraception as a whole was gradually weakening. Thus courts – which generally do not have the same need as legislators to avoid politically unwinnable, morally divisive issues – could accept birth control within a medical frame, as the frame appeared to be considerably less political and controversial than the frames that had been prominent in the 1910s. The medical frame included class biases, since many Americans could not afford to visit physicians; it gave a group that was mostly male the right to control women's access to contraception; and, while it did not inherently include a racial bias, it was at the time paired with eugenics, which could be virulently bigoted. But it did open the doors to the gradual acceptance of contraception and judicial rulings that hollowed out the power of the Comstock laws; and the class bias and bigotry often paired with advocacy of contraception gradually weakened as the twentieth century progressed.

The final nail in the coffin for Comstock laws was the 1965 U.S. Supreme Court case, *Griswold v. Connecticut*, striking down Connecticut's particularly restrictive Comstock law. The *Griswold* decision's emphasis on a constitutional right to privacy, including privacy in the marital bedroom (which itself built upon a trend in earlier cases concerning contraception),[116] served as a central precedent for those 1973 landmark abortion cases, *Roe v. Wade* and *Doe v. Bolton*. And so the elimination of laws that allowed the government to open U.S. mails to look for information about contraception, and in some states prohibited physicians from prescribing contraceptives (the result of Anthony Comstock's insisting that contraception was inherently obscene), ultimately contributed to the legal and political status of abortion, as we know it today.

---

[116] See, e.g., Garrow, *Liberty and Sexuality*, pp. 194–5, and indeed Garrow's book as a whole.

5

Abortion before Controversy: Quiet Reform within a Medical, Humanitarian Frame

Introduction

In the second half of the nineteenth century, American physicians led a movement that denounced the evils of abortion and commonly blamed women who sought abortions for moral ignorance and/or murder. Condemnation of abortion usually involved condemnation of the desire of some women to have some control over when they became mothers, and condemnation of any women who wanted a life outside of the role of homebound mother.[1] Yet nineteenth-century feminists supported the ban on abortion, though they saw women who resorted to abortion more as victims than perpetrators.[2]

Outside of occasional, publicized police raids of illegal abortion providers, abortion then generally disappeared from public view for nearly a century. For the most part, no one dared suggest making abortion more available. Nonetheless, when a quiet movement to liberalize state abortion laws emerged in the 1960s, for several years it met with

---

[1] James C. Mohr, *Abortion in America: The Origins and Evolution of National Policy, 1800–1900* (New York: Oxford University Press, 1978), esp. pp. 112–13; Kristin Luker, *Abortion and the Politics of Motherhood* (Berkeley: University of California Press, 1984), esp. pp. 20–7.

[2] Linda Gordon, *Woman's Body, Woman's Right: A Social History of Birth Control in America*, rev. ed. (New York: Penguin, 1990; orig. 1976), pp. 106, 409–10; Luker, *Abortion and the Politics of Motherhood*, pp. 112–13; Faye D. Ginsburg, *Contested Lives: The Abortion Debate in an American Community* (Berkeley: University of California Press, 1989), pp. 28–9.

little controversy. Furthermore, given a vastly different medical and social context, physicians had by then reversed themselves and generally favored liberalization, as did groups of legal and clerical reformers. We shall see that one of the puzzles of the history of U.S. abortion politics is that the quiet, elite movement to liberalize state abortion laws was particularly uncontroversial in the South. In recent years, the Christian Right, which opposes legal abortion and most other feminist causes, has been particularly strong in the South. In other parts of the country, some feminists initially supported the same type of laws,[3] then later, within the abortion rights movement, argued that the laws were still much too restrictive and challenged the new state laws in court.

The history of abortion politics provides an instructive comparison with the politics of contraception. Contraception entered the public arena early in the twentieth century as a morally charged, highly politicized controversy. But its legal status ultimately changed once the issue was placed within a medical, limiting frame. The medical framing that abortion inherited from the nineteenth century was so effective that abortion was not even an issue of public discussion for over half a century. But the path of abortion politics went in the opposite direction from contraception; abortion went from a politically invisible issue to one that is the quintessential example of an issue framed in highly politicized, morally divisive ways.

Abortion is also interesting in that, unlike contraception, it experienced a period of significant legislative change, before courts were much involved with the issue. The history of abortion legislation, then, helps us understand why moral vetoes exist at some times and not others. While contraception emerged on the public scene within the context of social movements, examining the emergence of abortion as a public controversy requires examination of activity in state legislatures.

Abortion is also highly significant for discussions of a supposed "culture war," a term that has made it into the popular language and indeed is a staple of journalists.[4] An influential sociological work of

---

3 Ginsburg, ibid., p. 31.
4 To take just a few examples that I gathered very easily in one short period (spring and early summer of 2002), news and opinion articles talked about culture wars over rock music lyrics ("Where's the Return Fire in Culture Wars?," *Washington Post*, July 2, 2002); the constitutional separation of church and state ("The Refining of Religious Neutrality," *New York Times*, June 28, 2002); funding of the arts ("Hail to City for

the early 1990s spoke about a culture war over the content and role of moral limits in American life on a broad array of issues, from education to sexuality, from the family to electoral politics and the arts.[5] In his famous – and in some quarters, infamous – speech at the 1992 Republican national convention, Patrick Buchanan spoke of the presidential election as a battle in the culture war between the forces of traditional, religious morality and the secularized, unpatriotic forces of secular relativism. I have even been at dinner tables, among friends, where some in the conversation took for granted the existence of a culture war between secular liberals and religious conservatives.

The claim that there are two hostile camps separated on every conceivable issue is a vast exaggeration. For example, a recent analysis of opinions surveys found that Americans are not experiencing, today, an unusually high level of polarization on social and political attitudes.[6] Americans today, as at other times, experience various cross-cutting cleavages, so that groups opposed on one issue often find common cause on another.[7]

Yet abortion is one issue that represents the idea of a culture war better than any other, and one with a particular ability to throw a monkey wrench into electoral campaigns and elicit vociferous protests. The

Summit on Culture," *The Plain Dealer* [Cleveland], May 17, 2002; "Art Review: 'Art and Outrage: The Exhibition,'" *New York Times*, June 14, 2002); gender equity in college athletics ("Time Fails to Lessen Title IX Furor," *USA Today*, June 19, 2002); racial and ethnic slurs ("The Nation: Adios, Speedy, Not So Fast," *New York Times*, April 7, 2002); and school prayer and abortion ("Does the Christian Right Understand Zionism?" *Pittsburgh Post-Gazette*, May 19, 2002). It is not difficult to locate hundreds of news media articles about "culture wars." Whether the culture wars were primarily a matter of the 1980s and 1990s or continue today, and what exactly are the two sides in any "culture war" sometimes varies quite a bit. Thus, for instance, cultural conservatives portrayed as opponents of liberalism are at other times portrayed as opposing hate speech in music lyrics, which is more typically a liberal position. If the identity of the participants varies greatly from battle to battle, then we have a series of battles that at best are loosely connected, not a war.

5 James Davison Hunter, *Culture Wars: The Struggle to Define America* (New York: Basic Books, 1991).

6 See Paul DiMaggio, John Evans, and Bethany Bryson, "Have Americans' Social Attitudes Become more Polarized?" *American Journal of Sociology* 102(1996):690–755, which includes both evidence against the polarization thesis and further examples of claims that there is such polarization.

7 See also Nancy J. Davis and Robert V. Robinson, "Are the Rumors of War Exaggerated? Religious Orthodoxy and Moral Progressivism in America," *American Journal of Sociology* 102(1996):756–87.

study I just mentioned found that abortion was the one issue on which polarization had increased since 1970.[8] More to the point, abortion is an issue that has often stymied attempts at compromise and, at its most extremes, has involved ideologically inspired antiabortion violence. The violence is probably more extensive than many Americans realize. Murders of clinic workers and particularly damaging bombings of clinics will often make national headlines, but many bombings and acts of arson and vandalism are such regular occurrences at abortion clinics that they often receive little or no notice in the news.[9] And, of course, pro-life activists claim that abortion providers regularly engage in murder.

The abortion debate is filled with uncompromising claims, about the morality of abortion itself, and about the rights of women. This book examines how debates over reproductive choices and reproductive morality develop in such a direction. It does so partly by discussing the current politics of abortion. But it attempts to provide insight into contemporary divisions by examining how it is that we came to this point, and what alternatives we have experienced in this century. There have been numerous, valuable analyses of the legal history of the 1973 *Roe v. Wade* decision and other U.S. Supreme Court abortion decisions since then. There have been accomplished studies of how activists have approached the abortion issue,[10] and what motivates medical workers

---

[8] DiMaggio, Evans, and Bryson, "Have Americans' Social Attitudes Become more Polarized?," p. 715. But see the discussion in Michele Dillon, "The American Abortion Debate: Culture War on Normal Discourse?" *Virginia Review of Sociology* 2(1995). It is reasonable to argue that Dillon demonstrates that while the abortion debate is particularly polarized, that does not mean that it is inextricably linked to wider worldviews. And so I would interpret Dillon's findings to suggest that, as I argue in Chapter 7, institutionalizing limiting frames surrounding abortion is conceivable some time in the future.

[9] The National Abortion Federation, a professional association of abortion providers, regularly tracks such incidents: see their Web site, http://www.prochoice.org.

[10] I note here just a sampling of important works on activists: Luker, *Abortion and the Politics of Motherhood*; Carol Maxwell, *Pro-Life Activists in America: Meaning, Motivation, and Direct Action* (Cambridge and New York: Cambridge University Press, 2002); Ginsburg, *Contested Lives*; Suzanne Staggenborg, *The Pro-Choice Movement: Organization and Activism in the Abortion Conflict* (New York: Oxford University Press, 1991); Dallas A. Blanchard, *The Anti-Abortion Movement and the Rise of the Religious Right: From Polite to Fiery Protest* (New York: Twayne, 1994); Mary Jo Neitz, "Family, State, and God: Ideologies of the Right-to-Life Movement," *Sociological Analysis* 42 (1981):265–76. Also quite relevant are political analyses of public opinion

in the field.[11] Abortion is such a visible issue that there is a rich body of historical, social scientific, and legal research upon which to draw. But, while benefiting from such research, this books tries to understand the pivotal transition abortion underwent this century, from an issue off the radar screen of public policy to an apparently intractable conflict, perhaps the most difficult and divisive political and moral controversy of contemporary American politics.

This chapter and the next are not an attempt to survey the entire history of the politics of abortion. The pivotal period during which abortion went from an issue of quiet, primarily elite discussion, to an explosive moral controversy, was about a decade long, from the early 1960s through the 1973 Supreme Court decisions that overruled most state laws restricting abortion. It is important to set the context with brief discussions of developments before and after that. But this chapter focuses primarily on the years 1966–1970, during which many states liberalized their abortion laws without much controversy. The lack of controversy depended on the framing of abortion as a humanitarian, medical concern. That is, reformers emphasized that physicians were best prepared to decide when, for regrettable but necessary reasons, women with health or personal problems needed an abortion. The next chapter focuses on the breakdown of that frame starting about 1970, and the emergence of a moral polarization that has since become so familiar.

Setting the Stage: Abortion, Medicine, and Morality

The Nineteenth-Century Inheritance

Abortion law and abortion politics has always been tied to questions of medical practice (even today, as the availability of physicians to

and local abortion politics, including Mary C. Segers and Timothy A. Byrnes, eds., *Abortion Politics in American States* (Amonk, N.Y.: M. E. Sharpe, 1995); and the many works of Ted G. Jelen and his collaborators, including Jelen and Marthe A. Chandler, eds., *Abortion Politics in the United States and Canada: Studies in Public Opinion* (Wesport, Conn.: Praeger, 1994), and Elizabeth Adell Cook, Ted G. Jelen, and Clyde Wilcox, *Between Two Absolutes: Public Opinion and the Politics of Abortion* (Boulder, Col.: Westview, 1995).

[11] Carole Joffe, *The Regulation of Sexuality: Experiences of Family Planning Workers* (Philadelphia: Temple University Press, 1986); Joffe, *Doctors of Conscience: The Struggle to Provide Abortion before and after Roe v. Wade* (Boston: Beacon, 1995).

perform abortion is often the greatest barrier to access). There are numerous accomplished works that trace this historical linkage.[12]

In the second half of the nineteenth century, American physicians initiated an antiabortion movement that resulted in laws in every state prohibiting abortion, but typically excepting cases where licensed physicians judged that an abortion might save a woman's life (and, in some states, when physicians judged the pregnancy to be the result of rape or incest). In mobilizing support for stricter control of women's access to abortion, physicians took advantage of the fact that they could push in a misogynist direction without severe political consequences. For example, their framing of the issue delegitimated the concerns of women contemplating unwanted pregnancies. They denounced the evils of abortion and commonly blamed women who sought abortions for moral ignorance and/or murder. Condemnation of abortion usually involved condemnation of the desire of some women to have some control over when they became mothers, and condemnation of any women who wanted a life outside of the role of homebound mother.[13]

Exactly why new, very restrictive abortion laws were passed is not just a scholarly debate but one that feeds into contemporary political debates about the moral status of abortion. Pro-life advocates sometimes claim that abortion was never morally acceptable in Western society. Abortion rights advocates sometimes claim that the general public never found abortion per se troubling, and that antiabortion laws were only the result of self-interested, manipulative elites who found particular abortion laws consistent with their own economic interest or their patriarchal intolerance of women having any autonomy.

The good scholarly work on abortion history gets us away from sweeping statements that the meaning of abortion was always unambiguous. Because the history has some bearing on our understanding of the more recent moral politics of abortion, and because the topic is of great scholarly importance, it is worth trying to resolve some

[12] Mohr, *Abortion in America*; Luker, *Abortion and the Politics of Motherhood*; Carroll Smith-Rosenberg, "The Abortion Movement and the AMA, 1850–1880," pp. 217–44 in Smith-Rosenberg, *Disorderly Conduct: Visions of Gender in Victorian America* (New York: Knopf, 1985); Rosalind Pollack Petchesky, *Abortion and Woman's Choice: The State, Sexuality, and Reproductive Freedom* (New York and London: Longman, 1984).

[13] Mohr, ibid., esp. pp. 112–13; Smith-Rosenberg, ibid.

of the competing claims by comparing two central, partly conflicting scholarly analyses.

The most commonly cited history of abortion in nineteenth-century America is James C. Mohr's *Abortion in America*. Mohr argued that there is not a significant history of moral disapproval of abortion, especially before "quickening" (the woman's feeling fetal movement, usually in the fourth or fifth month). Furthermore, the prime reason that strict abortion laws were passed in the nineteenth century is that physicians advocated for such laws, to a large extent because they wanted to drive competitors, such as midwives, out of business. Thus the laws allowed for licensed physicians, only, to permit legal abortions when the physician judged a danger to the woman's life (and, in some states, when the physician judged the pregnancy to be the result of rape or incest).

Less known is the more uneven but often accomplished work by Marvin Olasky,[14] a pro-life historian quite explicitly linked with the Christian Right. Having an explicit religious and ideological agenda can get in the way of good scholarly analysis, if it allows for no historical nuance or uncertainty, and no conflicting motives. That problem appears when Olasky steps back to interpret the ultimate meaning of abortion history and implies, for instance, that women's working outside the home cannot help but result in the dramatic moral decline of civilization.[15] In order to claim that all that is bad results from irreligious moral relativism, Olasky claims for instance that abortion rates necessarily go up whenever there is any questioning of the conservative, evangelical Protestantism of which he is part. Thus he makes the untenable claim that, in addition to prostitution, it was primarily the rise of spiritualism and other departures from Christian orthodoxy that accounted for a rise in abortion rates among married women in the mid–nineteenth century. His evidence on this point is anecdotal, heavily overinterpreted, and thus unconvincing.[16]

[14] *Abortion Rites: A Social History of Abortion* (Wheaton, Ill.: Crossway/Good News, 1992).

[15] Ibid., pp. 295–8.

[16] Ibid., pp. 62–82, 115, 300; to his credit Olasky does specifically note that his actual numerical estimates of abortions among spiritists are necessarily speculative (p. 291).

   I am personally not convinced that there actually was a strong rise in abortion rates in this period among married women, as both Mohr (*Abortion in America*, pp. 86–94)

But when systematically presenting detailed historical evidence,[17] the book includes very good scholarship. Thus Olasky notes that his own findings challenge some common pro-life claims: "Essentially, I have found that pro-life forces have been wrong to assume that abortion was rare in the nineteenth century, that tough laws virtually ended the practice, that doctors and ministers led the way, and that the antiabortion consensus remained philosophically intact until the 1960s."[18]

Olasky and Mohr are best read together. Olasky's book is driven by a critique of Mohr, whose history Olasky sees as skewed toward a pro-choice interpretation. (Mohr is a professional historian but did sign a pro-choice legal brief for a U.S. Supreme Court case; the brief claimed that Mohr's historical work supported a pro-choice view.[19]) But when read together, as I will detail, the books provide considerable evidence that within U.S. society there has always been a mix of views about abortion. That is, it has probably always been possible to vilify those who seem to provide abortions casually, but simultaneously there has always been a deep well of sympathy, even nonjudgmental understanding, for women who feel a need to resort to abortion. Thus, for instance, while in some ways the physician-led antiabortion movement was remarkably successful in persuading the states to pass strict abortion laws, it has also been the case that prosecuting women for obtaining abortions has essentially never been a viable option in the United States. Even obtaining convictions of abortion providers who seem to show some sympathy with the women involved has generally been very difficult.[20] In short, moral queasiness about abortion has

---

and Olasky (focusing on married spiritists) believe was true. They have evidence that there were contemporary *claims* of such a rise, made by physicians who wanted to pass antiabortion laws and by white native-born, Protestant males who were worried that "their" women were selfishly avoiding reproducing enough and thus risked race suicide in the face of rising immigration (Mohr, pp. 90, 100, 166–9). That there were claims of a crisis of rising abortion rates, when such claims aided particular political agendas, is not itself sufficient evidence that the rates were indeed dramatically rising. On the other hand, as noted in Chapter 2, we do know that there was a dramatic decline in fertility rates among U.S. women in the nineteenth century. It is hard to be sure how much of that decline was due to the avoidance of pregnancy and how much to the termination of pregnancy.

[17] Especially in Chapters 5 and 7.
[18] Olasky, *Abortion Rites*, p. 283.
[19] Ibid., p. 287.
[20] Luker, *Abortion and the Politics of Motherhood*, pp. 53–4.

never been absolute and has not translated into clear condemnation of abortion.

But Olasky demonstrated that Mohr was probably wrong to say that abortion had long been thoroughly acceptable to most Americans and that the law changed only because physicians wanted it rewritten.[21] The fact that it was so difficult to defend abortion explicitly in the nineteenth century – in that almost no one was willing to claim publicly that abortion was more than an understandable tragedy – meant that physicians could succeed fairly well in making abortion appear a menace that needed to be stopped. And while physicians advocated laws that were consistent with their professional interest, it is unlikely that pushing for their professional interest alone could have led to each state passing such a law: The physicians needed to draw upon a well of moral queasiness about abortion. And they could do so much more easily in the nineteenth century when women were mostly marginal within the polity (still about a half century away from even having a right to vote): The voice of sympathy for women who resorted to abortion was much more muted then than it would be in the late twentieth century.

Let me address some telling findings from Mohr's and Olasky's works. First, important in Mohr's analysis is that the earliest abortion laws, especially the very first such law, an 1821 Connecticut law, were really only incidentally about abortion and were primarily about the regulation of medical practice.[22] And so, in the context of medicine that was ineffective, largely unregulated, and often very dangerous to patients, Connecticut was trying to prevent some of the more drastic and dangerous medical practices. Thus the law prohibited the use of deadly chemicals to induce abortion (before quickening); Mohr thought the aim of the law was to prevent pregnant women from being poisoned, rather than to outlaw abortion.

However, Olasky produced a smoking gun, so to speak, which showed that Mohr was wrong about the 1821 Connecticut law.[23] Olasky identified a criminal case that occurred just months before passage of the new law, a case involving a defendant charged with

---

[21] Luker (ibid., pp. 24, 28–31) saw the self-interest of physicians as more dominant a factor in the antiabortion legislation than even Mohr did.

[22] Mohr, *Abortion in America*, pp. 21–2.

[23] Olasky, *Abortion Rites*, pp. 91–3.

providing drugs for an abortion. The defendant was apparently widely believed to have gotten off with too light a sentence (since, in the absence of a specific state statute, the courts were bound to go by ambiguous common law on abortion inherited from British colonial days). It is almost certain that the 1821 Connecticut law was written to eliminate what were seen as loopholes in the law, directly as a result of that criminal case, and so was very much an attempt to allow conviction for abortion after quickening.

The evidence from the two books together suggests that the legal distinction of quickening sometimes reflected a belief that before quickening, the fetus was more inert tissue than a real life but sometimes was instead a means of writing the law to increase the chance of conviction. That is, there was sometimes a pragmatic attempt to assure that prosecution would not founder on a claim that the woman was not even yet pregnant.[24] But Mohr and Olasky for the most part agree that the quickening distinction really came under attack with the physicians' antiabortion campaign in the mid– and late nineteenth century.

Olasky's skepticism about Mohr's view that the laws came about pretty much solely because physicians pushed for the laws[25] does implicitly raise some important questions. That is, Mohr argued that those physicians who went to medical school (known as the "regulars") had the problem that nineteenth-century medicine really was not that effective, and so driving out competitors from the medical business was difficult. Physicians were not thought of as having a monopoly on medical skill. But Mohr argued that, because they were better educated and from more prominent families, the regulars could get their views into law. But which is it: Were regulars unusually powerful, or were they not? That is, if their relatively low professional standing was precisely the problem, how could they have had the power to get written into law sweeping abortion restrictions for which there was basically no social support? Again, the most likely conclusion is that physicians could draw on existing moral discomfort with abortion.

Olasky sometimes concluded that abortion was widely *un*acceptable, but in fact his evidence does not demonstrate that, as he

---

[24] Ibid., pp. 93, 101–2; Mohr, *Abortion in America*, pp. 67, 73–4. See also Luker, *Abortion and the Politics of Motherhood*, pp. 23–5.

[25] Olasky, ibid., pp. 109, 282–4.

sometimes implicitly acknowledges. Thus he noted that antiabortion forces sometimes had great trouble getting anyone – journalists or clergy, for instance – interested in their cause.[26] Furthermore, throughout the book, Olasky's evidence implied that it was often difficult to get abortion convictions unless the evidence was overwhelming and the abortion provider unusually sleazy.

In the end, Olasky and Mohr were not that far apart on the medical profession's stance on abortion: Olasky acknowledged that, when it came to abortion, physicians were often pursuing their self-interest.[27] And Mohr stated it was likely that important motivations for the regulars to restrict abortion were moral commitment and what many physicians may have seen as their duty to use scientific authority to counter ignorance and protect life.[28] But ultimately, as Mohr and Luker pointed out, the physicians managed to advocate laws compatible with their professional interests.[29]

Olasky, as occasionally does Mohr,[30] overreaches with his evidence and so cannot demonstrate, for instance, that abortion has long been considered a form of infanticide. For instance, he claims that the wording of a (colonial era) Delaware statute of 1719, and an 1811 Georgia law, treated abortion as a form of infanticide. But a close reading of the wording indicates that these statutes did no such thing: They concern infanticide and do not imply anything about abortion (p. 85).[31]

---

[26] Ibid., p. 94, 149, 161–6.

[27] Ibid., pp. 123–5.

[28] Mohr, *Abortion in America*, pp. 35–6, 163–4.

[29] Ibid., p. 163; Luker, *Abortion and the Politics of Motherhood*, pp. 30–1.

[30] This is not often true of Mohr. But Olasky (pp. 104–5) does, for instance, point out that when quickening was mentioned in early-nineteenth-century state laws, Mohr (pp. 24–5) takes that as evidence that abortion before quickening was widely acceptable. But, Olasky notes, when abortion was prohibited by law and quickening was *not* mentioned, Mohr (pp. 25–6) concludes that the quickening distinction was so common it did not even need mention. So no matter what the law said, Mohr's unfalsifiable claim was that there was evidence of the belief in the quickening distinction. (Olasky has his share of unfalsifiable claims: For example, throughout the book a "legal minimalism" argument that when there was no law against abortion, it was because everyone assumed that no moral person would accept abortion. But then laws were passed against abortion when it seemed moral disapproval alone was not sufficient to restrict the practice. So Olasky takes both the existence and the absence of abortion laws as evidence that hardly anyone ever found abortion morally acceptable.)

[31] Olasky, *Abortion Rites*, p. 85. Most centrally, the statutes make it illegal to advise someone to commit infanticide, even if the *advising* is done before the actual birth.

But the central matter here is that the physicians' antiabortion movement succeeded and left a very important legacy for the practice and politics of abortion. What was especially significant – and is a reason so many scholars have suspected the motives of the physicians who pressed for the new abortion laws – is that in practice these laws could allow quite a bit of discretion to individual doctors.

Although a literal interpretation of the typical state abortion law of the late nineteenth century would seem to imply that abortion was allowed only when the mother might die, many interpreted this restriction more broadly to legitimate "saving" the socioeconomic and psychological stability of a woman's life. Room for discretion also resulted from the fact that the further one goes back in time, the less certain anyone could be that a woman's life was endangered by any particular pregnancy.[32]

Interestingly, while the laws and practice were hardly advantageous to women seeking abortion, medical knowledge and technology at the time could allow leeway not only to doctors: Women (and their men) with means and knowhow did have some access to legal abortion. It could sometimes be difficult to prove even that an abortion had taken place:

> An unmarried girl who feared herself pregnant... could approach her family doctor and ask to be treated for menstrual blockage.... [The physician] had no totally reliable means of distinguishing between an early pregnancy, on the one hand, and the amenorrhea that the girl claimed, on the other. Consequently, he treated for obstruction, which involved exactly the same procedures he would have used to induce an early abortion, and wittingly or unwittingly terminated the pregnancy.[33]

Even after the new state laws were passed in the mid– to late nineteenth century, well into the twentieth century, physicians could generally choose to allow abortions liberally or not at all, depending on how strictly they interpreted their state's laws. The chances of physicians being prosecuted when they chose to allow what was termed a

---

But Olasky incorrectly reads the statutes as prohibiting *killing* that is done before birth. But that is simply not a plausible reading of the statutes' wording that Olasky himself provides.

[32] Luker, *Abortion and the Politics of Motherhood*, p. 33.

[33] Mohr, *Abortion in America*, p. 15.

"therapeutic abortion" were quite slim, especially since it was very difficult to prove that a physician could not reasonably have believed that a pregnant woman's life is in danger. For several decades into the twentieth century, pregnancy and childbirth had enough risks that a physician could almost always reasonably claim the woman was at a significant health risk. Most abortions, however, operated outside the law, and illegal abortion was at various times and in various locales quite available and sometimes fairly openly tolerated. Prosecutions were generally most likely in the event of the death of a woman from a botched abortion, which was actually a fairly rare occurrence given how common illegal abortion was.[34]

In any case, once physicians gained control over legal abortion in the second half of the nineteenth century, controversy over the issue died down, during what Luker calls "the century of silence." The medical framing of abortion – rather than, for example, a feminist frame emphasizing a woman's control over her body or a civil rights frame emphasizing abortion as part of an implicit right to privacy (a central aspect of the reasoning behind *Roe v. Wade*[35]) – was central in discussion of the issue until at least 1970. (We shall see in the next chapter that it was important to the 1973 Supreme Court decision, as well.) The medical frame could contain controversy precisely because it papered over the moral conflict that was (empirically) most divisive in American society: what ultimately *is* the moral status of abortion? Thus Luker has noted that the moral status of the fetus has always been ambiguous.[36]

However, as Luker and James Mohr[37] have demonstrated, medical advances increasingly made problematic discretion around the requirement that abortion be performed only to save a woman's life. By the mid–twentieth century, actual loss of life by women during a medically supervised pregnancy or delivery was an increasingly rare occurrence.

---

[34] Nanette J. Davis, *From Crime to Choice: The Transformation of Abortion in America* (Westport, Conn.: Greenwood, 1985), pp. 51–6, 89–107; Rickie Solinger, *The Abortionist: A Woman against the Law* (New York: The Free Press, 1994); Leslie J. Reagan, *When Abortion Was a Crime: Women, Medicine, and Law in the United States, 1867–1973* (Berkeley and Los Angeles: University of California Press, 1997), chapt. 3. For relevant context, also see Joffe, *Doctors of Conscience*, pp. 29–31.

[35] David J. Garrow, *Liberty and Sexuality: The Right to Privacy and the Making of Roe v. Wade* (New York: Macmillan/Lisa Drew, 1994).

[36] Luker, *Abortion and the Politics of Motherhood*, p. 3.

[37] *Abortion in America.*

And the circumstances were increasingly predictable, so that it became more plausible to prosecute doctors for allowing an abortion that was not necessary to save the woman's life. Leslie J. Reagan has argued that the increased visibility of abortion (partly as a result of increased demand during the Great Depression), and, even more so, the movement to return women to the home after so many entered the workforce during World War II (many of whom were quickly dismissed once large numbers of men returned to civilian life), led to increased prosecutions of abortion in the 1940s and 1950s. Those prosecutions, in turn, helped spur the movement for abortion law reform.[38]

Reform: The Medical, Humanitarian Frame

Murmurings in favor of reforming the nineteenth-century state abortion laws had started by the 1950s, indeed to a limited extent even earlier.[39] The frame that reformers used was based on the nineteenth-century frame, but under changed circumstances it necessarily included some revision. In both cases, medical gatekeeping was central. But in the twentieth century, rather than emphasizing restrictions on abortion, the argument was that the laws had to be liberalized. And to do so required expanding the legally allowable reasons for physicians to approve abortion.

Physicians were joined by other interested reformers, including lawyers and clergy who formed various organizations and state-level coalitions that lobbied for reform.[40] However, in the mid- to late 1960s, when many states considered abortion reform bills, abortion was still a fairly low-profile issue. (It was not even until 1967 that the American Medical Association officially supported abortion reform.)

In 1962, a reform group that regularly recommends new legal codes and legal language on a range of issues, the American Law Institute (ALI), recommended changes in state criminal codes on a number of matters.[41] On abortion particularly, the primary goal was to make

---

[38] Reagan, *When Abortion Was a Crime*, chapt. 6.

[39] Luker, *Abortion and the Politics of Motherhood*, pp. 54–5; Staggenborg, *The Pro-Choice Movement*, p. 14; Garrow, *Liberty and Sexuality*, pp. 272–82.

[40] Lawrence Lader, *Abortion II: Making the Revolution* (Boston: Beacon, 1973), pp. 42–51.

[41] See the very informative discussion of the medical and legal discussions, also involving Planned Parenthood, that led to the ALI model code in Reagan, *When Abortion Was a Crime*, pp. 218–22.

so-called therapeutic abortion – a term that itself connotes a medical frame – more available, under the control of physicians and hospitals. That is, in the place of the requirement that abortions be allowed only to save the life of the pregnant woman – a requirement that could be either restrictive or ambiguous in practice – many states amended their laws to allow abortion when, according to medical judgment, pregnancy resulted from rape or incest, threatened the physical or mental health of the woman, or could result in the birth of a physically or mentally impaired child. The ALI recommended that two physicians certify in writing that an abortion was justified, and that abortions take place in licensed hospitals. The ALI model code, as it was known, became the standard starting point for discussion of revision of state laws.[42]

In contrast to the nineteenth century, then, when physicians led a movement to restrict the availability of abortion as part of an effort to establish their own profession, in the 1960s they led a movement to remove the law as an obstacle to their professional autonomy. In Mohr's view,

Physicians were no longer members of a struggling profession, looking to the state to prosecute their competitors, such as midwives. Instead they were now at the height of their power and prepared to assert their right to make sensitive and tolerant decisions without the state looking over their shoulders. To put it crassly, now that they had finally cornered the medical market, physicians sought to reduce the market's restrictions; to put it less crassly, physicians went public with their desire for a nearly absolute degree of flexibility in providing what they thought, not what the state thought, their patients wanted or needed.[43]

In both the nineteenth century and in the 1960s, then, physicians pursued a medical frame, that is, a frame which portrayed abortion as an issue of medical judgment and medical authority. But I believe Mohr overemphasizes the self-interest of physicians as the determining factor.

[42] For the text of the ALI recommendations on abortion law, see Sagar C. Jain and Steven W. Sinding, *North Carolina Abortion Law 1967: A Study in Legislative Process* (Chapel Hill: Carolina Population Center, University of North Carolina at Chapel Hill, 1968), p. 61.

[43] James C. Mohr, "Iowa's Abortion Battles of the Late 1960s and Early 1970s: Long-term Perspectives and Short-term Analyses," *The Annals of Iowa*, 3rd series, 50 (1989), pp. 75–6.

The public presentation of what constituted a "medical" approach included a strong claim of humanitarian paternalism. Some leaders of the reform movement were not physicians and were attracted primarily by the promise of humanitarian outcomes rather than physicians' professional interests. Thus some of those reformers could later easily drop the medical frame and become supporters of abortion as a woman's right, once they thought therapeutic abortion was not working. But, for the most part, before about 1970 medical autonomy and humanitarian concern were presented as two sides of the same coin. In the 1960s, women who sought abortions were portrayed not as moral transgressors or moral idiots, as they had been in the nineteenth century. Instead, they were objects of sympathy in a regrettable situation that doctors, acting professionally, could alleviate. This was certainly not an abortion rights frame: The view of women was paternalistic. Of the California legislators involved in that state's reform law, for example, Luker noted,

> The reaction of state legislators of the 1960s, when asked what role women had played in securing passage of the Beilenson bill, could best be epitomized as a blank stare. All of them could name individual women who had been active in the reform group California Committee on Therapeutic Abortion (CCTA), but none of them believed that women *as a constituency* were central to the issue.[44]

The frame, then, was certainly not a feminist one. It was a medical, humanitarian frame in the sense that it portrayed abortion as both a medical and a humanitarian concern, *and* that it treated medical intervention as intrinsically humanitarian.

And the frame did indeed promise physicians a great deal of professional autonomy. That is, in practice, the ALI recommendations would make it extremely difficult to question a doctor's decision to allow a "therapeutic" abortion. For example, the model code allowed abortion if "The physician believed there was substantial risk that continuance of the pregnancy would gravely impair the physical or mental health of the mother. . . . "[45] There was no reference to verification that a woman's health was actually at risk. How could a prosecutor disprove

---

[44] Luker, *Abortion and the Politics of Motherhood*, p. 93. Emphasis is Luker's. See also Reagan, *When Abortion Was a Crime*, pp. 220–1.
[45] Quoted in Garrow, *Liberty and Sexuality*, p. 277.

that a physician *believed* there could be a grave mental health risk? Still, such a medical framing appeared to many state legislators to be a sensible, fairly uncontroversial initiative without extensive moral or social implications.

There were also legal and clerical groups that supported abortion law reform. But it was ultimately groups of elites, not widespread popular movements, that supported the medical, humanitarian frame. The elite nature of that support was the frame's strength, as well as its ultimate weakness. As we see below, the frame painted abortion law reform as sensible, not radical, and state legislatures that passed reform laws perceived a range of respectable (i.e., elite) opinion in favor of reform and mostly an absence of focused opposition. But we shall also see that the widening of public debate on abortion, and the emergence of an alternative framing of abortion liberalization – namely an abortion rights frame advocating total repeal of abortion laws – quickly undermined and overwhelmed this apparently broad, elite coalition.[46]

But this frame did drive most of the abortion law discussion in the 1960s, partly in response to widespread humanitarian reactions to health crises of the time. Oft-cited in support of abortion law reform was public fear of birth defects as a result of the communicable disease rubella (also known as German measles) and the drug thalidomide. Awareness of the risks of thalidomide arose in the early 1960s, and of rubella in 1965. Both added steam to the already extant elite movement for abortion law reform.[47] Such fears were central in the portrayal of abortion as a simultaneously medical and humanitarian concern.

Most notable was the highly publicized 1962 case of Sherri Finkbine.[48] In retrospect, one could not imagine a better candidate to

---

[46] Note Suzanne Staggenborg's view of the reform coalitions in various states (*The Pro-Choice Movement*, p. 27): "What is surprising about these ideologically diverse coalitions is not that they were short-lived but that they were created at all." I would argue that such coalitions can actually be very effective in mainstream politics and can be quite common, but I also agree with Staggenborg that they have an Achilles' heal, that is, they cannot withstand popular and passionate attention.

[47] Staggenborg, ibid., pp. 14–15; Davis, *From Crime to Choice*, pp. 59, 214; Garrow, *Liberty and Sexuality*, pp. 300–1.

[48] Described in detail in numerous accounts, e.g., Raymond Tatalovich and Byron W. Daynes, *The Politics of Abortion: A Study of Community Conflict in Public Policy Making* (New York: Praeger 1981), pp. 44–6; Luker, *Abortion and the Politics of Motherhood*, pp. 62–5; Garrow, *Liberty and Sexuality*, pp. 285–9.

promote (unwittingly) the cause of access to abortion for humanitarian reasons. Finkbine was a mother of four children who appeared on the local version of a then-popular children's show, "Romper Room." She lived in Arizona, which had a typical abortion law, inherited from the nineteenth century, that allowed abortion only to save the life of the woman. But more liberal practice sometimes ensued. While pregnant, Finkbine had used headache tablets her husband had bought in Europe, which contained thalidomide, a drug not approved for sale in the United States. After reading newspaper stories linking the drug to birth defects, Finkbine and her husband consulted with a doctor and arranged for an abortion. At that time, abortions in Arizona, as in many states, had to be approved by a hospital board. The board readily approved, until Finkbine called a newspaper, suggesting that they publicize her story to warn other women who may have taken the drug. The story quickly spread, and controversy emerged amid a local district attorney threatening prosecution, as the abortion did not qualify under a strict interpretation of the law. The hospital was then hesitant to go forward, and the Finkbines' attempts to end the ordeal appeared as a daily melodrama in major U.S. newspapers. The couple declared that they were not really in favor of abortion but did not think it was right to have a baby with such a high probability of serious deformity. As they tried to elude the press, the Vatican condemned them, and they received hostile letters about their decision. Ultimately they obtained an abortion in Sweden, and doctors told them the fetus was horribly deformed and could not have survived.

Although the Finkbine case elicited a great deal of controversy, its significance is more that it helped crystallize support for abortion law reform. Within the circles that discussed such issues (which would remain quite limited circles, in most states, through the 1960s), Finkbine's case was one that evoked sympathy for abortion law reform within a medical, humanitarian frame.

I will detail below why these reform-minded elites had considerable success in having their recommendations enacted into law until alternative feminist (i.e., abortion rights) and pro-life frames emerged. From 1966 to 1970, a number of states passed abortion law reforms resembling the ALI model code. The central point I want to demonstrate in this chapter is that such laws passed because the medical, humanitarian frame was not morally charged. Within the limited discussion of

abortion in reform circles and many state legislatures, this frame did
not widen the agenda: it played into mainstream thinking about abortion. Persistence of that frame depended on the discussion remaining a
quiet one, primarily among elites.

That is, while abortion was politically invisible, no one needed to
resolve, or even discuss, the potentially thorny issue of the morality of
abortion.[49] Luker notes: "Until the end of the 1950s . . . no one seems
to have paid much attention to the philosophical issues involved; medical abortions took place with little or no public overview; and public
interest in the issue was limited to the occasional news report detailing
the arrest of an illegal abortion ring."[50] I would extend the point to
argue that, especially if we are talking about the public (and not just the
medical profession and small groups of reformers), even up to about
1970, abortion simply was not framed very well in most Americans'
minds. Thus coherent moral opposition to abortion law reform could
not emerge.[51] Organized movements with a moral frame on *either* side
were still quite young. More particularly, there was little reason for
most people, including legislators, to think of the issue as primarily
moral in nature. Instead, groups of medical, legal, and clerical elites
initially monopolized the framing of abortion reform, presenting it as
a sensible initiative that would make medicine more workable and
humane.

Abortion Law Reform in the State Legislatures

In the period 1966–1970, then, an elite movement of physicians, clergy,
and legislators succeeded in convincing numerous state legislatures to
liberalize their abortion laws, before abortion law became primarily a
matter of court decisions. How different the politics of abortion was
at the time is demonstrated by two striking characteristics of those

---

[49] Luker, ibid., pp. 46–7, 58.

[50] Ibid., p. 68.

[51] An analogous situation emerged in recent years on the issue of physician-assisted suicide and, beginning even more recently (especially in the summer of 2001), stem cell
research. In both cases, Americans' opinions are mostly unformed: There is no clear
dominant frame defining what the issue, morally, is primarily about. Are these sensible, new approaches that are medically beneficial, or are they morally unacceptable
tampering with life?

state laws: First, those that passed did so with little controversy, and, second, Southern states were disproportionately likely to pass such laws. We shall see that it was states in which a medical, humanitarian frame dominated that were more likely to pass such laws. Following the patterns, then, of which states passed laws and which did not, and why, helps us understand why abortion is a very visible controversy today but has not always been so.

While a number of works on the political and legal aspects of the abortion controversy have commented on these laws, sociological (as well as most historical) work has typically mentioned the pre– *Roe v. Wade* liberalization efforts in passing, if at all. There are very useful case studies of the politics of abortion bills in particular states,[52] with Luker's[53] account of the 1967 California abortion law providing the broadest sociological context. Garrow's[54] monumental history of the right of privacy as developed in the context of contraceptive and abortion rights provides extensive historical discussion of a number of the state laws; also quite useful is Lader's account.[55] However, both Garrow and Lader focus on how different laws provided a wedge for the legal recognition of abortion rights, which they ultimately did. However, such an approach does not explain why the laws passed in the first place: As we shall see, rights language was in fact not the justification provided for most of the laws at the time.

Archon Fung's excellent analysis[56] of how *Roe* affected women's practical access to abortion includes some consideration of the state-level changes. But Fung is primarily interested in how the laws affected

---

[52] Patricia G. Steinhoff and Milton Diamond, *Abortion Politics: The Hawaii Experience* (Honolulu: University Press of Hawaii, 1977); Jain and Sinding, *North Carolina Abortion Law 1967*; Daniel J. O'Neil, *Church Lobbying in a Western State: A Case Study on Abortion Legislation* (Tucson: University of Arizona Press, 1970); Sagar C. Jain and Laurel F. Gooch, *Georgia Abortion Act 1968: A Study in Legislative Process* (Chapel Hill: Department of Health Administration, School of Public Health, and Carolina Population Center, University of North Carolina at Chapel Hill, 1972); Mohr, "Iowa's Abortion Battles of the Late 1960s and Early 1970s."

[53] *Abortion and the Politics of Motherhood.*

[54] *Liberty and Sexuality.*

[55] *Abortion II.*

[56] Archon Fung, "Making Rights Real: *Roe*'s Impact on Abortion Access," *Politics & Society* 21 (1993):465–504. Fung includes a critique of Mary Ann Glendon's and Ruth Bader Ginsburg's views of how state-level changes would have affected access in the absence of *Roe*, a matter I also address in Chapters 6 and 7.

women's access to legal abortion, not why some states passed such laws and others did not. Some studies[57] have briefly noted that arguments in favor of state-level abortion reform depended on medical legitimation, rather than an appeal to morality or rights. Luker[58] makes that point particularly thoroughly. Political scientists Christopher Z. Mooney and Mei-Hsien Lee's analysis is rare in attempting to discern patterns in which states passed new abortion laws and which did not by comparing contrasting political and demographic characteristics of those states.[59]

Legally and historically, it is indeed the case that the 1973 decision in *Roe v. Wade* is ultimately more important than the state-level laws that the U.S. Supreme Court decision made obsolete. However, sociologically and politically, the process by which states liberalized their laws before *Roe* is essential to understanding why *Roe* was so controversial, and more generally how the frames used to define particular social changes lead to overt political controversy and conflict. For example, some very prominent critiques of *Roe*, such as Mary Ann Glendon's,[60] depend upon particular assumptions about the relationship between the state-level reform and current conflict over abortion.

---

[57] Tatalovich and Daynes, *The Politics of Abortion*, pp. 43, 55–6.

[58] *Abortion and the Politics of Motherhood.*

[59] Mooney and Lee, "Legislative Morality in the American States: The Case of Pre-*Roe* Abortion Regulation Reform," *American Journal of Political Science* 39(1995):599–627. Their findings are consistent with some of the central features of the analysis presented below, but later notes in this chapter indicate where I think they have made incorrect assumptions about the political process or where I think their statistical analysis fails to capture central elements of that process. Rosemary Nossiff adds some interesting data to our historical understanding of opposition to abortion reform, especially the role of the Catholic hierarchy in Pennsylvania, and of the means by which the repeal cause gathered steam in New York (Nossiff, *Before Roe: Abortion Policy in the States* [Philadelphia: Temple University Press, 2001]). But while the book attempts to use case studies of New York and Pennsylvania to understand the reform and repeal process that preceded *Roe* in a number of states, the case studies are unable to provide that understanding. She does not look in depth at any state that passed a reform law, and without a wider comparison it is difficult to assess her argument that internal Democratic battles over party control were a central factor in the outcome of abortion legislation in both states. Indeed, I would add, comparison with other states casts great doubt on that explanation. Finally, Nossiff seems of two minds about the nature of pre-*Roe* liberalization of state abortion laws: Perhaps overgeneralizing from the New York case, she makes the erroneous statement that such laws were framed as a whole "within the rubric of privacy and equality" (p. 130). But some of her own historical summary contradicts that point (pp. 42–43).

[60] Glendon, *Abortion and Divorce in Western Law: American Failures, European Challenges* (Cambridge, Mass.: Harvard University Press, 1987).

The rest of this chapter, then, focuses on two central aspects of the wave of liberalization of state abortion laws preceding the 1973 U.S. Supreme Court decision, *Roe v. Wade*. First, it seeks to explain the pattern by which some states passed such laws and others did not. It does not seem to be the case, for example, that traditionally liberal states were the most likely to pass such laws. Indeed, the most obvious pattern seems counterintuitive, given the current strength of the Christian Right in the South: Southern states were especially likely to pass such laws, and, as we shall see, by more convincing floor votes in the state legislatures.

Second, once we understand how state legislatures dealt with abortion, we can see that framing abortion as a moral issue highlighted differences of opinion over the issue and thus made it highly unlikely that states would initiate any changes. More favorable toward consensus was framing abortion as a sensible, limited reform that would allow physicians to use their proper medical judgment as well as permit limited but humanitarian access to abortion. This frame obscured divisions and was much more favorable toward passage of an abortion reform bill.

In making this argument, I make use of sources, especially state legislative journals (which record legislative floor actions), that are central to understanding what frames actually guided legislative debates. However, until now, researchers have generally ignored those journals, perhaps because they are often tedious and difficult to use and are not widely available.[61] To supplement our understanding of how frames varied by state, I also use local newspaper accounts of many of the legislative debates.

Before entering that discussion in detail, it is worth noting here both the strengths and weaknesses of the sources I have used to provide a

---

[61] As far as I know, only the Library of Congress attempts to keep a full collection of these journals, although the journals of particular states are available in legislative libraries in state capitals. I used the Library of Congress, which was nevertheless missing some volumes, and also obtained various materials from state legislative libraries and local newspaper accounts. Even when available, some states' journals are almost useless. Some give no sense of the substance of debates, and some have no index of any kind. Their thousands of pages per year may include just a few scattered lines about a particular bill, in whatever order discussions happened to take place. These difficulties make it almost impossible to state with any certainty, e.g., which states never even considered abortion law reform.

more detailed account, across states, than have previous works. When used in combination with local newspaper accounts and some of the more accomplished secondary accounts,[62] state legislative journals provide a detailed picture of the kind of frames used in debating abortion reform legislation. However, the information available varies a great deal from state to state. For some states there are available essentially verbatim accounts of floor debates, whereas it is difficult to determine whether other states ever even considered an abortion reform bill. Some states have kept almost no records on legislation from the 1960s, other than the text of bills that passed, and abortion reform was uncontroversial enough that national media took no notice of some of the new laws, or of some of the states that rejected such laws. In most states, it is impossible to provide a detailed account of debate throughout the entire legislative process. However, there is enough information available for enough state legislatures that we can see a great deal of similarity in the kinds of discussions that took place across states. And there is more than enough information to understand which frames dominated the debates.

Framing Abortion Law Reform

State legislators were often more than willing to allow physicians and other supporters of abortion reform to dominate the framing process, but they did have their own distinct concerns. What emerges from an examination of the reform process across states is that legislators operated on a few basic principles: First, in shaping abortion reform, because it was new territory, they were heavily influenced by the legal precedents set by other states. This seems particularly to have been the case given how little in-state concern there often seemed to be on the issue. Second, however, legislators frequently legitimated their positions by reference to some in-state constituency that agreed with them; to suggest that pressure for a certain position *originated* out of state was to delegitimate that position.[63] That is, once an in-state constituency

---

[62] Especially Garrow, *Liberty and Sexuality*; Luker, *Abortion and the Politics of Motherhood*; and Lader, *Abortion II*.

[63] State of Nevada, *Journal of the Assembly of the Fifty-fifth Session of the Legislature of the State of Nevada* (1969), p. 827; Jain and Gooch, *Georgia Abortion Act 1968*, pp. 44–5.

raised the issue, the state could consider abortion law reform and learn from the experience of other states. Third, legislators were happy to approve something that seemed a sensible initiative, one relatively uncontroversial within the state. However, if they perceived significant controversy and moral polarization within the legislature itself or within the state, support could quickly diminish.

The reliance on other states' precedents seems to have been what made the ALI model code as influential as it was: Once one state passed such a law, there was a snowball effect. Colorado, the first state to pass an ALI-type law, was particularly heavily cited in other states' legislative discussions. California, which like Colorado passed a law in 1967, was also a standard precedent.

I could document, for instance, that the Colorado law was invoked in Oklahoma,[64] Maine,[65] North Carolina,[66] New Hampshire,[67] and South Carolina.[68] In Florida in 1967, a legislator proposed waiting until seeing how the new Colorado and North Carolina laws worked out.[69] A Denver lawyer who chaired a reform group that had favored the Colorado law testified to the Georgia Senate.[70] It is quite likely additional states also considered the Colorado precedent in their discussions.

But Colorado was not the only precedent: For example, in 1968 the state Senate of Michigan consulted with California state Senator Anthony Bielenson,[71] who had sponsored California's reform law of 1967.[72] The 1967 Maine debate included references to laws of numerous states.[73] A 1967 Subcommittee on Abortion Law of the Maryland House Judiciary Committee studied the new laws of Colorado, North Carolina, and California before proceeding to recommend passage of

[64] *Daily Oklahoman* (Oklahoma City), March 30, 1967.
[65] State of Maine, *Legislative Record of the One Hundred and Third Legislature* (1967), pp. 2807, 2809–10, 3305, 3309.
[66] Jain and Sinding, *North Carolina Abortion Law 1967*, p. 46.
[67] State of New Hampshire, *Journal of the Honorable Senate: January Session of 1969* (1969), p. 626.
[68] *The State* (Columbia, S.C.), January 21, 1970.
[69] *Miami Herald* (Miami, Fla.), June 8, 1967.
[70] Jain and Gooch, *Georgia Abortion Act 1968*, p. 42.
[71] State of Michigan, *Journal of the Senate of the State of Michigan: 1969 Regular Session* (1969), p. 157.
[72] Luker, *Abortion and the Politics of Motherhood*, pp. 70–3, 89fn., 93.
[73] Maine, *Legislative Record of the One Hundred and Third Legislature*, pp. 3303, 3305–6.

a similar bill in Maryland.[74] The New Mexico law was invoked in Kansas.[75] In general, then, it was routine for legislators to cite laws passed by other states (but not bills that other states failed to pass, probably because considerably less was known about those).

Usually it was supporters who cited such precedents, but sometimes opponents did so, in order to argue that the precedent was a bad one. Precedents were not always cited accurately: A Florida proponent of reform claimed the bill he supported was more stringent than those passed in Colorado, North Carolina, and California[76]; but the Florida bill does not, in fact, appear to have been stricter. An opponent of the 1967 bill in Maine asserted that "very few states" had such liberal laws on abortion, and he went on to name eight states.[77] In fact, only one of the eight had actually passed such a law at that time, and so the legislator somewhat undercut his own opposition. Three of the remaining seven states he mentioned would pass a reform bill in 1968 and 1969; it is, however, doubtful that the legislator had such accurate foresight. Likewise, press reports that cited other states committed occasional errors. In 1969, the main newspaper in Delaware asserted quite erroneously that despite the close vote in that state (which in fact was atypically close), "passage came more easily than in any of the other nine states that have changed their abortion laws since 1967."[78]

Moving to legislators' concerns with in-state matters, this aspect of legislative perspective and process led to certain revisions in the ALI code on abortion. These revisions, though they did vary by state, took predictable forms. Thus, once again, many states' laws looked alike, even as they deviated from the model code.

In general, the most central concern was that the state not become an "abortion mill."[79] The intention was that legal abortion be

---

[74] State of Maryland, House of Delegates, Report of the Subcommittee on Abortion Law (Judiciary Committee), 1968 (2-page mimeo).

[75] *Wichita Eagle* (Wichita, Kan.), April 11, 1969.

[76] *Miami Herald*, June 9, 1967.

[77] Maine, *Legislative Record of the One Hundred and Third Legislature*, 1967, p. 3305.

[78] *Evening Journal* (Wilmington, Delaware), June 13, 1969.

[79] See, e.g., State of Maine, *Legislative Record of the One Hundred and Third Legislature* (1967), pp. 2807, 2810; *Miami Herald*, June 8, 1967; State of Nevada, *Journal of the Assembly of the Fifty-fifth Session of the Legislature of the State of Nevada* (1969), pp. 825–6; *Wichita Eagle*, February 26, 1969; *The Oregonian* (Portland, Or.), May 23, 1969; *Anchorage Daily News* (Anchorage, Al.), April 10, 1970; State of Alaska, *House*

"therapeutic" and humanitarian, something charitably granted rather than available on demand. One solution to the abortion mill problem, then, was to require that hospital review boards clear abortion decisions, so that individual physicians could not independently give the law an overly liberal interpretation. Such boards had begun in many hospitals in the 1950s, before the reform movement, as institutions worried about their legal liability under the old laws. In practice, they often became arbitrary quota systems that favored middle-class women. Hospitals did not want to appear to allow too many abortions, and middle-class women generally had greater success than poorer women in convincing the boards that an abortion was justified.[80] These boards would later become a source of dissatisfaction with the reform laws.

Another standard way that states dealt with the abortion mill problem, and one that seemed to generate more discussion than the review board requirement, was to mandate residency, of somewhere between one and four months. Almost every state that passed a reform or repeal law between 1966 and 1970 had either a residency requirement or some kind of requirement of oversight of physicians' decisions, or both.[81] Even where a bill never passed,[82] or a bill passed without a residency requirement,[83] there was evidence of considerable support for preventing so-called abortion tourism.

While citing the need for doctors to make professional judgments without worry of prosecution, then, legislators still wanted to assure that those professional judgments resulted in limited access to abortion, and only for women whose circumstances the legislators found sympathetic. They did not want to establish any new rights or take a position that seemed to ally with one particular moral position. Much

---

Journal (1970), suppl. 12. This four-page supplement was the Judiciary Committee Report on Alaska's 1970 abortion repeal bill, dated April 9, 1970. It follows p. 833 of the *House Journal* but has its own pagination.

[80] Luker, *Abortion and the Politics of Motherhood*, pp. 56–7.

[81] Davis, *From Crime to Choice*, pp. 254–7; B. J. George, Jr. "State Legislatures versus the Supreme Court: Abortion Legislation into the 1990s," in J. Douglas Butler and David F. Walbert, eds., *Abortion, Medicine, and the Law*, 4th ed. (New York and Oxford: Facts On File, 1992), p. 16; Jain and Sinding, *North Carolina Abortion Law 1967*, p. 31, 40, 70; Jain and Gooch, *Georgia Abortion Act 1968*, p. 39.

[82] State of Alabama, *Journal of the Senate of the State of Alabama: Regular Session of 1967* (1967), p. 930; *Daily Oklahoman*, March 30, 1967.

[83] *Baltimore Sun* (Baltimore, Md.), February 24, 1969.

as many Americans today may find it unimaginable that it's possible to pass a new abortion law without taking a moral position, the belief that states could and should take such a position was central to many legislators at the time. Proponents of reform stated quite directly that they considered the legislation "humanitarian and not a moral issue or based on any type of doctrine."[84] We will see below how this framing of reform helps explain regional differences, when considered in light of the legitimation of positions through reference to in-state support. Citing in-state support was usually a purely anecdotal affair, so that legislators did not necessarily accurately gauge in-state opinion. Still, we shall see below that Southern legislators were particularly unlikely to encounter vociferous, moral framings of abortion within their own states.

Promoters of abortion law reform often felt compelled to state that the law was only "permissive," that it did not require anyone to do anything against their will. For example, typically hospitals and medical professionals could choose not to participate in abortions. This freedom-of-choice rhetoric sounds familiar today, in a general sense. However, the "permissive not mandatory" defense typically included a component that sounds odd decades later: That is, it also was used to make the point that the legislation would not force any woman to have an abortion against her will.[85] It is clear some legislators thought of this as a real problem,[86] perhaps because the terrain was so unfamiliar at the time.

State-Level Patterns, 1966–1970

The lack of attention to the state-level reform and repeal process that has emerged in studies of abortion politics after *Roe v. Wade* has apparently led to confusion about such basics as which states actually passed such laws (see Tables 5.1 and 5.3). Recent studies of abortion politics that are otherwise quite accomplished have included some errors in

---

[84] Quotation from State of Maine, *Legislative Record of the One Hundred and Fourth Legislature* (1969), p. 2115; see also *Daily Oklahoman*, March 30, 1967.

[85] State of Maine, *Legislative Record of the One Hundred and Third Legislature* (1967), p. 2809; Maine, *Legislative Record of the One Hundred and Fourth Legislature* (1969), p. 2115; State of Vermont, *Journal of the House of the State of Vermont: Adjourned Session, 1970* (1970), p. 77.

[86] See, e.g., *Daily Oklahoman*, March 30, 1967.

TABLE 5.1. *Legislative votes in states that passed ALI-type abortion reform laws, 1967–1970*[87]

State	Year	House[88]	Senate
Colorado[89]	1967	40–21	20–13
North Carolina[90]	1967	N.A.[91]	?–2
California[92]	1967	48–30	21–17
Maryland[93]	1968	86–47	28–11
Georgia[94]	1968	126–3	33–17
Arkansas[95]	1969	75–10	N.A.
New Mexico[96]	1969	36–34	25–15
Kansas[97]	1969	81–16	38–1
Oregon[98]	1969	50–9	N.A.
Delaware[99]	1969	N.A.	10–9
South Carolina[100]	1970	67–37	Unanimous
Virginia[101]	1970	58–35	32–3

[87] (i) Given are the initial votes in each chamber on the bill that passed, before the two chambers reconciled any differences. (The two chambers may have voted on different versions of the bill, but these initial votes better indicate the level of support, as conference bill votes may be influenced by the fact that opposition by that time is often futile.) (ii) Those absent or otherwise not voting are not included here or in any other table. (iii) States are listed in the order in which they completed the full legislative process, i.e., either the date the governor signed the bill (typically a few months before the law actually took effect) or the date the bill became law without the governor's signature. In some state-to-state comparisons (e.g., Maryland vs. Georgia), the ordering is not substantively significant, given that the difference is a matter of a few days and could have easily been reversed if, e.g., a governor had acted more quickly.

[88] States' lower chambers go by various names, including House of Representatives, House of Delegates, and state Assembly. For simplicity's sake, throughout this book I refer simply to the "House."

[89] State of Colorado, *Journal of the House of Representatives* (1967), p. 989; State of Colorado, *Journal of the Senate* (1967), p. 1000.

[90] Jain and Sinding, *North Carolina Abortion Law 1967*, p. 33. The authors note two votes opposed in the Senate but do not give the number of votes in favor.

[91] "N.A." means not available.

[92] *New York Times*, June 14, 1967; *Miami Herald*, June 7, 1967.

[93] State of Maryland, *Journal of Proceedings of the House of Delegates of Maryland: Session 1968* (1968), p. 824; State of Maryland, *Journal of the Proceedings of the Senate of Maryland: Regular Session, 1968* (1968), p. 1443.

[94] Jain and Gooch, *Georgia Abortion Act 1968*, pp. 26, 53.

[95] *Arkansas Gazette* (Little Rock, Arkansas), February 6, 1969.

[96] State of New Mexico, *Journal of the Senate* (1969), p. 562; Garrow, *Liberty and Sexuality*, p. 369.

[97] State of Kansas, *House Journal: Proceedings of the House of Representatives of the State of Kansas* (1969), p. 598; State of Kansas, *Senate Journal: Proceedings of the Senate of the State of Kansas* (1969), p. 472.

[98] *The Oregonian* (Portland, Oregon), 23 May 1969.

[99] *Evening Journal*, June 13, 1969.

[100] *The State*, January 21 and 28, 1970.

[101] Virginia, *Journal of the House of Delegates of the Commonwealth of Virginia: Regular Session* (1970), p. 866; *Richmond Times-Dispatch*, March 15, 1970.

TABLE 5.2. *"Yes" votes for ALI-type bills as a proportion of total votes (for states that passed reform laws, 1967–1970)*[102]

State	Year	House	Senate
Colorado	1967	.66	.61
North Carolina[103]	1967	.8	.91
California	1967	.62	.55
Maryland	1968	.65	.72
Georgia	1968	.98	.66
Arkansas	1969	.88	N.A.
New Mexico	1969	.51	.62
Kansas	1969	.84	.97
Oregon	1969	.85	N.A.
Delaware	1969	N.A.	.52
South Carolina	1970	.64	1.0
Virginia	1970	.62	.91

Mean for votes in all chambers in all states: .74
Mean for votes in all chambers in states of the former Confederacy: .82
Mean for votes in all chambers for states not in the former Confederacy: .68

TABLE 5.3. *Legislative votes in states that passed repeal laws*[104]

	Year	House	Senate
Hawaii[105]	1970	31–20	17–7
New York[106]	1970	76–73	31–26
Alaska[107]	1970	29–10	11–9
Washington[108]	1970	60–36	25–23

[102] All proportions in all tables are rounded to two decimal places, but means are calculated before rounding. Proportions in Table 5.2 were calculated from votes listed in Table 5.1, except for North Carolina (see following note). I used proportions, rather than absolute number of votes, to control for the size of legislative chambers.

[103] The *New York Times*, May 6, 1967, provides estimated proportions and implies that these, if anything, are slightly lower than the actual vote. But cf. Jain and Sinding, *North Carolina Abortion Law 1967*, p. 33.

[104] See note 87 for Table 5.1, which applies to this table as well.

[105] In Hawaii, the state Senate amended an ALI-type reform bill already passed by the House to make it a repeal bill, then passed the bill. That is the vote I count for the Senate. The chambers then had a conference committee, and the House voted in favor of the bill with further changes, but still committed to repeal rather than reform. That is the vote I count for the House, not the initial vote in favor of reform. Steinhoff and Diamond, *Abortion Politics*, pp. 167, 146.

[106] *Facts on File Yearbook 1970* (New York: Facts on File, 1971), p. 274

[107] *Anchorage Daily News*, April 10, 1970.

[108] The legislative vote in Washington approved repeal only subject to approval in a subsequent referendum, which came in November 1970. Garrow, *Liberty and Sexuality*, p. 411.

TABLE 5.4. *"Yes" votes for repeal bills as a proportion of total votes (for states that passed repeal laws)*[109]

	Year	House	Senate
Hawaii	1970	.61	.71
Alaska	1970	.74	.55
New York	1970	.51	.54
Washington	1970	.62	.52

Mean for votes in all chambers in all four states: .60

their lists of such states.[110] Perhaps indicating that the obscurity of these pre-*Roe* legislative initiatives is increasing with time, these recent errors do not appear in the more influential works published closer to the enactment of those laws.[111]

Case studies of particular states that changed their abortion laws in this period have made the point that there was little politicization

[109] Proportions calculated from Table 5.3.

[110] Lee Epstein and Joseph F. Kobylka, *The Supreme Court and Legal Change: Abortion and the Death Penalty* (Chapel Hill: University of North Carolina Press, 1992), p. 152; Marian Faux, *Roe v. Wade: The Untold Story of the Landmark Supreme Court Decision That Made Abortion Legal* (New York: Macmillan, 1988), p. 59; Elizabeth Adell Cook, Ted G. Jelen, and Clyde Wilcox, *Between Two Absolutes: Public Opinion and the Politics of Abortion* (Boulder, Col.: Westview, 1992), p. 14; Davis, *From Crime to Choice*, p. 58. It is possible Davis excluded Georgia, the one state missing from her list, because it did not include certain allowances for abortion that the ALI recommended, such as pregnancy from incest or pregnancy that might threaten mental health. (For the Georgia 1968 law, see Jain and Gooch, *Georgia Abortion Act 1968*, pp. 82–5.) However, although the criteria are slightly different, overall the Georgia law was no more conservative than Arkansas's (as shown in Davis's useful table, pp. 254–6), but Davis does include Arkansas as a reform law in her text (p. 58).

[111] Lader, *Abortion II*; Tatalovich and Daynes, *The Politics of Abortion*, pp. 23–6. Although Luker's invaluable account (with the greatest detail provided in her case study of California), *Abortion and the Politics of Motherhood*, holds up remarkably well, and is by far the best published guide to the framing of these state-level changes, she does make a few small errors. She states (p. 272n.3) that California "passed its bill on Nov. 8, 1967." The state Senate passed the bill on June 6 (*Miami Herald*, June 7, 1967), the Assembly on June 13 (*New York Times*, June 14, 1967), and Gov. Ronald Reagan signed it on June 15. Luker may instead be referring to the date the law took effect, which is typically the date indicated in state statute books. Luker (p. 143) also states that Colorado's law had a residency requirement, but it did not; and her statement (p. 143) that the Washington state referendum on abortion (considered in the next chapter of this book) "bypassed the legislature entirely" should be qualified, as it was the legislature that mandated the referendum.

of the issue. As Jain and Gooch note,[112] the state debates over reform bills did not easily divide along liberal–conservative or Democratic–Republican lines. And, as noted below, there seems to have been no significant racial component. That is, the typical ideological divisions of American politics were not there: For example, legislators did not think of the medical frame as a liberal cause.[113] It was distant from what people usually thought of as politics.

Instead, uppermost in the minds of legislators and expert witnesses were the fetal effects of rubella and thalidomide and the ability of physicians to make medical judgments without fearing prosecution, not such issues as the rights of women or the moral status of the fetus.[114] Among the central points of Jain and Sinding's study of North Carolina and Jain and Gooch's study of Georgia[115] is that the bills attracted little notice and little controversy. My own research confirms these points as they apply to states that passed reform laws (but not those that passed repeal laws), as we see below.

However, there has not emerged a coherent explanation of the state-level process as a whole, perhaps because we know so little, in particular, about states where attempts to change the laws *failed*.[116] In addition, explanations of the state reform laws have been based primarily on case studies; some of the explanations hypothesized in the case studies do not hold up well when we attempt to apply those explanations more generally, that is, by comparing a number of states.

Lader,[117] for example, notes the skillful legislative strategy of the proponents of the Colorado bill. Garrow[118] agrees with the assessment of Jain and Sinding and Jain and Gooch that the bills in North Carolina and Georgia benefited from the facts that their sponsors were legislatively skilled, other controversial and/or time-consuming

---

[112] *Georgia Abortion Act 1968*, p. 3fn.14.
[113] Jain and Sinding, *North Carolina Abortion Law 1967*, p. 43; Steinhoff and Diamond, *Abortion Politics*, p. 210.
[114] Jain and Sinding, ibid., pp. 19–22, 28; Luker, *Abortion and the Politics of Motherhood*, pp. 81, 86–7, 89–90; Jain and Gooch, *Georgia Abortion Act 1968*, pp. 12–14, 16–17, 24, 61; Steinhoff and Diamond, *Abortion Politics*.
[115] Both cited in previous note.
[116] With the notable exceptions of O'Neil, *Church Lobbying in a Western State*, and Mohr, "Iowa's Abortion Battles."
[117] *Abortion II*, pp. 62–3.
[118] *Liberty and Sexuality*, pp. 327–30, 348.

legislative activity tended to overshadow the abortion bills, and Catholic opposition was fairly muted given the very small Catholic population in Georgia (2%) and North Carolina (1%). What opposition pro-life Catholics did mount benefited more than harmed the chances of passage, as such opposition was perceived as sectarian and unrepresentative; in such states, for instance, morally passionate Catholics may have been perceived as a fringe group.[119] Jain and his colleagues, as well as Garrow, also noted that the fairly quick passage of the bill took opponents of legal abortion by surprise, especially in the case of North Carolina. Thus little effective, organized opposition arose.

However, there are a couple of problems with these explanations. First, the contention that other more controversial legislation overshadowed the reform bills skirts the central question of why *abortion* did not become the focus of legislative controversy. Second, as detailed below, the sponsors in Colorado, North Carolina, California, and Georgia were all novices in elected office, so that it is unlikely that their legislative skill was so determining. Third, while these explanations still may not be erroneous as they apply to particular states, they cannot explain the pattern as a whole.

We need to consider a larger context. Between 1966 and 1970, abortion reform passed in enough states – in a *diverse* group of states (and typically fairly easily) – that the idiosyncracies of a state's population, legislative process, or legislators themselves cannot explain the trend as a whole. For example, a bit more than a fifth of U.S. population was Catholic: As a very rough indicator, having either very high or very low Catholic populations probably affected the likelihood there would be pro-life activists and, thus, affected the chances of passing a new abortion law. Thus, in New England, with some of the country's most Catholic states (especially Rhode Island, Massachusetts, and Connecticut), no abortion reform or repeal bills passed and, in the South, with very small Catholic populations (outside of Louisiana), reform bills were more likely to pass.[120] Still, some of the states that changed

---

[119] Jain and Gooch, *Georgia Abortion Act 1968*, pp. 43–5.

[120] Mooney and Lee, "Legislative Morality in the American States," on the basis of a statistical analysis of demographic and political variables of states that passed new abortion laws versus those that did not, argued that high numbers of evangelicals and Catholics made a new law less likely. However, they lump together measures

their abortion laws (New York, Hawaii, and New Mexico) had significantly more Catholics than the national average, while others were not far below that average (Alaska, California, Delaware, Maryland, and Colorado).[121]

I would argue that the explanation of why some states passed liberal abortion reform laws and others did not is even more simple than these authors have suggested: Typically, as long as the medical, humanitarian frame dominated discussion, legislators saw the reform as sensible and passed reform easily precisely because they did not see it as momentous. In states where reform passed, moral arguments did often enter the debates, but usually sporadically, without coming to dominate discussion. However, when debate became primarily a matter of supporting or refuting moral frames (pro-life frames being a more common example of a moral frame than an abortion rights frame, at least in state legislatures, in this period), the bills generally failed. State legislators were generally happy to pass a reform that seemed humanitarian, sensible, and even technocratic, and thus neither particularly liberal nor conservative. But they had trouble coming to agreement when the vote on an abortion bill was framed as taking a particular moral position. Legislators preferred to avoid taking positions perceived to be controversial and morally divisive among in-state constituencies. As was

of these two religious groups, and so it is unclear what this finding really means. In the 1960s, what pro-life activism existed was almost entirely Catholic; evidence strongly suggests evangelicals were not even aware of the abortion issue and did not have a specifically antiabortion stance. Although it is possible Catholics and evangelicals were more instinctively likely to oppose abortion (even in the absence of activism), that is highly unlikely, since the South was the best territory for reform laws, even though the dominant denomination there is Southern Baptists, an evangelical denomination. I suspect the fact that a Catholic presence made a moral veto a bit more likely, and the fact that two-thirds of the states did not pass a law (so that evangelicals had significant numbers in some states that – for reasons having nothing to do with evangelicals – did not pass abortion laws) allowed a spurious statistical relationship to emerge.

[121] Statistics of Catholic adherents by state taken from 1971 data from a study sponsored by the National Council of Churches in Christ (Douglas W. Johnson, Paul R. Picard, and Bernard Quinn, *Churches and Church Membership in the United States* [Washington, D.C.: Glenmary Research Center, 1974], pp. 3–4; and from the "General Summary" of the *Official Catholic Directory 1969*, Charles R. Cunningham, ed. (New York: P. J. Kenedy & Sons, 1969). One cannot expect precision in estimates of how many adherents a particular religion has in a given state, as it is difficult to establish (or even define) unambiguously who is a religious adherent (versus, e.g., an ex-Catholic) at a given time. In addition, note that the *Official Catholic Directory* organizes data by dioceses, which sometimes cross state borders.

the case for bills on contraception in the U.S. Congress in the 1920s and 1930s, state legislators considering abortion bills preferred inaction and the status quo over alienating a visible, morally passionate constituency.

Although no one variable could predict whether morally passionate frames came to dominate discussion of abortion reform in any particular state, certain political variables increased the chance that frames explicitly widening the moral agenda would receive extensive discussion in a legislature. For example, a large Catholic population within the state and an activist Catholic bishop could be a factor: At this time, what pro-life movement (and thus what publicly mobilized opposition to these laws) existed was almost exclusively Catholic.[122] Still, in some states the legislative momentum for passage developed too quickly for public controversy to arise, even when there was a large Catholic population. In such cases legislators presumably were unaware that there was much of a constituency that would get excited about the issue. And sometimes it just so happened that a small group of legislators or lobbyists, sometimes Catholic and sometimes not, were alarmed enough about the bill that they managed to organize opposition.

In most of the states that passed reform laws, there had been little significant discussion of the issue before passage of the new law. Most people had not heard enough about the issue to think of it in very detailed terms – there was an ideological vacuum.[123] In a study of the liberalization of divorce laws during approximately the same period, Herbert Jacob[124] found that reform of the divorce laws emerged not despite the lack of organized movements with strong feelings on the issue, but because of the lack of such movements. Similarly, in the 1960s, in most states, there were no vocal movements concerned with abortion per se.

Luker[125] noted that abortion reform at first seemed both novel and sensible, so that it was first-term legislators who initially attempted to sponsor abortion reform bills in California. They were looking for

[122] Tatalovich and Daynes, *The Politics of Abortion*, p. 75; Luker, *Abortion and the Politics of Motherhood*, pp. 127–8; O'Neil, *Church Lobbying in a Western State*.

[123] Steinhoff and Diamond, *Abortion Politics*, p. 207.

[124] *Silent Revolution: The Transformation of Divorce Law in the United States* (Chicago and London: University of Chicago Press, 1988).

[125] *Abortion and the Politics of Motherhood*, pp. 69–72.

a cause that could make a mark without being controversial. Indeed, the youth of the promoters of reform is striking in a number of states, including the first three states to pass ALI-type reform laws (Colorado, North Carolina, and California). The sponsor of the reform bill in North Carolina was a first-term legislator with personal experience in family planning issues; he initially submitted his own bill but readily substituted an ALI-type bill once he became aware of the ALI model code.[126] Colorado's sponsor was also a first-term legislator named Richard Lamm, who would later become Governor and ultimately, in 1996, Ross Perot's rival for the Reform Party's presidential nomination. Lader[127] reported that Lamm even came from a district with a heavy Catholic constituency. According to a South Carolina newspaper, the chief promoter of the reform bill in the South Carolina state House was just twenty-seven years old.[128] In Georgia, the sponsor introduced the bill in 1967 (which passed in 1968, because the 1967 legislature ran out of time), when he had been in office just two years. He had hoped that Georgia would be the first to approve such a bill, as he expected that would lead to favorable national publicity for his state.[129]

Still, portending the division that would come later, even where the medical, humanitarian frame dominated debate, there were usually at least some rumblings of controversy, albeit among a definite minority. For example, the bill in South Carolina, after easily passing the Senate, originally encountered a House filibuster,[130] implying a passionate minority. Debate in many states included references to murder, the devaluation of the lives of the handicapped (by allowing abortion when there was a risk of fetal deformity) and other supposed undesirables, usurping God's role, and occasional charges of Nazi eugenics.[131] This

---

[126] Jain and Sinding, *North Carolina Abortion Law 1967*, pp. 16, 20–2, 48.
[127] *Abortion II*, p. 62.
[128] *The State*, January 22, 1970.
[129] Jain and Gooch, *Georgia Abortion Act 1968*, pp. 12–14, 22–3.
[130] *The State*, January 21 and 28, 1970.
[131] *Clarion-Ledger* (Jackson, Miss.), March 10, 1966; State of Maine, *Legislative Record of the One Hundred and Third Legislature* (1967), pp. 2807–8, 3300–1; *Miami Herald*, June 8, 1967; *Baltimore Sun*, March 9 and 26, 1968; State of New Jersey, Commission to Study the New Jersey Statutes Relating to Abortion, (transcript of) *Public Hearing* [that took place in Trenton, N.J.], October 28, 1968, pp. 11–17, 46–54; (transcript of the same commission's) *Public Hearing* in Newark, N.J., November 13, 1968, pp. 26, 151–8; and *Public Hearing* in Camden, N.J., November 26, 1968, pp. 5–8; State of Michigan, *Journal of the Senate of the State of Michigan: 1969 Regular Session*,

did lead to some bit of tension in committee hearings and floor debates over a matter that had initially struck legislators as an uncontroversial reform.

But, as I will detail, available evidence indicates that in states where reform bills passed, the reason was that such controversy did not stick. It involved a few legislators or some isolated testimony at public hearings, but it did not fundamentally change the nature of the debate. If the typical legislator found such rhetoric extreme or inappropriate, bills were more likely to pass.[132] Again, it is difficult to explain with certainty why, in each and every state, moral frames did or did not come to dominate; state records are not detailed enough, and probably in some cases the idiosyncratic opposition of just a few legislators was central. The nature of legislatures is that, on any particular bill, dominant individuals can often have enormous influence setting the terms of debates, even when a larger group of less powerful legislators calls for a different approach. But we can see that legislative outcomes depended on which type of frame – medical or moral – did indeed guide debate as a whole.

Why Did So Many Southern States Liberalize Their Abortion Laws?

Because the medical framing of abortion was quite different from post-*Roe* discussion of the issue, the pattern of state-level reform in 1966–1970 does not follow our expectations. That is, one of the most striking aspects of this wave of change is that the states that liberalized their laws in this period were disproportionately Southern, a rather surprising fact given the current strength of the pro-life, Christian Right in the South. While Alaska, Hawaii, Washington, and New York entirely eliminated restrictions on abortion up until varying stages of pregnancy (all of these repeals occurring in the final year of legislative initiatives, the significance of which I address in the next chapter) and thus went beyond the ALI recommendations, the twelve states that enacted ALI-type laws by 1970 included North Carolina, Georgia, Arkansas, South Carolina, and Virginia (see Table 5.1).

---

pp. 1499–1500; *The State*, January 21, 1970; Jain and Gooch, *Georgia Abortion Act 1968*, pp. 30–1, 43.

[132] Jain and Gooch, ibid., p. 43; Jain and Sinding, *North Carolina Abortion Law 1967*, pp. 45–6.

In addition, Mississippi – hardly a liberal state, by any measure – was the first state to liberalize the criteria for legal abortion during this period. True, the 1966 legislation[133] was quite limited in scope: It simply added rape as an acceptable circumstance for legal abortion. But it was indeed the first state to change its law in the wake of elite calls for liberalization. And, although the records[134] are not sufficient to allow a definitive judgment, it is quite possible that the law was inspired by ALI recommendations, as the legislature also considered including a provision to allow abortion when there was a risk of fetal deformity.[135]

If we complete the entire list, in addition to those states already mentioned, the remaining states that passed ALI-type laws by 1970 were Colorado, California, Maryland, New Mexico, Kansas, Oregon, and Delaware. Note that even among this group there was no clear pattern of traditionally liberal states predominating. For example, Kansas is not obviously a particularly liberal state, and yet the two chambers agreed on and overwhelmingly approved an ALI-type reform bill, by a vote of eighty-one to sixteen in the House and thirty-eight to one in the Senate. And this was after the state Senate first passed (twenty-five to twelve) a *repeal* provision.[136] (The Senate's repeal provision, however, was bundled with a larger criminal code revision, so we do not know if it would have passed as a distinct bill. Still the Senate could have chosen to edit out the abortion repeal provision.[137] In any case, the House acted on a separate reform bill, and the Senate was then happy to concur.[138])

The only apparent pattern for the list of states as a whole, then, remains the striking predominance of Southern states. (I should note here that if one defined the Eastern border states Delaware and Maryland as "Southern," then Southern states become a majority of those that passed ALI-type laws. However, while Delaware and Maryland

---

[133] State of Mississippi, *Laws of the State of Mississippi 1966* (1966), vol. 1, p. 661.
[134] State of Mississippi, *Journal of the House of Representatives* (1966), pp. 284, 410–11; Mississippi, *Journal of the Senate* (1966), pp. 419, 931, 1069.
[135] *Clarion-Ledger*, March 10, 1966.
[136] State of Kansas, *House Journal: Proceedings of the House of Representatives of the State of Kansas* (1969), p. 598; Kansas, *Senate Journal: Proceedings of the Senate of the State of Kansas* (1969), p. 472; Garrow, *Liberty and Sexuality*, p. 369; *Topeka Daily Capital* (Topeka, Kan.), April 25, 1969; *Wichita Eagle*, April 13 and 25, 1969.
[137] Kansas, *Senate Journal* (1969), pp. 299–300; *Wichita Eagle*, February 26, 1969.
[138] Kansas, *House Journal* (1969), pp. 580–1, 594–5, 598; Kansas, *Senate Journal* (1969), pp. 698–9, 707; *Wichita Eagle*, April 11, 1969.

each have regions that could culturally and politically be described as Southern, I do not include them because overall they do not, and did not in the 1960s, display typical aspects of Southern politics. For example, today Maryland is one of the more liberal states overall, Democratic but certainly not Southern Democrat, and with clear two-party competition.[139] Delaware has long had effective two-party competition, and both states are dominated politically by metropolitan areas – Wilmington, Baltimore, and the Washington suburbs – where political dynamics are much more similar to the Northeast than to the South.)

Some sources list Mississippi's 1966 law as an ALI-type reform,[140] which is not unreasonable, as states did differ in exactly what ALI criteria they included in their final laws. Georgia, for example, did not include reference to mental health or to incest. However, given that Mississippi's liberalization was particularly limited, allowing just one new acceptable reason for legal abortion, I follow Lader and Luker in excluding it from the list of states with ALI reform laws.[141]

Garrow, however, is the only analyst I have encountered who has specifically explained why he excludes the Mississippi law. Indeed, he is the only analyst who attempted in passing to explain the origins of the law (as opposed simply to including it in a list) and who hinted, though quite indirectly, that there may have been a Southern politics of abortion. Garrow stated briefly in a footnote[142] that he did not consider the 1966 Mississippi law an actual reform, suggesting that the allowance of rape was prompted not by an interest in abortion but was tied up with Southern racial fears about the rape of white women by black men. However, in a book whose level of documentation is, in most cases, extraordinarily impressive, Garrow offered no evidence for this conjecture.[143]

---

[139] Eliza Newlin Carney, "Maryland: A Law Codifying *Roe v. Wade*," in Mary C. Segers and Timothy A. Byrnes, eds. *Abortion Politics in American States* (Armonk, N.Y., and London: M. E. Sharpe, 1995), pp. 51–3.

[140] Tatalovich and Daynes, *The Politics of Abortion*, p. 24; Epstein and Kobylka, *The Supreme Court and Legal Change*, p. 152.

[141] Lader, *Abortion II*; Luker, *Abortion and the Politics of Motherhood*, p. 272n.3.

[142] *Liberty and Sexuality*, p. 815n.50.

[143] However, I cannot emphasize enough that these state-level details – which, in most cases, are extremely well covered – are not Garrow's central focus and that the book as a whole is a definitive, unequaled study that goes far beyond the relatively modest focus of the analysis here.

In fact, there is little or no evidence that race was a significant factor in the Southern abortion reform laws, including Mississippi's. The evidence supports neither an interpretation that changes were prompted by myths about black men raping white women, nor that they were attempts to keep down black birth rates. Legislative records and local newspaper accounts certainly make no explicit references to race, nor do they use anything remotely suggesting coded racial language, for example, no reference to "state's rights," Southern "tradition," or protection of "our" women. There is mention of legislative concern for women's reputations in one local newspaper account of the Mississippi law (i.e., the shame associated with bearing a child out of wedlock as a result of rape), but the article says nothing at all about rapists or the circumstances of rape.[144] That is, there is no concern for perpetrators' identity, only for the consequences that women face from pregnancy as the result of rape. Garrow might also have trouble explaining why, if the primary concern was protection of whites, there was as much opposition in the Mississippi House as there was: It did draw forty-five opponents in the final House vote (as opposed to sixty-eight in favor, and nine absent or otherwise not voting).[145] Reflecting the fact that passion on Southern abortion reform was usually more sporadic than prolonged, however, the Senate approved the bill with forty-six in favor and only two opposed.[146] The next day, the state capital's daily newspaper reported, on the front page, controversy in the state Senate over the governor's latest nominee to the state's college board. In contrast, a continuation of the same article noted (on p. 18), the Senate's approval of the abortion bill after "no debate."[147]

There was an instance, in Georgia, of a pro-reform lobbyist attempting to sway right-wing Gov. Lester Maddox by raising the specter of white women becoming pregnant as a result of rape by black men.[148] It is clear from Jain and Gooch's account that the more standard issues of medical practice, humanitarianism, and occasional pro-life sentiments actually drove the discussion of Georgia's abortion reform bill, but in

---

[144] *Clarion-Ledger*, March 10, 1966.
[145] Mississippi, *Journal of the House of Representatives* (1966), pp. 410–11.
[146] Mississippi, *Journal of the Senate* (1966), p. 1069.
[147] *Clarion-Ledger*, May 19, 1966.
[148] Jain and Gooch, *Georgia Abortion Act 1968*, p. 57.

any case the evidence strongly suggests that the racial ploy did not work. Maddox declined specifically to endorse the bill and instead allowed the bill to become law without his signature. Jain and Gooch believe he was particularly influenced by the strong endorsement of the bill by the Christian Council of Metropolitan Atlanta, representing thirty-two denominations.[149] And other aspects of the politics of the Georgia reform law suggest very much that race was not a factor: Both in 1965 and again in 1968, the year the abortion bill was passed, there was effective lobbying to kill two separate bills that some opponents thought could be used in a racist way to promote sterilization (in the first bill, of minors and the legally incompetent) and eugenic abortion (in the case of a 1968 bill, concerning patients' consent to medical procedures, although the bill did not mention sterilization or abortion). Yet one of the prime opponents of the two sterilization bills (because of perceived racist potential), the executive director of the Jewish Community Council, saw no racial component in the abortion reform bill that passed, and no strong movement arose to oppose it.[150]

The case of North Carolina also questions any claims that abortion laws were part of an attempt at race-selective birth control. That is, in the legislative hearings on the North Carolina bill, a pro-reform psychiatrist's references to family planning and a world population explosion drew opposition from legislators. The family planning comments, which were not again repeated by reform advocates, were apparently the result of those advocates' not having fully thought through their strategy at that point.[151] It is difficult to imagine that family planning discussion would have been taboo if the intent of the bill had been to limit the African American population. (I do not deny that contraception has, at times, been attractive in the South for racist reasons, as noted earlier in this book. But the evidence is that, far from being

[149] Ibid., p. 58.
[150] Ibid., pp. 9–11.
[151] Jain and Sinding, *North Carolina Abortion Law 1967*, p. 28. There were arguments in favor of abortion reform in Iowa that included considerable reference to the need for population control (Mohr, "Iowa's Abortion Battles," pp. 73–4). But in Iowa, attempts to pass reform bills failed several times, attempts that in Mohr's words (p. 71) were at times "bitterly and strongly contested." There is no evidence that the population control issues caused the controversy, but it also remains the case that there is no evidence that states that passed reform laws depended upon family planning or population control arguments.

linked to such initiatives, there was a clear boundary drawn between abortion and birth control, in the South and elsewhere.)

It is true that Mississippi's racial politics of the time were especially charged; resistance to the civil rights movement's efforts to register blacks to vote probably met more resistance in Mississippi than in any other state. And it is true that Southern state records are often sparse enough that we cannot be absolutely certain that racist motivations were irrelevant. However, the records that do exist demonstrate pretty clearly that the content of Southern debates looks exactly like that of debates elsewhere, except that there was less opposition. The standard points of contention arose, that is, about guarding against abortion mills, and so forth, rather than anything remotely related to race. The only way to maintain the thesis that racial politics favored abortion reform in Southern states, in the face of no significant evidentiary support, is the unfalsifiable claim that race was so prominent a concern that legislators did not even need to mention it. But it is hardly difficult to find evidence of racial links in the rhetoric used to defend other contemporary concerns, such as segregation and "states' rights"; why should only abortion require such silence?

Also casting doubt on the racial politics thesis, the content of the Southern abortion reform laws was pretty much the same as the content of most Northern abortion reform laws. It is just that, in the South, these laws were particularly likely to pass.[152]

---

[152] Mooney and Lee, "Legislative Morality in the American States," argued from their statistical analysis that new abortion laws, as many types of laws, clumped together in certain regions because, when dealing with unfamiliar legislative initiatives, states look for guidance in the precedents of other states in their own region that presumably share political orientations. This initially is plausible given that they argued that similar stances on morally controversial laws like abortion laws will be found in similar political cultures. However, they assumed that all new abortion laws between 1966 and 1970 were morally controversial, which simply was not the case. The South formed a pro-reform regional bloc precisely because it is there that moral controversy was particularly unlikely. The clumping in the South probably accounts for much of the statistical variance that they found, but they draw invalid conclusions about its meaning.

Mooney and Lee's regional thesis also has the limitation that it does not enlighten why abortion law reform ever started in the first place: one cannot begin something new by copying others. Mooney and Lee count Mississippi as the first state to pass a reform law (see discussion above), but other Southern states hardly copied this supposed regional innovator: Of all the laws in the South passed in this period, Mississippi's is most different. And the first three states to pass ALI-type reform

To turn to a more compelling explanation, then, most significant about the Southern states was the strength of the medical, humanitarian frame, and the relative lack of controversy over therapeutic abortion. There was opposition mounted by Catholic bishops and priests and some (generally quite small) pro-life groups. But the medical frame was particularly dominant, and moral passion particularly absent, in the South: In the 1960s South, especially, there was a paucity of the type of groups that would organize abortion rights or pro-life movements. Thus accounts of the early, loosely organized abortion rights groups of the mid-1960s, for example, do not have much to say about the South.[153] There was not as developed a feminist movement as there was in the Northeast or on the west coast, and there was not the strong Catholic presence that was instrumental in early pro-life activity. Compared to most parts of the country, in the South, Catholics were relatively scarce. Thus, for example, North Carolina legislators received numerous letters from physicians supporting abortion law reform, but pro-life advocates had little success stimulating a mail campaign.[154] As I noted, when legislators cited in-state opinion on abortion reform, they used purely anecdotal evidence, so that it was not necessarily the case that they accurately read the distribution of pro- and anti-reform sentiment in their states. But, in the South, it was extremely unlikely that they would come across even anecdotal evidence of strong moral frames, whether pro-life or abortion rights frames. Reform laws, based on a medical, humanitarian frame, met particular success in the South; alternative frames were particularly lacking. In many other parts of the country, as Ginsburg noted, "it became clear by the early 1970s that right-to-life forces, though small in number, could successfully block moves to liberalize the existing law on abortion through legislative reform."[155] But that kind of moral veto was rare in the South before *Roe v. Wade.*

Note the type of developments that were *not* prominent in the South: In California, as Luker has demonstrated, an abortion rights movement

---

laws – Colorado, North Carolina, and California – are not at all close to each other and so did not follow regional precedents from politically and socially similar states.

[153] Lader, *Abortion II*; Staggenborg, *The Pro-Choice Movement*; Reagan, *When Abortion Was a Crime*, pp. 222–8.

[154] Jain and Sinding, *North Carolina Abortion Law 1967*, p. 34.

[155] Ginsburg, *Contested Lives*, p. 67.

(not just an individual plaintiff in court) quickly came to challenge the restrictions that still remained after an ALI law was passed in 1967. And Alaska, Hawaii, New York, and Washington states went further than the ALI model code by repealing restrictions entirely (for abortions performed before viability of the fetus), essentially foreshadowing *Roe v. Wade*; but no Southern state came close to choosing repeal over a medically framed reform law. That is, in the South, the medical frame usually did not meet opposition via a pro-life frame (which would have ignited controversy), but not because there were attempts to do away with restrictions on abortion entirely. In the South, there was neither a strong abortion rights movement nor a strong Catholic pro-life movement: Southern evangelicals would about a decade later be important in the pro-life movement, but at the time they simply were not very involved, taking little note of the issue. Abortion was far enough off the radar screen in the South that George Wallace's 1968 running mate, Curtis LeMay, pronounced in favor of legal abortion without fanfare. The Wallace–LeMay ticket won the electoral votes of five Southern states, and this statement came less than two weeks before the election, usually a time of great attention to any hint of bold statements among candidates. But neither LeMay nor the *New York Times*,[156] which ran a story on page 40, seemed to find the comments particularly momentous.

In the South, then, the ALI model code had particular success. And yet this was not because the South was actively liberal on the issue, reflected in the fact that no Southern state took the path of repealing its abortion restrictions; the medical frame held. Reform was not a way station on the path to repeal: The two involved different dynamics. Repeal efforts in the South made little headway; there were such bills introduced in 1972 in Florida, Georgia (and, if one wants to count the following as Southern), Texas, and Oklahoma.[157]

The relative lack of controversy surrounding reform bills passed by the North Carolina and Georgia legislatures, as I have already noted, has been amply documented by Jain and his colleagues.[158] The 1966

---

[156] October 24, 1968.
[157] Garrow, *Liberty and Sexuality*, pp. 538–9.
[158] Jain and Sinding, *North Carolina Abortion Law 1967*; Jain and Gooch, *Georgia Abortion Act 1968*.

Mississippi legislature, although it passed such a limited bill, nevertheless looks similar to Georgia and North Carolina legislatures in that attempts to inject moral passion into the debate made little headway. In the House, opponents objected that the measure was an "instrument of murder"; it would assume "God's prerogatives" and legitimate "the right to kill."[159] However, as is typically the case in states where reform laws passed, the moral arguments were merely episodic; that is, they did not succeed in reframing the debate as a whole. Even with the controversy, the House passed the bill just seventeen days after it was introduced. Actual floor debate and approval of the bill took place in a single day.[160] And although the House considered the bill first, the controversy was not sufficient to have any effect on the Senate, which passed the bill by an overwhelming vote of forty-six to two.[161] The daily newspaper of Jackson, Mississippi, the state capital, referred to the earlier House debate on the bill as "bitter" but noted that the Senate had no debate at all.[162] Indeed, indicative of the fleeting and low level of controversy surrounding abortion, just ten days before,[163] the same newspaper had listed the following as the "important issues to be decided" before the legislature adjourned: "Legal liquor, sheriff succession, the touchy problem of reapportionment and how to raise money to fix potholed highways are major questions." Potholes were a major question; abortion was not. (Incidentally, the "reapportionment" issue did have a racial component, involving court orders for legislative redistricting.)

The daily newspaper in South Carolina's state capital noted that that state's reform bill had encountered "fights, filibuster, and fanfare"[164] but the newspaper[165] presented the bill for the most part the way proponents would have preferred, that is, as a medical, humanitarian matter. The paper quoted one House member who objected to what he saw as eugenic implications.[166] But, again, it is striking how little effect

[159] *Clarion-Ledger*, March 10, 1966.
[160] Mississippi, *Journal of the House of Representatives* (1966), pp. 284, 410–11.
[161] Mississippi, *Journal of the Senate* (1966), pp. 931, 1069.
[162] *Clarion-Ledger*, May 19, 1966.
[163] *Clarion-Ledger*, May 9, 1966.
[164] *The State*, January 28, 1970.
[165] See also January 22, 1970.
[166] *The State*, January 21, 1970.

such arguments seemed to have. First, the bill still passed easily in the House, sixty-seven to thirty-seven. Second, the newspaper noted that the Senate passed the initial version of the bill "almost routinely," and the final version (after receiving it back from the House) "without a whisper against it," by unanimous voice vote.[167] The Senate, then, did not follow up on the controversy that existed in the House. It is interesting that this 1970 account of a Southern reform bill, by which time polarization had increased in other parts of the country, takes no note of such controversy elsewhere, perhaps another indication that Southern discussion of abortion at that point was still quite remote from the emerging national debate.[168]

A Richmond newspaper described the "generally decorous manner" of Virginia's House debate, although again this was in 1970, by which time the debate had become quite acrimonious in other states.[169] This "decorous" process led to a convincing House vote of fifty-eight to thirty-one in favor. Though the same newspaper described the upcoming Senate debate as potentially controversial,[170] and, after the fact, said that "Senators clashed" in a "prolonged" and "sometimes emotional" debate,[171] the Senate vote was even more lopsided: thirty-two to three. That is, once again, it appears that in the South moral arguments were introduced by individual legislators but failed to reframe the debate as a whole. There were sparks but no fire.

In understanding the Southern pattern, perhaps even more convincing than these narrative examples is an examination of the average voting margin (in statistical terms, the mean voting margin) by which Southern states passed ALI-type bills. As Table 5.2 indicates, of the states that passed ALI-type laws, legislatures in the states of the former Confederacy passed those laws by particularly large margins. Taking "yes" votes as a proportion of total votes (with those absent or not voting excluded), on average these states passed the laws with a bit more than four-fifths of the legislators voting in favor. In other

---

[167] *The State*, January 28, 1970.

[168] And Garrow noted (*Liberty and Sexuality*, p. 412) that the South Carolina law drew no national attention; indeed, the South Carolina law made no appearance in the *New York Times Index* or *Facts on File Yearbook 1970*.

[169] *Richmond Times-Dispatch*, March 4, 1970.

[170] *Richmond Times-Dispatch*, March 14, 1970.

[171] March 15, 1970.

states that passed such laws, about two-thirds voted in favor. The table probably slightly underestimates the difference: Specific tallies were not available for the state senates of Arkansas and South Carolina, for example, but they were probably quite convincing. I have already noted that a newspaper reported the South Carolina senate acted by unanimous voice vote. It is likely that in Arkansas as well, the state Senate and the governor accepted the measure easily: The Arkansas statute book lists final approval of the measure as having come just twelve days after initial House approval.[172]

In examining the voting margins, it is important to keep in mind as well that, in state legislatures in general, the range of voting margins for bills that pass is, in practice, probably limited. College textbooks on state government emphasize that there are multiple avenues for state legislators to kill bills with significant opposition, so that most bills die, often before ever coming to a floor vote.[173] It seems likely then that most bills that pass probably need a strong consensus in favor, except for those matters perceived as important enough (e.g., the state budget) that the legislature has no choice but to deal with them. A mean difference of four-fifths versus two-thirds in favor of particular bills is thus probably substantively quite significant.

The South, then, displayed a pattern of limited, episodic moral objections, within a discussion that remained focused on medical, humanitarian reform. However, while this pattern was particularly pronounced in the South, there were similar dynamics in some non-Southern states that passed reform bills. For example, some Kansas legislators objected to "diminishing the value of human life" and the "attempt to legislate morals,"[174] which, as we have seen, proponents denied they were doing. However, while newspaper accounts of the Kansas abortion reform (cited in the discussion of Kansas, above) were fairly thorough, they overwhelmingly focused on the medical requirements and procedures outlined in the bill. It appears the

---

[172] State of Arkansas, *Acts of Arkansas* (1969), Act 61, pp. 177–80.

[173] Robert S. Lorch, *State and Local Politics*, 6th ed. (Upper Saddle River, N.J.: Prentice Hall, 2001), p. 180; Michael Engle, *State and Local Government* (New York: Peter Lang, 1999), pp. 171–2.

[174] Kansas, *House Journal: Proceedings of the House of Representatives of the State of Kansas* (1969), p. 595.

pro-life rhetoric made little or no lasting impression, and the bill passed by overwhelming margins in both legislative chambers.

Of course, not every state that passed a reform law followed the same pattern. Delaware had a particularly close vote, for example. The 1969 reform bill squeaked by in both the House, by two votes, and the Senate, by one vote. The Senate victory came only after there was initially a tie, then a legislator who originally abstained decided to change his vote to "yes."[175] But merely sporadic attempts at moral framing, and thus a relative lack of passion, was clearly the typical pattern in states that passed reform laws, especially in the South.

Defeating Reform Bills: Moral Polarization

In contrast, when challenges to the medical frame were more than sporadic, but instead pushed the concerns of physicians to the background, reform bills generally failed. In such cases, the typical dynamic was that supporters continued to invoke humanitarian concerns, but they were forced to use their humanitarian arguments less to advocate *for* a medical frame than to defend *against* a strong pro-life challenge. Occasionally an abortion rights frame was invoked to challenge the pro-life frame. But in either case the debate became primarily a matter of explicitly supporting a pro-life reframing of the issue versus explicitly rejecting that reframing, while issues of medical autonomy receded to the background. Participants approached the issue of abortion passionately, not technocratically or incidentally, as was the case in many states that passed reform.

Let me begin with a rare example of a Southern state where abortion reform made headway but did not pass, amid considerable rancor. I will then move on to non-Southern states where reform bills failed.

The Southern example, Florida in 1967, is the exception that proves the rule in the sense that, even in the South, where the debate as a whole was passionate, the bill failed. Florida is a state whose politics is not typically Southern; for example, in 1967 in most of the South, Southern Democrats were so dominant that the Republican Party was not much of a contender. But that was not true in Florida.[176] And the

---

[175] *Evening Journal* (Wilmington, Del.), June 13, 1969; *New York Times*, June 13, 1969.

[176] My point is not that the strength of Southern Democrats or Republicans determined the fate of abortion reform bills. It is instead that, had Florida's state politics been more typically Southern, perhaps the discussion of its reform bill would have been more similar to that in other Southern states.

Southern abortion debate was also different: It was not a quiet affair. The Senate took up the bill, first, amid debate hardly typical of the low-key Southern approach to reform: "The galleries were crowded with women spectators and the presiding officer twice had to call down the crowd for applauding or talking."[177] One senator suggested that proponents might as well add what he called the "Sack Amendment," which "would allow deformed children to be taken at birth, 'put in a crocker sack and dropped in a fast-running stream.'"[178] The Senate did manage to pass the bill, by a close vote, twenty-six to twenty-two.[179] The bill then went to the House,[180] where differences over the bill in a House committee involved walkouts from committee meetings and a threat of a court order to force the recalcitrant chairman to act on the bill.[181] Reporting on House action to kill the bill, the *Miami Herald* described a "bitterly debated"[182] bill that was the "most fiercely fought legislation of the year."[183]

Moving beyond the South, in the same year, 1967, Arizona's reform effort also fell to defeat. In Arizona, the Catholic hierarchy managed to portray an image of grassroots opposition to abortion reform. While O'Neil[184] cited a lack of coordination in the Catholic church effort, comparatively speaking it was a well-organized opposition, several years ahead of pro-life activists in other parts of the country. The church hierarchy managed to organize a heavy mail campaign, with lay Catholic constituents writing to legislators to oppose reform.[185] A similar dynamic operated in North Dakota, where reform bills were introduced in 1967, 1969, and 1972. As was true of the sponsors of successful bills in other states, the North Dakota sponsor first introduced a bill during her first year in office; Ginsburg noted that she, "like many of the early participants in the abortion reform movement, did not see it as explosive or highly charged...."[186] But the

---

[177] *Miami Herald*, June 8, 1967.
[178] Ibid.
[179] State of Florida, *Journal of the Senate* (1967), p. 712.
[180] Florida, *Journal of the House of Representatives: Regular Session* (1967), p. 1069.
[181] Ibid., pp. 1518–19; *Miami Herald*, June 27, 1967.
[182] *Miami Herald*, June 27, 1967.
[183] *Miami Herald*, June 28, 1967.
[184] *Church Lobbying in a Western State*, p. 58.
[185] Ibid., p. 41.
[186] Quotation from Ginsburg, *Contested Lives*, p. 65, who cites Luker, *Abortion and the Politics of Motherhood*, p. 108, on the substantive point about early reformers.

bill elicited a quickly organized, passionate response, largely but not entirely Catholic. Hearings on the bill had to move to a larger building to accommodate the crowd, and the sponsor was deluged with hate mail.[187] Note the contrast with states that passed reform laws. In North Carolina, as noted above, pro-life advocates' attempt at a mail campaign failed. In Georgia, it appears that many state senators had the impression that there was little in-state opposition to reform,[188] even though the Catholic archbishop of Atlanta and a few other pro-life Catholics testified in favor of a pro-life view. The comparison confirms the point that state legislators do not like to take action on measures where they feel there is in-state moral polarization.

As the cases of Arizona and North Dakota are already summarized in published form, let us turn to Maine, which provides a good illustration of the process that could lead to defeat of reform efforts. That process depended more on the active pursuit of alternative frames rather than a Catholic presence per se. Bills to liberalize the Maine abortion law failed in the state legislature in 1967 and again in 1969. (The legislature met only every other year, a not uncommon practice of state legislatures.) Fortunately we can follow the legislative process reasonably well, as Maine publishes detailed accounts of floor debates.

In 1967, a joint state House–Senate committee divided on the proposed reform bill. A senator in the committee's minority, in favor of reform, opened floor debate on June 5, 1967, by invoking the medical frame:

None of us, including the signers of the Minority Ought to Pass report, are in favor of abortion. On the other hand, I think most of us recognize that on certain occasions an abortion is medically justified and medically advisable.[189]

The senator noted that they had revised the American Law Institute's bill to require that a hospital board, not just individual doctors, approve an abortion.

We couldn't see how, with this system, abuses could creep into this and make the State of Maine, as some people would suggest, an abortion mill.

As you all know, a law somewhat similar to this has been passed in the State of Colorado. It is perhaps interesting that this state has already performed two

---

[187] Ginsburg, ibid., pp. 66–7.
[188] Jain and Gooch, *Georgia Abortion Act 1968*, pp. 43–5.
[189] Maine, *Legislative Record of the One Hundred and Third Legislature* (1967), p. 2806.

abortions since the law went into effect a month or so ago under this law. Curiously enough, both abortions arose because of a possible rape. One of them was a twelve year old girl.[190]

The attempt, then, was to frame legal abortion as a regrettable necessity, a medical and humanitarian option that should be available, but only in limited quantities.

However, opposition legislators from the split committee asserted that abortion was murder, referred to "killing unborn people,"[191] and argued that allowing abortion of fetuses considered possibly deformed (the most common reason cited being rubella) was to imply that hand-icapped persons had less claim on life and were not fully human. There was invocation of the great accomplishments of Beethoven (who lost his hearing) and Helen Keller (born deaf and blind). Though the state Senate initially voted on June 5 to base further debate on the minority committee report, that is, which recommended passage of the reform bill, opposition remained strident.[192] In the next floor debate, in the House on June 14, after a number of opponents made strongly worded pro-life arguments, a proponent began his remarks, "I feel about as popular as a skunk at a lawn party on this particular bill. . . . "[193] Oppo-nents, meanwhile, claimed that thousands of people had signed letters or petitions opposing abortion reform.[194]

Extended consideration of the moral implications of a reform bill, as well as evidence of in-state passion, made passage more difficult. Both tended to push aside the medical frame that favored reform. Although the New Hampshire records are not as detailed as those of Maine, a similar dynamic may have operated in that state's Senate in 1969. That is, there appears to have been polarization over the relevance of moral and theological approaches to the issue of abortion, and the bill was set aside.[195]

There was another attempt in Maine to pass a reform bill in 1969; again, controversy was the order of the day. By this time, the topic attracted more attention than it had a couple years before, not only in

---

[190] Ibid., p. 2807.
[191] Ibid., p. 2808.
[192] See ibid., pp. 2807–9, 3299–304, 3306–7, 3312, 3315.
[193] Ibid., p. 3307.
[194] Ibid., pp. 3310, 3314.
[195] State of New Hampshire, *Journal of the Honorable Senate: January Session of 1969* (1969), pp. 624–7, 981–2.

Maine.[196] A supporter of reform opened the floor debate of May 15, 1969, invoking humanitarian concerns and noting,

Probably more has been written and said about this specific piece of legislation than any before us this session. . . . Now I know that the opposition will stress all of the mail that they have received against this bill. I too have received a great deal of mail, and I will admit that much of it was not flattering. However, as the sponsor, in the final analysis I had more mail in favor of this than against it, and many of the letters told of actual experiences, vividly portraying tragedy and heartbreak.[197]

Under these conditions, however, medical concerns fell to the wayside, and humanitarian concerns faced a passionate, pro-life opposition. Great public interest did not mean that the public was primarily opposed to abortion reform. But it did involve expressions of moral passions among at least some in-state residents, which legislators found uncomfortably controversial. Maine's abortion reform bill failed in 1969, as it had in 1967.

As noted earlier, within legislative debates, frames explicitly attempting to widen the moral agenda most commonly took a pro-life form. But abortion rights frames also occasionally drowned out the medical frame. In Michigan, a proponent of a 1969 reform bill, Senator Lorraine Beebe, made an impassioned plea for abortion as a right important for women's full equality.[198] She stated that she was an Episcopalian who had "had a therapeutic abortion at a Roman Catholic Hospital performed by a Roman Catholic doctor and supervised by the mother superior."[199] Beebe's case was a sympathetic one fitting the medical frame of therapeutic abortion, as physicians at the time apparently suspected that the fetus had already died.[200] But her appeal to the senate framed abortion as an issue of a woman's rights:

Her priest, her minister, her rabbi, her doctor, her husband and her friends all can give her advice and directives, but in the final analysis, gentleman, she

---

[196] See, e.g., Nevada, *Journal of the Assembly of the Fifty-fifth Session of the Legislature of the State of Nevada* (1969), p. 825.

[197] Maine, *Legislative Record of the One Hundred and Fourth Legislature* (1969), p. 2114.

[198] Michigan, *Journal of the Senate of the State of Michigan: 1969 Regular Session* (1969), pp. 1493–5.

[199] Ibid., p. 1494.

[200] *New York Times*, June 13, 1969. It is not clear from the article whether the doctors were right on this point.

and she alone must make this decision whether to have or not to have an abortion.... What is happening here is the fact that you are trying to impose your will on that of a woman's decision. You cannot do this. Women were emancipated in 1964. Oh yes, we got in under the Civil Rights Act of 1964 and it was because of the tenacity of women in the Congress that the one little word, sex, was added to the 1964 bill. We were not even second class citizens, Senator, and we have been third class citizens and we still remain that because men cannot represent us.... [W]e are responsible for what happens to us and to our bodies.[201]

This was unusual rhetoric in a state legislature at that time. Beebe went on to state that this was also an issue of religious freedom (a somewhat more common assertion), that one set of religious convictions could not be written into abortion law. A (male) supporter of Beebe's position argued, "You know this really shouldn't be called an abortion bill. This should be called a civil rights bill for womanhood, for our second-class citizens.... [Y]ou are destroying the right of women, you are keeping them subjugated as slaves."[202] An opponent countered that a child exists at conception, "created in the image of God...."[203]

Beebe's dramatic plea was recounted in a *New York Times*[204] story titled, "State Senator Defends Abortion by Tearfully Telling of Her Own," and in an Associated Press story reprinted, for example, in the main Delaware newspaper[205] the day after the Delaware legislature passed its own bill. The Associated Press story included the senator's photo and stated: "The chamber hushed as attractive, red-haired Mrs. Beebe, in her late 40s, told of her own operation 20 years ago." When such passion, moral polarization, and publicity drove the debate, it was very difficult to persuade a majority of legislators to take the active step of changing the law on such an apparently controversial issue: The bill failed in the Michigan Senate, sixteen to seventeen.[206]

New Jersey is a case that, in retrospect, could not have been designed better to encourage moral polarization and thus greatly dampen the

---

[201] *Journal of the Senate of the State of Michigan: 1969 Regular Session*, p. 1494.
[202] Ibid., p. 1496.
[203] Ibid., p. 1500.
[204] June 13, 1969.
[205] *Evening Journal*, June 13, 1969.
[206] Michigan, *Journal of the Senate of the State of Michigan: 1969 Regular Session* (1969), p. 1497. As noted in the next chapter, an attempt to repeal Michigan's abortion law by referendum in 1972 also failed.

chances of passing a reform bill. The state legislature established in 1968 a nine-member commission – including state legislators, clergy, a county prosecutor, and a gynecologist representing the New Jersey Medical Society[207] – to investigate whether a change in abortion laws was warranted. The intent of the legislators who created the commission was fairly clearly the legitimation of reform,[208] but a series of hearings, and a commission life of over a year and a half, allowed time for conflict to develop over the framing of abortion law reform. The commission encountered pro-life testimony, much of which was moderate in tone, emphasizing that life was sacred. But some such testimony talked of abortion as murder, compared it to Nazi views of the value of life, said that abortion in cases of rubella implied that handicapped persons were not fully human, and so forth. And those who made such testimony were diverse enough that they presumably gave the impression that there was in New Jersey a substantial constituency morally opposed to liberalization. Among the pro-life witnesses were, for example, a radiologist from a Catholic hospital, two Catholic sisters, an obstetrician-gynecologist, an Episcopal priest, and someone associated with the New Jersey Association for Brain Injured Children.[209] Also supporting the pro-life cause was one of the commission's clergy, who was the Director of the Family Life Bureau in the Catholic Diocese of Trenton at a time the state's Catholic bishops were actively opposing abortion. The commission also encountered arguments, from representatives of the National Organization for Women and the American Civil Liberties Union, that access to abortion was a right.[210]

---

[207] State of New Jersey, Commission to Study the New Jersey Statutes Relating to Abortion, *Final Report to the Legislature*, December 31, 1969, p. ii. Incidentally, although this *Final Report to the Legislature* is dated December 31, 1969, according to later legislative testimony by the chair of the commission, it was actually issued in March 1970 (New Jersey Legislature, General Assembly, Judiciary Committee, Transcript of public hearing on Assembly Bill No. 762, April 9, 1970, p. 3).

[208] Commission to Study the New Jersey Statutes Relating to Abortion, (transcript of) *Public Hearing* October 28, 1968, Trenton, p. 11; and same commission's *Final Report to the Legislature*, December 31, 1969, p. 1.

[209] Commission to Study the New Jersey Statutes Relating to Abortion, (transcript of) *Public Hearing* of October 28, 1968, Trenton, pp. 11–17, 46–54; *Public Hearing*, November 13, 1968, Newark, pp. 26, 151–8; *Public Hearing*, November 26, 1968, Camden, pp. 5–8.

[210] Ibid., pp. 66–7; same commission's (transcript of) *Public Hearing* (held in Newark, N.J.), November 13, 1968, pp. 73–80, 88–95, 126–8.

Not surprisingly, the commission's final report to the legislature gave an impression of controversy rather than consensus.[211] A bare majority of the commission (five members of nine total) recommended in favor of reform of the law, that is, liberalization along ALI lines, but three separate minority reports disagreed. Even the majority position was a compromise, as three members apparently would have preferred total repeal of the law.[212] Two of the minority reports were of pro-life sympathies, one of which was from the commission's Catholic priest and was titled "Let the Children Live!"[213] A third minority report, by the county prosecutor, noted that there had developed conflict around the difficult issue of "when does human life begin?"[214]

And, although this commission member was the only one who recommended that the law remain as it was (in order to see how the Supreme Court might respond to court challenges of abortion laws in other states), that was ultimately the outcome: New Jersey never passed abortion reform legislation.

While certainly not definitive, voting patterns support the points made in these narrative examples. We saw earlier that passage of reform bills by large margins was quite common. If we use an unscientific sample of states where tallies on reform bills were available, it appears, however, to have been rare for a legislative vote to *reject* an abortion reform bill by an overwhelming vote. An exception was the thirty-nine to ninety vote in the Maine House in 1967. This comparison suggests that rejection of a reform bill was accompanied by division, rather than a strong consensus opposed to abortion reform. But a strong consensus in favor of reform, that is, before moral polarization emerged, was common enough. (This cannot be a definitive finding: It is impossible to know whether, in many states, a reform bill was tabled – i.e., never came to a final vote – because it was particularly unpopular. State records simply do not provide adequate documentation.)

To note another apparent pattern, it is interesting to consider cases in which the bill passed in one chamber and not the other (as opposed

---

[211] Commission to Study the New Jersey Statutes Relating to Abortion, *Final Report to the Legislature*, December 31, 1969, esp. pp. 62–4, 81–132.

[212] New Jersey Legislature, General Assembly, Judiciary Committee, Transcript of public hearing on Assembly Bill No. 762, April 9, 1970, pp. 6–7.

[213] *Final Report to the Legislature*, December 31, 1969, p. 82.

[214] Ibid., p. 126.

to a number of cases where the bill lost in both chambers). When there was this split decision, typically the chamber that considered the bill first passed it by a small margin, and the second chamber voted it down. This suggests the possibility that controversy was already substantial and/or snowballed as the bill went through the legislative process. (As with much of the data available on state legislative process, this component is only suggestive, but there are enough such components to paint a compelling picture overall.) For example, in Florida in 1967, the Senate first approved the bill, twenty-six to twenty-two, then the House tabled it. In the same year the Oklahoma House approved a bill fifty-one to forty, with fifty apparently the minimum required for passage[215]; the bill then failed to make it through the Senate. The 1969 New Hampshire House vote was 204–171,[216] followed by the Senate's negative vote of six to twelve.[217] The same year, the Vermont House approved, seventy-four to seventy-one,[218] and then the Senate voted down the measure, ten to twenty.[219]

In Maine in 1967, although the first vote in favor of the bill (in the Senate, twenty to twelve) was not as close as in these other states, we have already seen – through examining Maine's detailed legislative journal – that controversy was indeed substantial in the Senate. So Maine is consistent with the substantive point even though the indicator (a close vote in the first chamber) is not present. The Senate Committee on Judiciary split on the bill six to four, with the majority recommending against passage.[220] Far from being considered a simple, popular reform, as originally perceived by the sponsors in, for example, Georgia and California, the sponsor in Maine (a Mrs. Sproul of Lincoln County) stated that she had known "it would cause a great deal of comment" and "in some quarters hurt me politically."[221] The debate became one of opponents who talked of "killing unborn people" versus proponents who spoke of the "political courage"[222] involved in

---

[215] *Daily Oklahoman*, March 30, 1967.
[216] State of New Hampshire, *Journal of the House of Representatives: January Session of 1969* (1969), pp. 344–7.
[217] New Hampshire, *Journal of the Honorable Senate: January Session of 1969*, p. 982.
[218] Vermont, *Journal of the House of the State of Vermont: Adjourned Session, 1970*, p. 91.
[219] *Facts on File Yearbook 1970*, p. 275.
[220] Maine, *Legislative Record of the One Hundred and Third Legislature* (1967), p. 2806.
[221] Ibid., p. 2809.
[222] Ibid., p. 2809.

supporting it. As one supporter of reform put it, the bill was "probably the most sensitive measure that has been before the Legislature this winter, and a person doesn't like to allow himself to be in a position where the opposition feels that he is taking the side of those who would murder or kill."[223] He went on to say that there was a bias in the legislature because it was dominated by men. His chamber nevertheless approved the bill, but the House voted it down thirty-nine to ninety.

Conclusion

In sum, abortion law reform depended upon a medical, humanitarian frame, which in turn depended upon a discussion limited to legislative and professional elites. On the one hand, the progress that abortion law reform made in a few short years demonstrates the power of frames that limit moral discussion, that is, limit the agenda: If a policy or legislative initiative seems not to have sweeping moral implications but instead is successfully portrayed as a limited reform that is not oriented toward settling fundamental moral divisions, legislative assent can be readily forthcoming. And thus significant legal change can emerge – change that in the case of abortion did make abortion more available in some states. The few short years in which reform laws were passed was the most dramatic period of *legislative* change on the issue of abortion this century. The movement for abortion law reform was an elite movement, not a mass movement; and thus it may not qualify as a "social movement," as most of us probably envision more than discussions among clergy, lawyers, and doctors, outside of public view, when we think of a "social movement." But, it was some sort of movement, and one that was arguably much more successful than most, at least for a few years. The typical movement does not so easily find numerous state legislatures readily agreeing to pass a statute that the movement, for the most part, had written.

On the other hand, the particular limiting frame that abortion reform represented could not withstand extensive public scrutiny: It depended on an elite willingness to limit the agenda to exclude moral passion. We shall see in the next chapter that the very legislative discussion

[223] Ibid., p. 2810.

that produced the reform laws ultimately paved the way for a more public and morally divisive discussion. Once that discussion emerged, legislatures were for the most part paralyzed. Even during the period 1966–1970, in some legislatures, where the medical, humanitarian frame happened to encounter sustained attack, it could not prevent a morally divisive debate from emerging.

Ultimately, as I argue at the end of the book, the history of medical framing of abortion demonstrates that limiting frames, when institutionalized in an effective way, can very powerfully prevent open conflict. But the particular limiting frame that the reform laws represented was ultimately, at the legislative level, a paper tiger: It fell apart quickly, once challenged. Ironically, though, the U.S. Supreme Court overruled the abortion reform laws, in favor of wider legal access to abortion, but by using arguments that were prominent within the medical, humanitarian frame that produced the reform laws in the first place. The next chapter examines these developments.

6

Abortion and Legislative Stalemate: The Weakness and Strength of the Medical, Humanitarian Frame

Introduction

In the case of both contraception and abortion, framing the issue in terms of a doctor's need to make medical decisions free from interference was central to the liberalization of legal restrictions. But we shall see in this chapter that such a medical frame does not easily win in a struggle against politicized frames that base themselves explicitly in a moral worldview and thus widen the agenda. The moral worldviews that had framed contraception declined as the social movements that spawned them declined. Liberalization of contraception had entered the public stage as a cause intertwined with broad agendas for social change; it became associated with respectable medicine only with great effort, and only once those causes lost their steam. Abortion reform had the advantage that it began among quiet circles of elites; but once discussion moves beyond such circles, frames based explicitly in moral worldviews are much more likely to emerge. The worldviews themselves rarely make much legislative progress but instead are more likely to take the form of moral vetoes, preventing any new statutory developments.

As we saw in the previous chapter, in the late 1960s, there emerged a movement for abortion reform, that is, liberalization of abortion laws to allow physicians wider discretion to grant legal abortions, most notably when physicians judged the physical or mental health of the pregnant woman, or deformity of the fetus, to be a significant risk.

These laws certainly did not give women any right to abortion and, in most of the (minority of) states that passed such laws, legal abortion rates hardly rose. Women seeking legal abortions often had to receive approval from hospital boards, reflecting that abortion reform was framed as a matter of the medical profession *granting* abortions based on humanitarian, therapeutic criteria.

In the first few years of the 1970s, both the weakness and strength of a medical, humanitarian framing of abortion became apparent. The very discussion that legislative reform efforts had initiated ultimately undermined the conditions for passage of abortion reform laws: Other groups started noticing the discussion and objected that the reform laws violated their moral convictions. And so, we shall see below, legislative reform came to a stop after 1970: A weakness of the medical frame is that it was a limiting agenda based on discussion not going beyond a limited circle of elites.

Legislatures are hesitant to act when any action will necessarily offend some politically significant constituency with strong convictions. But, as was significant in the case of contraception, unelected courts generally do not have to worry about constituencies in any direct fashion. Federal courts accepted a medical framing of contraception in the 1930s and thus overruled statutory restrictions on physicians' decisions about the contraceptive needs of their patients. But it is often forgotten today that the 1973 U.S. Supreme Court decision overruling most state restrictions on access to legal abortion also depended, to a great extent, on a medical framing of reproductive decisions. And so while the medical, humanitarian framing of abortion lost legislative steam in 1970, so that reform bills became increasingly controversial, the Supreme Court just three years later framed abortion law in a very similar way but used that frame to institute even more dramatic legal change. *Roe v. Wade* and *Doe v. Bolton* suggest that U.S. government officials, and probably the society as a whole, are culturally invested in the idea of benign medical authority: With those decisions, the Supreme Court greatly widened the availability of legal abortion partly by insisting that doctors, not laws, should be entrusted with such decisions.

Let us first examine why the state legislative reform process ground to a halt, and then turn to the 1973 Supreme Court decision. This chapter then examines legal and political developments on abortion in the United States and speculates why the United States has a particularly divisive abortion debate.

Repeal Laws and the End of Reform

Dissatisfaction with Reform

The apparent paradox of abortion reform laws is that many state legislators reacted to them very positively, but without passion. Those legislators who were passionate were usually quite opposed to reform bills.

We have seen that, in the state legislatures, proponents typically argued that the reform initiatives were a sensible, humanitarian reform in the interest of good medicine. Within the legislative chamber, what passion there was came from opponents, mostly on the pro-life side. But outside the legislatures there was also developing a small pro-life movement and an abortion rights movement. The former was, at that time, almost exclusively Catholic and was so small and diffuse that it was almost insignificant compared with the pro-life movement that would develop after *Roe v. Wade* (1973).[1] But when they were visible (which, in many states, they were not), their position on the reform laws was clear: Such laws were an abomination because, in the pro-life view, they encouraged and sanctioned murder.

There was also an abortion rights movement developing in the 1960s, whose supporters argued that only women had a right to control their bodies. What had begun as abortion referral services, for example, among liberal clergy, developed in some places into underground networks of safe but illegal abortion services that rejected the legitimacy of laws restricting women's access to abortion, even the liberalized reform laws.[2] Like the emerging pro-life movement, the abortion rights movement in the late 1960s, working to repeal legal restrictions on abortion

---

[1] Kristin Luker, *Abortion and the Politics of Motherhood* (Berkeley: University of California Press, 1984), pp. 127, 143–4; Suzanne Staggenborg, *The Pro-Choice Movement: Organization and Activism in the Abortion Conflict* (New York: Oxford University Press, 1991), pp. 34–5; Faye Ginsburg, *Contested Lives: The Abortion Debate in an American Community* (Berkeley: University of California Press, 1989), p. 42.

[2] Rosalind Pollack Petchesky, *Abortion and Woman's Choice: The State, Sexuality, and Reproductive Freedom* (New York and London: Longman, 1984), pp. 125–6; Staggenborg, *The Pro-Choice Movement*, pp. 21–4; Luker, *Abortion and the Politics of Motherhood*, pp. 120–5; John H. Evans, "Multi-Organizational Fields and Social Movement

entirely, was not particularly large. A leader in such groups, Lawrence Lader, noted: "The drive to build repeal organizations throughout the country was haphazard at best."[3] In some cases such groups developed in places and times in which the nineteenth-century laws were still in effect.[4] But they also developed in opposition to the new reform laws.

Small as the pro-life and abortion rights movements were in the 1960s, they were a contrast to support for reform laws, which was elite and out of public view; the reform movement had not been a grassroots movement. Tactically, repeal supporters often initially supported reform as a first step, since in most places in the 1960s reform was the only game in town. But a feminist abortion rights movement, dominated by women, quickly abandoned reform as insufficient. Some participants in the reform alliance – some clergy, for example, who helped women obtain safe, illegal abortions – defected to the abortion rights movement favoring a complete repeal of abortion laws.[5] One of the more dramatic actions of the movement was in 1969, when abortion rights picketers protested at the American Medical Association convention in New York, demanding that the AMA support repeal.[6] Liberalized medical control of the abortion decision, as instituted by the reform laws, was always unpopular with pro-life sympathizers. But it quickly lost support among abortion rights supporters, as well, even in California, where unusually liberal interpretation of a reform law had, unlike in any other state with a reform law, effectively eliminated most legal barriers to abortion, so that almost every application for therapeutic abortion was approved.[7] Despite the liberal interpretation, as noted,[8] abortion rights supporters were so ideologically

---

Organization Frame Content: The Religious Pro-Choice Movement," *Sociological Inquiry* 67(1997):451–69.

[3] Lawrence Lader, *Abortion II: Making the Revolution* (Boston: Beacon, 1973), p. 60.

[4] Ibid., pp. 26–8.

[5] Ibid., pp. 57–67; Luker, *Abortion and the Politics of Motherhood*, pp. 122–3.

[6] Petchesky, *Abortion and Woman's Choice*, pp. 127–9; Staggenborg, *The Pro-Choice Movement*, pp. 13–16; David J. Garrow, *Liberty and Sexuality: The Right to Privacy and the Making of Roe v. Wade* (New York: Macmillan/Lisa Drew, 1994), pp. 297–9.

[7] Luker, *Abortion and the Politics of Motherhood*, p. 94; Archon Fung, "Making Rights Real: *Roe*'s Impact on Abortion Access," *Politics & Society* 21(1993):472. See also Garrow, *Liberty and Sexuality*, pp. 360, 375, 411.

[8] *Abortion and the Politics of Motherhood*, pp. 120–1.

opposed to medical control that they pushed further in court cases and ultimately received a California state Supreme Court decision that anticipated *Roe v. Wade*.[9] Luker attributed this abandonment of reform to an ideological imperative of abortion rights groups: That is, the feminist ideology behind the movement was that no physician, or anyone else, had a right to decide what happened to a woman's body. Only the woman herself could decide whether or not to have an abortion.

The ideological passion that Luker cited is the most sensible explanation of the politics of abortion in California in the late 1960s and early 1970s. However, in many states, criticism of a recently passed reform law could have been based on disappointment with the subsequent level of access to legal abortion; that is, it was not solely ideological in origin. Depending on one's state of residence, reform may have appeared to have done little or nothing at all. If interpreted strictly, abortion reform laws only moderately changed access to legal abortion; there was wide variation across states, though again it would be incorrect to generalize from California's experience, because that state's dramatically increased access was atypical.[10] (California's Society for Humane Abortion appears also to have been unusually militant, compared to movements in other states, in its defiance of abortion laws, openly referring women to illegal abortionists judged to be safe.[11]) And so, even in most states that had passed reform laws, the concrete matter of limited abortion access would have been sufficient reason for abortion rights supporters to push for total repeal.

In any case, within a few years, even many original proponents of reform came to be dissatisfied with the new law. Many reformers, after a couple of years' experience with the application of the new laws, were disappointed with restrictive interpretations of the reform laws and thus receptive to the increasing calls for repeal. The *New York Times* reported on December 3, 1969, for example, that the two-year-old Colorado law was under considerable attack from medical personnel and others who had originally backed the law. A few months later, an

[9] Garrow, *Liberty and Sexuality*, pp. 377–80, 410–11.
[10] Fung, "Making Rights Real."
[11] Staggenborg, *The Pro-Choice Movement*, pp. 31, 191n.3; Luker, *Abortion and the Politics of Motherhood*, pp. 98–9, 122.

Associated Press story quoted the chief sponsor of Colorado's 1967 law, state Representative Richard Lamm, criticizing that very law.

> We tried to change a cruel, outmoded, inhuman law—and what we got was a cruel, outmoded, inhuman law. . . . We still force women either to have a baby or to have an illegal abortion.[12]

The newspaper story went on to state that "Lamm estimated that 19 of every 20 women who seek a legal abortion in Colorado are refused because they do not meet the legislated criteria." Similarly, the disappointed sponsor of the 1967 reform law in North Carolina came out for repeal in 1969.[13] Less than a year after the 1968 Maryland law passed, the sponsor proclaimed that the new law discriminated against poor women.[14] It seems, then, that humanitarian support for reform, in many cases, was transformed into support for repeal, and for court challenges to the reform laws. That is, presumably some of the supporters for reform had originally found medical gatekeeping reasonable because it seemed initially compatible with their humanitarian goals. But if the humanitarian goals were really primary, then such supporters could quickly jettison medicalization, in favor of repeal, if it appeared that medicalization (i.e., the ALI-type reform laws) did not provide sufficient access to legal abortion. From such a viewpoint, repeal would seem to be more humanitarian than would reform. In any case – whether such legislators had secretly supported abortion rights all along, or instead had had a change of heart in favor of repeal and not just reform – starting about 1969 many who had supported reform now came out in favor of repeal.

The National Organization for Women (NOW) had endorsed repeal of abortion laws in 1967; but NOW had just been founded the year before and was primarily preoccupied with economic issues at that time.[15] The National Association for the Repeal of Abortion Laws (NARAL, later the National Abortion Rights Action League[16]) was founded in 1969 and was instrumental in publicizing and lobbying for a position that all restrictions should be eliminated entirely. On

---

[12] Quoted in *Richmond Times-Dispatch* (Richmond, Va.), April 13, 1970; see also Garrow, *Liberty and Sexuality*, pp. 482–3.

[13] Garrow, ibid., pp. 482–3. Lader, *Abortion II*, pp. 85–6.

[14] *Evening Sun* (Baltimore, Md.), February 24, 1969.

[15] Staggenborg, *The Pro-Choice Movement*, p. 20.

[16] And now known as the National Abortion and Reproductive Rights Action League.

the pro-life side, the founding of the National Right to Life Committee was not until 1973, and the pro-life movement was much more
vibrant after *Roe* than before. Still, at the end of the 1960s and beginning of 1970s, social movement forces developed more systematic and
organized responses to proposed abortion reform legislation and effective movement strategies, lobbying legislatures intensively, organizing
protests, and attracting publicity.[17]

When considering how this mobilization related to the preexisting
reform movement, however, the contrasting time frames are interesting:
It took at least a decade or so for discussion among medical and other
elites to ferment to the point that it actually effected legal change,
beginning in 1967.[18] But for a couple of years momentum seemed to
be on the side of reform: By about 1969, it probably would have been
reasonable for contemporaries to judge the elite reform movement to
be immensely successful, even unstoppable. But we shall see that by
the end of 1970 the medical, humanitarian frame ceased to be relevant
to the broader public debate.

In one sense, organized abortion rights groups, and even more so,
pro-life organizations, were latecomers.[19] The abortion rights groups
initially often supported reform laws, for strategic reasons, at a time
when such groups were just getting started; thus they appear overall
to have been quite insignificant in the passage of reform laws. State
legislative records give little indication that such groups were heard
in many of the state discussions of reform laws. During the 1960s,
such groups, as well as pro-life groups, do not appear to have been
very big. In 1969 or 1970, it would have been reasonable to view
abortion rights and pro-life groups as quite marginal to the debate as a
whole. Yet, very quickly, abortion rights and pro-life activists stopped
the reform movement in its tracks, sometimes primarily by making
their voices heard before they had much of an organization behind
them.

---

[17] Raymond Tatalovich and Byron W. Daynes, *The Politics of Abortion: A Study of Community Conflict in Public Policy Making* (New York: Praeger, 1981), pp. 62–5.
[18] Or the previous year, if one includes the 1966 Mississippi law. See the previous chapter's discussion of that law.
[19] Just to clarify: Pro-life arguments were considerably more prevalent in debates over
reform laws than were abortion rights arguments. However, the abortion rights *movement*, while still somewhat small, was more developed by 1970 than was the pro-life
movement.

So why did the reform movement collapse so quickly? Why did a national movement with widespread elite support, which had had significant success in the state legislatures, fail to control the debate when it went public, as soon as some scattered groups mounted a challenge? True, the reform movement was a quiet movement, but one would think that elites who had been working on legal change for a number of years would have had more influence than a few disparate pro-life and abortion rights groups who had only recently appeared on the scene. One could easily imagine intuitively reasonable historical or sociological arguments that an elite political movement, with substantial evidence of trustworthy reputation and political success, would be a very difficult movement to stop.

I would argue, as I have elsewhere in this book, that one can explain the collapse of the medical, humanitarian frame – and thus the collapse of the movement for reform laws – only by focusing on the power of frames that broaden the moral agenda, a power that is somewhat independent of the apparent, mobilized power of particular interest groups. Such frames can have a veto power over frames that try to restrict the agenda, and yet the morally charged frames themselves are not usually written into law. At the legislative level, especially, their greatest success is in blocking alternatives, not in being written into law themselves.

Repeal Laws

The year 1970 was a turning point, one that may have appeared at the time as the beginning of victory for an abortion rights frame (in favor of repeal of restrictions on access to abortion). Each year from 1967 through 1970, as we have seen, at least two, and usually more, states passed an abortion reform law, so that twelve states had passed such laws (thirteen if Mississippi's less liberal 1966 law is included). In 1970, in addition, for the first and only time, several states passed repeal laws. That is, four states passed repeal laws that decriminalized abortion up to varying points in the pregnancy, allowing any reason for abortion as long as it was medically supervised. Alaska, Hawaii, and New York passed these laws through the usual legislative process, while Washington state passed a repeal referendum put to the voters by the legislature. These four states, then, legislated something very close to what the Supreme Court would mandate in 1973.

After 1970, the only state legislature to pass any new abortion law prior to *Roe* – Florida's in 1972 – did so as the result of a state Supreme Court ruling in February 1972, invalidating the nineteenth-century state law on abortion. The court gave the legislature 60 days to enact a new law, or be faced with an automatic reversion to English common law, allowing abortion before quickening. Even so, the Florida legislature, which had rejected a reform bill in 1967, did not easily come to agreement in 1972. After considerable legislative rancor during which many legislators thought a bill would not pass, Florida finally accepted an ALI-type bill, that is, a reform bill, at the end of its session.[20] Florida's 1972 law, then, was not typical; legislatively initiated reform laws stopped in 1970.

For the states that passed reform laws, public controversy was more the exception than the rule; states that did encounter a great deal of public controversy usually failed to pass such laws. But, for the repeal laws that passed in 1970, controversy was the norm rather than the exception: Hawaii was the only one of the four that could be described as primarily uncontroversial.[21] In the other three states, repeal laws were the result of a different dynamic than the reform laws: They were unusual cases of moral frames coming head to head and one winning over the other. Just as no Southern state passed a repeal law, no state that passed a repeal law did so after first passing a reform law. Maryland did come very close; it passed a reform law in 1968, and both houses of the legislature passed a repeal bill in 1970. But Governor Marvin Mandel vetoed it.[22] By this time, rhetoric was strong and publicity substantial; for example, Cardinal Patrick O'Boyle, the Catholic archbishop of Washington, D.C. (a diocese that includes substantial parts of Maryland), had a letter read in all churches condemning this "legalized killing."[23] But in general, the reform laws were not a way station on legislatures' paths to repeal laws: The two followed distinct dynamics. For example, feminist groups that supported repeal had little to do with the reform movement, as we have seen. And the only two cases of abortion bills eliciting a governor's veto from 1966 to

---

[20] *Miami Herald*, March 28, 1972, April 7, 1972.
[21] Patricia G. Steinhoff and Milton Diamond, *Abortion Politics: The Hawaii Experience* (Honolulu: University Press of Hawaii, 1977).
[22] *New York Times*, May 27, 1970.
[23] *Washington Post*, April 11, 1970.

1970 were repeal bills, in Maryland and Alaska. In at least two states (Georgia and New Mexico), governors allowed reform bills to become law without their signatures, but it appears that none decided actually to veto a reform bill.[24] Reform passed when controversy was minimal; repeal was almost always highly controversial.

New York's law, the most highly publicized of the four repeal laws, was the result of years of legislative battles that had begun with attempts in 1967 to pass a reform bill.[25] Each year after that abortion was a highly publicized and politicized cause, with highly mobilized Catholic opposition and feminist support. Moral polarization was such that the state failed ever to pass a reform law, but abortion rights forces did win a narrow victory on the 1970 repeal bill (which Republican Gov. Nelson Rockefeller supported). In a dramatic, emotional moment, a member of the New York Assembly who represented a heavily Catholic district, and had been lobbied by family members to support repeal, broke a tie by changing his vote from "no" to "yes." He suspected the vote would end his political career, and he was right.[26]

Alaska's bill, which received extensive local press coverage, initially passed without any votes to spare in the state senate. Gov. Keith H. Miller, whose devout Catholic wife's opposition was cited a number of times in the local press, then faced intense lobbying, including petition drives by the Alaska Right to Life Committee and the Alliance for Humane Abortions. Miller vetoed the bill, stating in a letter to the legislature that was reprinted in an Anchorage newspaper: "The central issue is the right to life. . . . Humans may decide to avoid conception but only God decides when a life is formed."[27] Supporters were not

---

[24] For some states, e.g., Arkansas, the availability of records is such that I have not been able to definitively establish what action the governor took when a reform law is passed. However, the most reasonable judgment is that no governor vetoed a reform law. For example, in Arkansas the time between the legislature's passing the bill, and its officially becoming law (dates I have been able to establish) was almost too short to allow for a governor's veto and then a legislative override of that veto.

[25] Those political battles in New York state are addressed extensively in Garrow, *Liberty and Sexuality*, passim.

[26] Lader, *Abortion II*, pp. 142–7; *Facts on File Yearbook 1970* (New York: Facts on File, 1971), p. 274.

[27] State of Alaska, *Senate Journal* (1970), pp. 792–3; *Anchorage Daily News* (Anchorage, Alaska), April 18, 1970.

Thus Gov. Miller accepted that contraception and abortion were distinct issues, a point that is typical of the politics of these issues.

initially expected to be able to mobilize a two-thirds vote to override the veto, given the close Senate vote. But they did so – the first time Miller faced an override since taking office two years before – amid considerable emotion.[28] In Washington state, a rancorous, very public debate led to the most restrictive of the four repeal laws, as it applied to abortion only through the first sixteen weeks of pregnancy. (New York allowed twenty-four weeks[29]; in Alaska and Hawaii, the standard was fetal viability,[30] which in 1973 the Supreme Court, in *Roe v. Wade*, judged to be about twenty-eight weeks.) Furthermore, the Washington bill would take effect only if approved in a referendum ten months later, which it was, 55.5 to 44.5 percent. The referendum of course invited and elicited considerable pro-life and abortion rights mobilization.[31] But once set in motion, a referendum, unlike a bill, cannot be killed in committee.

Hawaii was a bit of an exception to the controversy over repeal bills: While the process started, as in New York, with reform proposals in 1967, the issue had not been nearly as public or divisive a controversy. In Hawaii, the process was similar to the typical passage of a reform bill amid relatively little controversy, except that legislators happened to be convinced that repeal would be even more humanitarian and workable than a reform law. Steinhoff and Diamond, for instance, describe the Hawaii initiative as a sudden, quantum leap, which developed quickly enough that moral division did not have time to develop. "The state did not even have a movement to repeal its existing restrictive abortion laws until six months before the landmark law was enacted. Nor ... did that state have an acute abortion problem."[32] It is probably no accident that Hawaii's repeal law, which of the four produced the least controversy, was also the first to pass. Still, the Catholic governor did consider vetoing the bill; instead he allowed the bill to become law without his signature.[33]

---

[28] *Anchorage Daily News*, April 10, 11, 12, 14, 17, 18, and 30, 1970; May 1 and 2, 1970.

[29] Garrow, *Liberty and Sexuality*, p. 483.

[30] *Anchorage Daily News*, May 1 and 2, 1970; Steinhoff and Diamond, *Abortion Politics*, p. 199.

[31] Garrow, *Liberty and Sexuality*, pp. 384–5, 411; Lader, *Abortion II*, pp. 170–3; Tatalovich and Daynes, *The Politics of Abortion*, pp. 68–9.

[32] Steinhoff and Diamond, *Abortion Politics*, p. 1.

[33] Garrow, *Liberty and Sexuality*, pp. 412–14.

If we examine the legislative votes in all four of these states together (see the four tables in the previous chapter), we see that the
repeal bills received an even smaller proportion of "yes" votes, only
about sixty percent, than did the reform bills in non-Southern states.
In non-Southern states that passed reform bills, bills passed on average with about two-thirds of the votes, and in Southern states, with
about four-fifths of the votes (see Table 5.2). That is, by about 1970,
abortion had become a public and controversial enough concern that it
had become increasingly difficult to pass legislative initiatives. As noted
above, six states did pass new abortion laws in 1970, including three
that received little national attention and were relatively uncontroversial (two Southern reform laws and Hawaii's repeal law), and three very
controversial repeal laws. Garrow noted that, in 1971, abortion rights
activists were pessimistic about legislative success. While attempts to
reverse the New York abortion rights legislative victory faltered, it
was also the case that repeal bills were defeated in at least five states
in 1971 (sometimes before actually coming to a floor vote). Repeal
advocates had, for instance, been optimistic that a repeal law could
pass in Michigan, but they lost hope as the year progressed. (It was in
Michigan that a 1969 reform bill had narrowly failed, after a dramatic
plea by a female legislator who had told of her own abortion.) Garrow
quoted a founder of the clerical group that favored abortion liberalization, the Clergy Consultation Service, who, surveying the scene in
1971, noted that "the courts are the only real hope for change."[34] Repeal bills introduced in Oklahoma and Georgia in 1972 were never
brought to a floor vote.[35] Also in 1972, opinion polls into October
suggested a decisive victory for a Michigan repeal referendum of the
type Washington state had passed in 1970. But the pro-life side drew
on organized support from the National Right to Life Committee and
the Catholic Church, and anti-repeal TV ads started in mid-October.
In this volatile climate, the repeal referendum was decisively defeated
on Election Day, thirty-nine to sixty-one percent. The same day, North

[34] Ibid., pp. 495–6, quotation from p. 495. A long footnote in Garrow seems to indicate that this quotation, from New York Baptist minister Howard Moody, originally
appeared in *National Clergy Consultation Service on Abortion Newsletter*, vol. 2, no. 1
(July 1971).
[35] Garrow, ibid., p. 538.

Dakota's repeal referendum was defeated by the overwhelming vote of twenty-three to seventy-seven percent.[36]

As noted earlier, social movement mobilization, while still in somewhat formative stages, was at least a significant presence by about 1969 or 1970. With the presence of even formative social movements that claimed fundamental points of principle, and who were thus unwilling to compromise over abortion, a moral veto became operative, and the momentum for reform laws evaporated. In 1970, only in the South – which was relatively isolated from the heightened national debate over abortion, and where pro-life and abortion rights movements were essentially absent at this time – did any states pass reform laws (namely, South Carolina and Virginia).

It is true that it may have briefly appeared, in 1970, that suddenly the tide had switched in favor of repeal, or at least that there was a crisis in abortion law and practice that needed to be addressed. There is some evidence in a number of studies of the politics of public policy and of protest that a strong atmosphere of acute crisis – so that government officials feel considerable pressure to handle large protests, riots, or other social disorder – will sometimes open what John W. Kingdon called a "policy window." That is, if government moves quickly it can adopt policy initiatives that otherwise would not be politically feasible; the speed induced by a sense of crisis is essential, so that the usual political obstacles and political forces do not have time to develop and mobilize. There are, for example, various such instances in the history of civil rights legislation.[37] Even some elites and legislators, let alone protest movements, suggested a sense of crisis over abortion

---

[36] Ibid., pp. 496, 538, 562–3, 567, 576–7; Ginsburg, *Contested Lives*, pp. 69–71; Lawrence Tribe, *Abortion: The Clash of Absolutes* (New York and London: W. W. Norton, 1992), p. 50.

[37] John W. Kingdon, *Agendas, Alternatives, and Public Policies*, 2nd ed. (New York: HarperCollins, 1995), pp. 16–17, 96, 169; John Skrentny, *The Ironies of Affirmative Action: Politics, Culture, and Justice in America* (Chicago and London: University of Chicago Press, 1996), pp. 81–91, 103–10, 257n.2; Staggenborg, *The Pro-Choice Movement*, p. 28. An extreme example of such a crisis-induced window would be sudden revolutionary crisis: see Gene Burns, "Ideology, Culture, and Ambiguity: The Revolutionary Process in Iran," *Theory and Society* 25(1996):349–88. For related ideas on the emergence and effect of social movements in crisis situations, see Harvey Molotch, "Oil in Santa Barbara and Power in America," *Sociological Inquiry* 40, no. 1 (1970):131–44; Bert Useem, "Solidarity Model, Breakdown Model, and the Boston Anti-Busing Movement," *American Sociological Review* 45(1980):357–69;

policy at this time, as they spoke of inhumane abortion laws and the
tragedies that resulted. But this policy window, by its nature, depended
on quick action, before opponents of the policy could reach their full
strength. Thus repeal efforts passed only in 1970. In 1971 and 1972,
they suffered defeat after defeat.

Yet, as is true of moral vetoes in general, the defeat of repeal bills
did not mean legislatures could act on some more popular alternative or compromise. If one expected legislatures to function, on abortion, or any issue, as brokers for a compromise among mobilized constituencies, then one would have probably expected reform bills to
become *more* popular once early efforts at repeal bills were passed,
but then further efforts were stymied by pro-life opponents. But, in
fact, the reform option basically disappeared once repeal became a
central focus. If one expected political outcomes to depend on the sum
of interest group strengths, then abortion rights and pro-life mobilization would mean that more liberal states with abortion rights movements would pass repeal laws, moderate states with both movements
present would pass reform bills, and particularly conservative states
would retain nineteenth-century laws. But such attempts at explanation cannot comprehend the legal patchwork as it existed at the end of
1970. To give just a few examples, Michigan had more indications of
support for liberalization than most states, yet it retained its restrictive
nineteenth-century law. (Though pretty much all abortion rights and
pro-life movements were small before the early to mid-1970s,) some
states with particularly significant, early abortion rights movements,
such as Illinois,[38] failed to liberalize at all. To move to another region
of the country, New York had passed repeal, Delaware and Maryland
reform, yet New Jersey – not obviously less liberal than its neighbors –
retained a restrictive nineteenth-century law. Repeal showed no signs of
being popular in many states that had easily passed reform, particularly
in the South. Some states with particularly large Catholic populations
passed repeal laws, others reform laws, and others declined to pass any

Edward J. Walsh, "Resource Mobilization and Citizen Protest in Communities around
Three Mile Island," *Social Problems* 29(1981):1–21.
[38] Staggenborg, *The Pro-Choice Movement*, pp. 23–4, 26–7, 29–30, 39–40; Leslie J.
Reagan, *When Abortion Was a Crime: Women, Medicine, and Law in the United
States, 1867–1973* (Berkeley and Los Angeles: University of California Press, 1997),
pp. 224–7.

new abortion law. In fact, the dynamic that led to passage of reform bills was discontinuous with the dynamic favorable to repeal, and the latter undermined the former. By about late 1970 or early 1971, far from being able to reflect popular will on abortion, legislatures had become unable to take initiative.

As we have seen, then, abortion rights forces managed, amid increasing but still early mobilization, to have a few victories in 1970, most notably in New York, where a battle between pro-life and abortion rights frames was unusually explicit and lengthy. (New York's repeal law, and the fact that liberal interpretation of the California reform law made it in practice a repeal law, were especially important: Neither state had a residency requirement, so that their size and location made abortion accessible for many women. And New York's debate received particular national attention.[39]) But those very battles had heightened the public awareness and mobilization around abortion, thus undermining the conditions that had allowed passage of new abortion laws in 17 states[40] between 1966 and 1970.

Instead, court challenges against the reform laws that had just passed emerged throughout the country, along with challenges to nineteenth-century abortion laws in states that had passed neither reform nor repeal.[41] The 1973 U.S. Supreme Court abortion decision thus encompassed two cases, one invalidating the nineteenth-century restrictive abortion laws (in *Roe v. Wade*, a case involving the Texas law), and the other nullifying the reform laws (via the simultaneously issued *Doe v. Bolton* opinion, on Georgia's 1968 law).[42]

Medical Framing and the 1973 U.S. Supreme Court Decision

The state abortion laws reached the U.S. Supreme Court partly because the medical framing of abortion was faltering. Yet, ironically, the Court apparently found a medical framing – but one tied to repeal rather

---

[39] Garrow, *Liberty and Sexuality*, p. 457.

[40] If one includes Mississippi: see the discussion of the 1966 Mississippi law in the previous chapter.

[41] Eva R. Rubin, *Abortion, Politics, and the Courts: Roe v. Wade and Its Aftermath*, rev. ed. (New York: Greenwood, 1987), pp. 43–57; Garrow, *Liberty and Sexuality*, pp. 389–472.

[42] *Roe v. Wade*, 410 U.S. 113 (1973); *Doe v. Bolton*, 410 U.S. 179 (1973).

than reform – quite convincing. Luker[43] noted that the Court was probably influenced by the apparent support for legal abortion within the medical community, and the Court's opinion strongly emphasized physicians' medical autonomy as a reason to overturn both the reform laws and the nineteenth-century laws.

While current political discussions about *Roe* tend to focus on the right of a woman to privacy (and, indeed, *Roe*'s contribution to privacy rights is immensely important), the decisions in *Roe* and *Doe* justified legal abortion through a mixture of privacy rights and medical rationales. The argument for constitutionally protected privacy rights depended on a crucial precedent, the 1965 U.S. Supreme Court case, *Griswold v. Connecticut*.[44] The *Griswold* case concerned an 1879 Connecticut state Comstock law that forbade anyone to provide contraceptive information, and, in an unusually restrictive provision, forbade even the use of contraception.[45] Although most states had by that time ceased to enforce Comstock restrictions on contraception, a number of the laws remained on the books. It was easier to ignore the laws than for legislatures to initiate a change and thus invite the small number of diehard opponents to express their fury.

The Supreme Court ruled in *Griswold* that states cannot prohibit married couples' access to contraception. Perhaps more important than the substance of the decision on contraception, however, was the reasoning: The court ruled that the U.S. Constitution implies a right to privacy, including a married couple's right to make their own reproductive decisions, free of government intrusion.

In 1973, the Supreme Court built upon *Griswold* to decide on challenges to state abortion laws. The court handed down a somewhat complex decision that attempted to balance privacy rights with what it saw as constitutionally recognized compelling government interests, for example, to regulate medical practice and to protect the fetus. The court divided pregnancy into three-month periods, that is, trimesters, recognizing a different balance of rights and interests for each trimester.

---

[43] *Abortion and the Politics of Motherhood*, pp. 142–3.

[44] 381 U.S. 471 (1965). For discussions of the significance of *Griswold*, see Rubin, *Abortion, Politics, and the Courts*, pp. 39–44; and Garrow, *Liberty and Sexuality*, pp. 253–4.

[45] C. Thomas Dienes, *Law, Politics, and Birth Control* (Urbana, Ill.: University of Illinois Press, 1972), pp. 46–7.

Privacy rights were paramount in the first trimester, so that the abortion decision required only the assent of the doctor performing the operation. In the second trimester, the state was permitted to place restrictions in the interest of the woman's health, and in the third trimester the viability of the fetus could outweigh privacy rights. Here medical technology was implicated, for the Court defined viability as the point at which a fetus is "potentially able to live outside the mother's womb, albeit with artificial aid. Viability is usually placed at about seven months (28 weeks) but may occur earlier, even at 24 weeks."[46] Requirements such as approval by a hospital committee and state residency were invalidated by the logic that they had little or nothing to do with the woman's health. As Blackmun's *Roe* decision stated, until viability "the abortion decision in all its aspects is inherently, and primarily, a medical decision, and basic responsibility for it must rest with the physician."[47] In *Doe*, the Court noted that *Roe v. Wade* "sets forth our conclusion that a pregnant woman does not have an absolute constitutional right to an abortion on her demand."[48] Implicitly a greater right was the "woman's right to receive medical care in accordance with her physician's best judgment and the physician's right to administer it...."[49] In *Doe*, the Court, as well, took the position that medical intervention was inherently humanitarian. The justices took umbrage at what they perceived as the plaintiff's suspicions about doctors' motives and doctors' ability to respect a woman's privacy: "...we trust that most physicians are 'good' [and] will have sympathy and understanding for the pregnant patient that are probably not exceeded by those who participate in other areas of professional counseling."[50]

Even though the medical, humanitarian frame had died at the state level in about 1970, in 1973 the Supreme Court to a great extent accepted that frame and thus attempted to limit the moral agenda. The ironies abound, as the Court provided abortion rights supporters much of what they seemed to want, but used medical reasoning, which they had fought against.

[46] *Roe v. Wade*, p. 160.
[47] Ibid., p. 166.
[48] *Doe v. Bolton*, p. 189.
[49] Ibid., p. 197.
[50] Ibid.

The Court was quite consciously attempting not to ground its opinion within a particular moral worldview.[51] For instance, it chose not to speak on the question of when life begins. As Eva R. Rubin explained, "it would be wise to evade discussion of philosophical and religious doctrines on which there was no agreement and no hope of finding consensus...."[52] Instead, Rubin noted,

the strategy of emphasizing the integrity of doctors and the medical nature of abortion had the practical result of appearing to supply some kind of objective standards to govern the abortion decision. Doctors make many decisions involving life and death without the help of government. It would be appropriate to defer to the expertise of the medical profession and let individual doctors decide when abortion is in the best interests of the patient.[53]

As I noted in this book's discussion of contraception, courts have shown a particular willingness to consider issues of sexual and reproductive politics within a medical frame. The discussion of the previous chapter helps us understand why: This kind of discourse is apparently attractive to elites, especially elites involved in policy making. It allows for professional autonomy, and it appears not to be ideologically driven. It appears to judge policy on the basis of reasoned judgment rather than emotionalism. But it is probably not just elites who find the idea of medical professionalism appealing. For whatever reason, within our culture deference to medical judgment appears to be a knee-jerk reaction, at least until someone presents a morally charged critique of such judgment. Presumably, then, it is a common cultural assumption that medicine is humanitarian and rational until proven otherwise. Think how often potentially controversial matters – assisted suicide, stem cell research – initially have a large constituency arguing that giving physicians and medical researchers autonomy will result in humanitarian outcomes. That is, ultimately some assumptions may seem nonideological, and thus fair and balanced, precisely because most members of a culture never articulate or question those assumptions. (I discuss these issues further in the concluding chapter.) Thus there is the pattern, which initially seems very strange, that the idea of therapeutic abortion was eminently sensible at first to so many legislators.

[51] Rubin, *Abortion, Politics, and the Courts*, pp. 73, 77–9.
[52] Ibid., p. 73.
[53] Ibid., pp. 76–7.

And yet that idea also could not withstand even mild moral controversy, so that the term *therapeutic abortion* – the standard term in the 1960s – quickly disappeared from American discourse.

The States, *Roe*, and the Politics of Abortion

Critics of *Roe v. Wade* have pinned the blame for the divisive conflict surrounding abortion on that Supreme Court decision. Philip Selznick argues that *Roe v. Wade*, for example, while properly recognizing women's legitimate moral claim to a choice, was too absolutist and thus did not make room for large portions of the American public who have legitimate moral disagreements. His criticism of *Roe* is not in its substance but in its style: ". . . the [Supreme] Court's posture offered little room for compromise or for a spirit of reconciliation."[54] Numerous critics, including now-Justice Ruth Bader Ginsburg, have claimed that *Roe* was too broad and thus unnecessarily invited conflict.[55] Like Selznick, Ginsburg supported women's right to choose abortion, but she argued that the legal claims were too far-reaching and thus responsible for unnecessary conflict.

Mary Ann Glendon,[56] most notably, has made the argument that differences over abortion could best be worked out at the state level. If left to their own devices, she has argued, some states would have retained highly restrictive laws, many would have passed liberalizing, reform laws, and still others would have passed repeal laws. In addition, in practice many of the restrictions would have been "undermined by collusion between doctor and patient, by travel for those who had the means to do so, and by liberal interpretations of what constituted a threat to the life or health of the pregnant woman."[57] And the country would have then avoided polarization over the stunning *Roe* and *Doe* decisions.

---

54 Philip Selznick, *The Moral Commonwealth: Social Theory and the Promise of Community* (Berkeley: University of California Press, 1992), p. 415.

55 Ruth Bader Ginsburg, "Some Thoughts on Autonomy and Equality in Relation to *Roe v. Wade*," *North Carolina Law Review* 63(1985):375–86. Once on the Court, however, Ginsburg has voted to uphold *Roe*.

56 Mary Ann Glendon, *Abortion and Divorce in Western Law: American Failures, European Challenges* (Cambridge, Mass.: Harvard University Press, 1987).

57 Ibid., p. 48.

The meaning of the state-level reforms is not just an academic debate; the view that the Supreme Court abruptly and inappropriately interrupted a process that the states were working out themselves has even appeared in prominent news and public affairs magazines.[58]

On the one hand, such arguments point to an important aspect of discussion of abortion in states that passed reform laws: The discussion did take place within frames that were less divisive. The moral frames, including claims about fundamental rights,[59] that have dominated the abortion debate in the last quarter century are extremely difficult to resolve in any direct fashion. They imply a zero-sum battle in which one side necessarily loses something it considers fundamental and beyond compromise. A medical, humanitarian frame was acceptable to state legislatures because it did not seem to imply such a stark choice.

However, there are a couple of problems with the conclusions Glendon drew. First, as Fung[60] has demonstrated, it is highly questionable that actual access to abortion would have dramatically increased without the *Roe* decision. And so supporters of accessible abortion could not have found the state laws a reasonable compromise; indeed we have seen that even some of the state laws' sponsors were disappointed in the level of access to abortion effected by these laws and so came out in favor of repeal within a couple of years.

The history of state abortion laws, traced in this and the previous chapter, raises a second problem: In fact, the state-level reform process had reached its limits by about 1970, that is, before the *Roe* decision. There was so much judicial activity on abortion laws partly because the moral frames that Glendon and others have blamed on *Roe* had gathered enough steam to stymie further state-level legislative initiatives. Glendon's argument implies that the reform law states talked about the various views of abortion and decided on a moderate, mainstream compromise. In fact, they decided on such a course because they did not realize that this position was indeed a compromise; they operated within a medical frame that had largely collapsed by the end of 1970. Typically, they heard brief pro-life appeals and were essentially unaware of the abortion rights perspective. Those states that passed

---

[58] Garrow, *Liberty and Sexuality*, pp. 613–16.
[59] Mary Ann Glendon, *Rights Talk* (New York: Free Press, 1991).
[60] "Making Rights Real." See also Ferree et al., *Shaping Abortion Discourse*, p. 116.

reform laws did so because they did *not* reflect much upon pro-life and pro-choice arguments.

The medical frame, once it encountered strong moral frames, turned out to be something of a paper tiger, indicating that we need to qualify Mohr's comment, quoted earlier, that the reform laws were the product of physicians' grab for market dominance when they were "at the height of their power." As is typically true of framing battles, one cannot predict the outcome simply on the basis of interest group power; certain frames are culturally stronger than others. The medical, humanitarian reform supporting reform laws could not withstand extensive publicity, which would raise the visibility of pro-life and abortion rights sentiments. Under such circumstances, usually reform bills did not pass, and nineteenth-century statutes remained in place. Occasionally the result was a repeal law, typically amid divisive conflict. Thus these repeal laws passed by particularly small voting margins. These debates were unlikely to repeat in a great many more states. How many times could one realistically expect that legislators would be swept up in the moment and risk their political careers on an abortion vote? Presumably even many of the legislators who voted for repeal, when it was such a new issue, did so expecting that repeal was in the process of becoming the acknowledged, mainstream position. From a 1970 vantage point, few probably could have guessed how divisive the abortion controversy would become, and for how many years.

In short, while *Roe* made the conflict even more visible and thus more extensive, discussion of the issue was divided and morally charged by the end of 1970, over two years before *Roe* was issued in January 1973. Highly visible conflicts in large states like New York had helped bring awareness of the conflict to a national level. The state-level reform process had exhausted itself; the compromise positions that Glendon recommends were no longer viable. *Roe* did not *initiate* a period of divided moral sentiment over abortion; it did not serve as a sharp break from the point where state discussions had left off. It was part of a process that the state legislative discussions themselves had largely initiated and, ultimately, could not resolve.

And yet, ironically, the Supreme Court used a reasoning that was in important ways apparently intended to be a compromise: It consciously tried not to be extreme, not to emphasize absolute rights, and not to favor any particular worldview. Arguably, the Court did much of what such critics of *Roe* in fact wanted it to do; and so its actions suggest that a Court compromise *could* not prevent conflict, because it *did* not. The failure of the Court to bound the abortion controversy within a widely acceptable frame demonstrates precisely that such critics are wrong to think that the Court or anyone, by the early 1970s, had the power to make abortion anything but a morally charged controversy. Given how often claims about the need for "judicial restraint" have *Roe* in mind, it is striking how incorrect are the empirical assertions that often form the basis of such a critique of *Roe*.

Abortion Politics and Abortion Law since *Roe v. Wade*

Abortion politics today are beyond the stage of moral vetoes, because *Roe v. Wade* shapes existing abortion law to such a large degree that legislatures participate more at the margins than at the center. Moral vetoes work only on elected legislators who fear strongly alienating part of their constituency. There have been heated and important battles over a number of legislative attempts to challenge parts of the 1973 *Roe* decision; at times even relatively minor attempts at change have been occasions to rally the troops on both sides of the issue. But, while the Supreme Court has allowed states to enact legislation to move elements of abortion law in a more restrictive direction since *Roe*, the core of abortion law remains the *Roe v. Wade* and *Doe v. Bolton* decisions. When it is courts rather than legislatures that have the authority over a particular area of law, there is no moral veto to exercise: The Supreme Court will often consider public opinion but can choose not to. Any *dramatic* change in abortion law will almost certainly come from changes in the makeup of the U.S. Supreme Court rather than through legislative initiative.

Not that legislatures are irrelevant: Among the earlier legislative actions that restricted access to abortion was the Hyde Amendment of 1977,[61] which prohibited the use of federal Medicaid funds to pay for abortions, except to save the life of the pregnant woman. (During

---

[61] Numerous laws that affect access to abortion at the margins but have been important symbolic battles in Congress are too complex to describe here; a clear description is provided by Raymond Tatalovich, *The Politics of Abortion in the United States and Canada* (Armonk, N.Y.: M. E. Sharpe, 1997), esp. pp. 95–9. See also pp. 66–73. For a good summary of the major court decisions through the early 1990s, see Kathryn

most of the presidency of Bill Clinton, 1993–2001, the Hyde Amendment also allowed for exceptions when a woman's health was in danger.) Medicaid is a program involving both federal and state funding that provides health insurance for poor people; in 2000, sixteen states used state funds to provide Medicaid coverage of abortion,[62] and so Medicaid coverage for abortion was unavailable for most abortions in thirty-four states and the District of Columbia.

Among the more important and interesting changes in the nature of abortion politics since 1973 is that it has become divided along party lines, especially at the level of Congress and the presidency.[63] Positions on abortion were not clearly divided by party through the 1970s. Mainstream pro-life organizations still typically see themselves as officially nonsectarian, and there are significant numbers of pro-choice Republicans, including in the U.S. Congress. But, in the 1980s it became increasingly clear that the pro-life cause was more welcome in the Republican Party, largely because the Christian Right became a significant wing of that party. President Ronald Reagan, first elected in 1980 as the Christian Right was becoming a political force, courted and welcomed these cultural conservatives into the party. Pro-choice groups, on the other hand, became important supporters of the Democratic Party.

A number of scholars studying the pro-life movement, such as James Davidson Hunter, Faye Ginsburg, and Keith Cassidy have emphasized, and provided data indicating, that there is ideological diversity within the pro-life movement, including people who would be considered liberal on a number of other issues.[64] Indeed some pro-life advocates, for

---

Ann Farr, "Shaping Policy through Litigation: Abortion Law in the United States," *Crime and Delinquency* 39(1993):167–83.

[62] Stanley K. Henshaw and Lawrence B. Finer, "The Accessibility of Abortion Services in the United States, 2001," *Perspectives on Sexual and Reproductive Health* 35(2003):20, available at the Web site of Alan Guttmacher Institute, http://www.agi-usa.org/pubs/journals/501603.pdf (accessed October 11, 2003).

[63] Michele McKeegan, *Abortion Politics: Mutiny in the Ranks of the Right* (New York: Free Press/Macmillan, 1992); Geoffrey Layman, *The Great Divide: Religious and Cultural Conflicts in American Party Politics* (New York: Columbia University Press, 2001); and John H. Evans, "Have Americans' Attitudes become more Polarized? An Update," *Social Science Quarterly* 84(2003):71–90.

[64] Faye Ginsburg, "Saving America's Souls: Operation Rescue's Crusade against Abortion," pp. 557–88 in *The Fundamentalism Project, vol. 3: Fundamentalisms and the State*, Martin E. Marty and R. Scott Appleby, eds. (Chicago and London: University

instance small groups of pro-life feminists, would deny that a pro-life position should be placed on the right in the political spectrum.[65] I have used the term *pro-life* as a synonym for *antiabortion* (in a common social science approach that movements' self-labels should be accepted unless clearly inaccurate), but Cassidy and Hunter argue, for instance, that such advocates are not simply antiabortion but are truly pro-*life*. For instance, they are also particularly likely to oppose euthanasia.

However, Cassidy acknowledged that pro-life advocates are overall more likely than other Americans to be politically conservative, and Ginsburg noted that pro-life voters tend to be single-issue voters. Hunter, while disagreeing with Cassidy and Ginsburg on other important points, similarly saw pro-life advocates as ultimately having a more conservative worldview. So there may be some political liberals in the pro-life movement, but fewer than among Americans as a whole. Given also that pro-life voters to a great degree base their votes on abortion to the exclusion of other issues, in the end, they are ultimately a force for political conservatism and a Republican voting base.

President Reagan, the Republican president who first allied with the pro-life movement, gave symbolic and very public encouragement to the pro-life cause but delivered almost nothing in terms of legislative victories. For instance, he voiced clear approval for a constitutional amendment against abortion but did nothing that would make such an amendment happen. However, Reagan and his successor, George H. W. Bush (who had been Reagan's vice president and then served one term as president, from January 1989 to January 1993), did move federal policy in a pro-life direction. Both used federal funds and federal

of Chicago Press, 1993); Keith Cassidy, "The Right to Life Movement: Sources, Development, and Strategies," pp. 128–59 in *The Politics of Abortion and Birth Control in Historical Perspective*, Donald T. Critchlow, ed. (University Park, Pa.: Pennsylvania State University Press, 1996); James Davison Hunter, "What Americans Really Think about Abortion," *First Things* 24(1992):13–21.

[65] See, e.g., Sidney Callahan, "Abortion and the Sexual Agenda: A Case for Prolife Feminism," pp. 128–40 in *Abortion and Catholicism: The American Debate*, Patricia Beattie Jung and Thomas A. Shannon, eds. (New York: Crossroad, 1988); Lisa Sowle Cahill, "Abortion, Autonomy, and Community," pp. 85–97 in *Abortion and Catholicism*; and Denise Lardner Carmody, *The Double Cross: Ordination, Abortion, and Catholic Feminism* (New York: Crossroad, 1986).

agencies to promote the pro-life agenda. For instance, Reagan instituted in 1987 the "gag rule," mandating that family planning clinics
that received federal funding could not discuss abortion with patients.
Pro-choice advocates argued that this was interference with physicians'
medical obligations and with women's rights. Since that time, the gag
rule has been in effect during Republican presidencies but was nullified during Clinton's Democratic presidency (1993–2001). The second
President Bush, who took office in January 2001, reinstated the gag
rule.[66]

More important advancement of the pro-life cause has come as a
result of Republican Supreme Court appointments, which gradually
moved the Court to the right.[67] Again, any dramatic change in abortion
law can come only with the Supreme Court's approval.

The vote in favor of *Roe* was seven to two. But as a result of the
appointment of new justices, the majority in favor of preserving *Roe*
now stands at five to four. One of those five, Sandra Day O'Connor
(appointed by President Reagan), has voted for restrictions on abortion
rights and has indicated she would have voted against *Roe* if she had
been on the Court in 1973. But she also argues that it is important that
the Court uphold existing precedent and not change constitutional
interpretations simply because of a personnel change on the Court.
Otherwise, in her view, the Court loses its legitimacy and becomes
merely a partisan political institution.

Since 1973, the central components of *Roe v. Wade* (and *Doe v.
Bolton*[68]) have for the most part been upheld, but it is also the case
that the legal status of abortion is less secure now than it was in 1973.

---

[66] A good description of President Reagan's use of the federal bureaucracy to promote
the pro-life cause is Karen O'Connor, *No Neutral Ground? Abortion Politics in an Age
of Absolutes* (Boulder, Col.: Westview, 1996), pp. 88–95.

[67] One of George H. W. Bush's appointments, Clarence Thomas, is one of the two most
conservative justices now on the Court, including on abortion issues. Thomas replaced
one of the most liberal justices of recent decades, Thurgood Marshall. However, it
has turned out that the other appointment of George Bush, Sr., namely, David Souter,
whose views on many issues were not well known when he was nominated, votes
mainly with the liberals on the Court, again including on abortion cases. Overall,
the Court became more conservative on abortion as a result of Reagan and Bush
appointments, but not as conservative as pro-life advocates would have liked.

[68] As I noted earlier, I use the standard shorthand of mentioning only *Roe v. Wade* to
refer to the 1973 U.S. Supreme Court decision on abortion, but the decision really
was on a pair of cases, *Roe v. Wade* and *Doe v. Bolton*.

In 1989, in *Webster v. Reproductive Health Services,*[69] the Supreme Court ruled that states, if they so chose, could prohibit abortions in public hospitals (thus requiring that abortions take place only at privately owned facilities) and could require that physicians check for viability of the fetus at twenty weeks. *Roe* had explicitly assumed that viability outside the womb was typically at about 28 weeks, though possibly as early as twenty-four weeks; it was only after viability that the state's interest in protecting the fetus outweighed the woman's privacy rights (but not her and her doctor's interest in protecting her health). And so *Webster* implied that the Court might accept that states could restrict access to abortion, except when a woman's health was in danger, starting about halfway through the pregnancy, instead of after about six or seven months. To some Americans, it would make sense that improving medical technology would move viability earlier into the pregnancy, so that this part of *Webster* was consistent with the spirit of *Roe*. But to pro-choice advocates, Webster implied a whittling away at the right to privacy through which *Roe* originally gave women access to abortion fairly freely in the first two trimesters.

Before going on, I should note that keeping track of the meaning and implications of these decisions can be confusing if one forgets that many Supreme Court decisions, including most on abortion, set or revise *the range* of what is constitutional for states to legislate, and what factors states must consider (such as women's health, viability of the fetus, and so forth), *rather than mandate specific laws or policies* that states must institute. Further, the Supreme Court cannot rule on abortion matters unless it has before it a case involving a specific law, sometimes a federal law but more typically a state law. Often the state law is meant quite directly as a challenge to existing precedents and thus is passed in hopes that the Court will use approval of the law as a vehicle to hem in *Roe*. Thus, for instance, *Webster* upheld the restrictions of a Missouri law and so implicitly allowed other states also to institute such restrictions, including restrictions that seemed inconsistent with *Roe*. But *Webster* does not mandate that states actually institute such restrictions.

The 1992 *Casey* decision (i.e., *Planned Parenthood of Southeast Pennsylvania v. Casey*[70]) was a clear signal of the Court's moving to

---

[69] 492 U.S. 490 (1989).
[70] 505 U.S. 833 (1992).

the right, as the Court allowed new restrictions that it had rejected in a 1986 decision, *Thornburgh v. American College of Obstetricians and Gynecologists.*[71] The *Casey* decision upheld a Pennsylvania state law that required a twenty-four-hour waiting period between a woman's formally recorded decision to have an abortion and the abortion itself. It also required counseling of the woman, including the presentation of pamphlets and other information about the procedure that were written from an antiabortion perspective. And the Court upheld the portion of the Pennsylvania law that required doctors to keep records of each abortion and submit those records to the state, which could then make them available to the public. In *Casey,* however, the Court rejected requirements that a married woman obtain her husband's approval before having an abortion and for the most part rejected requiring proof that a woman had notified her husband (whether he approved or not).

All of these central decisions were decided by five to four votes, reflecting a Court very divided on the issue of abortion. Retirement of a single justice – especially if a justice in favor of upholding *Roe* retires when Republicans control the White House and the Senate (which must approve Supreme Court nominations) – could be enough to result in reversal of much of *Roe.*

As things stand, these Court decisions, and others, have also formally lowered the bar on what evidence and arguments are sufficient to justify restrictions on a woman's obtaining an abortion. In effect the Court has changed the burden of proof: The Court majority now requires proof that a restriction fundamentally violates *Roe* before *rejecting* the restriction, instead of requiring proof that a restriction is clearly compatible with *Roe* before *approving* it. (In legal terms, the Court has moved away from a "strict scrutiny" standard – which implies that the Court is suspicious of restrictions until proven otherwise – to the requirement instead that any given restriction not be an "undue burden," that is, not so strong that it substantially undermines rights.)

Other Supreme Court cases have allowed states to require parental notification before minors have an abortion, as long as there is some opportunity for such pregnant minors to make a case to a judge why

---

[71] 476 U.S. 747 (1986).

special circumstances (e.g., an abusive home) merit nullification of that requirement. Pro-life forces have been glad the Court has moved a bit away from *Roe* but also are very disappointed that the Court has not overturned *Roe*. Pro-choice forces have of course been very nervous about the direction of the Supreme Court, although they also have been relieved that *Roe*, though circumscribed, still survives. The pro-choice movement also had an unexpectedly strong victory in a 1994 case, in which the court unanimously agreed that a law originally intended to prosecute organized crime could be used against militant pro-life organizations who tried to close down legal abortion clinics.[72] That is, an antiracketeering statute used to prosecute conspiracy to use illegal means to interfere with a legal business, in the Court's view, also allowed for lawsuits against militant pro-life groups who attempted to close down abortion clinics via intimidation, violence, and other illegal means. Central to the case seemed to be that the antiracketeering statute did not require that the motive for conspiracy be economic gain. Organized crime used such methods to extort money, while militant pro-life groups were driven by ideological commitments.

This lawsuit ultimately was a response to the fact that the pro-life movement developed a more militant face starting in the 1980s, especially in the late 1980s and early 1990s. Violence against abortion clinics has waxed and waned, with spikes during the mid-1980s, late 1980s through early 1990s, and the first years of the new century. One of the central reasons was the beginning of more militant pro-life organizations and activists starting in the early 1980s but especially with the founding of Operation Rescue in late 1987. Operation Rescue was a new phase in pro-life politics, a militant, well-organized effort to use civil disobedience and other interference with the daily operations of abortion clinics, in the hope of drawing attention to what was seen as the evils of abortion and of shutting the clinics down. Operation Rescue – by far the largest and most significant of a number of militant pro-life groups – took the view that more standard pro-life methods of picketing, lobbying, and holding prayer vigils were ineffective and did not adequately respond to the reality of one and a half million murders through abortion annually in the United States. (In more recent

---

[72] In *National Organization for Women v. Scheidler* (510 U.S. 249 [1994]).

years, the number of abortions annually in the United States has fallen to about 1.2 million per year.) Operation Rescue and the pro-choice National Abortion Federation agree that, as a result of Operation Rescue's tactics, the number of arrests at abortion clinics went up dramatically in the late 1980s. Operation Rescue reported 35,000 arrests in its first three years of existence, and the National Abortion Federation reported that arrests went up during that period from perhaps the low hundreds to over 10,000 a year nationally.[73] (The statistics are not broken down by type of offense. Some of the arrests undoubtedly were linked to violent protests, and more to harassing and intimidating clinic staff and women obtaining abortions. But most were probably the result of protestors blocking clinic entrances.) Operation Rescue's position was that it condemned acts such as murdering doctors performing abortions, but that such a murder was no more heinous than the murder committed in every single abortion. Pro-choice activists saw such statements as implicitly condoning and inciting the murder of such doctors.[74]

Operation Rescue's methods included targeting particular cities and concentrating all its resources for several weeks or months on closing down abortion in that city. Perhaps because it is difficult to sustain the kind of committed mobilization – with heavy costs, including many arrests – that was characteristic of Operation Rescue, it became less of a presence after a few years, so that in the mid- to late 1990s the annual number of arrests at abortion clinics was much, much lower than it had been in the late 1980s and early 1990s.

Operation Rescue, though including some conservative Catholics, primarily involved conservative evangelical Protestants. It is almost certainly no accident that Operation Rescue emerged at a time the Christian Right was attempting to influence U.S. politics, as both draw

---

[73] Ginsburg, "Saving America's Souls," information on arrests at p. 557; National Abortion Federation, "NAF Violence and Disruption Statistics," as of June 30, 2003, at http://www.prochoice.org/Violence/Statistics/stats.pdf (accessed October 8, 2003). On militance in the pro-life movement, see also O'Connor, *No Neutral Ground?*, pp. 102–9, 137–8; and Carol J. C. Maxwell, *Pro-life Activists in America: Meaning, Motivation, and Direct Action* (Cambridge and New York: Cambridge University Press, 2002).

[74] See, e.g., Janette Kenner Muir, "Hating for Life: Rhetorical Extremism and Abortion Clinic Violence," pp. 163–95 in *Hate Speech*, Rita Kirk Whillock and David Slayden, eds. (Thousand Oaks, Calif.: Sage, 1995), esp. pp. 178–80.

primarily from the same pool of Americans, that is, white evangelical Protestants. In the late 1970s and 1980s, the dominant Christian Right organization was the Moral Majority, founded by Rev. Jerry Falwell, and in the 1990s it was the Christian Coalition, led by Rev. Pat Robertson and Ralph Reed. Somewhere between about a fifth and a quarter of Americans identify in some way with evangelical Christianity (and opinion surveys suggest a minority of those, but still millions of evangelicals, explicitly support the Christian Right). Evangelical Christianity is a religious tradition that historically has more often withdrawn into private religious expression but which has had a few periods of strong political involvement. While the typical evangelical Protestant even today does not see a strong relationship between religion and politics, it is the case that those involved in the Christian Right have been primarily white evangelical Protestants. Operation Rescue did however pursue different tactics than Christian Right organizations like the Moral Majority and the Christian Coalition; the latter organizations worked within legal political bounds and were sometimes criticized by Operation Rescue for not being militant enough.

The Christian Right emphasizes the importance of conservative religion in public life and takes a very conservative line on sexual and reproductive matters, including condemnation of homosexuality and abortion and very critical views of liberal approaches to sex education and sexual morality. The mobilization of the Christian Right surely contributed to the vehemence felt by hard-core opponents of President Bill Clinton. Political moderates and liberals had trouble understanding the venom directed at Clinton, especially as his economic and welfare policies were noticeably more conservative than those of Democratic leaders in the 1960s and 1970s. As Randall Terry, founder of Operation Rescue, stated after Clinton was first elected, "Our worst political nightmare has come upon us a pro-baby killing, pro-sodomite, pass-out-condoms-in-school President."[75]

During the Clinton presidency, there were legislative efforts on behalf of the pro-choice cause, which had the ability to take offensive as the result of the murders of physicians who worked at abortion clinics. The Freedom of Access to Clinic Entrances (FACE) Act passed in

---

[75] Quoted in ibid., p. 164. The (sparse) punctuation is faithful to Muir's quotation.

1994; it made blocking entrances to abortion clinics and harassment or violence directed at women seeking care at such clinics a federal crime. During the Clinton Administration there were also introduced into Congress bills to write the content of *Roe* into statute law, so that even if the Supreme Court overturned *Roe*, a federal law would uphold the abortion rights pronounced in *Roe*. (Or so was the hope; but if the Court ruled that only the states had authority over such matters, then any such federal law would be nullified along with *Roe*.) It is also highly significant that President Clinton made two Supreme Court appointments, of justices who are sure not to vote to overturn *Roe v. Wade*.

A high-profile legislative battle has taken place a number of times in recent years over the legal status of what the pro-life side calls "partial birth abortion" and the pro-choice side calls "intact dilation and extraction." This late-term abortion procedure, used for only about 1.5 percent of abortions overall, is more easily condemned because removal of the fetus seems gestationally and medically more similar to birth than are early-term abortions, which do not involve part of the fetus's intact body being extracted from the woman as part of the abortion procedure. Pro-life activists portray the next step in the procedure as the deliberate crushing of a baby's skull.[76] It is clear that this rare pro-life legislative success in Congress was possible because it makes enough legislators associate abortion with babies, leading even some otherwise consistently pro-choice members of Congress to vote for the ban.[77] That the pro-life side has won the framing battle is indicated by the fact that "partial birth abortion" is a much better known term than is "intact dilation and extraction." Congress passed a ban on this procedure in 1996 but it was vetoed by Democratic President Clinton. The ban was passed again in 2003, and President George W. Bush signed the bill into law. Although this measure drew more Democratic support than most proposals supported by the pro-life movement, it was no accident that the bill became law when Republicans had majorities in both houses of Congress and a Republican occupied the White House.

[76] Tatalovich, *The Politics of Abortion in the United States and Canada*, p. 99.
[77] See Sheryl Gay Stolberg, "Abortion Vote Leaves Many in the Senate Conflicted," *New York Times*, October 23, 2003.

In 2000, in *Stenberg v. Carhart*,[78] the Supreme Court overturned Nebraska's law against this procedure (which the Nebraska law called "partial birth abortion"), in a five to four decision. The central reasoning was that, while the Nebraska law did allow the procedure to save the *life* of the woman, otherwise there was no exception for the health needs of the pregnant woman, an exception that would seem to be mandated by *Roe v. Wade*. Assuming the Supreme Court accepts the inevitable court challenge, the Court can uphold the new federal statute, then, only by reversing itself and chipping away at *Roe* (which could happen if, for instance, by that time a justice wanting to overturn *Roe* replaces a justice who has upheld *Roe*). The federal statute explicitly asserts that this particular procedure is never medically necessary and that alternative procedures are available when there is a health threat. Although it is at least conceivable that the Court could accept this argument and thus claim that endorsing the federal statute is consistent with the health exception mandated by *Roe* (by allowing for alternative procedures for late-term abortions), it would still be chipping away at related aspects of *Roe v. Wade* and *Doe v. Bolton*. This is the case because those cases strongly upheld the autonomy and competence of physicians to make decisions over what measures are medically appropriate.

These judicial and legislative developments since *Roe* have made little impact on the incompatible frames that to a great extent define the contemporary abortion debate. In the current context, even legislative efforts that one side strongly opposes, for instance, can be framed as reasonable modifications rather than dramatic statements on the fundamental issues of the morality or legal status of abortion. For instance, FACE could be defended as a means for people engaged in a legal practice to avoid harassment and danger, especially in the context in which it was quite plausible to argue that close physical proximity of protestors and clinic workers increased the chances of additional violence. And the opposition to partial birth abortion/intact dilation and extraction can be painted as opposition to such an extreme procedure (and thus implicitly not necessarily typical of abortions) that it was unacceptable; that is precisely why some otherwise pro-choice

[78] 539 U.S. 914 (2000).

legislators voted for it. Of course many of the opponents of (what they call) partial birth abortion oppose all abortions, but they are unable to engage in a full, effective legislative debate while *Roe* is in effect. (But without *Roe*, moral vetoes would make any legislative action difficult anyway.)

For those heavily invested in the abortion issue, even changes at the margins of the national debate can be immensely important. In that sense, I do not want to downplay the importance of any of the judicial or statutory changes noted above. It matters a great deal to both pro-life militants and clinic workers, for instance, whether protestors are allowed to follow those workers from the parking lot to the clinic loudly protesting their view that the worker is engaged in murder. It matters a great deal to those who see abortion as a right and those who see abortion as murder whether access to abortion changes at all. But, in the big picture historically, access to legal abortion is much more similar to where it was in 1973 than it is different. There was more change between 1966 and 1970 than there has been since *Roe*.

Still, access to abortion in practice has been reduced since the 1970s. As long as *Roe* stays in effect, those who want to keep abortion accessible of course have the strong advantage of a Supreme Court precedent on their side, although the existence of *Roe* is also a strong motivating agent for the pro-life side. But the greatest success the pro-life side has had is probably not the result of legal changes but of the legal protests typical of the majority of pro-life activists and the intimidation and threats characteristic of a minority of protestors. The pro-life movement has made no progress on the central goal of obtaining a constitutional amendment to outlaw abortion; on the alternative, having the U.S. Supreme Court reverse itself on *Roe v. Wade*, so far it has made at most incremental progress. But it appears to have had some success driving medical personnel out of the practice of abortion: since 1973, actual access to abortion has probably been affected less by legal changes than by the fact that working in an abortion clinic can require very strong commitment, given protests, threats, and sometimes mortal danger. The militance of groups like Operation Rescue probably was a significant reason that, between 1982 and 2001, surveys indicate there was a thirty-seven percent drop in the number of clinics or other sites where abortion was available. The number of U.S. counties without an abortion provider rose from seventy-seven percent in 1978 to eighty-six percent in 1996 and seems to have held steady since that time. In interpreting the meaning of these statistics, we must remember that some proportion of those counties are so sparsely populated that one would expect few medical facilities of any kind; thus rural states are particularly likely to have many counties without abortion clinics. But the difference also reflects that clinics in rural areas are probably more easily targeted by disruptive protests and cannot draw on metropolitan resources for support. And so it is striking that only three percent of counties outside a metropolitan area have an abortion provider.[79]

It is likely that access is most restricted for poor women living in rural areas and in states that require in-person counseling and/or a waiting period. Although there is variety among states within a given region, in general these factors most affect access in the upper Midwest and the South. The burden of restrictions in access, then, falls disproportionately on a minority of women who seek an abortion. Fewer than ten percent of women nationally travel more than 100 miles to a clinic; but if one lives in a state with a twenty-four-hour waiting period before an abortion (allowed since *Casey*), and the only abortion clinic is 200 miles away, attending to the procedure would involve two or three days (which are days away from work and/or family) and additional expenses of lodging and so forth. (For instance, in the early and mid-1990s, North Dakota and South Dakota had one abortion clinic each; in 2000 each had two.) In that case, the Hyde Amendment, which prohibits federal Medicaid funds paying for abortions in most cases, might be one obstacle but probably not the biggest. A first-trimester abortion

---

[79] Stanley K. Henshaw and Lawrence B. Finer, "Abortion Incidences and Services in the United States in 2000," *Perspectives on Sexual and Reproductive Health* 35(2003):6, 9–11, 14, available at the Web site of Alan Guttmacher Institute, http://www.agi-usa.org/pubs/journals/3500603.pdf (accessed October 10, 2003); Henshaw and Finer, "The Accessibility of Abortion Services in the United States, 2001." It is difficult to know if there is a causal relationship, and if so how strong and in what direction, between the drop in the number of abortions performed in recent years and the drop in the number of abortion providers. For instance, at least partly relevant is that, in recent years, there has been a drop in teenage sexual activity and also an increase in teenagers' effective use of contraceptives ("Abortion Incidences and Services in the United States in 2000," pp. 6, 10).

typically costs about $400, not an irrelevant sum, as evidence suggests the majority of abortions are paid for not by medical insurance but out of pocket.[80] Still, for women in rural areas, distance and a waiting period could easily be bigger factors. (It is a standard pro-life claim that abortion doctors are making enormous profits off the suffering of women, but abortion is quite inexpensive as medical procedures go and thus an unlikely source of profiteering. Again, given the controversy and the obstacles, those who devote a great deal of time and effort to the abortion issue – including clinic workers, pro-life activists, and so forth – must have a very strong belief that what they are doing is worthwhile.)

Still, the restrictions on access that have resulted from legal changes and the closing of clinics since *Roe* is a much smaller story than *Roe* itself. For instance, the new ban on partial birth abortion will fit into the pattern of affecting abortion practice mostly at the margins: many of the existing post-*Roe* restrictions allowed as a result of *Webster* and *Casey* affect abortions during the second and third trimesters of pregnancy, but it has long been the case that nearly ninety percent of abortions occur during the first trimester.[81] Living in a rural versus an urban area does today mean a significant difference in access to legal abortion, but that difference pales in comparison to the difference between women in their child-bearing years before *Roe* versus after *Roe*. And in the future the big divide may be whether a woman is of child-bearing years now or in a few years, if a Republican president appoints a couple of new Supreme Court justices willing to overturn *Roe*.[82]

---

[80] Henshaw and Finer, "Abortion Incidences and Services in the United States in 2000," p. 10, 14; Henshaw and Finer, "The Accessibility of Abortion Services in the United States, 2001," pp. 18–20, 23.

[81] Alan Guttmacher Institute, "Trends in Abortion in the United States, 1973–2000" (January 2003), at http://www.agi-usa.org/pubs/trends.ppt (accessed October 10, 2003).

[82] There is important research that indicates that public opinion on abortion in a given state significantly affects practical access to abortion (e.g., whether and how aggressively a state will take advantage of the restrictions allowed by *Webster* and *Casey*): Matthew E. Wetstein, *Abortion Rates in the United States: The Influence of Opinion and Policy* (Albany: State University of New York Press, 1996). But this is true if one compares *contemporary* access to abortion, that is, when almost all abortion that actually takes place is legal. Before 1970 (when a few states passed repeal laws), and probably

Abortion, Medicine, and the Contemporary Abortion Debate

An interesting aspect of the contemporary American polarization over abortion since about 1970 is that, in other contexts, medical frames have survived and appear to have helped contain conflict over abortion. As we have seen, if we actually count the years, some version of a medical frame – where physicians' professional judgments are assumed to be a sensible prerequisite for legal abortion – has been the dominant one within the United States over the last 150 years. And if we compare across space as well as time, we can see, for example, that while the dynamics of the politics of abortion before World War II in Britain did not differ greatly from that in the United States, after the establishment of the National Health Service – and especially after the late 1960s – there is clear divergence. The medical establishment never lost control of the issue in Britain: The National Health Service institutionalized a system in which abortion was available on a restricted basis, with physicians' approval required. The result has been that in Britain, abortion has never been as accessible as it was in the United States in the years immediately after *Roe v. Wade*. However, it is also the case that Britain has not continually revisited the legal status of abortion in the way the U.S. Supreme Court has, and so in Britain the government gives less of a message that abortion policy is potentially forever up for grabs.

The actual delivery of abortion services also differs. In Britain access to legal abortion does not depend on one's economic circumstances as it could for some Americans, since all British citizens have access to medical care that is low-cost or free (depending on the procedure). Because Britain is a considerably more densely populated country, distance to medical facilities would not be so great as in parts of the United States. Finally, it appears that because the U.S. health care system is primarily a system of private enterprise, there was not much of a constituency for retaining the medical frame, outside of the medical industry itself. In Western Europe, however, it is more difficult to extract abortion from one's view of the national health care system, and so it appears

---

until 1973 (the year of *Roe*), most abortions that took place were illegal or at least of dubious legality.

to be less likely that abortion will be isolated as an issue of focused controversy.[83]

The loss of the medical frame in the United States, sociologically speaking, has then been a somewhat atypical situation, compared to the previous history of abortion in the United States, and to the continuing medicalization of abortion in western Europe. Actual access varies in Europe, but typically there is a system of physicians serving as gatekeepers and having at least formally to justify abortion according to accepted criteria. In the United States, with the loss of the medical frame, the debate came to center around mutually exclusive moral claims.[84] In practice institutionalizing the practice of abortion in a way that leaves unsettled the central moral questions may ultimately be conducive to social peace around the issue.

[83] See, e.g., Barbara Brookes, *Abortion in England, 1900–1967* (London: Croom Helm, 1988); Glendon, *Abortion and Divorce in Western Law*. See also the excellent discussion of British versus American feminist attitudes toward health provision in Mary C. Wright, "Separate or Equal? Integration and Separatism within Feminist Health Care Provision in the United States and England" (Undergraduate Senior Thesis, Dept. of Sociology, Princeton University, 1993). Wright found that for British feminists to question the medicalization of abortion would have meant to question health access via the National Health Service, whereas British feminist movements had generally been defending socialized medicine. Indeed they had attempted to involve the National Health Service in more services for women, exactly what the 1967 law provided.

[84] Cf. Glendon, ibid., and *Rights Talk: The Impoverishment of Political Discourse* (New York: Free Press, 1991); and Tribe, *Abortion: The Clash of Absolutes*.

7

Looking Back: Limiting Frames, Moral Vetoes, and Cultural Pluralism

Introduction

In the opening chapter, I used the metaphor of a conversation to describe the political and social dynamics of reproductive politics in the twentieth-century United States. In this final chapter, I want to explore that metaphor further, in order to draw out the theoretical implications. For most of the book so far, I have attempted to present the discussion in a way that is accessible to a variety of readers. That should be true of much of this final chapter as well, especially the beginning of the chapter. But, as the chapter proceeds, it will address more explicitly important theoretical debates within sociology, because those debates have a great deal to tell us about the history of American reproductive politics. Sociology's theoretical debates are ideally always strongly linked to empirical understanding, and so even the theoretical discussion will make continual reference back to that history.

Let me begin by saying a little more about the conversation metaphor. First, I should qualify its use: I mean "conversation" indeed as a metaphor, to indicate any time that people are involved in debate or discussion of a social issue. I do not mean to say literally that their "conversation," that is, their actual speaking to each other, is the only aspect worth examining. Indeed, by saying that people are engaged in a conversation, I mean they are *sociologically and politically* engaged: I mean there are groups of people who identify the issue as relevant to them and think the issue is a worthwhile political concern. I do not, for example, mean to refer to what is often called "conversation analysis" or "discourse analysis," modes of analysis heavily influenced by literary theory and primarily focusing on the actual words, and even grammatical structure, of statements within a discussion. While my own analysis very much emphasizes attempting to uncover what different speakers meant when they used particular terms, I would argue that one cannot possibly do this only by looking at the words themselves, in isolation from the conditions of life in which those words were spoken – economically, politically, culturally, and so forth. I see no reason to separate analysis of social organization from analysis of the debates and controversies that emerge within political rhetoric about that social organization.

Within such a sociological perspective, then, I have argued that we can understand much of reproductive politics in terms of who is involved in the conversation, and why they became involved in the conversation in the first place. Conversations can be civil and polite; they can be heated. Sometimes people who might in fact have some shared concerns are not engaged in conversation at all, either because they live socially or geographically apart, or because a previous conversation became so heated that it ended as a shouting match and with refusal to listen further. Thus the conversation essentially ends.

Within this chapter I want to explore why different groups would engage in conversations about reproductive politics, why they came to the conversation, and how that has affected the history of American debate over contraception and abortion. I also want to explore how important it is to examine who is left out of a conversation (especially in cases where a group is marginal to the political process and so has little voice), what happens when new groups enter an existing conversation, and why moral vetoes are particularly likely to result in the end of previous conversations. Theoretically, I want to make the case that there are predictable patterns why some political debates (a form of conversation) involve moral vetoes and others limiting frames. I also want to make the case that limiting frames can take two basic forms. In one, a frame works to limit the agenda of debate because it fits well with prevailing cultural assumptions. Such frames are to be expected as commonplace – most political debates are not going to interrogate the fundamentals of our culture. But that does mean that the prevailing cultural assumptions can at times include negative views of groups excluded from active participation in the polity, views implicitly built into the frame. However, a second type of limiting frame is more hopeful: This type of limiting frame builds upon and can help extend an actual pluralism by legitimating social arrangements that make it very difficult to come to a final resolution on some topic of potential dispute. That is, social arrangements are institutionalized in a way that allows for a stable moral pluralism, not requiring the suppression of a range of opinion in cases where there is no single moral vision in the society.

Along the way, I want to make the case that an understanding of the dynamics by which limiting frames and moral vetoes emerge requires a reorientation in how we think about social movements and social order. Recent sociological work, for instance by Belinda Robnet and Jo Reger,[1] points the way toward greater emphasis theoretically on the fact of social diversity as a central and dynamic factor in the construction of solidarity and collective identity within social movements. I argue that emphasizing the diversity not only in social movements, but also in society in general, allows us to account for the importance of framing in both the dynamics of social movements and in our understanding of the cultural bases of social order.

More specifically, within the study of social movements, this focus on diversity allows us to build upon the important developments within frame analysis (as applied to the study of social movements) by placing at the center a focus on the question how certain frames build a bridge across diverse constituencies that come at an issue from different perspectives. This focus on diversity also helps us move beyond one reading of Durkheimian social theory, a reading that equates social order with cultural consensus. This is by far the dominant theory of the cultural bases of social order; even within sociological analyses of politics and society that are not primarily Durkheimian, it is so easy to move in that direction when the question of the cultural bases of social order emerges. I argue that on some important questions,

---

[1] Robnett, "External Political Change, Collective Identities, and Participation in Social Movement Organizations," pp. 266–85 in *Social Movements: Identity, Culture, and the State*, David S. Meyer, Nancy Whittier, and Belinda Robnett, eds. (Oxford and New York: Oxford University Press, 2002); Reger, "More Than One Feminism: Organizational Structure and the Construction of Collective Identity," pp. 171–84 in *Social Movements*.

Durkheimian approaches could not be more wrong: That is, in a nut-shell, Durkheimian approaches call for a supposed return to an encom-passing, common value system that could not exist in a diverse society such as the United States. And because they have diagnosed the prob-lem wrong, Durkheimians call for a solution that would backfire: That is, the attempt to push a single moral agenda, when there is a reality of great moral diversity in a society, actually increases the possibility of moral vetoes and tense political stalemates and thus leads to the moral division that Durkheimians decry. I argue, on the contrary, that the institutionalization of the second type of limiting frames – that is, frames that institutionalize an acceptance of cultural diversity and thus specifically acknowledge that we will *not* pretend that it is possible to erase cultural diversity (including moral disagreements) – is essential to social order in a diverse society.

Political Debate and Social Change as Conversations: Focusing on Diversity

Two Types of Conversations: A Metaphor

Imagine two groups of people engaged in separate conversation at some social gathering, say a wedding reception. Each group consists of about three or four people. The first group is quite cliquish; the indi-viduals already know each other well and have a considerable history of comradery and insider language (e.g., jokes that outsiders would not understand). They have a lively time; they feel strong connections with each other.

Others may at first be drawn to this group, given the very lively con-versation. However, the clique is not interested in admitting outsiders into its conversation; they continue their insider discussion, ignoring those who have no history of friendship within the group. Perhaps the clique, at its worst, regularly deprecates some people it excludes. Even without such explicit deprecation, however, outsiders who attempt to join the conversation quickly feel excluded and wander away. Perhaps they come resent the clique and resolve never to act the way they do, or at least to stick with people like themselves so as to avoid feeling so much like an outsider.

Then there is another group of three or four who are not so exclusive; instead they attempt to make everyone feel comfortable and engage everyone in a common conversation. Most likely, this group will be more diverse, in some way, than the clique, by the mere fact that any random wedding guest is welcome to join in the conversation and thus become part of the group. Conversation may be a little more difficult in this group, because at first there is little or no obvious common history, and the attempt to include all comers can mean abrupt changes in conversation whenever the group enlarges. The inclusiveness of the group necessarily limits what the individuals, collectively, can discuss. They will probably avoid controversial topics and engage in discussion that members of the clique (or perhaps even members of this second, more inclusive group) would find banal. There are a limited number of available topics that can include even three or four strangers, and a good number of topics that only one or two has an interest in discussing. There are even some issues that might be of interest to most of the discussants except one or two, so that the presence of each individual makes a difference in the conversation. Thus, for example, if one is to include a newcomer in the conversation, it may be necessary to change the conversation abruptly and find a new, inclusive topic, perhaps by asking directly, "What brings you here?" or, "Do you know the bride or the groom?" Still, the group will likely discover that many of them have something in common. As they were invited to the same wedding, they probably are involved in some of the same social networks, that is, they learn that they in fact have some mutual friends or acquaintances. A few might even discover that they are distantly related.

If the group continues to grow, however, as more people attempt to join the conversation, it may become increasingly difficult to find a truly inclusive topic. A general feeling of welcome and friendliness prevails, but smaller groups break off from the larger group and start their own, new conversations. It is here that the conversations may be a little more personal, a little more lively (because they do not need to be quite so inclusive and polite). A few of these smaller conversations probably build upon the fact that some of the people who had been strangers find that they have mutual friends or common interests. But the context also allows for conversations built precisely on the diversity that may exist in the group: one person learns about an interesting profession, or place, or political topic, of which she had previously been ignorant and thus find this new acquaintance interesting company.

Such an encounter is less likely among those who remain in the orbit of the clique.

While the large, fully inclusive group is thus not enough to hold everyone's attention indefinitely, the participants nevertheless will probably generally have a good feeling about this original, larger group of discussants. That may be especially true of those who felt rebuffed by the clique (which has remained a close group of just three or four people). And that is true even though the larger groups' conversation had clear limitations, so that most participants eventually decided to break down into smaller groups that could involve more in-depth conversations.

In many ways, the dynamics of such conversations give us a model for what might happen in political debates and in society as a whole.

First, if one focuses only on an intense history of common perspectives and common experiences, it can be difficult or impossible to reach out and win over other people. That is, the cliquish group maintains close bonds and has a long history tying its members together. But that intensity includes a process of isolating themselves from others, and little likelihood of discovering new bases for social connections. The more inclusive group as a whole will never have the common history and inside jokes of the clique, but it has considerably less trouble welcoming newcomers. Even when the newcomers ultimately break off into their own conversations, knowing they will never have an intense experience or live much of their lives in such a loose grouping, they may retain a certain loyalty to the more inclusive group. And certainly anyone who approached both the clique and the large, inclusive group feels better about the latter.

Second, it would be a good bet that any two members of the clique are likely to feel close to each other far into the future. With the large, inclusive group, that is considerably less likely. But the large group is not necessarily a purely ephemeral and superficial phenomenon. Imagine that the next week, or at another wedding months later, a couple of participants in the larger, inclusive group run into each other. Each recognizes a friendly face and they strike up a new conversation. In most cases, the two will never become fast friends, but after a few such encounters the face looks less like that of a stranger, even if conversations remain at the level of polite small talk. Furthermore, not often, but occasionally, these kinds of interactions do lead to new friendships, that is, new social bonds. (There is e.g. the folk wisdom that a wedding is a good place to meet a potential partner.) And so, although the large inclusive group does not itself have intensive, deep social bonds, such inclusive interactions ultimately do produce new social bonds. Furthermore, it is only when we encounter the unfamiliar that we can find the type of friend or associate we have never known before, the kind who gives us insight into a part of life or of society about which we would otherwise remain ignorant. In any single loose grouping of people, we are unlikely to make such connections; but if we have numerous such encounters, ultimately we are likely to meet people different from those we usually encounter, people who intrigue us precisely because they are different.

If, at a social gathering, we do find that close friends are present, most of us will probably immediately gather with those friends rather than enter a polite, inclusive discussion among strangers. Thus, it is a common experience at weddings that the groom's side never really gets to know the bride's side. But, when something is new and unfamiliar, when we must necessarily talk to strangers (because, e.g., we find ourselves with children at the same school), the dynamic of the large, inclusive group is probably what most of us would like to find.

The history of reproductive politics demonstrates that a social movement with a moral worldview is like the clique, and that social movements (as well as political institutions) that build broad coalitions are more like the large, inclusive group. In the latter, the overall bonds are weaker, and forging those bonds may be difficult and take some time. Often nothing much will happen with any given initiative, and the more exciting experience of "bonding" within a homogeneous group, as Robert Putnam put it, may often seem more rewarding than attempting to bridge differences across groups that might share perspectives on only a small part of their overall agendas.[2] But ultimately that latter type of bridging coalition is also capable of including and/or fostering multiple groups (each with strong internal social bonds) within it. Furthermore, similar analogies hold for understanding society and social order as a whole: A society like the United States is too big ever to have the intense bonds of the clique. Those social analysts who expect social

---

[2] Robert Putnam, *Bowling Alone: The Collapse and Revival of American Community* (New York: Simon & Schuster, 2000), pp. 22–4.

order to be based on strong normative consensus unrealistically expect everyone to join and experience the same clique; in fact, building such a clique necessarily alienates those who do not and cannot belong. Building cliques divides people into mutually exclusive groupings. Social order in a diverse society instead has to work like the larger, inclusive group. But that does not at all mean that people cannot have intense connections to other members of the society. It just means they have those experiences without being quite as exclusive as the clique. Their primary feelings of security and social connection are not to be found within national society as a whole – instead those bonds are found within families, among groups of friends, within religious congregations, within social clubs, within the neighborhood, and so forth.[3] But if they live in a society in which diverse people regularly encounter each other on inclusive terms, they will occasionally form entirely new types of bonds, bonds built upon the diversity they experience. And the ability to do this can mean greater rewards and advantages within the society. But it cannot be the end of social interaction: Political society is not simply the experience of close-knit groups writ large. It is a different kind of bond.

In a now-classic discussion, sociologist Mark S. Granovetter demonstrated the "strength of weak ties" in economic transactions: That is, people with better-paying jobs rely more on a larger network of acquaintances than they do on close friends to obtain those jobs.[4] In a complex economy, they are more likely to learn about relevant jobs, and be introduced to potential employers, if they have a larger network of communications. Those larger networks necessarily involve people who do not go to the same churches, live in the same neighborhoods, or go to the same parties. And while one person may connect to a large network of acquaintances, many or most of those acquaintances do not know *each other*. Those who rely on very tight-knit communal bonds

---

[3] It is interesting to note that James Madison painted a similar portrait even of the eighteenth-century American polity, which by today's standards was quite homogeneous: "Federalist #10," in *The Federalist Papers*, Clinton Rossiter, ed. (New York: Mentor/Penguin, 1999), p. 51.

[4] Mark S. Granovetter, "The Strength of Weak Ties," *American Journal of Sociology* 78(1973):1360–80; Granovetter, "The Strength of Weak Ties: A Network Theory Revisited" [hereafter referred to as "A Network Theory Revisited"], *Sociological Theory* 1(1983):201–33.

(which sometimes of course is not their choice but is a function of opportunities they do or do not have) lead more insular lives[5] and have
greater trouble recovering from economic setbacks. Building upon a
similar argument by Rose Coser, Granovetter pointed out further that
such diverse ties – where connection is built on some mutual but limited perspective or interest, rather than complete homogeneity – are not
just of economic importance. They can be central to social order as a
whole. That is, a true society – as opposed to a bunch of small groups
who have little to do with each other – does not exist without there
being people who bridge different kinds of groups. And such bridges
would be essential to work out disagreements so that every tension does
not escalate into mutual misunderstanding and all-out hostility. Those
whose lives are tied to one very tight-knit group are poor candidates
to build bridges to members of other groups. Again, any such bridge
is likely to be built on the fact that different groups often hold a bit
in common even while they are in other ways – perhaps most ways –
quite different from each other.[6]

Although the political implications of his argument were not
Granovetter's central concern, he made an argument on which this
book draws. That is, internal cohesiveness is not the same thing as –
and indeed may work against – political effectiveness, because internally cohesive groups may not have many links to other social and
political networks. Although ties to groups in which one is not a central member are by definition weak ties, those weak ties are essential to
form the kind of alliances, and exert the kind of influence, necessary to
make governmental bodies or public opinion responsive to demands.[7]
To have a political impact on a large scale, one has to move beyond
bonds of tight solidarity, to engage and at times win over those who

---

[5] That tight social networks leads to commitment to distinct subcultures is a central premise of network theory, a dominant perspective within the study of social
movements: Mustafa Emirbayer and Jeff Goodwin, "Network Analysis, Culture, and
the Problem of Agency," *American Journal of Sociology* 99(1994): 1411–54, at p. 1419.
[6] Granovetter, "The Strength of Weak Ties," p. 1376; Granovetter, "A Network Theory
Revisited," pp. 203–4, 208, 218; Rose Laub Coser, "The Complexity of Roles as a
Seedbed of Individual Autonomy," pp. 237–63 in *The Idea of Social Structure: Papers
in Honor of Robert Merton*, Lewis Coser, ed. (New York: Harcourt Brace Jovanovich,
1975).
[7] Granovetter, "The Strength of Weak Ties," pp. 1373–6; Granovetter, "A Network
Theory Revisited," pp. 224–5.

hail from different corners of society and in fact may not fully agree on a number of other potential political concerns. The ability to find common ground and to downplay potential differences at strategic moments is a central political skill. A brief tour through some important issues in the study of social movements helps us understand why some movements seize such strategic moments, and others cannot.

Building Bridges to Diverse Constituencies

Social Movement Theory: From Resource Mobilization to Frame Analysis

I now turn to an effort to account theoretically for the political dynamics of limiting frames and moral vetoes. The best path to do so is to begin with frame analysis within the study of social movements and then move to a consideration of the cultural bases of social order.

From about the mid-1970s, and to some extent still today, research agendas within the study of social movements have been guided by the resource mobilization approach[8] and related rational choice theories. Resource mobilization argued against social psychological approaches to social movements, often referred to as "collective behavior" theory.[9] In the view of resource mobilization theorists, changes in group psychology were not the primary basis for the emergence and success of social movements. The resource mobilization critique of collective behavior theory was probably oversimplified, but suffice it to say that the former rejected any implication that a massive change in group perceptions, or acute social breakdown, explained the emergence of

---

[8] See John D. McCarthy and Mayer N. Zald, *The Trend of Social Movements in America: Professionalization and Resource Mobilization* (Morristown, N.J.: General Learning Corporation, 1973); McCarthy and Zald, "Resource Mobilization and Social Movements: A Partial Theory," *American Journal of Sociology* 82(1977):1212–41.

[9] Central works from this perspective include Neil Smelser, *Theory of Collective Behavior* (New York: Free Press, 1962), and Ralph H. Turner and Lewis M. Killian, *Collective Behavior* (Englewood Cliffs, N.J.: Prentice Hall, 1957). Two particularly good works that discuss the ideas that fed into resource mobilization theory are Doug McAdam, *Political Process and the Development of Black Insurgency, 1930–1970* (Chicago: University of Chicago Press, 1982), pp. 5–35; and Mayer N. Zald, "Looking Backward to Look Forward: Reflections on the Past and Future of the Resource Mobilization Research Program," pp. 326–48 in *Frontiers in Social Movement Theory*, Aldon D. Morris and Carol McClurg Mueller, eds. (New Haven and London: Yale University Press, 1992).

social movements. Especially objectionable were collective behavior arguments (related to Durkheimian social theory[10]) that alienation from society, or a somewhat irrational mob psychology, were fundamental features of social movements. Among the central contributions of the resource mobilization approach has been to point out that persons involved in social movements, especially movement leaders, often are far from alienated but are instead typically well-networked, even prominent, individuals within their communities. These communities are aware that they are disadvantaged in systems of social stratification, but usually they are powerless to do anything about it.

The "political process" approach is sometimes distinguished from resource mobilization theory but the two are really components of a unified approach, as rarely is one emphasized without the other being at least implicit. (I will then mean to include "political process" as an essential component when I refer to the resource mobilization approach.) The reference to "political process" involves an emphasis that social movements need political opportunities, not simply internal strength, to succeed, and political opportunities typically develop independently of the movement. For instance, economic downturns, political crises, and changes in political administrations might create opportunities for social movements to attain some of their goals.

The resource mobilization approach began, then, with the premise that grievances were normal in a society, not an indicator of abnormal social conditions. But oppressed groups needed organization, resources (such as time, money, and social networks), and political opportunities to make a movement to challenge their situation. Movements did not need some collective, social psychological transformation to come to believe that they were dissatisfied with their lot. But by the nature of social stratification, oppressed groups are usually short on resources; one of the apparently paradoxical realities of social movements, then, is that the most downtrodden groups generally do not rebel (because they do not have resources or effective organization), and disadvantaged groups often rebel when their social situation is improving rather than declining. Increased social standing often brings – pretty much by

[10] Charles Tilly, *From Mobilization to Revolution* (Reading, Mass.: Addison-Wesley, 1978), pp. 16–24.

definition – more access to resources, and thus ability to rebel, as well as more effective social institutions within the community. The research agenda of resource mobilization, then, included an examination of the ways that social movements mobilize resources, including via social networks and the building of professionalized social movement organizations. Thus among the progeny of resource mobilization has been the use of network analysis of the leadership and memberships of social movements.

A cousin to resource mobilization theory is rational choice theory, the application of neoclassical economic theory to the study of social phenomena. (Political scientists generally refer to "public choice" to mean the same thing that sociologists call "rational choice.") The most influential use of rational choice analysis in the study of social movements comes from Mancur Olson.[11] The approach has numerous subtleties, but at its core is the argument that there is a basic paradox in motivating people to organize into a social movement. The problem is that mobilizing a movement involves a lot of costs, that is, time, money, and energy. To translate into resource mobilization language, mobilizing a movement requires a lot of resources, and someone has to provide or pay for those resources. Thus, even when one agrees with the goals of a movement, it is individually more rational to wait to see if someone else will do all the work, that is, to be a free rider. The problem is that then no individuals have clear incentive to start and maintain a social movement, even when all those individuals would benefit. Usually the costs (of time, money, and so forth) of organizing a movement will not match the benefits that most individuals can expect from a successful movement. And so the result can be the absence of a movement, even when large numbers of individuals would benefit from such a movement.

One solution is to offer "selective incentives," that is, special rewards for making that extra effort, that is, for contributing to a movement. One makes membership in the movement a valuable, scarce commodity. It then becomes worthwhile to participate.

Resource mobilization had a great deal in common with rational choice theory, and at times they have been treated as essentially

---

[11] Mancur Olson, *The Logic of Collective Action: Public Goods and the Theory of Groups* (Cambridge, Mass.: Harvard University Press, 1965).

equivalent theories. In both cases, mobilizing resources into an effective movement organization is crucial, and the central practical problem for any movement to overcome. Both also assume that people's grievances are fairly predictable, given the system of social stratification in the society. There is little or no attempt to explain ideological change, for example. Rational choice, more than resource mobilization, sometimes follows economic theory in seeing social movements as primarily concerned with increasing participants' economic well-being. But both focus primarily on how movements relate to economic distribution and/or state power.

However, as sociologists are less apt to argue for stripped-down and deductive models of social action, resource mobilization quickly fed into sociological arguments that diverged from the way that economists would think of social movements. An early indicator of the different orientation sociologists take was the integration of "political process" into resource mobilization theory: That is, one could not look at movements simply as an aggregate of individuals pursuing their self interest, but also the social-structural context. Indeed, pretty much all of the central figures in early resource mobilization theory – for instance, John McCarthy, Mayer Zald, and Doug McAdam – fairly quickly came to more expanded views of collective action, including approaches quite compatible with cultural analyses.[12]

In recent years, important figures in resource mobilization theory and their associates have developed frame analysis, which takes its name from the creative microsociological work of Erving Goffman.[13] Within the study of social movements, frame analysis makes the case that it matters how people perceive a social issue; for example, looking at a certain conflict in society, they may side with different participants in the conflict depending on how they perceive the nature of the conflict. For example, do they think the conflict is a matter of a bully picking on a victim? Do they think of the conflict as a matter simply of different people having different preferences, each of which is legitimate?

---

[12] See, e.g., the work of John McCarthy, Mayer Zald, and Doug McAdam in *Frontiers of Social Movement Theory*, Morris and Mueller, ed.; and in *Comparative Perspectives on Social Movements: Political Opportunities, Mobilizing Structures, and Cultural Framings*, McAdam, McCarthy, and Zald, eds. (Cambridge: Cambridge University Press, 1996).

[13] Erving Goffman, *Frame Analysis: An Essay on the Organization of Experience* (New York: Harper, 1974).

David Snow, William A. Gamson, Robert D. Benford, and Hank Johnston have led the way in applying frame analysis to the study of social movements.[14] Frame analysis takes the sociological literature even further from rational choice.

Some of the critiques of resource mobilization theory that ultimately paved the way for frame analysis began very soon after resource mobilization emerged. In 1979, Bruce Fireman and William Gamson[15] drew attention to resource mobilization's unwarranted assertion that grievances are constant, as well as the assumption that the cultural meanings of social movements automatically follow from material interests.[16] Indeed, by now, arguing against these original assumptions of resource mobilization theory is rather easy to do, given that almost no sociologists actively defend them, at least in print.

Still, social movement theory's development away from the rationalist, materialist legacy of resource mobilization has moved, at best, in fits and starts. For example, Friedman and McAdam[17] claimed to

[14] David A. Snow and Robert D. Benford, "Master Frames and Cycles of Protest," pp. 133–55 in *Frontiers of Social Movement Theory*, Aldon D. Morris and Carol McClurg Mueller, eds. (New Haven and London: Yale University Press, 1992); Snow and Benford, "Ideology, Frame Resonance, and Participant Mobilization," *International Social Movement Research* 1 (1988):197–217; David A. Snow, E. Burke Rochford, Jr., Steven K. Worden, and Robert D. Benford, "Frame Alignment Processes, Micromobilization, and Movement Participation," *American Sociological Review* 51(1986):464–81; William A. Gamson, *Talking Politics* (Cambridge: Cambridge University Press, 1992).

[15] Bruce Fireman and William A. Gamson, "Utilitarian Logic in the Resource Mobilization Perspective," pp. 8–44 in *The Dynamics of Social Movements*, Mayer N. Zald and John D. McCarthy, eds. (Cambridge, Mass.: Winthrop, 1979).

[16] Myra Marx Ferree and Frederick D. Miller, "Mobilization and Meaning: Toward an Integration of Social Psychological and Resource Perspectives on Social Movements," *Sociological Inquiry* 55(1985):38–61, p. 57fn.2; Sidney Tarrow, "Mentalities, Political Cultures, and Collective Action Frames: Constructing Meanings through Action," pp. 174–202 in *Frontiers of Social Movement Theory*, Morris and Mueller, eds.; Tarrow, *Power in Movement: Social Movements, Collective Action and Politics* (Cambridge: Cambridge University Press, 1994).

[17] Debra Friedman and Doug McAdam, "Collective Identity and Activism: Networks, Choices, and the Life of a Social Movement," pp. 156–73 in *Frontiers of Social Movement Theory*, Morris and Mueller, eds. It is interesting to note, however, that McAdam has recently questioned a central assumption of social movement theory of the last quarter century, i.e., that organization is a central facilitator of social movement activity. Doug McAdam, "Beyond Structural Analysis: Toward a More Dynamic Understanding of Social Movements," pp. 281–98 in Mario Diani and Doug McAdam, eds., *Social Movements and Networks: Relational Approaches to Collective Action* (Oxford:

incorporate the concept of "collective identity" – which, for most social scientists, inherently implies a cultural focus on shared meanings –
but treated it as a type of selective incentive offered to individuals to
solve the free rider problem. The entire notion of a free rider problem implies that utility maximization, experienced at the individual
level, is the driving force behind all social movement participation.
And so *collective* identity becomes an *individual*'s reward for donating
resources, not a defining aspect of the movement itself. This assumption
is at odds with a cultural approach, which assumes that an essential
part of social activity is the creation and reinterpretation of collective
understandings.

The movement away from models partly borrowed from economics
needs to proceed more quickly and dramatically, as such models assume
individualist motivation and see collective action only as an aggregate
of individual action, assumptions that simplify social reality beyond
recognition and thus lose sociology's central insights. For instance, the
focus on selective incentives may help solve the free rider problem, but
only because – as is often true of economic models of social action –
the "problem" emerges as an attempt to solve a streamlined, deductive
model of how social dynamics work, one that seems artificial and sim-
plistic to many sociologists and historians who actually study movements in detail. That is, the typical movement does not emerge and
grow when some social change entrepreneur suddenly starts offering rewards for participation, as rational choice theory implies. A movement
grows when people are passionate enough to sacrifice for the cause,
and when political opportunities arise; certainly success is invigorat-
ing and can help sustain movements, but exactly what personal, self-
interested benefits participants receive is not usually in the forefront
of their minds. And as Fireman and Gamson pointed out nearly two
decades ago, within the rational choice cost–benefit analysis, the value
of selective incentives needs to outweigh the costs of participation: Actual benefits from movement success cannot be a major part of the

Oxford University Press, 2003). McAdam argues there has been neglect of the many
cases when established organizations instead inhibit such activity. In a general sense,
this book's argument would be complementary to McAdam's observations, in that
I argue that the cultural process of framing is as central to a movement's prospects,
that movements with high internal solidarity (and thus usually well-organized) may
have trouble reaching out to other audiences.

cost–benefit calculation, because those are also available to free riders. And so, within this rational choice model, there is no particular reason to think membership in a movement depends especially on those who would benefit from the movement or otherwise feel some identification with it, a patently false empirical implication.[18]

I would add further that the costs of participation – although certainly important – are only part of what social movements are about: The concept of selective incentives cannot account for solidarity within a movement. It involves ignoring the obvious ideological commitment and cultural bonds of solidarity that are observable within social movements. In addition, the focus on free riders and selective incentives has particular trouble explaining why anyone is willing to serve in the leadership of a social movement, since typically their lives are consumed by what are mainly mundane tasks of communicating, propagandizing, and soliciting funds. Leaders may also be putting themselves at significant personal risk, for instance, if a government is willing to arrest, torture, or kill movement leaders. The only plausible explanation within rational choice theory is that leaders receive psychological satisfaction by aiming for some principle or by attaining social status within the movement. But these "benefits" can be explained in utilitarian terms only by making the argument tautological (again, as Fireman and Gamson pointed out[19]) to include as incentives things that do not at all seem to be in people's self-interest, for example, a commitment to principle.[20] Even the attainment of social status makes sense only within a shared culture and solidarity within the movement, that is, in a context in which the criteria and existence of social status are established within the culture of the group. To use social status as an explanation, then, still begs the question of where and how movement solidarity originates.

It is indeed in examinations of social solidarity within movements that an investigation of the cultural dynamics of social movements has

---

[18] Fireman and Gamson, "Utilitarian Logic in the Resource Mobilization Perspective," p. 14.

[19] Ibid., p. 20.

[20] An example is Samuel Popkin's argument in *The Rational Peasant* (Berkeley: University of California Press, 1979), esp. p. 254, in which he identified conscience and altruism as motivations for revolutionary behavior, undermining his view that self-interest motivates such behavior.

been most promising, for instance in work by Francesca Polletta, Nina Eliasoph, Paul Lichterman, Marc Steinberg, and Rhys Williams.[21] I might also note that in such works sociologists display another strength that is usually absent when sociologists borrow from economic models: That is, such cultural work is interesting reading for people who care about the social movements and not just about social science theory. The typical sociological study that depends on network analysis or rational choice models does not inform the reader about what the movement was actually like – it is not *about* the movement but is instead an abstracted model of the movement – and is opaque to all but specialists.

The central difference between frame analysis and resource mobilization is that the former does not take the perception of grievances for granted. But, as Steinberg makes clear,[22] it still assumes that grievances, and the framing of grievances, develops before a person is actually involved in a movement. Thus most frame analysis looks only at how individuals frame a social problem: Again, as with resource mobilization theory, once a person is acting collectively, within a movement, the grievances are implicitly assumed to be fixed and thus not worth investigating in themselves. That is, the central focus in such research remains an explanation of how people manage to build social movement organizations, mostly taking for granted that they are interested in the same social movement goal. And so for both approaches, once a social movement becomes organized, there is no need to reinvestigate why people are involved: Movement organizations do not change the grievances but only make it possible to act on the grievances.

[21] Francesca Polletta, *Freedom is an Endless Meeting: Democracy in American Social Movements* (Chicago and London: University of Chicago Press, 2002); Nina Eliasoph, "Making a Fragile Public: A Talk-Centered Study of Citizenship and Power," *Sociological Theory* 14(1996):262–89; Paul Lichterman, *The Search for Political Community* (New York and Cambridge: Cambridge University Press, 1996); Lichterman, "Talking Identity in the Public Sphere: Broad Visions and Small Spaces in Sexual Identity Politics," *Theory and Society* 28(1999):101–41; Marc Steinberg, "Toward a More Dialogic Analysis of Social Movement Culture," pp. 208–25 in *Social Movements*, Meyer, Whittier, and Robnet, eds.; Rhys H. Williams, "From the Beloved Community to Family Values": Religious Language, Symbolic Repertoires, and Democratic Culture," pp. 247–65 in *Social Movements*.

[22] Steinberg, ibid., pp. 209–10.

But there have been sporadic calls for frame analysis and related theories of social movements to become more cultural,[23] including by emphasizing that shared meanings within a movement are not simply a reflection of shared interests but are central to what the movement is about, and also central to enabling the movement to attempt to effect social change.[24] Frame analysis has remained somewhat distant from truly cultural analyses of social movements. The questions *not* much asked in the frame analysis literature would lead us into a deeper analysis of the cultural aspects of framing: How, for example, do people ever work together in a social movement, given that any given issue might be framed in multiple ways? Where does a particular social movement framing originate? Might changes in the nature of grievances (as people come to build a new collective understanding of social issues) explain some of the rhythms of social movement politics?

The closest that most framing literature gets to addressing the question of how a movement develops what Snow and Benford call a "master frame" (that defines a movement as a whole) is to say that different people use a combination of their own experiences and media information to apply different frames to understanding the same issue.[25] I would argue that the emphasis on media's ability to supply frames (while always qualified) is really too strong and that it leads frame analysis away from investigating empirically what happens *within movements* to allow for the diverse elements of a movement to cohere. Thus there has been little attention to how these differences

[23] Emirbayer and Goodwin, "Network Analysis, Culture, and the Problem of Agency," p. 1425; Ann Mische, "Cross-talk in Movements: Reconceiving the Culture-Network Link," pp. 258–80 in Diani and McAdam, eds., *Social Movements and Networks.*

[24] Polletta's analysis (*Freedom is an Endless Meeting*) included emphasis on a point important in this book, that a strong subculture within a social movement builds its identity but can hamper its ability to have wider influence. Emirbayer and Goodwin's argument, ibid., focuses more on shared cultural identity as not being simply epiphenomenal but central to a movement's ability to act, strategically or otherwise.

[25] For example, Gamson, *Talking Politics*, pp. 58, 81–2, 117; Gamson, "The Social Psychology of Collective Action," pp. 53–76 in *Frontiers in Social Movement Theory*, Morris and Mueller, eds., p. 71; Bert Klandermans, "The Social Construction of Protest in Multiorganizational Fields," pp. 77–103 in *Frontiers in Social Movement Theory*, Morris and Mueller, eds., p. 89; John D. McCarthy, Jackie Smith, and Mayer N. Zald, "Accessing Public, Media, Electoral, and Governmental Agendas," pp. 291–311 in *Comparative Perspectives on Social Movements*, McAdam, McCarthy, and Zald, eds.; Theodore Sasson, *Crime Talk: How Citizens Construct a Social Problem* (New York: Aldine de Gruyter, 1995), p. 141; Tarrow, *Power in Movement*, pp. 126–9.

within a movement become coordinated into a perspective that can unite a movement as a whole. Why do people find some frames rather than others appealing and unifying, for example? If we acknowledge that grievances change, why do they change in one direction rather than another? Frame analysts sometimes raise such questions,[26] but there has been little or no attempt to answer them, directly and empirically.

These questions do not guide such research partly because frame analysis, methodologically, typically investigates how *individuals* use and respond to frames. Again, frame analysis, and social movement theory in general, needs to approach cultural approaches less gingerly and make a cleaner break with models derived partly from economic analyses and thus centered on individual motivation that aggregates into collective, rather than collective action being dependent on social solidarity that cannot be understood at the individual level. Frame analysis talks primarily about individuals' cognitive reactions to different frames but relatively little about the cultural history of meaning that would make a frame appeal *collectively* to different kinds of people. It is the progeny of the rationalism of resource mobilization and thus primarily attempts to explain how individuals interpret a material world whose structure is logically prior to, and independent of, their

---

[26] For example, Klandermans, ibid., pp. 77, 83–5. Mayer Zald has suggested that relying too much on media determinism can be a problem in social movement research (Zald, "Looking Backward to Look Forward: Reflections on the Past and Future of the Resource Mobilization Research Program," pp. 326–48 in *Frontiers in Social Movement Theory*, Morris and Mueller, eds., p. 338). Zald's "Culture, Ideology, and Strategic Framing" (pp. 261–74 in *Comparative Perspectives on Social Movements*) raises some of the questions involved in cultural interaction and diversity within movements but mostly gives a literature review of some of the issues involved rather than attempting to account theoretically for such cultural matters. I should note here that another recent framing study of abortion discourse uses a different approach to frame analysis than do I: Myra Marx Ferree, William Anthony Gamson, Jürgen Gerhards, and Dieter Rucht, *Shaping Abortion Discourse: Democracy and the Public Sphere in Germany and the United States* (New York and Cambridge: Cambridge University Press, 2002). This study talks of multiple frames in a way that treats a frame as an different issue or component within the abortion debate: it is a part more than a whole; the focus is not on master frames. Thus the study provides a rich and fascinating analysis of the many individual issues raised in German and American discourse on abortion. There is a focus on the nature of change in the background assumptions, or master frames, and what political circumstances might make change on such matters more or less likely at any given time, but that is not as central a focus as it is in this book. Also, Ferree et al. do not focus as much on which kinds of frames are most likely to be strategically successful, though again there is some discussion of that issue.

readings of that world.[27] That partly explains the overreliance on explaining the origins of frames by referring to mass media messages: Mass media are a cognitive influence immediately accessible to individuals, as a coherent package. It is accessible to an individual watching television or reading a newspaper, alone.[28] But a focus on the cultural *history* of people involved in movements would take research away from this overly exclusive emphasis on contemporary mass media, and away from frames experienced only at the individual level.[29] Culture is not possible without social interaction, and the history that is an integral part of culture is not immediately accessible: It is learned and experienced over time, in a variety of social encounters.

It is, then, a significant limitation of frame analysis and resource mobilization that they emphasize how important collective action is to social change, and yet they imply that collective experience has little influence on how individuals frame social problems and movement goals. Marc Steinberg, who develops a particularly rich approach to the cultural dynamics of the construction of identity within a movement, has found such limitations of frame analysis reason to abandon the framing approach altogether.[30] I would argue, however, that the concept of framing has the distinct advantage that it captures the need for

[27] (See, e.g., the telling footnote in Snow and Benford, "Master Frames and Cycles of Protest," pp. 140–1.) There is, then, not much of a focus on how people come to shape each other's understanding of the world in a mutually reinforcing, interdependent way. (I am not one to claim that human beings act on the world in any way their interpretations point, but the problem with frame analysis is that it implies that the problem a movement addresses exists in its essential form no matter what frame is used to understand it. I would argue instead that, while movement participants are usually reacting to events and structures over which they have little control, they can categorize and define social problems in multiple ways. The problem is indeed different to some extent, depending on how it is talked about.)

[28] The focus on media messages also results from the fact that print media are often the most available source of documentation on the actions of social movements. See, e.g., Pamela E. Oliver and Daniel J. Myers, "Networks, Diffusion, and Cycles of Collective Action," pp. 173–203 in Diani and McAdam, eds., *Social Movements and Networks*, p. 184.

[29] Snow, especially, has written unambiguously from a cultural perspective, in other contexts (David A. Snow and Susan E. Marshall, "Cultural Imperialism, Social Movements, and the Islamic Revival," pp. 131–52 in *Research in Social Movements, Conflict and Change*, vol. 7, Louis Kreisberg, ed. [Greenwich, Conn.: JAI, 1984]), and Snow and Benford's idea of a master frame is considerably more cultural in focus than most frame analysis, which is social psychological rather than cultural. That is, group sharing of meanings does not figure in most frame analyses.

[30] Steinberg, "Toward a More Dialogic Analysis of Social Movement Culture."

movements to focus on and define agendas, within a world in which it is never possible to include everything within a given frame. The concept of framing captures something very important in the dynamics of social movements, that is, if we conceptualize framing as a process including cultural dynamics and not simply static perceptions. And, again, unlike too much of the social science literature on social movements, the concept of framing shows promise of conveying important sociological insights to an audience wider than that of specialized sociological journals.

The Bridging Function of Frames

Greater attention to the empirical reality of diversity within movements can retain the strengths of frame analysis, while expanding it to include a rich analysis of the cultural dimensions of the construction of collective identity. There are hints in the frame analysis literature that the construction of social movement frames is a process of bridging ideas from diverse sources. For example, Snow and Benford note that

> frames simplify and encode the "world out there" by selectively punctuating and encoding ... threads of information [which] may be diverse and even incongruous, but they are woven together in such a way that what was previously inconceivable, or at least not clearly articulated, is now meaningfully interconnected.[31]

On this point I would agree; however, this literature tends to focus on the frames that individuals hold and thus neglects the importance of the "master frame" that defines the public discourse of a movement as a whole. There are occasional references to such diversity but no attempt to link this diversity to an explanation of how movements nevertheless manage to cohere.[32]

---

[31] Snow and Benford, "Master Frames and Cycles of Protest," pp. 137–8.

[32] Starting with Fireman and Gamson, "Utilitarian Logic in the Resource Mobilization Perspective," p. 25. See also Robert D. Benford, "Frames Disputes within the Nuclear Disarmament Movement," *Social Forces* 71(1993):677–701; and Snow and Benford, "Master Frames and Cycles of Protest," p. 140, who also mention such diversity but do not emphasize it as a central feature of social movements. Myra Marx Ferree and Frederick D. Miller make a related point in "Mobilization and Meaning: Toward an Integration of Social Psychological and Resource Perspectives on Social Movements," *Sociological Inquiry* 55(1985):38–61, p. 56n.2.

The "new social movements" literature that emerged primarily from European sociologists a couple of decades ago more explicitly takes note of diversity within

The answer, I would argue, begins with Sidney Tarrow's brief discussion of how frames bridge the concerns of different groups.[33] Tarrow[34] notes that a "rights" frame in the U.S. Civil Rights Movement could

movements. But in practice this is not a strong focus within that literature, either. In general, the new social movements literature is full of interesting insights but there are fundamental problems in applying its theoretical perspective. First, it implicitly takes the position that Marxist class analysis had no trouble explaining the world until about the mid–twentieth century and thus generally takes for granted that before our "new" era, social movements were formerly organized around class divisions only. This is a problematic empirical assumption that, e.g., cannot make sense of movements surrounding birth control and abortion. Second, it assumes that the "new" feminist, environmental, and peace movements are reacting against a bureaucratized state and society (Alberto Melucci, "Symbolic Challenge of Contemporary Movements," *Social Research* 52[1985]:794; Claus Offe, "New Social Movements: Challenging the Boundaries of Contemporary Politics," *Social Research* 52[1985]:830, 841). But it is often unclear exactly what about postindustrial society, "modernization," or the "state" the movements are reacting against. And whether in the "old" or "new" eras, the implication is that all movements of a given era originate for the same basic reasons, an assumption that is not empirically tenable. Look, e.g., at the first third of the twentieth century in the United States, when there were movements organized around class issues, feminist issues, peace issues, evangelical religion, and so forth. It may be that this view of contemporary social movements is empirically more accurate in Europe, perhaps especially in Germany, than in the United States (see, e.g., Bert Klandermans, "New Social Movements and Resource Mobilization: The European and the American Approach," *International Journal of Mass Emergencies and Disasters* 4[1986]:13–37, esp. pp. 17–18). Given feminist support for the welfare state, the wing of (perhaps especially United States) environmentalism interested in state regulation, the argument that these movements are an entirely new phenomenon attempting to reappropriate private domains from the state is questionable. Third, this theoretical approach does not adequately specify why some movements meet the "new" criteria and others do not. It is unclear, for instance, why conservative, laissez-faire trends in much of Europe and the U.S. are not discussed in this literature as examples of reactions against the postindustrial state.

The "new social movements" approach is partly a postmodernist approach to sociology. See the discussion of postmodernism in note 54 in this chapter.

33 Some other social movement scholars use the similar concept of "brokerage," but "bridging" seems to me the preferable term, as "brokerage" is on its face more ambiguous. It could be taken to imply a market transaction and even a process of one party getting the better end of the deal, as in a brokered commodities deal. For the use of the term brokerage, see Mario Diani, "Leaders' or Brokers? Positions and Influence in Social Movement Networks," pp. 105–22 in Diani and McAdam, eds., *Social Movements and Networks*, pp. 106–7; Roberto M. Fernandez and Roger V. Gould, "A Dilemma of State Power: Brokerage and Influence in the National Health Policy Domain," *American Journal of Sociology* 99(1994):1455–91. Fernandez and Gould's analysis is complementary to the analysis of bridging frames here in that they noted, for instance, that effective brokerage requires remaining noncommittal on specific policy agendas.

34 *Power in Movement*, p. 130.

bridge the concerns of Southern blacks and of white conscience constituents. Why would that be? I would argue it did so because first, it linked the need for concrete change in the lives of Southern blacks – establishing equal rights, meaning the end of segregation – with the perspective of whites and others outside the South who were not directly affected by segregation but were moved by conscience. Second, the idea of literal, civil rights – legal and political rights guaranteed to all individuals – was uncontroversial within American political discourse. Extending the point, I would argue that the clearly stated, apparently simple point that segregation is wrong was a very effective limiting frame, and limiting frames will usually build more bridges than will framing an issue within an explicit worldview. The limiting civil rights frame did not seem to question the moral fundamentals of the society; quite the contrary, it appealed to what most Americans thought were the society's moral fundamentals: that individuals could not have fewer rights for nonmeritocractic reasons. It appeared, in the American context, as a limiting frame, not a moral worldview. If the movement had instead, for example, argued at the same time that the entire economic system of the United States was unjust because historically it had descended from slavery, such a frame would not have bridged the orientations of different constituencies quite so successfully.[35] For instance, some of the white liberals who supported the movement might have felt that the movement was going too far.

How Limiting Frames Bridge Distinct Collective Identities

What frames will serve as bridging frames for particular social movement causes? To answer this question, we need to move beyond the dominant theoretical assumption in the study of social movements that motivation and framing occurs only at the individual level. We must begin by asking what brings different groups to a conversation. The history of reproductive politics makes clear that people enter the conversation for very different reasons. A number of sociologists have noted that there can often be numerous logics to the way people pursue their goals, and which define which kinds of goals

---

[35] I am not addressing here whether any particular claim is a better or more justifiable frame than another, just how different claims work strategically within social movements.

matter.[36] Max Weber, for example, wrote of different orientations toward social action, such as a means–ends instrumental orientation, orientation toward the pursuit of some normative value, action motivated by emotional attachments, and traditional, customary means of action.[37] The point here is not to explore the intricacies of Weber's conceptual scheme but to note that his approach suggests we need to ask why a group or faction is involved in a debate and to ask what makes them a collectivity. Why are they, as a group, involved in this particular conversation? What unites them? For example, physicians have been involved in debates over contraception and abortion. Any individual physician might be a Catholic, an evangelical, a feminist, or a conservative. But what brings physicians *as a group* into a discussion of contraception or abortion? Professional concerns in the practice of medicine. Thus, although individual physicians might agree or disagree with, for example, positions taken by the American Medical Association, in general their individual reasons will not explain the logic of the AMA's involvement in a political conversation.

There are certainly cases when individuals have a significant effect on how an issue is framed. Such was the case with legislators who sometimes could assist or prevent an abortion reform bill getting out of committee. Margaret Sanger had unusual influence, much more than is typical in social movements. But, more often, movements and frames come from people who have something in common, who can share meaning (and thus agree on a frame), and who can pool and mobilize resources to lobby, protest, go to legislative hearings, and do the other things social movements do. To join a mobilized group, devote one's time, and make those sacrifices, then, participants must have something in common. Again, there are many different bases to sharing a collective identity, including profession, ideology, and shared history. (These might respectively correspond, roughly, to Weber's means–ends orientation, normative orientation, and customary ways of acting.)

---

[36] For such an argument, but one that addresses only collective action, with socio-economic goals explicitly oriented towards capitalism, see Claus Offe and Helmut Wiesenthal, "Two Logics of Collective Action," pp. 170–220 in Offe, *Disorganized Capitalism: Contemporary Transformations of Work and Politics*, John Keane, ed. (Cambridge, Mass.: MIT Press, 1985).

[37] Max Weber, *The Theory of Social and Economic Organization*, ed. Talcott Parsons (New York: Free Press/Macmillan, 1964), pp. 89–94, 115–18.

In great contrast to the professional bonds shared by reform-minded physicians, early participants in the pro-life movement and the abortion rights movement worked more from an explicitly moral orientation. Without a basic moral commitment to seeing the fetus as a life, there would be no reason to be involved in the pro-life movement; more specifically, the early activists shared a religious identity, as they were almost exclusively Catholic. And without a basically feminist perspective, there would have been no abortion rights movement in the 1960s and early 1970s. This is not to say that there might be other – perhaps even more fundamental – reasons that motivate and define these movements.[38] But still we can see a basic difference in the collective orientation that physicians would have toward abortion – one of professional commitment and professional interest – versus the more normative orientation of pro-life or pro-choice activists.

The orientation of any collective actor in a debate will make certain kinds of frames more or less likely and set the parameters for what type of bridging frame, if any, might be adopted. The importance of this difference in collective orientation, and in turn the importance of framing, can be demonstrated by Luker's discussion of the emergence of the pro-life movement in California. California had a version of the standard, restrictive nineteenth-century American state abortion law, which remained in effect until the state passed an abortion reform law in 1967. In the years just preceding the 1967 law, before there was much grassroots pro-life movement, some physicians had voiced what would later come to be known as pro-life positions. That is, they regarded fetal life as akin to a baby's life. So, on the central issue, small numbers of pro-life physicians held basically the same position the grass-roots pro-life movement held. But physicians kept their distance from the grassroots activists, because pro-life physicians were accustomed to being engaged professionally (and probably also socially) with other

---

[38] For example, central to Luker's *Abortion and the Politics of Motherhood* is a status politics argument that moral positions on abortion (at least as they apply to activists) are strongly dependent on the role of motherhood in women's lives. Women whose social status depended primarily on their role as wives and mothers tended to be pro-life, whereas women oriented at least partly toward the job market and career were more likely to be pro-choice. (Like many studies of abortion politics, Luker focused on activists; arguments based on studies of activists may not explain very well abortion politics among the general population. For one, activists – no matter what the cause – are more likely to see that cause in moral worldview terms, an approach that in fact may turn off much of the general population.)

physicians. In contrast, the new pro-life grassroots activists knew very few people who found legal abortion morally acceptable; the grass roots condemned legal abortion as a moral scandal. Thus, to the pro-life physicians, the pro-life grass roots appeared shrill and hysterical. Even though the physicians and the grass roots had basically the same views of the fetus and abortion, the pro-life physicians found it extreme to call other physicians murderers. They had been involved in different conversations, or as Luker described it, "cross pressures,"[39] reflecting a different group identity. Abortion was an important part of the conversations they considered relevant to the practice of medicine, but they engaged in many medical conversations with their fellow physicians, most of which had nothing to do with abortion. And so they could not see even physicians who were liberal in granting abortions as evil people beyond redemption.[40] They could not frame abortion within only a single, unambiguous moral worldview. As a result, although of course they strongly opposed any liberalization of abortion laws, they did not feel completely comfortable with the new, grassroots pro-life movement. Becoming part of that movement would have required that they ignore the professional medical identity that brought them to the abortion issue in the first place. As was the case of physicians who supported abortion law reform, the pro-life physicians quickly fell to the margins of the debate. Abortion was no longer a medical issue.

Physicians as a group, then, could be part of a movement only to the extent that the professional concerns that they shared as a group, that is, that gave them a collective identity, were part of the frame. Once the frames became explicitly moral, with professional medical concerns discarded, physicians could not act as a group. Some individual physicians could peel off into the new pro-life or abortion rights movements, but for the most part physicians, *qua* physicians, were no longer relevant to the debate.

The same pattern happened with physicians who were in favor of abortion reform laws. They saw the matter in humanitarian terms but also, crucially, as a problem of legal restrictions on medical practice. The humanitarian component of their frame initially allowed nonmedical allies to join them and, in some cases, to be more proactive than

39 Ibid., p. 145.
40 Ibid., pp. 73, 79, 86–7, 129–33, 138–42, 145–7.

even the physicians. But physicians were involved because they shared professional concerns; once there was large-scale rejection of the claim that abortion was primarily a medical matter, the pro-reform physicians fell to the margins of the debate.

To explore further how mobilized, collective identities highly constrain the kind of frame possible at any given time, let us draw parallels to coalitions within the history of contraceptive politics. There was a great deal of intensity, of a feeling of common purpose, in the socialist movement before World War I. Those associated with the movement felt loyal to it, as there was a coherent U.S. Left that could encompass one's entire life: There were social gatherings, favored neighborhoods, and political associations addressing numerous causes, from union organizing to economic justice, to peace, to internationalism, and to women's rights. These causes were not entirely overlapping, but there were many people who participated in more than one and who saw the causes as a seamless web. Thus, birth control advocates paraded their socialism.

The strength of collective identity is a central reason social movements do not simply do whatever it takes to win. If we are to understand why they do things that may seem irrational, that is, act in ways that seem to hamper their cause, we must understand social movement participants as people who have come to share in a cultural experience. Like most of us, they will find the strong bonds of an exclusive community more immediately and intensely meaningful than the weak bonds of an amorphous, larger network. They will value the social and political ties that brought them into existence, indeed perhaps more than the specifics of manifest ideology itself. That is, for example, proponents of various causes referred to their valued links with the socialist movement, but ideologically it was often unclear what their specific cause (e.g., feminism or birth control) had in common ideologically with socialism. But they did have in common a strong identity with a socialist movement that was at its peak in U.S. history.

With that kind of strong collective identity, it can be very difficult to find allies: Potential supporters of birth control who perceived socialism as an undesirable ideology would not feel comfortable with the conversation. They might have an interest in birth control but were not going to talk about birth control as a socialist cause. And so a possible alliance never developed.

The socialists feared, quite rightly, that including too many diverse people in a cause would necessarily water down the intensity. Indeed, to build a broad coalition of birth control advocates would mean mainstreaming the cause of birth control. That did mean that a socialist framing of birth control was never going to give the cause of birth control mainstream success. It could not build strategically effective bridges.

And so, moving the cause of birth control beyond the socialist movement did not occur until the community of socialists was no longer available: A limiting, bridging frame was possible only once the morally charged worldview that defined the birth control movement in the 1910s had faded. Those birth control advocates committed to socialist groups did not voluntarily leave such an intense movement with strong internal ties. The socialist movement greatly weakened after World War I for reasons that had nothing to do with birth control. At that point, it was easier for birth control advocates to reach out to other potential allies, who might start to believe that supporting birth control did not, contrary to previous perceptions, make one a socialist. But the socialist advocates of birth control did not do this simply because that was the way to win: They did it only when the previous alternative – remaining tied to a socialist movement that had strong social bonds – was taken away from them. Still, some former allies from the 1910s held to the position that Sanger and her allies had betrayed the movement. In their eyes, Sanger had sold out to respectable, capitalist society. The political meaning and identity provided by socialist and related left-wing causes was not something they could all simply discard.

The Entry of New Players into a Debate

Bridging frames serve to link different people into a working alliance, and so the entry of new players into a debate will often strain existing frames and thus existing alliances, although it may also allow the building of new bridging frames. No bridge can accommodate everyone, so that it may be that different factions find themselves out in the cold at different points in a debate. As I suggested in my metaphor of the wedding reception, when conversation is a halting attempt to find common ground among people who have little common history, the addition of even one new participant can require dramatic transformation in the topic of conversation. While not discussing the importance of frames, Kristin Luker's analysis of abortion politics nearly two decades ago – which continues to hold up remarkably well on a number of dimensions – made the entry of new players a prominent part of her analysis.[41]

Limiting frames will usually serve most effectively as bridging frames, because they limit the agenda and thus, when constructed effectively, avoid the issues that most divide the different factions within the movement. But the entry of new players into a debate can undermine an existing limiting frame, and some times a moral worldview may serve a new alliance quite well: New participants may find that an existing, limiting frame is incapable of addressing their central concerns, concerns built on a collective identity that is very strong.

The complexities of how the entry of new players affect the framing possibilities within a movement is perhaps most dramatically clear when we examine why support for abortion reform laws evaporated in about 1970. As noted above, a coherent voice speaking from the point of view of professional medicine could not withstand the turn to frames of moral outrage. But the exodus of the medically focused reform frame also made way for new bridges.

Physicians had every professional reason to emphasize the particular medical framing of abortion law reform. When physicians act collectively, they are informed by a world of conversations focused upon the professional practice of medicine. Within this world, the assumption is that medicine is inherently humanitarian. But as I noted earlier in this book, for others involved in the reform movement, the humanitarianism of the frame was potentially separable from the medical part of the frame. Such would likely be the case, for example, for clerics in the Clergy Consultation Service, or lawyers and other activists (such as the prominent activist Lawrence Lader, author of two books chronicling this early history of abortion reform[42]). We saw in Chapter 6 that even some legislators who had been central in passing reform bills became disillusioned with the limited increase in access that followed and so, within a couple years, came out in support of repeal.

This is not to say that no physicians could see things in terms beyond the narrow world of medicine, nor that it was impossible for

---

[41] Ibid., p. 7.
[42] Lader, *Abortion* (New York: Bobbs-Merrill, 1966); Lader, *Abortion II: Making the Revolution* (Boston: Beacon, 1973).

lawyers, legislators, or clerics to think about abortion in primarily medical terms. But for physicians as a group, there was a different set of conversations going on, which would tend to emphasize the particular problems that the nineteenth-century laws posed for the practice of medicine. Physicians would not have acted as a group, *as physicians*, if they did not perceive a directly medical issue involved. Any individual physician might also be a parent, a spouse, a member of a church, a community member, a Northerner, a Southerner, or whatever. But, as a group, physicians (though a small minority of physicians) were involved in the discussion of abortion because they saw, collectively, relevance to their practice of medicine.

The medical, humanitarian frame guiding the reform laws emphasized the legal and professional problems that the existing abortion laws (inherited from the nineteenth century) posed for the practice of medicine. Reformers presented women's problem pregnancies in sympathetic, humanitarian terms. Those behind the reform laws presumably genuinely cared about the crises such women faced, but the frame was implicitly paternalistic. It was these elites, for example, not women with problem pregnancies, who testified in state legislative discussions in favor of the reform proposals. As far as I can determine (and as Luker noted[43]), in most cases it did not really occur to those involved in the reform movement to seek or publicize the perspective of the women themselves. The reform laws were meant to give physicians the means to practice medicine as they thought appropriate, and to *assist* women and make it easier for women (in those circumstances the physicians considered sympathetic) to *ask* for an abortion. The point was certainly not to encourage women to *demand* abortion rights.

And thus it would be difficult for the medical profession as a whole to buy into an abortion rights frame, stressing women's rights to complete control over their bodies and aiming at total repeal of abortion laws. But other wings of the reform movement would have less trouble switching frames: Consider humanitarian reformers not greatly concerned with the details of medical practice, such as lawyers and other nonmedical elites and activists who had come to support the reform movement. For those not actually involved in medicine themselves, but

---

[43] Luker, *Abortion and the Politics of Motherhood*, p. 93.

who had a humanitarian interest in liberalizing abortion laws, at first the abortion law reform movement was the obvious route to take. It was the only game in town until the later years of the 1960s: It seemed new and progressive in making abortion laws less punishing. It had not yet occurred to many people to think of total repeal as an option. And so, during the reform law process, medical and humanitarian components merged into a single frame. However, while those motivated by humanitarian concerns apparently had no particular suspicions about medicine, the professional welfare and autonomy of medicine was not necessarily the top priority for nonmedical humanitarians. When physicians looked at the Sherri Finkbine case, they may have seen primarily a problem in medical practice; humanitarians, on the other hand, may have focused primarily on the plight of Finkbine herself, not her doctors or hospital.

Repeal did not necessarily or originally occur to the humanitarian reformers themselves as the most obvious, necessary path. Their basic, humanitarian goal was to make safe, legal abortion more available: At first it seemed that could be done (only) in alliance with physicians. But then feminist abortion rights groups offered what was to the humanitarians an even more thorough assault on restrictive abortion laws. So, once abortion rights feminist groups raised the banner of repeal, many humanitarian reformers abandoned reform and allied with the repeal movement, because repeal promised to make legal abortion more available than would reform.

As we have seen, then, in some parts of the country, some abortion rights feminist groups had formed by the late 1960s. At least one group was formed as early as 1961, but such groups generally did not become very publicly visible before 1969 or 1970.[44] Sometimes these groups were actively involved in helping women obtain safe, but still illegal, abortions; also important were the consciousness-raising sessions of speak-out groups, which encouraged women to share accounts of their negative experiences with illegal abortion. But, whatever the ultimate source of involvement in these groups, they had come to frame restrictive abortion laws as an unjust oppression forced upon

[44] Ibid., pp. 93–113; Lader, *Abortion II*, pp. 88–97; Suzanne Staggenborg, *The Pro-Choice Movement: Organization and Activism in the Abortion Conflict* (New York and Oxford: Oxford University Press, 1991), pp. 21–7, 43–54.

women. Their emergence on the scene was a nail in the coffin of the medical, humanitarian frame and thus also in the coffin of the reform movement.

A medical, humanitarian frame, supporting reform, could build a bridge between the humanitarians and the physician reformers. An abortion rights frame, supporting repeal, could build a bridge between the humanitarians and the abortion rights feminists. But it is difficult to see how anyone could have built a bridge between the medical profession and feminists. They were involved in the same issue – liberalizing abortion laws – for quite different, even opposed, reasons, because they disagreed who should ultimately control the abortion decision. And so their goals differed, but more important, their reasoning (i.e., their frames) differed. Having different goals is itself not necessarily an obstacle: Experienced political actors generally realize that they sometimes have to compromise on their goals and will often do so if the compromise at least takes social change in the right direction. But framing the issue in an incompatible way is much more difficult to overcome. And so a great deal of tension developed between these two groups. Abortion rights feminists had generally not been involved in the reform law discussions; once they took note of the issue, they found the medical gatekeeping and medical paternalism of the reform laws offensive. Thus, they often perceived the medical profession as their antagonists, rather than as their allies in the cause of liberalization.

But that did mean that another bridging function served by the medical frame, that is, a link to legislators, had been lost. Legislators could find appealing and uncontroversial the idea of paternalistic, humanitarian medicine – a limiting frame that involved explicit appeals that abortion was not a moral issue. But repeal in the interest of a feminist view of abortion rights was hardly uncontroversial in the early 1970s. And so repeal did not have nearly the legislative success that reform had had. A passionate abortion rights stand could build a movement but could not easily convince legislators or the public at large. It appears that a focus on abortion as part of a woman's right to control her body motivates a solid minority of the American public, but only a minority. Thus, even as early as the early 1970s, some abortion rights groups concerned with winning broad support tried to frame legal abortion as a reasonable concern rather than a dramatically feminist imperative.[45] There can be considerable tension between affirming the collective identity of a movement and reaching out to potential allies.

Granted, there was a moral component implied in the medical, humanitarian frame – in the form of sympathy for women facing unwanted pregnancies under some, but not all, circumstances – but it did not have a very specific content of moral imperatives. It did not delve too deeply into the specific moral questions abortion raised. It positively avoided those questions, so that proponents literally claimed they were addressing "humanitarian" *not* "moral" issues. It was a limiting frame, not a moral worldview, and the frame succeeded to the extent that it did not seem to address fundamental, uncompromising moral principles, the kind of principles found when issues are framed within explicit moral worldviews.[46]

Again, the limiting frame, although more effective within legislatures, could not withstand the entrance of Catholic pro-life activists or feminist abortion rights activists into the debate. The entry of new players undermined the existing frame. But it also follows that the elimination of players from debate can be as decisive as the entry of new players, as we saw in the case of the emergence of a medicalized procontraception frame in the 1920s. For reasons that had little to do with birth control per se, socialism and feminism became considerably less relevant to birth control starting in about 1920. (Socialism foundered given the problem of relating and retaining socialist ideals in the midst of World War I, and the repression of antiwar dissidents during that time; feminism weakened and divided in the wake of attaining a central goal, i.e., women's suffrage.) As a result, a fundamental reframing was possible, and it emerged quite quickly once socialism and feminism faded from the scene. By the early 1920s, Sanger was having

---

45 Staggenborg, ibid., pp. 30–2, 40.
46 Such may be the case with Gamson's "injustice" frames (*Talking Politics* and Gamson, "Constructing Social Protest," pp. 85–106 in *Social Movements and Culture*, Hank Johnston and Bert Klandermans, eds. [Minneapolis: University of Minnesota Press, 1994]). They may win broad support to the extent that such frames can build a consensus that someone or something is the source of a problem, without requiring that everyone also agree on the specific, positive moral principles that are to map out an alternative. Indeed, Gamson ("Constructing Social Protest," pp. 91–2) notes that specifying the source of a problem may be flexible enough to be compatible with a range of other political and moral positions.

some success portraying birth control in much more mainstream terms than she had just a few years earlier.

And that new birth control frame was now built on a new set of collective identities – in effect a narrower set of such identities, since key players had left the debate. The new frame reflected the loss of those players: It became more strategically effective, and it took an inegalitarian turn. Without the partnership with movements that were basically more egalitarian than inegalitarian in nature (despite their own forays into racism), the eugenic component of the birth control movement took an ugly turn toward more explicitly negative portrayals of those it deemed to be of inferior stock. And because a strategic alliance with pro–birth control members of the medical profession became possible (and because Sanger chose that path), the procontraception frame became considerably more medicalized. But those who did not want to separate birth control from a larger radical agenda – Mary Ware Dennett most prominently – for the most part could not stomach the new direction Sanger was taking the movement.

Limiting Frames and Moral Worldviews

Social Solidarity and Social Division: Two Sides of the Same Coin?

Moral worldviews do not usually serve effectively as bridging frames because they invite too many paths of opposition. They require such a broad ideological commitment that, outside of the close circle of true believers, almost anyone can find something they do not like. A moral worldview by its nature does not allow the movement to submerge points of disagreement: When a cause is framed as a moral worldview, it offers to potential supporters (and opponents) an all-or-nothing proposition. Because it makes strong moral claims and refuses to compromise, coalition building is extremely difficult or impossible. Mary Ware Dennett's principled, uncompromising stance was inimical to coalition building, as was the socialist framing of birth control in the 1910s, and as the pro-life framing of abortion may be today. Each required, or requires, too much of its audience to make it a broadly supported cause; it requires diverse audiences to agree on more than is realistic within a diverse polity.

Moral worldviews unite on a societal level when, and only when, no one is willing or able to voice an alternative opinion. Thus Durkheim spoke of unanimity of opinion and extremely tight bonds, that is, what he called "mechanical solidarity," as a possibility only in societies in which there was no social diversity.[47] Unanimity of opinion on one given issue, of course, does not require a total absence of social diversity. For example, a society or a movement might be extremely diverse economically but be linked culturally by a common ethnicity or common religion, so that, on some issues, that strong cultural bond includes a near unanimity of opinion. Or there may have been a common political experience, such as a war, that makes it unlikely that one will hear public affirmation of certain taboo opinions (e.g., friendliness toward an enemy in war). Such opinions, even if held by some segment of the population, may be politically impossible to express within mainstream society. Thus the politically acceptable view of a war or other defining political experience might be stated explicitly in worldview terms, with very strong moral force, with no significant possibility that it will encounter public contradiction.[48]

But, in the case of social movements that address issues on which there is some diversity of opinion in a given society, there is the irony that movement solidarity may be inversely proportional to the ability of that movement to frame issues in ways that can build bridges to potential allies. In contrast to limiting frames, moral worldviews have a great deal to offer those who want to mobilize and join social movements; for instance they have a great deal to offer both sides of the abortion issue. They offer a collective identity, a strong sense of purpose (which a resource mobilization view of collective identity cannot comprehend[49]). But, if the moral element is offensive to a large segment of the polity – which is perhaps likely, or else there would

---

[47] Emile Durkheim, *The Division of Labor in Society*, W. D. Halls, trans. (New York: Free Press/Macmillan, 1984).

[48] As another example, in a country as large and internationally powerful as the United States, I think it may be more feasible to express a wide range of foreign policy stances in moral worldview terms than to express domestic policy. That is, most foreign policy matters that the U.S. government addresses publicly have little obvious direct effect on most citizens, and so there is less likely to be organized, effective opposition in general on foreign policy matters than on domestic matters. The moral worldviews that politicians express in favor of their foreign policy may simply not mean much to the general population. And those likely to object to the moral worldview may mostly be people in foreign countries.

[49] Tarrow, *Power in Movement*, pp. 15, 19.

be no need for the movement – that moral frame may be the central obstacle preventing the movement from winning allies and thus attaining its goals. Politicians and public officials, for example, will find the goal too risky, too controversial. Thus the paradox that in the early and mid-1990s, pro-life, right-wing populist Patrick Buchanan could whip up a frenzied support that other politicians envy. Many of his supporters wildly affirmed his framing of American electoral politics as a "culture war" in which abortion, homosexuality, progressive politics, secularism, and so forth are all a unified moral evil that cannot be tolerated. Yet by the very nature of his uncompromising, comprehensive moral worldview, his strong support never showed any signs of translating into concrete electoral or legislative victory.

The same is true of the hard core of the pro-life movement. It has had fervent support, but among a small minority. Operation Rescue was sure that its ability to focus attention on abortion clinics and shut the clinics down would awaken the country to abortion's horrors and ultimately put abortion clinics out of business. In fact, the political reaction tipped in favor of a pro-choice view. A pro-life constitutional amendment remains a pipe dream.

A limiting frame, on the other hand, is not so explicit about addressing a range of issues. It limits its claims – whether moral or pragmatic – so that its intended audience (which might be small factions of social movements or legislators, or perhaps an entire nation) does not feel that it must commit itself to new views on a range of issues all at once.

Implicit Assumptions within Limiting Frames

But a limiting frame may avoid being explicit about certain issues because it includes implicit assumptions that are widely shared and go without challenge within a social movement, or within a society as a whole. An audience may interpret a frame to mean it does not involve radical new commitments precisely because it implicitly reaffirms long-standing commitments. That can be true in a number of ways.

For instance, there may simply be ideas and rhetoric that are uncontroversial throughout mainstream society as a whole. In certain societies, for instance, Christian rhetoric would simply not be controversial, in others Islamic rhetoric. In still others, secular rhetoric would be typical within political discussions and thus implicit secular assumptions may not be questioned, whereas religiously inspired frames would at least raise an eyebrow. In some societies, it may be assumed by most people that individual initiative is a good thing until proven otherwise; in others, the instinctive reaction might be to suspect that individualism is brazen and selfish.

A second way that widespread cultural assumptions can be implicit in a limiting frame – without ever being the topic of explicit discussion – lay in the danger, that I have noted repeatedly in this book, that some limiting frames may appear uncontroversial partly because they assume or perpetuate a negative view of groups that are not significant players in the polity. Such was the case in the eugenic component of the procontraception frame, especially in the 1930s. Even when not so directly bigoted, limiting frames may favor some groups over others without acknowledging that they are doing so, as was the case in the middle-class bias of the medical framing of birth control and abortion. The poor typically have less access to medical care; in the 1930s, even middle-class jobs did not include health insurance as they typically do today, and there was no national program to help provide health insurance for poor people. And so the mainstreaming of birth control into a medical frame in the 1920s – culminating in 1930s court decisions that physicians must be able to dispense contraceptives to their patients as physicians see fit – simply did not address the needs of poor and immigrant women and families who were unlikely to have much access to licensed physicians. Similarly, the medical framing of therapeutic abortion in the 1960s resulted, in many states, in hospital review boards having to approve such abortions. But in hindsight it is clear that the class status of a client greatly affected the chances that she would be granted a legal abortion. Educated women more easily convinced boards of professionals that an abortion was justified than did poorer, less educated women not accustomed to professional settings and professional rhetoric.[50] The portrayal of medicine as humanitarian and morally neutral may have its strengths, but it may also implicitly ignore the needs of those who are socially and culturally distant from the professional world of medicine. Even conversations that seem to be inclusive may not encounter the perspectives of those it did not occur to us to invite to participate. To return to the

[50] Luker, *Abortion and the Politics of Motherhood*, pp. 56–8.

wedding reception metaphor, even a table that is welcoming to those who know few of the guests might easily end up consisting of guests who are, for instance, all of the same race. Even in situations where we encounter new faces, some process of social filtering has often determined that certain kinds of people are unlikely to end up in the same room.

Limiting frames can work precisely because we often do not make our central cultural assumptions and cultural practices explicit, and we do not engage in debate about them. We do not make them explicit for multiple reasons: First, as just noted, we may not even be aware of what issues, or what parts of the population, we leave out of our conversations. We may not think much about the fact that we often associate with people with whom we have a great deal in common.

But it is also the case that, in almost any group, it would be impossible to imagine having to explain every decision and every action within an explicit, articulated system of thought and values. Some readers will then conclude that that means whole worldviews are in fact always implied in limiting frames, and then we hide those worldviews. But I would argue that the same logic implies that that is not always the case. In a complex and diverse society, there are always large aspects of our view of the world for which we do not need to think out detailed, logically consistent positions. And, in fact, we often do not *hold* entirely consistent or worked-out positions, which at times allows us to be open to diverse sets of values and justifications. As Alfred Schuetz argued, we use "recipes," or what Weber might call customary patterns of behavior, to address social situations because we know unconsciously that the recipe is expected and effective. So, for instance, on a daily basis we use the "recipe" that money (or its substitute, such as a credit card) allows us to buy things; when we offer money for purchases, everyone knows that this is normal and everyone knows how to respond. But most of us have at best only a vague idea why money has the particular value it does. If we go to a foreign country we exchange money and are reminded that there are things called exchange rates, but most of us have about as much of a grasp of the determinants of particular exchange rates as we have of why our solar system has nine planets rather than fifteen (or a hundred or a thousand). To use a recipe as a repertoire of interaction, we do not *need* to know where a recipe originated or why exactly it works.[51] To take another example, we do not need to know – and again most of us do not know – what exactly are the chemical properties of baking soda or yeast to know that we need to include such an ingredient in a successful cake recipe.

We can use a frame in the same sense that we use a recipe: If we are told that abortion law reform is a medical matter and had never heard anything that would suggest the contrary, that limiting frame may make sense and not lead us to think about larger moral implications for abortion law reform. If we have never heard, for example, that abortion necessarily has implications for women's reproductive freedom, it may not occur to us that the two issues are related. And so we might then take a position on abortion without actually developing a particular commitment on all its moral implications. For instance, it may not have occurred to humanitarian supporters of abortion law reform in the mid-1960s that abortion could be considered a woman's right, rather than a physician's privilege. Once an abortion rights movement emerged, many of the humanitarians might have quickly rethought the issue.

That our moral commitments might be amorphous and flexible, even on important issues, is most clear on issues on which dominant frames have not congealed. Thus, for instance, is being in favor of stem cell research a conservative or liberal position? Is stem cell research a lot like abortion, or is it more like life-saving medical research? That the Bush administration, dominated strongly by conservatives, could not in mid-2001 settle on one unambiguous position on stem cell research demonstrated that the framing of the issue is in early, undetermined stages. It is therefore not clear what it would mean to declare oneself a "conservative" on stem cell research. In 1965 it would not have been obvious what was the "conservative" position on abortion law reform.

Failing to make explicit all the implications of a frame may actually help institutionalize pluralism by, in effect, keeping our options open. And so there is a great deal of interesting sociological work that suggests that, in practice, people compartmentalize issues and ideologies. They may not contemplate all the moral and logical implications of everything they do, or they may put together ideas that we, who exist in

---

[51] Alfred Schuetz, "The Stranger," *American Journal of Sociology* 49(1944):499–507.

other worldviews, cannot anticipate. There has been interesting ethnographic research that argues, for example, that some women may be able to find incipiently feminist messages in romance novels that others find profoundly antifeminist, given story lines that imply that women's happiness is possible by finding the perfect man. Some women might find incipient feminist ideas in evangelical Protestantism,[52] despite the fact that that religious tradition has often seemed overtly antifeminist (as well as the source of energy for the more militant wing of the pro-life movement) in recent years. Some might too easily conclude that that religious tradition is inevitably and inherently patriarchal.[53] Even if it typically tends toward antifeminism, however, it does not follow that the antifeminism is inevitable.[54]

[52] Janice Radway, *Reading the Romance: Women, Patriarchy, and Popular Literature*, 2nd ed. (Chapel Hill: University of North Carolina Press, 1991); Susan D. Rose, "Women Warriors: The Negotiation of Gender in a Charismatic Community," *Sociological Analysis* 48(1987):245–58; John P. Bartkowski, *Remaking the Godly Marriage: Gender Negotiation in Evangelical Families* (New Brunswick, N.J.: Rutgers University Press, 2001).

[53] Rosalind Pollack Petchesky, *Abortion and Woman's Choice: The State, Sexuality, and Reproductive Freedom* (New York and London: Longman, 1984), pp. 257–60. Petchesky notes that it is not evangelical Protestantism that is inherently conservative and antifeminist, but that the New Right's use of the religious tradition in the pro-life movement has taken that path.

[54] Some of the points here are often made by those who consider themselves analysts of postmodernism. Although sustained discussion of the diverse family of approaches termed "postmodernist" is beyond the scope of this book, I can note briefly here why I resist joining such approaches, despite the fact that this book very much agrees with a general postmodernist point that diversity of viewpoint is central to contemporary society. First, as addressed in note 32 in this chapter, I do not think we somehow abruptly moved from a "modern" world of social-structural categories to a "postmodern" world of diverse, identity-oriented politics. There has always been diversity – explicit and hidden – and any kind of political or social identity has always had to have an element of cultural construction. (See Craig Calhoun, "Postmodernism as Pseudohistory," *Theory, Culture, and Society* 10[1993]:75–96.) We are not an obviously more fractured society than we used to be. For instance, a mid–nineteenth century Eastern European immigrant to the United States was hardly obviously closer to the dominant white Protestant world of that time than a contemporary environmentalist is to a contemporary pro-business politician.

Second, typically linked with postmodernist approaches is the "deconstruction" of discourses, which, in a glaring self-contradiction, often works from the premise there is a dominant, hidden worldview (or discourse of power) present in most rhetoric, and strengthened by that rhetoric. It would seem more consistent with a postmodernist approach instead to emphasize that any given rhetoric might allow for a true multiplicity of interpretations linked to social location, so that one cannot "deconstruct" the rhetoric down to one hidden, essential core. For illustrative examples and

Limiting frames may leave open multiple, though not infinite, future paths that a movement or a debate may take. Some options from the past may be closed off because of paths already taken. Any one of us may like or dislike the particular range of limited paths a limiting frame leaves open, or like or dislike that it has left certain paths behind. But closing off some paths does not imply closing off all paths; and so a limiting frame does not necessarily imply an entire, specified worldview.

Later in this chapter I explore further why limiting frames are essential in the institutionalization of pluralism, precisely because they can allow people to avoid commitments to entire worldviews. But first it is important to explore constraints on the strategic effectiveness of limiting frames, because that exploration helps us learn more about how limiting frames relate to dominant cultural perspectives within a given society, at a given time.

Limiting Frames, Moral Vetoes, and Moral Worldviews

Successful Moral Vetoes Depend on Consistency with Widespread Cultural Assumptions

Throughout this book I have argued that limiting frames are usually more effective than framing an issue within an explicit moral worldview, in the case of a diverse polity with liberal political structures (i.e., with a political system reasonably competitive elections and legal systems that reasonably protect civil rights). In that case, limiting frames allow for the building of bridges that can connect a broad alliance. In a diverse polity, many political discussions will involve disagreements about the full nature and implications of any particular initiative, and so convincing diverse audiences that a given initiative is a sensible, but limited, change is generally more effective than convincing diverse audiences of the need for a cultural or political revolution.

---

relevant debates, see for instance Joel F. Handler, "Postmodernism, Protest, and the New Social Movements," *Law and Society Review* 26(1992):697–731, and the responses to Handler in the same issue (vol. 26, no. 4). It should be very clear from this book that I certainly do not deny that a given body of rhetoric can help further a particular power structure. My point here is that postmodernism's often vague theoretical stance, and typical lack of detailed sociological investigation, involves too much ungrounded speculation about power structures and too much theoretical inconsistency to help us understand the relationship between rhetoric and power.

But I have also argued that policy initiatives that depend on legislative approval can often be stymied by moral vetoes. Legislators do not like to face a vote that will result in some small but significant portion of their constituents thinking their vote was outrageous and morally illegitimate.

Why, then, is any political position, or any limiting frame, not subject to a moral veto? Is there not some way to frame just about any issue in a way that suggests that a particular direction would be morally disastrous?[55] Why, for example, do legislators ever pass new laws, especially on matters that obviously touch on such morally sensitive topics as families and sexuality?

In a purely idealist, philosophical sense, yes, even the most apparently mundane issue could be framed to imply that there is impending moral and social disaster. We have to remember that there are Americans on the social margins who find the most everyday operations of government to be part of some vast "new world order" conspiracy taking away citizens' rights.

But moral vetoes do not depend simply on some lone individual's spinning a theory of moral calamity; they involve appealing to significant segments of the polity: And so there are reasons moral vetoes are effective at particular times. First, the claim made in an attempted moral veto must be compatible with prevailing cultural assumptions: It has to be about something that is familiar and important within the society as a whole – even if there is strong disagreement about how important it should be or exactly what it means. So, for instance, a claim in the United States that a policy initiative is not compatible with Hindu religion is not going to be an effective basis for a moral veto, although the same claim may work in India.

Second, and very much related, the claim must not itself seem to impose an explicit, controversial moral worldview. That is, a limiting frame works precisely because it taps into unstated, common (but not necessarily universal) cultural perspectives. If it explicitly opposes widespread cultural proclivities – offering an alternative worldview – it will not work as a veto.

For instance, a moral veto was possible against legislative liberalization of birth control because there was anxiety about women's sexuality

---

[55] I am grateful to Mark Chaves for his insightful questions that pushed me to consider this issue more fully.

and changing sexual morality. That the moral veto could be advanced by the Catholic church hierarchy is very instructive here. As discussed in Chapter 5, it is apparently paradoxical that the early-twentieth-century Catholic Church was a somewhat unpopular social presence and yet successfully raised critiques of birth control legislation as furthering sexual promiscuity and the breakdown of the family. The Catholic Church did not itself have the power to stop birth control legislation: It had as a central ally the fact that it was still culturally unacceptable to talk about sexuality openly in mainstream circles or to suggest that a different approach to sexuality was desirable. What is very notable is that the Catholic church hierarchy, for the most part, did not frame its opposition to birth control as a specifically Catholic issue. The hierarchy's role in opposing birth control could have easily backfired if it had appeared that the church was using birth control as a wedge issue to have its doctrine as a whole written into law. In fact, the Catholic hierarchy had, for the most part, developed such a positive view of church–state separation that it never would have made such an attempt in the early twentieth century. However, many Protestants feared that Catholicism were basically a strange, un-American, and undemocratic religion; they would, for example, point to the U.S. Catholic church's insistence on running its own schools and the Vatican's opposition to church–state separation at that time. (The Vatican has since come to accept the basic legitimacy of church–state separation but still claims that states do not have authority to violate fundamental, God-given morality, such as the prohibition of abortion.[56])

And so, Catholic opposition to birth control would have failed if Catholics framed that opposition in terms of papal encyclicals and natural law theology. The hierarchy did occasionally make such references, but they were strategically aware enough that, for the most part, they did not put on a public face that simply promulgated Catholic doctrine. They spoke of promiscuity, dangers to the family, and so forth. Protestants had made similar arguments in preceding decades:

---

[56] It is the case, however, that the Vatican does not draw the church–state boundary exactly the way secular states do. It claims that certain moral fundamentals, including abortion, should not be subject to electoral, democratic caprice. Still, for the most part, Catholic doctrine has reversed its former opposition to church–state separation. See Gene Burns, *The Frontiers of Catholicism: The Politics of Ideology in a Liberal World* (Berkeley: University of California Press, 1992), pp. 63–7, 200–8.

There was not a new, distinctly Catholic message in anti–birth control arguments. It was essentially the same message that had appeared for decades, just a new messenger. Although the message now came from Catholics more than from Protestants, arguments that birth control could lead society down a slippery moral slope resonated not only with Catholics. A moral veto on birth control legislation could take advantage of the fact that there was enough moral queasiness about changing family structures and women's roles that, even though a majority of Americans might have opposed the Comstock laws if given a clear choice, legislators preferred not to touch a morally charged issue.

In trying to explain why some attempts at moral vetoes will succeed and others will not, there is the methodological problem that I am appealing to the significance of widespread cultural assumptions: But how does one know what are the widespread cultural assumptions in a particular time and place? What kind of empirical evidence will demonstrate that something is or is not part of the prevailing culture?

This is indeed one of the trickiest aspects of cultural analysis, especially if we want such analysis to be empirically based rather than to be mere speculation. Implicitly I have taken the approach in this book that we should reasonably presume particular cultural dispositions exist only if the mere mention of going against certain values or practices meets a very strong reaction. So, for instance, essentially no one in mainstream U.S. society before about the 1970s questioned in a public realm that sexuality belonged only within marriage and that promiscuity and sexual scandal was always a danger. Thus the claim that sexual impropriety could be advanced by contraception or abortion was almost always taken seriously, even among those who ultimately disagreed. Their actions demonstrated that the argument was one to be dealt with.

We also must remember to think in counterfactual terms, that is, to ask whether a particular situation or rhetoric is actually not what we would normally expect. For instance, when one thinks about the fact that Roman Catholicism of the early twentieth century was a distinct subculture, it is surprising that Catholic prelates would make arguments within American public affairs that actually had little specifically Catholic content. These are the types of clues that help us discover when a debate touches upon widespread cultural assumptions. A not particularly popular group, the Catholic hierarchy, could find itself on the winning side of legislative debate not because the group itself had positive power to force policy changes, but because it took a position consistent with widespread cultural assumptions and in fact played down the very distinctiveness that made it unpopular. And it took a position that was consistent with legislators doing nothing, as opposed to taking initiative. That is how a moral veto works.

And so when the message a group successfully promotes is strategically successful, but not what one would expect from that particular group, we are probably viewing something related to widespread cultural assumptions. I am hesitant, however, to make claims about the existence of cultural inclinations when the evidence is merely subtle: We are best able to avoid mere speculation when the evidence for a widespread cultural inclination involves patterns that at some level are unusually striking.[57]

Moral Vetoes Are Especially Successful at Widening Discussion Beyond Elites

In one sense, quiet elite discussions are especially likely to avoid addressing anyone's moral fundamentals. On the other hand, that means that they sometimes do not consider the moral implications of their discussions and so once there is public voice given to moral objections, a moral veto is especially likely. (Of course such a moral veto must meet the test discussed above: It must not itself require acceptance of an unorthodox, explicit moral worldview.)

In general, quiet discussions among people used to working with each other and elite discussions (which are often one and the same thing) produce limiting frames, not moral worldviews. In legislatures, for example, most bills are simply not of great concern to most people: The discussions are technocratic, not morally charged. There is little

---

[57] One might think of this approach as the "dummy variable" analysis of cultural trends. (A dummy variable can have just two values, usually zero or one. For instance, one might code opinion data so that all U.S. citizens are coded as zero on the citizenship variable, and everyone else is coded as 1.) That is, if we contrast times or social situations when an argument is strident versus times or contexts when it is completely absent, we are likely to have a finger on something important about cultural assumptions and can avoid empirically unconvincing, obscure cultural analysis.

public notice, and limiting frames dominate, whether or not elites care about the issue.

In U.S. reproductive politics, discussions have been quiet to the extent that they have indeed been primarily elite discussions. A medical, limiting frame gradually came to dominate the birth control debate once most of the grassroots social movement activity had faded. However, for a couple of decades moral vetoes emerged whenever the discussion threatened to widen, that is, whenever legislatures tried to take up the issue. As a limiting frame, a medical framing of birth control had the best chance when the discussion was limited to courts, where the discussion was shielded from direct politicization.

Similarly a limiting frame dominated the abortion debate before that grassroots activity emerged. Once the discussion widened, the medical, limiting frame collapsed.

Elite worlds are by definition small, and elites are involved in conversations oriented toward getting things done. Anyone who has climbed a career ladder, for example, knows that professional insiders can easily find the sudden involvement of an outsider in decision making to be troublesome and disruptive. An outsider may not be accustomed to the kinds of conversational and interpersonal boundaries implicit in professional, elite agendas. And so professors at state universities groan when internal academic discussions become politicized within state legislatures; corporate boards groan when a religious group or protest organization calls their decisions immoral.

It is nearly impossible to have a large meeting of professionals, business people, and so forth, if every aspect of every agenda item is fair game. Managers oriented toward efficient decision making, for example, work to prevent anyone from using agenda items to reopen old, deep wounds or revisit recurring tensions within an organization. It is easier to make decisions if there are clear boundaries to the collective conversations allowed, especially boundaries that keep everyone in the conversation focused on specific, even technocratic, goals, rather than divisive, morally charged battles.

Elites are particularly adept within, and accustomed to, such conversations, especially business, professional, and administrative elites: That is much of what they do as elites. Usually, then, elites disproportionately dominate discussions and decision making. Those heavily involved in a given line of policy or business would generally rather not allow morally charged rhetoric enter into their everyday decision-making processes. Within the routines of government, administration, and business, such rhetoric slows down decisions and gets people upset in ways that elites consider time-consuming and disruptive. Even those of us who like to think of ourselves as egalitarian quickly see in organizational settings that wide open agendas and frequent heated exchanges typically stymie efforts to make and implement decisions. When we are part of such an elite, we hardly see such limitation of agendas as elitist.

And so everyday policy making, business, and administration on its face involves a large dose of what Weber sees as characteristic of bureaucratic decision making.[58] That is, there are clear rules of procedure, and decisions are made impersonally. Authority depends on expertise and office (i.e., one's position within an organization) rather than simply personality or personal background. And so limiting frames dominate most of life in modern society. In a complex bureaucratic society, elites, almost intrinsically, are the masters of limiting frames.

Elite-led limiting frames, then, dominate most policy making and indeed much organized decision making in general. But the Achilles' heal of elite involvement in the routinization of decision making is that, while such discussions often truly are based primarily on impersonal expertise so that most people would find the discussions dry and uninteresting, others may not see it that way. Just because a discussion is "elite" does not mean there is any nefarious intent to keep things behind closed doors; but from the point of view of people who have strong moral opinions on an issue, that is how matters may appear. That is, discussions pursued in technocratic terms can easily implicitly assume that there are limits to who is involved in the conversation (perhaps by assuming few people would be qualified, or perhaps even interested). And sometimes the insistence on technocratic discussion can even consciously be an attempt to limit agendas. That is, at times, rules of debate in a bureaucratic setting (such as a hearing) may require participants to appeal to impersonal rules, even when the majority of people in the room know that the speaker in fact has a large personal stake in the decision. Many of us can think of examples of meetings

---

[58] Max Weber, *The Theory of Social and Economic Organization*, pp. 328–41.

that rhetorically would appear polite and formal, even boring, to outsiders, but in which insiders know that strong feelings of resentment and disagreement are just beneath the surface.

Elites are ill equipped to deal with those relatively rare, but substantively highly significant, periods when nonelites insist on being heard during a conversation that elites would like to deal with bureaucratically. This is the type of unbounded conversation that elites find disruptive and inefficient; indeed, one might say it certainly is disruptive and inefficient if the goal is actually to implement something new. If a limiting frame develops as an elite, quiet discussion, it quickly collapses when a debate becomes a widespread, grassroots concern.[59]

A limiting frame, then, is particularly likely to face a moral veto when it is purely an elite-held frame, but also when there exists a great deal of moral passion in the society at large on that same issue. That is, if elites at first control the political discussion of an issue outside of public view, but strong opinions emerge as a public discussion breaks out, the limiting frame quickly crumbles. Such was the case with abortion around 1970. Other people who deeply cared about abortion simply did not look at the world in the same way as reform-minded physicians and their allies.

On the other hand, limiting frames that are widely accepted because many groups have an interest in preserving them are not so subject to moral vetoes. Examples can be seen in the use of religious imagery in U.S. politics: The limit is that tying political appeals to particular denominations or particularly sectarian religious traditions usually backfires. That is, in a situation of religious pluralism and First Amendment rights, no single denomination is a majority and each has an interest in preventing law or policy framed in highly sectarian ways and/or favoring one denomination.[60] Now it remains the case that religious

---

59 This can be true even on technocratic initiatives that initially appear to have no reasonable basis of opposition: see Robert L. Crain, Elihu Katz, and Donald B. Rosenthal, *The Politics of Community Conflict: The Fluoridation Decision* (Indianapolis: Bobbs-Merrill, 1969).

60 Alan Wolfe presents evidence that suggests that a basic acceptance of religious pluralism has become the dominant position within American culture: *One Nation After All* (New York: Viking/Penguin, 1998). But there are also legal and political mechanisms that would make sectarian religious appeals difficult to sustain even without such a cultural predisposition: That is, it simply is the case that no one denomination and no one specific Christian tradition is close to being a majority, and so a sectarian

appeals, like limiting frames in general, can include implicit cultural assumptions. Thus, for instance, Christian appeals – even if only vaguely Christian – are more common than other appeals, and non-Western religions are implicitly excluded from religious imagery used in U.S. politics. But there are limits nevertheless, so that attempts to condemn a policy because it violates specifically Catholic or evangelical or Baptist beliefs not shared by most other Americans are generally insufficient to block a policy. (Claiming that a policy is discriminatory, on the other hand, may be more effective, because then it is not religious doctrine at stake but equality before the law and basic rights that are supposed to be available to all minorities, religious or not.) And so, for instance, while most Americans presumably learn that Martin Luther King, Jr., was a minister, how many know the denomination to which he belonged?[61] His powerful, religiously inspired appeals transcended denominational specifics.

Reproductive Politics, Moral Vetoes, and Social Conflict in Contemporary America

The Long-Term Strategic Advantage of the Pro-Choice Frame
Certainly some readers would find the birth control of the 1910s more appealing than the birth control movement of the 1920s and 1930s. In the 1910s, the movement had a broader set of commitments, including especially the socialist movement. In the 1920s and 1930s, it was less committed to birth control as a means of empowering poor women; it was less committed to rethinking social injustice as a whole. Indeed, in

---

movement that gets very far politically will make too many enemies and be reminded of its minority status. Still, again, a *vaguely* Christian perspective almost certainly is culturally dominant in the United States.

[61] The Christian Right in recent years, much more than has religiously inspired U.S. political movements, has often made political claims appealing implicitly or explicitly to sectarian religious ideals. But I would argue that, for the most part, the political reactions they receive in electoral contests demonstrate that the religiously sectarian political appeals typically backfire. For the most part, the Christian Right is not politically popular, and their few electoral successes have come in Republican caucuses where those eligible to vote are much more conservative than the electorate as a whole (e.g., Pat Robertson in the 1988 Iowa presidential caucus) or in school board elections where turnout is very low. Arguably they also have had success in affecting appointed positions, especially during the presidency of George W. Bush, and including in court appointments, which might give the Christian Right in the end considerably more influence than its quite limited electoral successes would suggest.

the 1930s, a crude and discriminatory eugenics was for some supporters an equally important commitment as birth control.

But the birth control movement of the 1920s and 1930s was more strategically effective than the movement of the 1910s. In its early years, the birth control movement asked not just that supporters and allies support the distribution of condoms and diaphragms; it asked for commitment to a morally charged worldview, with a wide agenda. It was difficult for the movement to change voluntarily, because that worldview was exciting and intensely meaningful to participants. They could not change the frame without, to a great extent, changing who they were.

One can see a similar dynamic in the pro-life movement today: It involves intense feelings of commitment, so that some participants are willing to go to jail for a moral crusade that they could not consider more important. In many ways, the pro-life movement appears to be a stronger movement than pro-choice: Its members seem more committed, and they seem to put in more time.[62] Moral certainty keeps the movement going, but it also keeps most other Americans away. The pro-life movement has not had that much success in changing the law. The intense solidarity of a movement that feels it possesses a stunning and comprehensive moral truth makes it very difficult to build allies. Even Americans who have some sympathy for the pro-life position find the moral certainty of pro-life activists to be extreme and unappealing. Some supporters admit that the American public perceives the pro-life movement to be more extremist in nature than the pro-choice movement.[63] Some leaders of the pro-life movement argue that, strategically, they need to face up to the fact that, to get anywhere, they have to make some strategic compromises. They have to support a moderately pro-life presidential candidate instead of a firebrand from the Christian Right; they have to accept legal abortion under some circumstances in order to build a coalition that will at least take away part of *Roe v. Wade*. A half loaf is better than none. But, for the purists, any pragmatic compromise is morally corrupt, and the pro-life movement seems to be dominated by the purists.

[62] Luker, *Abortion and the Politics of Motherhood*, pp. 250–1.
[63] Hunter, "What Americans Really Think about Abortion," *First Things* 24(1992), p. 20.

Like the Catholic Church's ability to affect the birth control debate in the early twentieth century, the pro-life movement's ability to influence contemporary U.S. politics is not the result of interest group power: The Christian Right cannot come close to getting its own agenda written into law. Instead it succeeds when it can tap into widespread cultural sympathies with babies as innocent creatures needing protection. When people on the fence think of abortion and babies at the same time, the pro-life side is on its way to victory.

But the pro-life side in the long term may undermine its own moral force by appearing to present a moral worldview at odds with mainstream U.S. society. Why? Because the nature of social solidarity within that movement makes it so difficult for the movement to limit its claims in a way compatible with the moral queasiness many Americans have about abortion. The majority of Americans have moral qualms about abortion in at least some circumstances but are not willing to see it as unambiguously unacceptable and evil in all circumstances. Not much more than about one-fourth of Americans are hundred percent opposed to, or in favor of, legal abortion under all circumstances (with just a bit more than half of that minority in the pro-choice camp). The typical American is sympathetic toward women seeking abortion for "hard" reasons like serious health dangers, rape, and incest but becomes less supportive of legal abortion the more they perceive women to be resorting to abortion for elective, less serious reasons. Although there has been some fluctuation over the last three decades, and overall support for a pro-choice position has risen a bit, survey data indicate more stability than change in attitudes toward abortion.[64] The majority of Americans, then, are balancing what they see as understandable reasons for resorting to abortion versus the fact that they see serious moral issues involved.

But the dominant view in the pro-life movement seems to be that abortion is not *only* about babies, and not about balancing difficult priorities. And again, there is considerable evidence that commitment

---

[64] See, e.g., Elizabeth Adell Cook, Ted G. Jelen, and Clyde Wilcox, *Between Two Absolutes: Public Opinion and the Politics of Abortion* (Boulder, Col.: Westview, 1992); Barbara Norrander and Clyde Wilcox, "Public Opinion and Policy Making in the States: The Case of Post-*Roe* Abortion Policy, *Policy Studies Journal* 27(1999):707–22, p. 709.

to the core of the pro-life movement involves a belief that abortion is a moral cataclysm, degrading and threatening the morality of society as a whole. It is very difficult to sell a broad agenda of moral cataclysm in a diverse society, with a functioning electoral system, regardless of whether the messenger is right or wrong. Whenever the pro-life movement attempts to claim that abortion has disastrous implications even beyond the practice of abortion itself (e.g., in claiming, as has Pope John Paul II, that abortion is part of a "culture of death"[65]), they may heighten the commitment of their core supporters, but they fail to persuade the public as a whole. I would argue that when the pro-life movement claims that abortion is like the Nazi Holocaust, or that legal abortion will lead to the decline of Western civilization, most Americans find such claims implausible. They do not pay attention to such claims, except perhaps to the extent that they see them as evidence that the pro-life movement consists of extremist zealots.

Another central reason that the pro-life movement may appear to many Americans to be pushing a controversial moral worldview is that antiabortion violence has been visible for well over a decade. Seven abortion workers, primarily doctors, were targeted and murdered in the 1990s, and on average there was about one bombing of a U.S. abortion clinic per year in the last decade. According to statistics maintained by the professional association of abortion providers, vandalism and threatened or attempted violence, including anthrax attacks (especially in 2001), have been very common, typically more than fifty incidents nationally per year, peaking in the early 1990s and in the first few years of the new century. The vandalism is probably too common (and not as dramatic as a bombing or shooting) for the media to take much interest. In the early 1990s, there were typically ten to twenty incidents of arson and attempted arson at U.S. abortion clinics nationally, though arson has become quite uncommon in recent years. While pro-life activists might be skeptical of statistics kept by abortion providers, data concerning the more serious crimes of murder, bombings, and arson, as well as attempted bombings and arson, are taken from the data of law enforcement authorities. Considerably more frequent, and also

---

[65] See Ronald R. Burke, "*Veritatis Splendor*: Papal Authority and the Sovereignty of Reason," pp. 119–36 in *Veritatis Splendor: American Responses*, Michael E. Allsopp and John J. O'Keefe, eds. (Kansas City: Sheed & Ward, 1995).

reflecting the data of law enforcement agencies, has been stalking of clinic personnel, typically with more than ten incidents per year nationally, and during the mid-1990s typically more than sixty incidents per year.[66]

Those who engage in bombings and shootings of abortion workers – although they certainly see the fight against abortion in epochal terms, which thus supplies them with a great sense of personal purpose – are typically only marginally associated with pro-life organizations. Mainstream pro-life leaders condemn such violence (though, in the minds of pro-choice leaders, not always as unambiguously as they should).[67] But opposition to abortion is most visible when such violence receives press coverage. Such violence has of course immediate and traumatic effects on clinic workers,[68] while probably also hardening the resolve of those most committed to the pro-choice movement. But here I am concerned with the political effects of such a fallout within American society as a whole. Once associated, rightly or wrongly, with the pro-life movement as a whole, such violence is incompatible with a "limiting" agenda. That is, a movement that is thought to engage in illegal acts of violence, including murder, is hardly going to be seen as a movement that aims for limited and legitimate social change and an agenda acceptable to people who have a variety of viewpoints. Indeed, it is clear that pro-life militance and violence against abortion clinics, especially at one of its peak periods in the early 1990s, resulted in more negative public opinion about the pro-life movement.[69] Operation Rescue claimed to be a nonviolent movement in the tradition of the Civil Rights Movement, and undoubtedly many of its members are sincerely committed to the classic nonviolent protest techniques that the organization professes. But antiabortion violence escalated with the

---

[66] National Abortion Federation, "NAF Violence and Disruption Statistics," as of June 30, 2003, at http://www.prochoice.org/Violence/Statistics/stats.pdf (accessed October 8, 2003).

[67] See, e.g., Dallas Blanchard and Terry J. Prewitt, *Religious Violence and Abortion: The Gideon Project* (Gainesville: University Press of Florida, 1993); Ginsburg, "Saving America's Souls," p. 53.

[68] See, e.g., Kevin M. Fitzpatrick and Michele Wilson, "Exposure to Violence and Post-traumatic Stress Symptomatology among Abortion Clinic Workers," *Journal of Traumatic Stress* 12(1999):227–42.

[69] Karen O'Connor, *No Neutral Ground? Abortion Politics in an Age of Absolutes* (Boulder, Col.: Westview, 1996), pp. 137–8.

growth of Operation Rescue. Sociologist Victoria Johnson has argued
that Operation Rescue, while clearly drawing partly from traditions
of nonviolent protest, frames the abortion conflict in a way that easily
slides into tactics that depart from that tradition. That is, in comparing different kinds of civil disobedience movements, Johnson argues
that framing the struggle as an epochal struggle that needs immediate
resolution, and portraying the opposition as so fundamentally evil to
the point of dehumanizing them, results in tactics of intimidation and
harassment of opponents, endorsement of vandalism, and aggressive,
rather than passive, civil disobedience, for instance in the blockades of
clinic entrances.[70]

The pro-choice side, on the other hand, has generally gone the more
pragmatic route, and the "pro-choice" frame is more of a limiting frame
than is an "abortion rights" frame.[71] The pro-choice rhetoric often
implies that legal abortion, far from heralding a sweeping reform of
society, is simply a regrettable necessity. This was clearly the rhetoric of
prominent politicians like former New York Governor Mario Cuomo,
among the more prominent Catholic politicians in recent years (as there
was often speculation Cuomo would be a major presidential candidate)
who has claimed that he personally opposed abortion but thought it
was improper to impose a legal ban before building a national consensus and dealing effectively with the social problems that lead women
to need abortions.[72] Similarly, Bill Clinton, although clearly supporting legal abortion, framed his support in terms of making abortion
"safe, legal, and rare," that is, less necessary if social supports were
in place and contraception were easily available. And so he stated as
a presidential candidate in 1992: "We have to remind the American

[70] Victoria Johnson, "Operation Rescue, Vocabularies of Motive, and Tactical Action:
A Study of Movement Framing in the Practice of Quasi-nonviolence," *Research in
Social Movements, Conflict and Change* 20(1997):103–50.
[71] For an interesting discussion of how the pro-choice frame does not emphasize
women's rights, see Myra Marx Ferree, William Anthony Gamson, Jürgen Gerhards,
and Dieter Rucht, *Shaping Abortion Discourse: Democracy and the Public Sphere in
Germany and the United States* (New York and Cambridge: Cambridge University
Press, 2002), pp. 132, 149–51.
[72] See Mario Cuomo, "Religious Belief and Public Morality: A Catholic Governor's
Perspective," a September 13, 1984, lecture at the University of Notre Dame;
text available at the website of the University of Notre Dame Archives, http://
classic.archives.nd.edu/episodes/visitors/cuomo/cuomo.html (accessed October 30,
2003).

people once again that being pro-choice is very different from being pro-abortion."[73]

Pro-life forces of course scoffed at what they saw as Clinton's duplicity and at the notion that abortion under *Roe* would ever become rare. But the distinction often seems to be treated at face value. Now, there are certainly many Americans mobilized in favor of abortion as a right, and "pro-choice" is often used as a synonym for "abortion rights." But the pluralist version of pro-choice that seems to have gained ground, especially since *Webster*, implies that it is best not to impose a particular moral position by law. Furthermore, that frame implies that some abortions are necessary, and that other abortions will happen no matter what the law says, so it is best to make legal abortion accessible and thus safe. The humanitarian element, then, has resurfaced (and even includes a hint of medical justification), although the larger 1960s medical frame of which it had been a component has died. It is now tied to the pluralist frame implied in legislative arguments in the 1960s that abortion reform legislation was "permissive," not "mandatory." Pro-choice, to the extent that it is distinct from an abortion rights frame, emphasizes a humanitarian and pluralist rationale that does not require of the audience that they accept a particular, encompassing moral worldview. Perhaps they could do so precisely because, as Luker and others[74] have noted, the movement

---

[73] "Clinton Meets with Anti-Apartheid Leader," *St. Petersburg Times* (Florida), July 16, 1992.

[74] Kristin Luker, *Abortion and the Politics of Motherhood* (Berkeley: University of California Press, 1984), p. 241; Faye Ginsburg, *Contested Lives: The Abortion Debate in an American Community* (Berkeley: University of California Press, 1989), p. 72. William Saletan, a political reporter for *Slate* magazine, interprets this reframing of abortion rights into a pro-choice rhetoric as ultimately a move to the right, in a way that made it impossible for the pro-choice side to argue for Medicaid funding for abortions or for a broader government commitment to reproductive rights. (Saletan *Bearing Rights: How Conservatives Won the Abortion War* [Berkely: University of California Press, 2003]). He sees the pro-choice side thus as having help set up the conditions for its own defeat. I think Saletan is correct in saying that the pluralist pro-choice rhetoric is more conservative and limited in its claims than is an explicit rhetoric about abortion rights. But Saletan at times implies that American political realities pushed the pro-choice movement in that more conservative direction – an implication with which I would agree – but at other times implies a different argument, that an uncompromising abortion rights rhetoric would have had more success than does the mainstream pro-choice movement in defending and expanding reproductive freedom, including Medicaid funding for abortion. Here I would disagree: it is

somewhat lost its intensity after the apparent full-scale victory of *Roe v. Wade* in 1973. That is, perhaps by the time *Roe* came under assault, especially during the Reagan administration in the 1980s, the movement for legal abortion was not restrained by the intense solidarity the abortion rights movement had experienced in the years leading up to *Roe*, when abortion speak-outs (publicly speaking about one's own illegal abortion) and a fervent commitment to providing women what they considered a fundamental right were components of a passionate solidarity. After *Roe*, the movement for legal abortion was perhaps more like the birth control movement after World War I: The previously intense movement solidarity had weakened, so that pragmatic, limiting frames became an option that the remaining movement could support.

It is possible that some of the ideas that animate the pro-life frame might actually have more influence if the pro-life movement ceased to exist. Much as a birth control movement infused with socialism in the 1910s was too scary for too many Americans, a pro-life movement that seems to promote a sectarian and unorthodox moral worldview may invite too many paths of opposition for even some of its more mainstream ideas to have great cultural influence. The more culturally resonant issues of the movement may not be heard amid what seems to the majority of Americans to be too much shouting.

Still, it is not only having a culturally resonant message that is necessary for political victory. Throughout the analysis here, I have tried to be faithful to Paul Burstein's call for sociologists to pay more attention to how different types of governmental structures either facilitate or

unlikely an abortion rights framing could have become widely accepted in the United States. The pro-choice movement is better off fighting wider battles in the long run by not staking its identity immediately on battles it cannot currently win. Saletan's lamentations about the conservative nature of the pro-choice rhetoric is much like the complaints that the birth control movement should have stuck to its radical message of the 1910s: that is fine if you make the untenable assumption that such rhetoric would have led to political success. And like other analysts who overestimate pro-life successes, Saletan takes any modifications at all in *Roe v. Wade* – modifications which indeed have gone in directions opposed by the pro-choice movement – as indications that the pro-life side is winning the war. But any whittling away at *Roe* since 1973 pales into comparison with the enormous expansion in legal abortion that *Roe* instituted. Yes, the pro-life side has had some victories, but mostly at the margins: to say they are winning the war is not tenable when one compares access to legal abortion with such access four decades ago.

constrain responsiveness to the public.[75] For instance, central to understanding why laws may not reflect public opinion is that moral vetoes depend on the fact that, because they face the electorate, legislators are typically hesitant to delve into morally charged, publicly divisive battles. Even a frame that is culturally dominant is not necessarily written into law.

But courts have more autonomy from public controversy, especially courts characterized by lifetime appointments. And so the Supreme Court could act in the 1970s in the way that most legislatures could not. Similarly, even though the pro-choice frame has a cultural advantage, the Supreme Court could act in the future to curtail or even reverse *Roe*. I would predict that, if the Court does so, the United States will have a battle over abortion that may make the last few decades look tame: Much of America has had three decades to become accustomed to the access available since *Roe*, and taking away is much more difficult than never giving in the first place. There would be massive protests and civil disobedience, with surreptitious or perhaps deliberate and open flouting of the newly restrictive laws. Legislatures would be hounded by pro-life and pro-choice forces intent on seeing their vision either retained or instituted into law. The majority of states would find that their nineteenth-century laws would automatically again take effect, although only a small portion of the population believed that abortion should be so restrictive. And so states would be faced with the unpalatable choice of retaining such a law or having to take the initiative to change it, in which case the electoral and legislative process would be overwhelmed by the abortion issue: Significant portions of the electorate would become single-issue voters and punish any legislator who voted the wrong way on abortion.

But again, the Supreme Court consists of justices with lifetime appointments; they do not necessarily base decisions on whether resistance is likely to result.

---

[75] Burstein, "Bringing the Public Back In: Should Sociologists Consider the Impact of Public Opinion on Public Policy?" *Social Forces* 77(1998):27–62. Burstein's argument is consistent with the argument in this book that some social movements fail to affect policy primarily because they frame issues in a way that cannot gather widespread public support (Burstein, p. 50). I would, however, emphasize even more than Burstein (pp. 47–8) that governmental institutions and political processes do not simply respond to public opinion; they also help shape that opinion.

Limiting Frames, Moral Worldviews, and Cultural Pluralism

I have emphasized that limiting frames tap into cultural assumptions, typically assumptions that are too common even for people to think about them explicitly – that is, it does not occur to people that the world could be otherwise. That can mean that denigration of groups marginal to the polity, and maintenance of their marginal position, can be an implicit part of a limiting frame.

However, even a limiting frame that victimizes disadvantaged groups is probably more likely, in the long run, to allow for the expansion of pluralism than is a frame based explicitly in a moral worldview. Sanger's framing of birth control in the 1920s primarily emphasized a medical approach to birth control. Nevertheless, another component of the frame was its eugenics; as I have noted, the eugenics became more specific and thus more bigoted as the restraining influences of socialism and feminism faded into the background.

But ultimately eugenics itself could fade into the background, especially after the experience with Naziism in World War II. Because the eugenics was not the most prominent, specified part of the frame, eugenics could disappear without destroying the frame's primary rationale for supporting birth control.

Indeed, although the change was slow, after a couple of generations the idea that contraception was a sensible option for middle-class couples gradually undermined the attempt to keep contraceptives away from the public. And so for almost half a century it has been the exception rather than the rule that making contraception accessible to adults requires any particular justification.[76] Sanger achieved her goals much more slowly than she hoped, or even acknowledged. But ultimately birth control did become considerably more accessible. Access to contraception still is linked strongly to income, but I would argue that it is less the result of the medical framing in Sanger's time than the economics of health care in contemporary United States. (The cost of a number of contraceptive methods can be considerable for people on

---

[76] There remain controversies involving contraception, but only when other moral controversies are explicitly involved. Primarily controversy exists around the question of supplying birth control to minors. But it is not that contraception is itself considered inherently controversial, as demonstrated by the fact that adult use is unquestioned in most quarters. The controversy surrounds instead the issue of youth sexuality.

a low income. Many health insurance plans cover those contraceptives involving a trip to the doctor and a prescription, such as the pill, or the intrauterine device, i.e., the IUD. But the United States has a system in which health insurance is provided primarily by employers. Insurance is typically very good for those who have a middle-class or upper-class job in the family, reasonably good for those living in poverty and in states with comprehensive Medicaid programs, and poor or absent for everyone else. About forty-five million Americans have no health insurance.)

For now, let us again contrast the limiting birth control frame to the alternatives. What moral worldview frame might have instead promoted birth control, and what would have been the consequences? First, there was socialism, a strategic failure: If birth control advocates had never disentangled the cause of birth control from the cause of socialism, then birth control would have elicited even stronger opposition. Similarly with feminism, whose links to birth control were even less explicit than were the socialist links. The only other alternative moral worldview frame would appear to have been an even stronger version of eugenics: And that would hardly have helped the plight of the poor and people of color, or the cause of pluralism. Fortunately eugenics never threatened to become the dominant justification for birth control.

The specter of eugenics, however, raises the point that moral worldview frames can victimize disadvantaged groups more thoroughly and brutally than can limiting frames. If eugenics had become so prominent as to provide a broad and explicit view of how society should be structured, the negative aspects of eugenics would have been even more severe. In any frame – whether a limiting frame or a moral worldview – it is easy to pursue negative portrayals of groups without a voice in the polity. But a limiting frame, even when biased toward certain social groups, leaves open some possibilities: If we have left a group out of the conversation, a limiting frame at least does not call for a sweeping reordering of society while completely disregarding that group. There remains an opportunity for further change down the road: Even the bigotry of a limiting frame is not so brutally implemented as is the bigotry of a moral worldview.

This does not mean that social change must always be slow and incremental, nor that we are supposed to be only amoral pragmatists. A limiting frame may in fact draw attention and support for an issue resulting in dramatic social change – as long as that issue can rhetorically be stated with specific moral force, focusing on a specific outrage that is nearly impossible to justify when brought into the open. Limiting frames can be purely technocratic and amoral, or they can have a very targeted moral message that does not elicit fear that a moral *worldview* is being imposed. Ending the daily indignities, and the occasional violent brutality, of legally enforced segregation was a great victory, morally, socially, and politically. It required a limiting frame, one focused specifically on the evils of segregation. A limiting frame is a frame that limits rhetorical claims and limits the explicit *agenda*; it does not necessarily limit social or political impact to incrementalism. The early Civil Rights Movement has probably had the most far-reaching effect on U.S. society of any twentieth-century social movement; it did so not by calling for revolution but by demanding that Americans practice what they preached.

A limiting frame for birth control also in the end had profound significance for U.S. society. Making birth control more available affected the lives of many people, and even though abortion law reform in most states had only a small effect on actual abortion practice, such reform may have been a crucial step in making the abortion issue ultimately central to U.S. politics.

All these examples involved political success through limiting frames. Arguably, in fact, limiting frames are ultimately more effective in bringing about long-term social change than are moral worldview frames. The latter too easily involve moral vetoes, and thus stalemates.

A limiting frame does not necessarily deny the eventual relevance of a wider agenda, but it doesn't try to convince people that they must settle all agenda items at once. Preventing a limiting frame from quietly reinforcing existing, accepted social inequalities requires constant vigilance. But a limiting frame does not carry as great a risk as do moral worldview frames that it could create even more radical inequality and repression than already exists. And it may remove a crucial impediment, like segregation, from the path of egalitarian social change.

Durkheimian Social Order versus Cultural Pluralism
The preceding discussion partly develops my own reasoning for preferring limiting frames. But the central point of this book is the empirical,

sociological nature of limiting frames versus moral worldviews. To say that limiting frames "work" is not to say that they are necessarily good. I think it is possible to accept my argument about why limiting frames are strategically effective under certain empirical circumstances without agreeing that limiting frames are in fact desirable outcomes. Indeed all of us have limits to our pluralism and our willingness to limit the agenda: Certain moral stands are nonnegotiable, even if they happen to be unpopular or strategically difficult in certain settings. For pro-life activists, for instance, it is often the case that any kind of turmoil surrounding the abortion debate pales in comparison to the horror of what they consider over a million murders in the United States annually. We can disentangle sociological claims from normative claims.

That is precisely what we need to do in sociological discussions of the cultural bases of social order. That is, I would argue that discussions of the cultural bases of social order have included a Durkheimian theoretical bias that assumes that consensus over moral worldviews is always socially desirable. In this final section of the book, I want to demonstrate that the history of reproductive politics shows how problematic that assumption is.

Certainly not all social analysis accepts the premise, prominently associated with the social theory of Emile Durkheim, that moral consensus is a prerequisite of social order.[77] But this premise has been fundamental to a wide range of sociological work and arguably is one of the most commonly accepted sociological principles. Discussions of the cultural bases of social order usually assume Durkheimian premises,[78] and not just in the academic world of sociology. There is a strong presence in the public intellectual sphere of arguments that culture, in the words of James Hunter,

is first and foremost a *normative* structure of "commanding truths" – commanding, in the final analysis, because they derive from an understanding if

---

[77] For a discussion of the sociological tradition identifying normative consensus with social order, see Dennis Wrong, *The Problem of Order: What Unites and Divides Society* (New York: Free Press, 1994).

[78] See, e.g., Daniel Bell, *The Cultural Contradictions of Capitalism* (New York: Basic Books, 1976), p. 154; James Davison Hunter, *Culture Wars: The Struggle to Define America* (New York: Basic Books/Harper Collins, 1991), p. 313. I detail below how such assumptions have very directly informed sociological analysis of abortion politics.

not an encounter with the "sacred" (Emile Durkheim's word), or in a slightly less loaded term, what Paul Tillich called the "orienting principle" of one's life.[79]

Hunter even states that "any sociologist or anthropologist" would agree that "commanding truths" define a culture.

But there are indeed sociologists and anthropologists who would disagree. Included in that group are those who emphasize the interdependence and diversity implicit in Durkheim's "organic solidarity," a diversity that becomes increasingly important in complex societies but that, as a concept, has not been as popular as Durkheim's emphasis on moral consensus.[80] Durkheim argued that a shared, common culture is sufficient for social order only in a homogeneous society. In large, diverse societies, social order would be built instead on organic solidarity, that is, interdependence within the division of labor.[81] Durkheim used the concept of "division of labor" broadly, to mean any system of diverse and complementary social roles. But the concept of organic solidarity has had little impact on discussions of social order. The concept has its limitations: Within liberal societies, it is quite obvious that social order depends not just on interdependence, but also on some degree of autonomy for both individuals and social groups. Organic solidarity vaguely points to the idea of cultural pluralism, but it is not itself exactly what we usually mean by pluralism. That "organic solidarity" does not really seem to capture the nature of contemporary democratic society probably explains why, even when discussions of social order refer to it, the discussion is underdeveloped.

That wing of sociology most inclined to reject Durkheimian assumptions, that is, what is sometimes called "conflict theory" (really a family of approaches rather than a specific theory), does not offer a good, alternative explanation of the cultural bases of social order. Mostly, such approaches do not talk much about social order at all, because they

---

79 James Davison Hunter, *Before the Shooting Begins: Searching for Democracy in America's Culture War* (New York: Free Press, 1994), p. 252n.29. Emphasis is Hunter's.

80 Philip Selznick, *The Moral Commonwealth: Social Theory and the Promise of Community* (Berkeley: University of California Press, 1992), p. 369. The emphasis on moral consensus by sociologists who call themselves Durkheimian has been so strong that I generally describe my own argument as non-Durkheimian, even though arguably it is within the spirit of Durkheim's concept of organic solidarity.

81 Durkheim, *The Division of Labor in Society*.

do not value social order. While a bit of a simplification, it is generally accurate to say that such theories – including the work of Marxist sociologists, elite theorists in the C. Wright Mills tradition, and structural theories of social movements and revolutions – start from the premise that "social order" is built upon the repression of those exploited within a given social-structural distribution of power.

Thus explanations of social order, especially the cultural bases of social order, have mainly been the province of Durkheimians. And unfortunately, when sociological theories of conflict – or those that begin by arguing that social order is maintained by pure repression and domination – have taken cultural bonds seriously, they have usually tended toward a mirror-image version of the Durkheimian approach. Nicholas Abercrombie and his colleagues have noted that Gramscian, cultural Marxism, for example, tends toward a "dominant ideology thesis" that is ultimately rather similar to the Parsonian functionalism it attempts to oppose.[82] In both cases, social order emerges because of a shared, common culture, and there is little sense of how diversity and social coherence can exist simultaneously.

For whatever reason, the view that normative consensus is the basis of social order is highly pervasive, beyond simply social theory and beyond the academy. Perhaps it is an easy way to imagine society; it simplifies society and implies a harmony that at some level might be highly comforting. Political debates and ordinary conversation often assume that society is best served by agreement on fundamental principles, and that social conflict results from a decreasing social consensus. Indeed, some of the most visible American social movements of the last ten years are based on conservative religious assumptions that crime and poverty are ultimately due to a breakdown of moral consensus (on matters of sexuality, family life, patriotism, and so forth).[83]

When theorized with social science, there are two related problems with this overemphasis on moral consensus. First, following Durkheim, those who use the term "social order" commonly and often reflexively

---

[82] Nicholas Abercrombie, Stephen Hill, and Bryan S. Turner, *The Dominant Ideology Thesis* (London: George Allen & Unwin, 1980). Yet Abercrombie et al.'s solution, to return to pure materialism, is hardly satisfactory.

[83] See Hunter's discussion in *Culture Wars* and Alan Wolfe's companion discussion in *One Nation After All*, which argues that Americans are much less divided, and much less morally judgmental, than Hunter's argument implies.

imply that order is absolute good.[84] Since social order is based on normative consensus, the implication is that cultural diversity is therefore always potentially bad, because it is disruptive.

The second problem with Durkheimian approaches is they are inappropriate for liberal societies in which there is some opportunity for people to express political differences: Again, the Durkheimian approach expects an empirically unrealistic degree of cultural consensus. It seems to imply that political disagreement can only be about matters that are unimportant. Within a diverse society the attempt to pursue moral consensus and eliminate ideological diversity is actually more likely to divide than to unite.

Democratic societies do not need agreement on all moral fundamentals to cohere; they thrive instead on institutionalized social spaces that allow diversity on the many issues that people define as moral, and vitally important, but on which they are not of one mind.[85] Certainly societies do, and perhaps must, write into law those principles on which they do indeed strongly agree, and which they consider fundamental. But those points are likely to constitute a much smaller realm than the large range of disagreement. When some significant portion of society considers certain views fundamental, while others emphatically do not, attempts to enforce a definitive moral rule are self-defeating. As Philip Selznick has argued, the pursuit of a comprehensive moral consensus destroys rather than strengthens community:

[T]he very effort to achieve that wholeness tends to reduce the complexity of social reality. The world must be simplified in the interests of consistency. Although ideologues often yearn for community, they are at the same time

---

[84] For a related point, see Wrong, *The Problem of Order*, p. 9.

[85] I should note that I am not arguing that people can share absolutely nothing culturally and still have a functioning society. I am talking about normative positions, especially those expressed within comprehensive worldviews; there are some aspects of culture for which my argument may be of questionable relevance. For example, in societies with debates about the use of language – the central issue in Quebecois nationalism – it may not be possible simply to allow people to use languages as they wish, without using the state to make a language dominant. Neighbors, or even members of the same household, can go to different churches without there being much impact on the rest of their lives. But it is impossible for neighbors, coworkers, schoolmates, and so forth to use different languages and others have their interactions unaffected. (My thanks to Kathleen Dowley, Norman Graham, and Peter Dorman for raising this point with me.)

subversive of it. As they reach for their own truth, their own fellowship, their own moral identity, they undermine existing communities. Ideological orthodoxy is a breeder of factions.[86]

Selznick argued that *Roe v. Wade* properly recognized women's legitimate moral claim to a choice but was too absolutist and thus did not make room for large portions of the American public who have legitimate moral disagreements. His criticism of *Roe* is not in its substance but in its style: "... the [Supreme] Court's posture offered little room for compromise or for a spirit of reconciliation."[87] I argued in Chapter 6 that the claim that *Roe* was responsible for polarization on abortion is a misreading of the historical evidence: The polarization was strong a couple of years before *Roe*. But Selznick's point that there has to be room for moral disagreements is well taken.

It is worth exploring further, however, the view that *Roe* was disruptive of social order. As we saw in Chapter 6, a number of scholars, most notably Mary Ann Glendon, have made similar arguments. Glendon has argued that the Supreme Court should have left the regulation of abortion to the states, rather than declare a national policy and the uncompromising priority of a woman's right to privacy over fetal rights. In her view, such an approach would have led to a gradual expansion of the availability of abortion, but would not have produced polarization and intractable conflict. She can cite persuasive comparative evidence, for example, the fact that the less rights-oriented British abortion law of 1967 – which resembled the ALI legislation of the time, in the United States – appears to have had that effect in Great Britain. Perhaps additional evidence in favor of Glendon's view that polarizing conflict could have been avoided is the fact that two authors whose personal politics on abortion differ as much as Hunter's and Selznick's can make arguments so close to her own.[88] Still, as I noted at the end of the previous chapter another central difference between the United States and Britain is that the practice of abortion in Britain is embedded in a national system of health care in which it is difficult to talk about abortion separately from the structure of the health care system. This may help

[86] Selznick, *The Moral Commonwealth*, p. 412.
[87] Ibid., p. 415.
[88] Glendon, *Abortion and Divorce in Western Law*, pp. 48–9; Selznick, *The Moral Commonwealth*, pp. 412–17; Hunter, *Before the Shooting Begins*, pp. 246–7.

prevent the development of constituencies devoted to the single-issue politics of abortion.

The German case is also interesting in this context: it questions Glendon's implication that a legislative give and take can produce a clear, compromise consensus. In Germany, like Britain, it is the case that abortion requires approval by physicians; somewhat oddly, most abortion is technically illegal, but most women determined to press for physicians' approval and willing to undergo mandatory counseling do eventually obtain abortions. The illegal nature of the abortion is then in practice ignored and the abortion is paid for through a health insurance system that covers almost the entire German population. Again, medicalization of the process probably helps keep the level of polarization less intense than in the United States, but that's partly because abortion access is not greatly dependent on the accident of geography or the woman's economic status, as it can be in the United States. Furthermore, polarization is limited in Germany partly because the German political system prevents precisely the kind of open debate that Glendon recommends. That is, German government institutions can largely shield themselves from public lobbying on the issue. As a recent study has demonstrated, very relevant to the abortion debate is that the parliamentary democracy of Germany allows political parties to control the government agenda much more than in the United States. Parties can more easily choose to avoid potentially controversial issues like abortion, not least because they can essentially force out of office any elected official who strays too far from the party line. It is also the case that the German Constitutional Court has prohibited further liberalization of abortion law and, unlike the U.S. Supreme Court, the German Court makes many of its decisions largely out of public view. Its judges are chosen largely out of public view as well: without a process of public input, politicization of the Constitutional Court's role in abortion is not really possible.

And so the German case does not serve as a precedent for legislatures working out social peace and compromise on the abortion issue.[89] Chapter 6 demonstrates the weakness of this argument in trying to understand U.S. abortion politics, as well: The assumption that the

---

[89] Ferree et al., *Shaping Abortion Discourse*, esp. pp. 40–44, 64–69, 182, 287–291.

states could have resolved the abortion debate is empirically wrong. It is not true that the states had the ability to resolve the abortion debate until the Supreme Court took the issue away from them. Instead, they themselves reached an impasse as a result of moral vetoes before the case reached the Supreme Court.

But Glendon's argument concerns wider matters than the particular impact of *Roe*. Her argument is a subtle and interesting one, as she places her discussion of abortion in a context of comparative analysis of law, state policy, and social assumptions about both abortion and divorce in the United States and Europe. Here I can examine that part of her argument with implications of our understanding of the cultural bases of social order.

One of the more significant aspects of Glendon's perspective is the common argument – often hurled as a criticism of the Supreme Court but also made within a serious analysis of constitutional law – that legislatures should be left to resolve divisive social conflicts. As elected bodies, the argument goes, legislatures more directly reflect the popular will. The implication is that there needs to be public discussion so that the public can think the issue through and develop a fully informed compromise or consensus.

If my argument is correct, one problem with such arguments is that legislatures can in fact be held hostage by a morally charged minority. That is, when there is a group exercising a moral veto, legislatures can be paralyzed, as elected officials would rather avoid taking a stand on an issue in which *any* position necessarily alienates a substantial portion of the electorate. It may be that, given a choice between the current law and a change in the law, the majority within a society would choose a change, and yet legislators will not initiate a change. Such was the case concerning 1960s abortion reform laws, for example, in states where controversy developed: opinion polls for decades have shown that Americans, by a large majority, approve of legal abortion under the circumstances allowed in the reform laws.[90] The laws passed easily when the process had low visibility, but extensive public discussion resulted in a failure to deal with the issue. Once polarized public controversy emerged, the political path of least resistance for legislators

[90] Raymond Tatalovich and Byron W. Daynes, *The Politics of Abortion: A Study of Community Conflict in Public Policy Making* (New York: Praeger, 1981), pp. 116–18.

was to do nothing, which in that case meant keeping on the books a law that most people found too restrictive.

Perhaps even more striking is the fact that many states in the early 1960s still had on the books highly restrictive laws on contraception that were not enforced, because almost no one took them seriously. And yet the legislatures did not act to change the laws: Why stir up a hornet's nest when the hornets are sleeping? Not until 1965, in *Griswold v. Connecticut*, did the U.S. Supreme Court nullify laws restricting married persons' access to contraception.[91] In 1972 the Court forbade restrictions on any adult's access regardless of marital status.[92]

In such situations, a court, if it chooses to do so, can better represent the popular will than a legislature; courts can provide cover for legal initiatives that legislatures would probably be inclined to approve, if only there were no electoral consequences. But there are such consequences, and so the legislature lets stand whatever law happens to be on the books at the time. Yes, *Roe v. Wade* added to the flames of controversy (which were already blazing), but *Griswold v. Connecticut* did not.

I would also disagree with Glendon's implication that, on divisive issues, the society eventually has to come explicitly to a self-conscious compromise or consensus. Glendon's approach is interesting here. It implies a view of social order, including the relationship between law and culture, which is more subtle than that of many Durkheimians: She does not expect actual consensus on abortion, but more an acceptance that, in the legal realm, we should compromise so that, culturally, we can live with and respect each other. That is the nature of having a democracy. Furthermore, even when law is not enforced, it is important for law to state our ideals and to be a public acknowledgment that we consider certain matters of serious moral consequence. And so, even if we let physicians give legal abortions because we do not enforce in any specific sense the law's limiting under what circumstances women can have an abortion, the fact that there is such a law reminds us that abortion is not to be decided lightly.[93]

Applying this perspective to the abortion controversy, Glendon holds that both litigation and legislative initiative are part of the process

---

[91] *Griswold v. Connecticut*, 381 U.S. 479 (1965).
[92] *Eisenstadt v. Baird*, 405 U.S. 438 (1972).
[93] Glendon, *Abortion and Divorce in Western Law*, pp. 10, 13, 15, 17, 19, 32–3, 40.

of collectively working out a resolution, including a sense of what moral issues are involved. But it works only if the courts do not "unnecessarily decide such controversies on constitutional grounds."[94] In many or even most cases, Glendon is probably right. But given the stalemate that had emerged in the state legislatures over abortion in 1970, in a context in which some of the state laws appeared to be enormously unpopular, it is not clear what the Supreme Court could have done other than look to the Constitution.

I would argue, though, that there are some matters on which it is better not to seek an explicit compromise. Consider for instance the case of religion, a matter of immense moral seriousness to a substantial majority of Americans: What if we used laws to assure that we were constantly reminded that religion is of serious moral import? How would we do that? Would we, for instance, have laws that mandated specific religious teaching in schools, both public and private? Or should we tell students that there is no exception to the requirement that they recite prayers publicly but that it is OK if they do not really believe those prayers? Or we do teach some "compromise" religion that seems to cover as many Americans as possible, one that is kind of Christian but only vaguely so?

No, of course not: That would arguably mock religion more than show respect for it. We do not force people to compromise on religious belief because we want them to be able to hold and practice their own commitments. I would argue that *there are some moral commitments that are so important to people in a diverse society that it is a mistake to force them to compromise within the electoral and legislative arena.* Laws can mandate reasonably specifically what even private schools must teach in the way of math and social studies, but not on religion, because we consider religious freedom more important than specific knowledge of math or social studies.

I would turn Durkheimian logic on its head: For a devoutly religious person, nothing could be more important than their beliefs about their God. Precisely because those beliefs are so important, but are not universally held, the First Amendment does not allow Americans to use government institutions to settle theological debates. It does not force

[94] Ibid., p. 45.

them into an explicit compromise. Instead it allows them to believe what they want, within communities that government leaves alone. The First Amendment's approach to religion is, in a sense, a limiting frame: It frames the role of religion in politics, greatly circumscribing the ability of religious worldviews to go head to head when it comes to constructing legislation and government policy. But it does not then imply that religion is unimportant: quite the opposite.

The result is that the United States is particularly distinctive in how many new religious communities are continually created, and to which people have very strong commitments, because it is relatively easy to find or create a religious community to one's liking. Americans join and leave different religious communities at rates unheard of in most of the world.[95] Some Americans will not find any religion appealing, and any given religious American will not find most available religious options appealing, just as meeting any one particular stranger is unlikely to result in a significant new social bond. But with enough opportunities to meet strangers, eventually new friendships will form. And given enough opportunities to develop themselves spiritually free of legal restraints, some Americans will build new religious communities, often with other people who were once strangers or mere acquaintances. Many people will find their primary communal attachments outside religion, while typically at least tolerating religious people. Both religious and secular people will get along better given they have the freedom to live their values without forced compromise, and given that they do not have the freedom to destroy communities who have values with which they disagree.

The problem with a politicized debate like abortion is that mutually incompatible worldviews, rather than being limited in their ability to go head to head, do precisely that in the political arena. Indeed that is much more true now than it was in 1970: Killing legislative initiative on abortion then took less mobilization around abortion than we have currently. New political communities, and new collective identities, have formed around the abortion debate since the demise of the reform

---

[95] Theodore Caplow, "Contrasting Trends in European and American Religion," *Sociological Analysis* 46(1985):101–8; R. Stephen Warner, "Work in Progress toward a New Paradigm for the Sociological Study of Religion in the United States," *American Journal of Sociology* 98(1993):1044–93.

laws. The formation of new identities and new frames within the debate have changed political options and constraints, making it difficult to find true resolution.

It is possible that a different Court decision would have worked better than *Roe* in getting people who disagree passionately about abortion to live together with tolerance. But it is not clear what such a decision could have looked like in 1973, and it is even less clear now. It *is* clear that simply reversing *Roe*, especially now that *Roe* has been the law for over three decades, will not result in social peace over abortion. The normative argument that *Roe* was wrongly decided often depends upon an incorrect historical, empirical assertion, that is, that the state legislatures can resolve such matters much more amicably than can courts, and that it was *Roe* in particular that *caused* the abortion debate.

Upholding versus reversing *Roe* has been the main axis in the debate over the legal status of abortion for some time. Some people's value commitments mandate that they value social order less than a morally correct abortion law. But for those who indeed want peace over abortion, I would argue that it is time to get beyond the question of whether we reverse *Roe*. The debate needs to be more along the lines of, "if not *Roe*, then what?" And it does not work to answer that question while pretending that it is possible just to erase decades of debate: We are no longer where we were when a number of states passed abortion reform laws.

If, then, you want something different than *Roe*, and you would like to get there while maintaining social peace, tell us, how do we get there *from here*?

Works Cited

Archival Collections

Margaret Sanger Papers, Library of Congress, Washington, D.C. (abbreviated as MSP-LC)

Margaret Sanger Papers, Sophia Smith Collection, Smith College (abbreviated as MSP-SS)

Mary Ware Dennett Papers, Schlesinger Library, Radcliffe College (abbreviated as MWD)

Newspapers

Anchorage Daily News. Anchorage, Alaska.
Arkansas Gazette. Little Rock, Arkansas.
Baltimore Sun. Baltimore, Maryland.
Clarion-Ledger. Jackson, Mississippi.
Daily Oklahoman. Oklahoma City, Oklahoma.
Evening Journal. Wilmington, Delaware.
Evening Sun. Baltimore, Maryland.
Miami Herald. Miami, Florida.
New York Times. New York, New York.
The Oregonian. Portland, Oregon.
Pittsburgh Post-Gazette. Pittsburgh, Ohio.
The Plain Dealer. Cleveland, Ohio.
Richmond Times-Dispatch. Richmond, Virginia.
The State. Columbia, South Carolina.
St. Petersburg Times. St. Petersburg, Florida.
Topeka Daily Capital. Topeka, Kansas.
Washington Post. Washington, D.C.
Wichita Eagle. Wichita, Kansas.

State Government Documents

Alabama. 1967. *Journal of the House of Representatives of the State of Alabama: Regular Session of 1967.*

———. 1967. *Journal of the Senate of the State of Alabama: Regular Session of 1967.*

Alaska. 1970. *House Journal.*

Alaska. 1970. *House Journal*, supplement no. 12. Four-page supplement (Judiciary Committee Report on Alaska's 1970 abortion repeal bill, 9 April).

———. 1970. *Senate Journal.*

Arkansas. 1969. *Acts of Arkansas*, Act 61.

Colorado. 1967. *Journal of the House of Representatives.*

Colorado. 1967. *Journal of the Senate.*

Florida. 1967. *Journal of the House of Representatives: Regular Session.*

———. 1967. *Journal of the Senate.*

Kansas. 1969. *House Journal: Proceedings of the House of Representatives of the State of Kansas.*

———. 1969. *Senate Journal: Proceedings of the Senate of the State of Kansas.*

Maine. 1967. *Legislative Record of the One Hundred and Third Legislature.*

———. 1969. *Legislative Record of the One Hundred and Fourth Legislature.*

Maryland. 1968. *Journal of Proceedings of the House of Delegates of Maryland: Session 1968.*

———. 1968. *Journal of the Proceedings of the Senate of Maryland: Regular Session, 1968.*

———. House of Delegates. 1968. Report of the Subcommittee on Abortion Law (Judiciary Committee). (2-page mimeo.)

———. 1970. *Journal of Proceedings of the House of Delegates of Maryland: Session 1970.*

Michigan. 1969. *Journal of the Senate of the State of Michigan: 1969 Regular Session.*

Mississippi. 1966. *Journal of the House of Representatives.*

———. 1966. *Journal of the Senate.*

———. 1966. *Laws of the State of Mississippi 1966*, vol. 1.

Nevada. 1969. *Journal of the Assembly of the Fifty-fifth Session of the Legislature of the State of Nevada.*

New Hampshire. 1969. *Journal of the House of Representatives: January Session of 1969.*

———. 1969. *Journal of the Honorable Senate: January Session of 1969.*

New Mexico. 1969. *Journal of the Senate.*

New Jersey. 1968. Commission to Study the New Jersey Statutes Relating to Abortion. (Transcript of) *Public Hearing* (that took place in Trenton, N.J.), October 28.

———. 1968. Commission to Study the New Jersey Statutes Relating to Abortion. (Transcript of) *Public Hearing* (in Newark, N.J.), November 13.

———. 1968. Commission to Study the New Jersey Statutes Relating to Abortion. (Transcript of) *Public Hearing* (in Camden, N.J.). November 26.

———. 1969. Commission to Study the New Jersey Statutes Relating to Abortion. *Final Report to the Legislature.* December 31.

———. 1970. Legislature. General Assembly, Judiciary Committee. Transcript of public hearing on Assembly Bill No. 762, April 9.

Vermont. 1970. *Journal of the House of the State of Vermont: Adjourned Session, 1970.*

Virginia. 1970. *Journal of the House of Delegates of the Commonwealth of Virginia: Regular Session, 1970.*

United States Supreme Court Cases

Doe v. Bolton, 410 U.S. 179 (1973).

Eisenstadt v. Baird, 405 U.S. 438 (1972).

Griswold v. Connecticut, 381 U.S. 479 (1965).

National Organization for Women v. Scheidler, 510 U.S. 249 (1994).

Planned Parenthood of Southeast Pennsylvania v. Casey, 505 U.S. 833 (1992).

Roe v. Wade, 410 U.S. 113 (1973).

Stenberg v. Carhart, 539 U.S. 914 (2000).

Thornburgh v. American College of Obstetricians and Gynecologists, 476 U.S. 747 (1986).

Webster v. Reproductive Health Services, 492 U.S. 490 (1989).

Books, Articles, and other Scholarly Works

Abercrombie, Nicholas, Stephen Hill, and Bryan S. Turner. *The Dominant Ideology Thesis.* London: George Allen & Unwin, 1980.

Alan Guttmacher Institute. "Trends in Abortion in the United States, 1973–2000" (January 2003), at the institute's website, http://www.agi-usa.org/pubs/trends.ppt (accessed October 10, 2003).

Banks, J. A., and Olive Banks. *Feminism and Family Planning in Victorian England.* New York: Schocken, 1964.

Bartkowski, John P. *Remaking the Godly Marriage: Gender Negotiation in Evangelical Families.* New Brunswick, N.J.: Rutgers University Press, 2001.

Beisel, Nicola. "Class, Culture, and Campaigns against Vice in Three American Cities, 1872–1892." *American Sociological Review* 55 (1990):44–62.

———. *Imperiled Innocents: Anthony Comstock and Family Reproduction in Victorian America.* Princeton, N.J.: Princeton University Press, 1997.

Bell, Daniel. *The Cultural Contradictions of Capitalism.* New York: Basic Books, 1976.

Benford, Robert D. "Frames Disputes within the Nuclear Disarmament Movement." *Social Forces* 71(1993):677–701.

Blanchard, Dallas A. *The Anti-abortion Movement and the Rise of the Religious Right: From Polite to Fiery Protest.* New York: Twayne, 1994.

_____ and Terry J. Prewitt. *Religious Violence and Abortion: The Gideon Project.* Gainesville: University Press of Florida, 1993.

Brodie, Janet Farrell. *Contraception and Abortion in Nineteenth-Century America.* Ithaca, N.Y., and London: Cornell University Press, 1994.

Brookes, Barbara. *Abortion in England, 1900–1967.* London: Croom Helm, 1988.

Buechler, Steven M. *Women's Movements in the United States.* New Brunswick, N.J., and London: Rutgers University Press, 1990.

Burke, Ronald R. "*Veritatis Splendor*: Papal Authority and the Sovereignty of Reason." Pp. 119–36 in *Veritatis Splendor: American Responses*, Michael E. Allsopp and John J. O'Keefe, eds. Kansas City: Sheed & Ward, 1995.

Burns, Gene. "Abandoning Suspicion: The Catholic Left and Sexuality." Pp. 67–87 in *What's Left? Progressive Catholics in America*, Mary Jo Weaver, ed. Bloomington, Ind.: Indiana University Press, 1999.

_____. *The Frontiers of Catholicism: The Politics of Ideology in a Liberal World.* Berkeley: University of California Press, 1992.

_____. "Ideology, Culture, and Ambiguity: The Revolutionary Process in Iran." *Theory and Society* 25(1996):349–88.

Burstein, Paul. "Bringing the Public Back In: Should Sociologists Consider the Impact of Public Opinion on Public Policy?" *Social Forces* 77(1998):27–62.

_____ and April Linton. "The Impact of Political Parties, Interest Groups, and Social Movement Organizations on Public Policy." *Social Forces* 81(2002):380–408.

Cahill, Lisa Sowle. "Abortion, Autonomy, and Community." Pp. 85–97 in *Abortion and Catholicism: The American Debate*, Patricia Beattie Jung and Thomas A. Shannon, eds. New York: Crossroad, 1988.

Callahan, Sidney. "Abortion and the Sexual Agenda: A Case for Prolife Feminism." Pp. 128–40 in *Abortion and Catholicism: The American Debate*, Patricia Beattie Jung and Thomas A. Shannon, eds. New York: Crossroad, 1988.

Caplow, Theodore. "Contrasting Trends in European and American Religion." *Sociological Analysis* 46(1985):101–8.

Calhoun, Craig "Postmodernism as Pseudohistory." *Theory, Culture, and Society* 10(1993):75–96.

Carlen, Claudia, ed. *The Papal Encyclicals. Vol. 3: 1903–1939.* Raleigh, N.C.: McGrath/Consortium, 1981.

Carmody, Denise Lardner. *The Double Cross: Ordination, Abortion, and Catholic Feminism.* New York: Crossroad, 1986.

Carney, Eliza Newlin. "Maryland: A Law Codifying *Roe v. Wade.*" Pp. 51–68 in *Abortion Politics in American States*, Mary C. Segers and Timothy A. Byrnes, eds. Armonk, N.Y., and London: M. E. Sharpe, 1995.

Cassidy, Keith. "The Right to Life Movement: Sources, Development, and Strategies." Pp. 128–59 in *The Politics of Abortion and Birth Control in Historical Perspective*, Donald T. Critchlow, ed. University Park, Pa.: Pennsylvania State University Press, 1996.

Chafe, William H. *The Paradox of Change: American Women in the 20th Century.* New York and Oxford: Oxford University Press, 1991.

Chen, Constance M. *"The Sex Side of Life": Mary Ware Dennett's Pioneering Battle for Birth Control and Sex Education.* New York: New Press, 1996.

Chesler, Ellen. *Woman of Valor: Margaret Sanger and the Birth Control Movement in America.* New York: Doubleday/Anchor, 1992.

Condit, Celeste Michelle. *Decoding Abortion Rhetoric: Communicating Social Change.* Urbana and Chicago: University of Illinois Press, 1990.

Cook, Elizabeth Adell, Ted G. Jelen, and Clyde Wilcox. *Between Two Absolutes: Public Opinion and the Politics of Abortion.* Boulder, Col.: Westview, 1992.

Coser, Rose Laub. "The Complexity of Roles as a Seedbed of Individual Autonomy." Pp. 237–63 in *The Idea of Social Structure: Papers in Honor of Robert Merton*, Lewis Coser, ed. New York: Harcourt Brace Jovanovich, 1975.

Cott, Nancy F. *The Grounding of Modern Feminism.* New Haven and London: Yale University Press, 1987.

Crain, Robert L., Elihu Katz, and Donald B. Rosenthal. *The Politics of Community Conflict: The Fluoridation Decision.* Indianapolis: Bobbs-Merrill, 1969.

Cuomo, Mario. "Religious Belief and Public Morality: A Catholic Governor's Perspective," a September 13, 1984, lecture at the University of Notre Dame. Text available at the website of the University of Notre Dame Archives, http://classic.archives.nd.edu/episodes/visitors/cuomo/cuomo.html (accessed October 30, 2003).

D'Antonio, William V. "Autocracy and Democracy in an Autocratic Organization: The Case of the Roman Catholic Church." *Sociology of Religion* 55(1994):379–96.

Darnton, Robert. *The Great Cat Massacre and Other Episodes in French Cultural History.* New York: Basic Books, 1984.

Davis, Nancy J., and Robert V. Robinson. "Are the Rumors of War Exaggerated? Religious Orthodoxy and Moral Progressivism in America." *American Journal of Sociology* 102(1996):756–87.

Davis, Nanette J. *From Crime to Choice: The Transformation of Abortion in America.* Westport, Conn.: Greenwood, 1985.

Degler, Carl N. *In Search of Human Nature: The Decline and Revival of Darwinism in American Social Thought.* New York and Oxford: Oxford University Press, 1991.

Dennett, Mary Ware. *Birth Control Laws: Shall We Keep Them Change Them or Abolish Them.* New York: Frederick H. Hitchcock/The Grafton Press, 1926 (reprinted New York: Da Capo Press, 1970).

Diamond, Sara. *Not by Politics Alone: The Enduring Influence of the Christian Right.* New York and London: Guilford, 1998.

Diani, Mario. "'Leaders' or Brokers? Positions and Influence in Social Movement Networks." Pp. 105–22 in *Social Movements and Networks*, Diani and McAdam, eds.

———— and Doug McAdam, eds. *Social Movements and Networks: Relational Approaches to Collective Action.* Oxford: Oxford University Press, 2003.

Dienes, C. Thomas. *Law, Politics, and Birth Control.* Urbana, Ill.: University of Illinois Press, 1972.

Dillon, Michele. "Cultural Differences in the Abortion Discourse of the Catholic Church: Evidence from Four Countries." *Sociology of Religion* 57(1996):25–8.

————. "The American Abortion Debate: Culture War or Normal Discourse?" *Virginia Review of Sociology* 2(1995):115–32.

DiMaggio, Paul, John Evans, and Bethany Bryson. "Have Americans' Social Attitudes Become more Polarized?" *American Journal of Sociology* 102(1996):690–755.

Douglas, Emily Taft. *Margaret Sanger: Pioneer of the Future.* New York: Holt, Rinehart and Winston, 1970.

Drinnon, Richard. *Rebel in Paradise: A Biography of Emma Goldman.* Chicago: University of Chicago Press, 1961.

DuBois, Ellen Carol. *Woman Suffrage and Women's Rights.* New York and London: New York University Press, 1998.

Durkheim, Emile. *The Division of Labor in Society,* W. D. Halls, trans. New York: Free Press/Macmillan, 1984.

Eliasoph, Nina. "Making a Fragile Public: A Talk-Centered Study of Citizenship and Power." *Sociological Theory* 14(1996):262–89.

Emirbayer, Mustafa, and Jeff Goodwin. "Network Analysis, Culture, and the Problem of Agency." *American Journal of Sociology* 99(1994):1411–54.

Engle, Michael. *State and Local Government.* New York: Peter Lang, 1999.

Epstein, Lee, and Joseph F. Kobylka. *The Supreme Court and Legal Change: Abortion and the Death Penalty.* Chapel Hill, N.C.: University of North Carolina Press, 1992.

Evans, John H. "Have Americans' Attitudes become more Polarized? An Update." *Social Science Quarterly* 84(2003):71–90.

————. "Multi-Organizational Fields and Social Movement Organization Frame Content: The Religious Pro-Choice Movement." *Sociological Inquiry* 67(1997):451–69.

Facts on File Yearbook 1970. New York: Facts on File, 1971.

Farr, Kathryn Ann. "Shaping Policy through Litigation: Abortion Law in the United States." *Crime and Delinquency* 39(1993):167–83.

Faux, Marian. *Roe v. Wade: The Untold Story of the Landmark Supreme Court Decision that Made Abortion Legal.* New York: Macmillan, 1988.

Fernandez, Roberto M., and Roger V. Gould. "A Dilemma of State Power: Brokerage and Influence in the National Health Policy Domain." *American Journal of Sociology* 99(1994):1455–91.

Ferree, Myra Marx, William Anthony Gamson, Jürgen Gerhards, and Dieter Rucht. *Shaping Abortion Discourse: Democracy and the Public Sphere in Germany and the United States.* New York and Cambridge: Cambridge University Press, 2002.

Ferree, Myra Marx, and Frederick D. Miller. "Mobilization and Meaning: Toward an Integration of Social Psychological and Resource Perspectives on Social Movements." *Sociological Inquiry* 55(1985):38–61.

Fireman, Bruce, and William A. Gamson. "Utilitarian Logic in the Resource Mobilization Perspective." Pp. 8–44 in *The Dynamics of Social Movements,* Mayer N. Zald and John D. McCarthy, eds. Cambridge, Mass.: Winthrop, 1979.

Fitzpatrick, Kevin M., and Michele Wilson. "Exposure to Violence and Post-traumatic Stress Symptomatology among Abortion Clinic Workers." *Journal of Traumatic Stress* 12(1999):227–42.

Friedman, Debra, and Doug McAdam. "Collective Identity and Activism: Networks, Choices, and the Life of a Social Movement." Pp. 156–73 in *Frontiers of Social Movement Theory,* Morris and Mueller, eds.

Fung, Archon. "Making Rights Real: *Roe*'s Impact on Abortion Access." *Politics & Society* 21(1993):465–504.

Gamson, William A. "Constructing Social Protest." Pp. 85–106 in *Social Movements and Culture,* Johnston and Klandermans, eds.

———. "The Social Psychology of Collective Action." Pp. 53–76 in *Frontiers in Social Movement Theory,* Morris and Mueller, eds.

———. *Talking Politics.* Cambridge: Cambridge University Press, 1992.

Garrow, David J. *Liberty and Sexuality: The Right to Privacy and the Making of Roe v. Wade.* New York: Macmillan/Lisa Drew, 1994.

George, B. J., Jr. "State Legislatures versus the Supreme Court: Abortion Legislation into the 1990s." Pp. 3–77 in J. Douglas Butler and David F. Walbert, eds., *Abortion, Medicine, and the Law,* 4th ed. New York and Oxford: Facts On File, 1992.

Ginsburg, Faye D. *Contested Lives: The Abortion Debate in an American Community.* Berkeley: University of California Press, 1989.

———. "Saving America's Souls: Operation Rescue's Crusade against Abortion. Pp. 557–88 in *The Fundamentalism Project, vol. 3: Fundamentalisms and the State,* Martin E. Marty and R. Scott Appleby, eds. Chicago and London: University of Chicago Press, 1993.

Ginsburg, Ruth Bader. "Some Thoughts on Autonomy and Equality in Relation to *Roe v. Wade.*" *North Carolina Law Review* 63(1985):375–86.

Glendon, Mary Ann. *Abortion and Divorce in Western Law: American Failures, European Challenges.* Cambridge, Mass.: Harvard University Press, 1987.

———. *Rights Talk: The Impoverishment of Political Discourse.* New York: Free Press, 1991.

Goffman, Erving. *Frame Analysis: An Essay on the Organization of Experience.* New York: Harper, 1974.

Goldstone, Jack A. "Ideology, Cultural Frameworks, and the Process of Revolution." *Theory and Society* 20(1991):405–53.

Gordon, Linda. "Why Nineteenth-Century Feminists Did Not Support 'Birth Control' and Twentieth-Century Feminists Do." Pp. 40–53 in *Rethinking the Family: Some Feminist Questions*, Barrie Thorne and Marilyn Yalom, eds. New York and London: Longman, 1982.

———. *Woman's Body, Woman's Right*, rev. ed. New York: Penguin/Vintage, 1990.

Gould, Stephen Jay. "William Jennings Bryan's Last Campaign." *Nebraska History* 77, nos. 3–4 (1996):177–83; Willard H. Smith, "William Jennings Bryan and the Social Gospel," *Journal of American History* 53(1966):41–60.

Granovetter, Mark S. "The Strength of Weak Ties." *American Journal of Sociology* 78(1973):1360–80.

———. "The Strength of Weak Ties: A Network Theory Revisited." *Sociological Theory* 1(1983):201–33.

Grant, George. *Grand Illusions: The Legacy of Planned Parenthood*, 4th rev. ed. Nashville: Cumberland/Highland, 2000.

Handler, Joel F. "Postmodernism, Protest, and the New Social Movements." *Law and Society Review* 26(1992):697–731.

Henshaw, Stanley K., and Lawrence B. Finer. "Abortion Incidences and Services in the United States in 2000." *Perspectives on Sexual and Reproductive Health* 35(2003):6–15. Available at the website of Alan Guttmacher Institute, http://www.agi-usa.org/pubs/journals/3500603.pdf (accessed October 10, 2003).

———. "The Accessibility of Abortion Services in the United States, 2001." *Perspectives on Sexual and Reproductive Health* 35(2003):16–24. Available at the website of Alan Guttmacher Institute, http://www.agi-usa.org/pubs/journals/3501603.pdf (accessed October 11, 2003).

Herrnstein, Richard J., and Charles Murray. *The Bell Curve: Intelligence and Class Structure in American Life*. New York and London: Free Press, 1994.

Hunt, Scott A., and Robert D. Benford. "Identity Talk in the Peace and Justice Movement." *Journal of Contemporary Ethnography* 22(1994):488–517.

Hunter, James Davison. *Before the Shooting Begins: Searching for Democracy in America's Culture War*. New York: Free Press, 1994.

———. *Culture Wars: The Struggle to Define America*. New York: Basic Books/Harper Collins, 1991.

———. "What Americans Really Think about Abortion." *First Things* 24(1992):13–21.

Jacob, Herbert. *Silent Revolution: The Transformation of Divorce Law in the United States*. Chicago and London: University of Chicago Press, 1988.

Jain, Sagar C., and Steven W. Sinding. *North Carolina Abortion Law 1967: A Study in Legislative Process*. Chapel Hill: Carolina Population Center, University of North Carolina at Chapel Hill, 1968.

——— and Laurel F. Gooch. *Georgia Abortion Act 1968*: A Study in Legislative Process. Chapel Hill, N.C.: Department of Health Administration, School of

Public Health, and Carolina Population Center, University of North Carolina at Chapel Hill, 1972.

Jelen, Ted G., and Marthe A. Chandler, eds. *Abortion Politics in the United States and Canada: Studies in Public Opinion.* Wesport, Conn.: Praeger, 1994.

Joffe, Carole. *Doctors of Conscience: The Struggle to Provide Abortion before and after Roe v. Wade.* Boston: Beacon, 1995.

———. *The Regulation of Sexuality: Experiences of Family Planning Workers.* Philadelphia: Temple University Press, 1986.

Johnson, Douglas W., Paul R. Picard, and Bernard Quinn. *Churches and Church Membership in the United States.* Washington, D.C.: Glenmary Research Center, 1974.

Johnson, Victoria. "Operation Rescue, Vocabularies of Motive, and Tactical Action: A Study of Movement Framing in the Practice of Quasi-nonviolence." *Research in Social Movements, Conflict and Change* 20(1997):103–50.

Johnston, Hank, and Bert Klandermans, eds. *Social Movements and Culture. Social Movements, Protest, and Contention,* vol. 4. Minneapolis: University of Minnesota Press, 1994.

Kennedy, David M. *Birth Control in America: The Career of Margaret Sanger.* New Haven, Conn., and London: Yale University Press, 1970.

Kingdon, John. *Agendas, Alternatives, and Public Policies.* New York: Harper Collins, 1995.

Klandermans, Bert. "New Social Movements and Resource Mobilization: The European and the American Approach." *International Journal of Mass Emergencies and Disasters* 4(1986):13–37.

———. "The Social Construction of Protest in Multiorganizational Fields." Pp. 77–103 in *Frontiers in Social Movement Theory,* Morris and Mueller, eds.

Kraditor, Aileen S. *The Ideas of the Woman Suffrage Movement, 1890–1920.* New York and London: Columbia University Press, 1965.

Lader, Lawrence. *Abortion.* New York: Bobbs-Merrill, 1966.

———. *Abortion II: Making the Revolution.* Boston: Beacon, 1973.

———. *Politics, Power, and the Church: The Catholic Crisis and Its Challenge to American Pluralism.* New York: Macmillan, 1987.

Layman, Geoffrey. *The Great Divide: Religious and Cultural Conflicts in American Party Politics.* New York: Columbia University Press, 2001.

Lichterman, Paul. *The Search for Political Community.* New York and Cambridge: Cambridge University Press, 1996.

———. "Talking Identity in the Public Sphere: Broad Visions and Small Spaces in Sexual Identity Politics." *Theory and Society* 28(1999):101–41.

Lienesch, Michael. *Redeeming America: Piety and Politics in the New Christian Right.* Chapel Hill, N.C., and London: University of North Carolina Press, 1993.

Lindblom, Charles E. "The Science of Muddling through." *Public Administration Review* 14(1959):79–88.

Lorch, Robert S. *State and Local Politics*, 6th ed. Upper Saddle River, N.J.: Prentice Hall, 2001.

Luker, Kristin. *Abortion and the Politics of Motherhood*. Berkeley: University of California Press, 1984.

———. *Dubious Conceptions: The Politics of Teenage Pregnancy*. Cambridge, Mass.: Harvard University Press, 1996.

Madison, James. "Federalist #10." Pp. 45–52 in *The Federalist Papers*, Clinton Rossiter, ed. New York: Mentor/Penguin, 1999 (orig. 1787).

Maxwell, Carol J. C. *Pro-life Activists in America: Meaning, Motivation, and Direct Action*. Cambridge and New York: Cambridge University Press, 2002.

McAdam, Doug. "Beyond Structural Analysis: Toward a More Dynamic Understanding of Social Movements." Pp. 281–98 in *Social Movements and Networks*, Diani and McAdam, eds.

———. *Political Process and the Development of Black Insurgency, 1930–1970*. Chicago: University of Chicago Press, 1982.

McAvoy, Thomas T. *The Great Crisis in American Catholic History, 1895–1900*. Chicago: Regnery, 1957.

McCann, Carole R. *Birth Control Politics in the United States, 1916–1945*. Ithaca and London: Cornell University Press, 1994.

McCarthy, John D., and Mayer N. Zald. "Resource Mobilization and Social Movements: A Partial Theory." *American Journal of Sociology* 82(1977): 1212–41.

———. *The Trend of Social Movements in America: Professionalization and Resource Mobilization*. Morristown, N.J.: General Learning Corporation, 1973.

McCarthy, John D., Jackie Smith, and Mayer N. Zald. "Accessing Public, Media, Electoral, and Governmental Agendas." Pp. 291–311 in *Comparative Perspectives on Social Movements*, McAdam, McCarthy, and Zald, eds.

McCarthy, John D., Mayer Zald, and Doug McAdam, eds. *Comparative Perspectives on Social Movements: Political Opportunities, Mobilizing Structures, and Cultural Framings*. Cambridge: Cambridge University Press, 1996.

McKeegan, Michele. *Abortion Politics: Mutiny in the Ranks of the Right*. New York: Free Press/Macmillan, 1992.

Melucci, Alberto. "Symbolic Challenge of Contemporary Movements." *Social Research* 52(1985):789–816.

Meyer, David S. "Opportunities and Identities: Bridge-Building in the Study of Social Movements." Pp. 3–21 in *Social Movements*, Meyer, Whittier, and Robnett, eds.

———, Nancy Whittier, and Belinda Robnett, eds. *Social Movements: Identity, Culture, and the State*. Oxford and New York: Oxford University Press, 2002.

Mische, Ann. "Cross-talk in Movements: Reconceiving the Culture-Network Link." Pp. 258–80 in *Social Movements and Networks*, Diani and McAdam, eds.

Mohr, James C. *Abortion in America: The Origins and Evolution of National Policy, 1800–1900*. New York: Oxford University Press, 1978.

_____. "Iowa's Abortion Battles of the Late 1960s and Early 1970s: Long-term Perspectives and Short-term Analyses." *The Annals of Iowa*, third series 50(1989):75–6.

Molotch, Harvey. "Oil in Santa Barbara and Power in America," *Sociological Inquiry* 40, no. 1 (1970):131–44.

Mooney, Christopher Z., and Mei-Hsien Lee. "Legislative Morality in the American States: The Case of Pre-*Roe* Abortion Regulation Reform." *American Journal of Political Science* 39(1995)599–627.

Morris, Aldon. *The Origins of the Civil Rights Movement: Black Communities Organizing for Change*. New York: Free Press/Simon & Schuster, 1984.

Morris, Aldon D., and Carol McClurg Mueller, eds. *Frontiers of Social Movement Theory*. New Haven and London: Yale University Press, 1992.

Muir, Janette Kenner. "Hating for Life: Rhetorical Extremism and Abortion Clinic Violence." Pp. 163–95 in *Hate Speech*, Rita Kirk Whillock and David Slayden, eds. Thousand Oaks, Calif.: Sage, 1995.

Murray, Charles. *Losing Ground: American Social Policy, 1950–1980*. New York: Basic Books, 1984.

National Abortion Federation. "NAF Violence and Disruption Statistics," as of June 30, 2003, at http://www.prochoice.org/Violence/Statistics/stats.pdf (accessed October 8, 2003).

Neitz, Mary Jo. "Family, State, and God: Ideologies of the Right-to-Life Movement." *Sociological Analysis* 42(1981):265–76.

Noonan, John T., Jr. *Contraception: A History of Its Treatment by Catholic Theologians and Canonists*. Cambridge, Mass.: Harvard University Press/Belknap, 1966.

Norrander, Barbara, and Clyde Wilcox. "Public Opinion and Policy Making in the States: The Case of Post-*Roe* Abortion Policy." *Policy Studies Journal* 27(1999):707–22.

Nossiff, Rosemary. *Before Roe: Abortion Policy in the States*. Philadelphia: Temple University Press, 2001.

O'Connor, Karen. *No Neutral Ground? Abortion Politics in an Age of Absolutes*. Boulder, Col.: Westview, 1996.

Offe, Claus. "New Social Movements: Challenging the Boundaries of Contemporary Politics." *Social Research* 52(1985):817–68.

_____ and Helmut Wiesenthal. "Two Logics of Collective Action." Pp. 170–220 in Offe, *Disorganized Capitalism: Contemporary Transformations of Work and Politics*, John Keane, ed. Cambridge, Mass.: MIT Press, 1985.

Official Catholic Directory 1969, ed. Charles R. Cunningham. "General Summary." New York: P. J. Kenedy & Sons, 1969.

Olasky, Marvin. *Abortion Rites: A Social History of Abortion*. Wheaton, Ill.: Crossway/Good News, 1992.

Oliver, Pamela E. and Daniel J. Myers. "Networks, Diffusion, and Cycles of Collective Action." Pp. 173–203 in *Social Movements and Networks*, Diani and McAdam, eds.

Olson, Mancur. *The Logic of Collective Action: Public Goods and the Theory of Groups*. Cambridge, Mass.: Harvard University Press, 1965.

O'Neil, Daniel J. *Church Lobbying in a Western State: A Case Study on Abortion Legislation*. Tucson: University of Arizona Press, 1970.

Pashute, Lincoln. "Economic versus Racial Discrimination in the Provision of Birth-control Services in the United States." Pp. 189–196 in *Research in Population Economics*, vol. 1, Julian L. Simon, ed. Greenwich, Conn.: JAI, 1978.

Pennington, Jon Christopher. "The Role of Culture in Explaining the Failure of Social Movement Mobilization: Why Framing Is not Enough." Paper presented at the Annual Meeting of the American Sociological Association, Atlanta, August 2003.

Petchesky, Rosalind Pollack. *Abortion and Woman's Choice: The State, Sexuality, and Reproductive Freedom*. New York: Longman, 1984.

Pickens, Donald K. *Eugenics and the Progressives*. Nashville: Vanderbilt University Press, 1968.

Piven, Frances Fox, and Richard A. Cloward. "The Civil Rights Movement." Chapter 4, pp. 181–258, in *Poor People's Movements*. New York: Vintage, 1979.

Polletta, Francesca. *Freedom is an Endless Meeting: Democracy in American Social Movements*. Chicago and London: University of Chicago Press, 2002.

Popkin Samuel. *The Rational Peasant*. Berkeley: University of California Press, 1979.

Putnam, Robert. *Bowling Alone: The Collapse and Revival of American Community*. New York: Simon & Schuster, 2000.

Radway, Janice. *Reading the Romance: Women, Patriarchy, and Popular Literature*, 2nd ed. Chapel Hill: University of North Carolina Press, 1991.

Reagan, Leslie J. *When Abortion Was a Crime: Women, Medicine, and Law in the United States, 1867–1973*. Berkeley and Los Angeles: University of California Press, 1997.

Reed, James. *The Birth Control Movement and American Society: From Private Vice to Public Virtue*. Princeton, N.J.: Princeton University Press, 1983.

Reger, Jo. "More than One Feminism: Organizational Structure and the Construction of Collective Identity." Pp. 171–84 in *Social Movements*, Meyer, Whittier, and Robnett, eds.

Reher, Margaret Mary. "Leo XIII and Americanism." *Theological Studies* 34(1973):679–80.

Robnett, Belinda. "External Political Change, Collective Identities, and Participation in Social Movement Organizations." Pp. 266–85 in *Social Movements*, Meyer, Whittier, and Robnett, eds.

Roh, Jongho, and Donald P. Haider-Markel. "All Politics Is not Local: National Forces in State Abortion Initiatives," *Social Science Quarterly* 84(2003):15–31.

Rose, Susan D. "Women Warriors: The Negotiation of Gender in a Charismatic Community." *Sociological Analysis* 48(1987):245–58.

Rubin, Eva R. *Abortion, Politics, and the Courts: Roe v. Wade and Its Aftermath*, rev. ed. New York: Greenwood, 1987.

Ryan, John A., and Moorhouse F. X. Millar. *The State and the Church*. New York: Macmillan, 1922.

Saletan, William. *Bearing Right: How Conservatives Won the Abortion War*. Berkeley: University of California Press, 2003.

Sanders, Scott, and James M. Jasper. "Civil Politics in the Animal Rights Conflict: God terms versus Casuistry in Cambridge, Massachusetts." *Science, Technology, & Human Values* 19(1994):169–88.

Sanger, Margaret. "A Plan for Peace." *Birth Control Review* (April 1932): 107–8.

———. *An Autobiography*. New York: W. W. Norton and Company, 1938.

———. *Motherhood in Bondage*. New York: Brentano's, 1928.

———. *The Pivot of Civilization*. New York: Brentano's, 1922.

———. *Woman and the New Race*. New York: Truth Publishing, 1920.

Sarch, Amy. "Dirty Discourse: Birth Control Advertising in the 1920s and 1930s." Ph.D. dissertation, Annenberg School for Communication, University of Pennsylvania, 1994.

Sasson, Theodore. *Crime Talk: How Citizens Construct a Social Problem*. New York: Aldine de Gruyter, 1995.

Schuetz, Alfred. "The Stranger." *American Journal of Sociology* 49(1944):499–507.

Segers, Mary C., and Timothy A. Byrnes, eds. *Abortion Politics in American States*. Armonk, N.Y., and London: M. E. Sharpe, 1995.

———. "Introduction." Pp. 1–15 in *Abortion Politics in American States*, Segers and Byrnes, eds.

Selznick, Philip. *The Moral Commonwealth: Social Theory and the Promise of Community*. Berkeley: University of California Press, 1992.

Shorter, Edward. "Female Emancipation, Birth Control, and Fertility in European History." *American Historical Review* 78(1973):605–40.

Skrentny, John. *The Ironies of Affirmative Action: Politics, Culture, and Justice in America*. Chicago and London: University of Chicago Press, 1996.

Smelser, Neil. *Theory of Collective Behavior*. New York: Free Press, 1962.

Smith, Willard H. "William Jennings Bryan and the Social Gospel." *Journal of American History* 53(1966):41–60.

Smith-Rosenberg, Carroll. "The Abortion Movement and the AMA, 1850–1880." Pp. 217–44 in Smith-Rosenberg, *Disorderly Conduct: Visions of Gender in Victorian America*. New York: Knopf, 1985.

Snow, David A., and Robert D. Benford. 1992. "Master Frames and Cycles of Protest." Pp. 133–55 in *Frontiers of Social Movement Theory*, Morris and Mueller, eds.

_____. "Ideology, Frame Resonance, and Participant Mobilization," *International Social Movement Research* 1(1988):197–217.

Snow, David A., and Susan E. Marshall. "Cultural Imperialism, Social Movements, and the Islamic Revival." Pp. 131–52 in *Research in Social Movements, Conflict and Change*, vol. 7, Louis Kreisberg, ed. Greenwich, Conn.: JAI, 1984.

Snow, David A., E. Burke Rochford, Jr., Steven K. Worden, and Robert D. Benford. "Frame Alignment Processes, Micromobilization and Movement Participation." *American Sociological Review* 51(1986):464–81.

Solinger, Rickie. *The Abortionist: A Woman against the Law.* New York: The Free Press, 1994.

Staggenborg, Suzanne. *The Pro-Choice Movement: Organization and Activism in the Abortion Conflict.* New York: Oxford University Press, 1991.

Steinberg, Marc. "Toward a More Dialogic Analysis of Social Movement Culture." Pp. 208–25 in *Social Movements*, Meyer, Whittier, and Robnet, eds.

Steinhoff, Patricia G., and Milton Diamond. *Abortion Politics: The Hawaii Experience.* Honolulu: University Press of Hawaii, 1977.

Sulloway, Alvah W. *Birth Control and Catholic Doctrine.* Boston: Beacon, 1959.

Tentler, Leslie Woodcock. "'The Abominable Crime of Onan': Catholic Pastoral Practice and Family Limitation, 1875–1919." *Church History* 71(2002): 307–40.

Tribe, Lawrence. *Abortion: The Clash of Absolutes.* New York and London: W. W. Norton, 1992.

Useem, Bert. "Solidarity Model, Breakdown Model, and the Boston Anti-Busing Movement." *American Sociological Review* 45(1980):357–69.

Valenza, Charles. "Was Margaret Sanger a Racist?" *Family Planning Perspectives* 17, no. 1 (Jan–Feb 1985):44–5.

Wells, Robert V. *Revolutions in Americans' Lives: A Demographic Perspective on the History of Americans, Their Families, and Their Society.* Westport, Conn.: Greenwood, 1982.

Walsh, Edward J. "Resource Mobilization and Citizen Protest in Communities around Three Mile Island." *Social Problems* 29(1981):1–21.

Williams, Rhys H. "From the 'Beloved Community' to 'Family Values': Religious Language, Symbolic Repertoires, and Democratic Culture." Pp. 247–265 in *Social Movements*.

Steinhoff, Patricia G., and Milton Diamond. *Abortion Politics: The Hawaii Experience.* Honolulu: University Press of Hawaii, 1977.

Tarrow, Sidney. "Mentalities, Political Cultures, and Collective Action Frames: Constructing Meanings through Action." Pp. 174–202 in *Frontiers of Social Movement Theory*, Morris and Mueller, eds.

_____. *Power in Movement: Social Movements, Collective Action and Politics.* Cambridge: Cambridge University Press, 1994.

Tatalovich, Raymond. *The Politics of Abortion in the United States and Canada.* Armonk, N.Y.: M. E. Sharpe, 1997.

_____. and Byron W. Daynes. *The Politics of Abortion: A Study of Community Conflict in Public Policy Making.* New York: Praeger, 1981.

Tilly, Charles. *From Mobilization to Revolution.* Reading, Mass.: Addison-Wesley, 1978.

Turner, Ralph H. and Lewis M. Killian. *Collective Behavior.* Englewood Cliffs, N.J.: Prentice Hall, 1957.

Warner, R. Stephen. "Work in Progress toward a New Paradigm for the Sociological Study of Religion in the United States." *American Journal of Sociology* 98(1993):1044–93.

Weber, Max. *The Theory of Social and Economic Organization*, Talcott Parsons, ed. New York: Free Press/Macmillan, 1964.

Wetstein, Matthew E. *Abortion Rates in the United States: The Influence of Opinion and Policy.* Albany: State University of New York Press, 1996.

Whittier, Nancy "Meaning and Structure in Social Movements," pp. 289–307 in *Social Movements*, Meyer, Whittier, and Robnett, eds.

Williams, Rhys H. "From the 'Beloved Community' to 'Family Values': Religious Language, Symbolic Repertoires, and Democratic Culture." Pp. 247–65 in *Social Movements*, Meyer, Whittier, and Robnett, eds.

Wright, Mary C. "Separate or Equal? Integration and Separatism within Feminist Health Care Provision in the United States and England." Undergraduate Senior Thesis, Dept. of Sociology, Princeton University, 1993.

Wolfe, Alan. *One Nation After All.* New York: Viking/Penguin, 1998.

Wrong, Dennis. *The Problem of Order: What Unites and Divides Society.* New York: Free Press, 1994.

Zald, Mayer N. "Culture, Ideology, and Strategic Framing." Pp. 261–74 in *Comparative Perspectives on Social Movements*, McAdam, McCarthy, and Zald, eds.

_____. "Looking Backward to Forward: Reflections of the Past and Future of the Resource Mobilization Research Paradigm." Pp. 326–48 in *Frontiers in Social Movement Theory*, Morris and Mueller, eds.

Index

Abercrombie, Nicholas, 306
abolition (of slavery), movement for, 36
abortion. *See also* abortion laws; framing;
    pro-choice movement; pro-life
    movement
  access to, post–*Roe v. Wade*, 239–41
  access to, under reform laws, 208,
    210–11, 212, 221, 226
  as an uncontroversial issue, 3, 168–9,
    172
  Americans' mixed views on, 157–8
  birth control movement's view of, early
    20th-century, 50
  eugenics and, 104
  fetal viability and, 217, 223, 232
  framed as a civil right, 162
  framed as a medical, humanitarian
    issue, 5, 8, 104, 154, 162, 164,
    165–6, 167–9, 198–9, 213, 223–5,
    242–3, 272–3
  framed as a woman's right (feminist
    abortion rights frame), 5, 8, 162,
    165, 196, 200–1, 273–6
  frames affected by whether women
    were disenfranchised, 155
  hospital boards to approve, 167, 175,
    198, 200, 223, 280
  humanitarian frame separated from
    medical frame, 165, 210, 269–70,
    272–5, 282
  legally acceptable reasons for, 155, 164,
    165–6, 186, 187–8

  "partial birth" (intact dilation and
    extraction), 24, 237
  party politics and, 229–31
  polarization over the issue of, 152–3,
    225–8, 242, 313–14
  pro-choice frame, 7, 9–10, 297–8
  pro-life frame, 7–8, 10–11, 167, 182,
    188, 196, 200, 277–9
  public opinion on, 294, 310
  race and, 187–90
  "therapeutic," 164, 165, 174, 191, 200,
    208, 210, 224–5, 280
  violence, antiabortion, 19, 153, 234–7,
    295–7
Abortion in America. See James C. Mohr
abortion law, federal. *See also* individual
    U.S. Supreme Court cases
  antiracketeering law applied to
    antiabortion protests, 234
  constitutional amendment to outlaw
    abortion, proposed, 19, 22, 230,
    239, 279
  gag rule, 231
  revisions since *Roe v. Wade*, 228–9,
    233–4, 239
  role of courts, 12, 87, 221
abortion law, state-level. *See also* South
  "abortion mills," state legislators'
    concerns about, 174–5, 190
  clergy involved in liberalization
    movements, 163, 168, 205, 210,
    218

abortion law, state-level (*cont.*)
  controversy surrounding repeal laws,
    215
  eugenics and, 184, 189, 193
  lawyers involved in liberalization
    movements, 163, 168, 205
  legislators' approach to, 172–3, 174–6,
    191, 198
  morally charged frames and, 185, 193,
    195–205, 289
  moral vetoes of, 17, 191, 219–21, 310
  physicians' discretion within, 161–3
  referenda on, 214, 217, 218–19
  reform bills defeated, 182–3, 196–205,
    220
  reform laws passed (with medical,
    humanitarian frame), 1, 166, 168,
    182, 183–4, 214
  reform movement, 151, 163–8
  repeal bills defeated, 215, 218–19
  repeal laws, 180, 186, 192, 209–21
  repeal movement following
    dissatisfaction with reform, 210–14,
    272–5
  residency requirements, 175, 223
  restrictive laws, 19th-century, 155–62
  voting patterns in legislatures, 177–9,
    194–5, 203–5, 218, 227
abortion rights groups, 191–2, 209–11,
  212–13, 268–70, 274–5, 299. *See
  also* pro-choice movement
African Americans, 33–4, 69, 73, 74, 77,
  96, 103, 129, 131, 145, 189. *See also*
  eugenics
Alaska, 185, 192, 214, 216–17
Alaska Right to Life Committee, 216
Alliance for Humane Abortions (Alaska),
  216
American Birth Control League, 89, 90,
  91, 92, 93, 100, 111, 121
American Civil Liberties Union, 202
American Eugenics Society, 90, 93–4,
  98
American Law Institute (ALI),
  recommendations for abortion law
  reform, 163–4, 167, 173, 174, 184,
  185–7, 192, 194, 198, 212, 215,
  308
American Medical Association (AMA),
  163, 210, 267

anarchists, 55, 59–60, 74–5
Anglican Church, 131
Arizona, 167, 197–8
Arkansas, 185, 195
Associated Press, 201, 212

Bauer, Gary, 20
Beebe, Lorraine, 200
Beethoven, Ludwig van, 199
Beilenson, Anthony, 165, 173
Beisel, Nicola, 41
Benford, Robert D., 257, 261, 264
birth control. *See* abortion; birth control
  movement; contraception
birth control movement. *See also*
  Comstock laws; contraception;
  Margaret Sanger
  abortion, view of, 50
  eugenics and, 54, 89–93, 103–5, 125
  feminism and, 42, 58–9, 61–3, 67–8,
    93, 103
  grew in context of high social
    movement activity, 42, 51–9
  legislative failures, 4, 85
  socialism and, 1, 2, 8, 42, 48, 52–7, 93,
    270–1
Birth Control Review, 53, 81, 90
black Americans. *See* African Americans
Blackmun, Justice Harry, 223
Bolshevism, 56
Bryan, William Jennings, 73
Buchanan, Patrick, 18, 152, 279
Burstein, Paul, 299, 300
Bush, President George H. W., 18, 19, 24,
  230
Bush, President George W., 20, 231, 237,
  282
Byrne, Ethel, 44

California, 165, 169, 173–4, 181–2,
  183–4, 186, 191–2, 204, 210–11,
  221, 268
California Committee on Therapeutic
  Abortion, 165
Casti Connubii ("On Christian
  Marriage"), 120, 138, 140
Catholic Church. *See* Roman Catholic
  Church
Catt, Carrie Chapman, 36, 116
Chen, Constance M., 114

Chesler, Ellen, 26, 61, 75–6, 78, 89, 90, 94, 96, 99–101, 112–13
Christian Coalition, 19, 236
Christian Council of Metropolitan Atlanta, 189
Christian Right, 17–20, 22, 122, 151, 156, 171, 229, 235–6, 293
Church of England. *See* Anglican Church
Civil Rights Movement, U.S., 14–15, 34, 265–6, 296, 303
Civil War, U.S., 7, 33–4, 36
class bias
    eugenics and, 27, 71, 74, 78, 82, 94–7, 98, 99, 101, 104
    medical frames and, 31, 104, 112, 126, 129, 148–9, 280
Clergy Consultation Service, 218, 272
Clinton, President Bill, 229, 231, 236–7, 297
Colorado, 173–4, 180–2, 184, 186, 198, 211–12
communism, 56
Communist Party, American, 17
Comstock, Anthony, 29–30, 39–40, 41, 46, 78, 130, 149
Comstock laws, 29–30, 39–41, 42–8, 85, 123–4, 126
    birth control movement and, 31–2, 50, 51, 53, 54, 81, 132
    Catholics and, 129–30, 133, 136, 146–7, 148
    Connecticut, 142
    Massachusetts, 141–2
    nullified by court decisions, 86–7, 88, 125, 148–9
    opposition to, as a point of unity in birth control movement, 121
conflict theory, 305
Congress, U.S., 63, 85–6, 87, 89–90, 94, 95, 117, 125, 183
Connecticut, 40, 141–2, 157–8, 159–62
contraception. *See also* birth control movement; eugenics
    arguments against, 36, 47–8, 58
    arguments in favor of, 48–51
    contemporary access to, 301–2
    framed as a feminist issue, 30, 32–3, 77–9

framed as a socialist issue, 8, 16, 30–1, 32–3, 77–9, 277
framed within a moral worldview, 52, 70, 77–8, 293
laws liberalized by courts, 4, 11, 31–2, 311
legislatures' hesitance to address, 31–2, 85–6, 117, 129–30
methods of, 37–8, 40, 137, 139–40, 302
minorities and immigrants derogated in framing of, 25, 69, 103, 280
opposition to, within women's movements, 37, 64–5
popular support for, 1, 31, 39, 48, 86, 141–2
reframed as a medical issue, 4, 31, 107, 128 (*See also* Margaret Sanger)
taboo nature of, 37, 38–9, 62, 123
Coser, Rose, 252
Cott, Nancy, 58–9, 64, 66, 110
Coughlin, Rev. Charles, 134
Creationism, 72
cultural pluralism, 306–7, 314. *See also* limiting frames
culture war. *See also* abortion
    as a popular concept, 18–19, 151–2, 279
    as a sociological concept, 151–3
Cuomo, Mario, 297

Darwin, Charles, 71, 72, 73
Debs, Eugene V., 30, 53
Degler, Carl N., 72
Delaware, 160, 174, 186–7, 196, 201, 220
Democratic Party, 18, 92, 180, 196, 229
Dennett, Mary Ware, 25, 27, 43, 111
    birth control as part of larger social justice agenda, 106, 108, 114–19, 126, 127
    Catholicism, view of, 119–21
    Comstock laws and, 40–1, 44, 45–6, 51, 109–10, 124, 127, 128
    eugenics and, 72, 122–3
    her politics misunderstood, 110–14
    feminism and, 60, 61
    opposed Sanger's medical framing of contraception, 30–1, 81, 82–3, 109, 112, 116–17

Dennett, Mary Ware (*cont.*)
  role in birth control movement,
    111–12, 121–2, 128
  strategically less effective than
    Margaret Sanger, 83, 106, 108, 110,
    116–17, 122, 126–7, 128, 143, 277
Diamond, Milton, 217
Dickinson, Robert L., 83–4
Dienes, C. Thomas, 129, 130, 136–7, 142
discourse analysis, 245
Dillon, Michele, 135, 153
Doe v. Bolton (1973), 3, 5, 12, 149, 208,
    221–8, 231. *See also Roe v. Wade*
Dole, Bob, 19
Durkheimian sociology, 21–2, 246–7,
    254, 277, 304–5, 308, 312

Eisenstadt v. Baird (1972), 31
Eliasoph, Nina, 260
Ellis, Havelock, 76
Equal Rights Amendment (E.R.A.),
    proposed, 59
Essay on the Principle of Population, 71
eugenics. *See also* birth control movement;
    class bias; Margaret Sanger
  contraception and, 27, 32, 69–80
  immigration and, 48–51, 72, 74, 77,
    101, 103
  harsher versions in the 1930s, 90–102,
    301
  not an intrinsic component of birth
    control frame, 103–5, 122–3, 128–9,
    301
  Naziism and, 75–6, 91, 97–8, 104,
    184, 202, 301
  race and, 74, 77, 78, 102
  socialism and, 74–5, 76, 103
  variety of perspectives within, 70–7
Europe, 167
  abortion in, 242–3, 308–10
  contraception, advocacy of, 80, 131,
    137
  Catholic opposition to contraception,
    120, 131–2
  eugenics in, 75, 93
  socialism in, 114
evolution. *See also* eugenics; social
    Darwinism
  Darwinian theory of, 72–3
  Lamarckian (and neo-Lamarckian)
    view of, 73–4

Falwell, Rev. Jerry, 17, 18, 236
Family Limitation (birth control
    pamphlet), 43, 53
"Family Limitation" (Catholic anti–birth
    control article), 132
feminism, 283. *See also* birth control
    movement; contraception; suffrage
  abortion and, 150, 230, 268
  equal rights approach to, 59, 62
  limiting frames within, 62–5
  separate spheres approach to, 64–5, 85
  socialism, relationship to, 59–60
  use of the term, historically, 58, 65,
    85
fertility rates, U.S., 38, 40, 42, 47,
    58
Finkbine, Sherri, 166–7
Fireman, Bruce, 257, 258–9
First Amendment (to the U.S.
    Constitution), 291, 312–13
Florida, 173–4, 196–7, 204,
    215
framing. *See also* limiting frames, moral
    worldviews; moral veto
  affected by entry or elimination of
    players, 271–7
  bridging frames, 11, 246, 252–3,
    264–77, 284
  collective identity and, 267–75, 276,
    278
  comparing history of abortion frames
    and contraception frames, 151
  concept explained, 7, 8–9
  disenfranchised groups, derogated
    within, 24–5, 69, 78–80, 280–1, 301
  "injustice" frames, 276
  reflecting who is included in a
    conversation, 11, 25, 69–70, 244–5,
    266–7
Freedom of Access to Clinics Act (FACE),
    236, 238
Friedman, Debra, 257
Fung, Archon, 169, 226

Gamson, William A., 257, 258–9, 276
Garrow, David J., 169, 180–1, 187–8,
    218
George, Henry, 114–15, 116
Georgia, 160, 173, 180–1, 184, 185, 187,
    188–9, 192–3, 204, 216, 218
Germany, 137, 262, 265, 309

Ginsburg, Faye, 10, 191, 197, 229–30
Ginsburg, Justice Ruth Bader, 225
Glendon, Mary Ann, 170, 225–7, 308–12
Goffman, Erving, 256
Goldman, Emma, 30, 36, 43, 46, 52–3, 57, 60, 74, 111, 124
Gooch, Laurel F., 180, 188–9
Gordon, Linda, 26, 56, 81, 105, 113, 114
Granovetter, Mark S., 251–2
Great Britain, 242, 308–9
Griswold v. Connecticut (1965), 31, 84, 88, 142, 149, 222, 311

Hatfield, Henry D., 89–90
Hawaii, 182, 185, 192, 214, 215, 217
health care system (affecting reproductive politics), 242–3, 301–2, 308–9
Heterodoxy (feminist group), 61, 116
Hitler, Adolf, 97
homosexuality, 19, 236, 279
Hoover, President Herbert, 146
Hunter, James Davison, 229–30, 304, 308
Hyde Amendment, 228–9, 240

immigrants (to the United States), 33, 34–5, 129–38 *See also* eugenics
interest groups, explanatory problems with the concept of, 21, 87, 147–8, 294
International Workers of the World (Wobblies), 53, 74, 132
infanticide, 160
Illinois, 220
Iowa, 18, 189

Jacob, Herbert, 183
Jain, Sagar C., 180, 188–9, 192
Japan, 137
Jewish Community Council (Atlanta, Georgia), 189
Jews, 33–5, 76
Johnston, Hank, 257
John Paul II, Pope, 295
Johnson, Victoria, 297
Jones, Eleanor (a.k.a. Mrs. F. Robertson Jones), 111, 121

Kansas, 174, 186, 195
Keller, Helen, 199

Kennedy, David M., 26, 49, 85, 94, 101, 133
Kennedy, President John F., 147
Keyes, Alan, 20
King, Martin Luther, Jr., 292
Kingdon, John W., 219
Knowlton, Charles, 38
Ku Klux Klan, 119, 146

Lader, Lawrence, 169, 180, 187, 210, 272
Ladies' Home Journal, 102
Lamarck, Jean Baptiste de Monet, 73
Lamm, Richard, 184, 212
Latz, Leo J., 138, 139
Lee, Mei-Hsien, 170, 181–2, 190–1
LeMay, Curtis, 192
Leo XIII, Pope, 131
Lichterman, Paul, 260
limiting frames. *See also* framing; moral worldviews, social movements
  concept explained, 13–14, 16, 24, 80, 276
  courts' use of, 86–8, 288–9, 291
  cultural pluralism and, 21–2, 28, 246, 281–4, 301–3
  elite nature of some, 166, 167–8, 205, 210, 214, 224, 273
  leaving future options open, 301–3
  medical frames as, 28, 70, 80–5, 86–8 (*See also* contraception; abortion)
  political vulnerabilities of, 206, 207–8, 227, 288–91
  relationship to moderation of movement goals, 65–7, 88
  religious pluralism and, 291–2, 312–13
  strategic effectiveness of, 84–5, 109, 266, 272, 284
  widespread cultural assumptions and, 279–84, 301
Louisiana, 181
Loyola University Medical School, 138
Luker, Kristin, 162, 165, 168, 169–70, 183, 187, 191, 210–11, 222, 268, 269, 272, 273, 298

McAdam, Doug, 256, 257
McCann, Carole R., 26, 50, 60, 79, 100–1, 114
McCarthy, John, 124, 256
Maddox, Lester, 188–9

Maine, 173, 198, 200, 203, 204–5
Malthus, Thomas, 71
Malthusianism (and neo-Malthusianism), 74
Mandel, Marvin, 215
Massachusetts, 141–2, 181
Marxism
    Marxist sociology, 306
    Marxists and birth control, 55, 131
Maryland, 173–4, 186, 212, 215–16, 220

mechanical solidarity, 278
Medicaid, 228–9, 240, 302
medical framing. *See* framing,
medical profession, United States,
    267–70 *See also* abortion; birth
    control movement, framing limiting
    frames
    Comstock laws and, 4, 40, 44, 45, 104
    favoring abortion reform laws, 1950s
        and 1960s, 1, 151, 163–4
    opposition to abortion, 19th-century,
        1, 36, 50, 78, 150, 157–8, 159–62
    "regulars," 159
methodological challenges to studying
    culture, 287–8
Michigan, 173, 200–1, 218, 220
Midwest, 240
midwives, 156, 164
Miller, Keith H., 216–17
Mills, C. Wright, 306
Mississippi, 186, 187–8, 190, 193, 214
Missouri, 232
Mohr, James C., 156–7, 160, 162, 164,
    227
Mooney, Christopher Z., 170, 181–2,
    190–1
Moral Majority, 17, 236
moral veto. *See also* abortion law; Roman
        Catholic Church
    concept explained, 22–4
    conditions under which moral vetoes
        are effective, 285–7, 291
    legislatures, relevance to, 23, 86, 87,
        125, 300, 310–11
    policy windows and, 219–20, 227
    relationship to prevailing cultural
        dispositions, 23–4, 144, 285–7
    role of courts in resolving, 23, 86–8,
        148, 300, 310–11

moral worldviews. *See also* framing
    among activists, 268
    concept explained, 16–17
    danger of strong victimization of
        disenfranchised groups, 302
    political obstacles, 19, 21–2, 266, 277,
        278
    social movement solidarity and, 19,
        270, 272, 278–9, 293
    societal level, 277–8
Motherhood in Bondage, 60–1, 76

National Abortion Federation, 235
National Birth Control League, 49, 71,
    112, 115, 123
National Committee on Federal
    Legislation for Birth Control, 56,
    86
National Health Service (United
    Kingdom), 242
National Liberal League, 47
National American Woman Suffrage
    Association, 61, 63, 113, 116
National Association for the Repeal of
    Abortion Laws (NARAL, later
    renamed National Abortion Rights
    Action League), 212
National Organization for Women, 202,
    212
National Right to Life Committee, 213,
    218
National Woman Suffrage Association,
    30
National Woman's Party, 30, 59, 63
Native Americans, 73
Nebraska, 238
neo-Malthusianism. *See* Malthusianism
New Deal, 92–4, 104, 129, 133, 136,
    147
New England, 181
New Hampshire, 173, 199, 204
New Jersey, 201–3, 220
New Jersey Association for Brain Injured
    Children, 202
New Jersey Medical Society, 202
New Mexico, 174, 182, 186, 216
New York Society for the Suppression of
    Vice, 39
New York, state of, 87, 182, 185, 192,
    210, 214, 216, 217, 218, 220–1

New York Times, 192, 201, 211
Nichols, Thomas Low and Mary Gove, 38
Noonan, John T., Jr., 140
North Carolina, 173–4, 180–1, 184, 185, 189, 191, 192–3, 198, 212
North Dakota, 197–8, 218, 240
Nosiff, Rosemary, 170

O'Boyle, Cardinal Patrick, 215
O'Connor, Justice Sandra Day, 231
Oklahoma, 173, 204, 218
Olasky, Marvin, 123, 156–7, 160
Olson, Mancur, 255
O'Neil, Daniel J., 197
Operation Rescue, 234–6, 239, 279, 296–7
Oregon, 119, 186
organic solidarity, 305
Origin of Species (On the Origin of Species by Means of Natural Selection), 71

Parsonian sociology, 306
Pennsylvania, 233
People's Council of America, 115
Perot, Ross, 184
Petchesky, Rosalind Pollack, 26
physicians. *See* medical profession
Pius XI, Pope, 120, 138, 140
Pius XII, Pope, 138
Pivot of Civilization, The, 100
Planned Parenthood, 105, 122, 141
    Connecticut, Planned Parenthood of, 142
Planned Parenthood of Southeast Pennsylvania v. Casey (1992), 232–3, 240, 241
Polletta, Francesca, 260
postmodernism, 276, 283–4
pro-choice movement. *See also* abortion rights groups
    Democratic party and, 229, 236–7
    historical perspective on abortion and, 155, 157
    less movement solidarity than pro-life movement, 298–9
    pluralist frame distinct from "abortion rights" frame, 297–8

pro-life movement, 181–91, 212–13, 229–31
    Catholic pro-life movement, 183, 197–8, 209–10, 216, 218, 268–9, 276
    historical perspective on abortion and, 155
    limited success of, 12, 23–4, 153, 156–7, 239, 279, 293, 299
    militant wing of, 234–6, 239
    moral worldview within, 293–7
    Republican party and, 230–1, 237, 241
    South, in the, 1, 181, 185, 191, 192
prostitution, 39, 60, 61, 133, 156
Protestantism
    Catholicism, suspicion of, 145, 286
    contraception, opposition to, 130, 135, 286–7
    eugenic concerns with dominance of, 32, 33, 58, 69, 71, 131, 134
    evangelical, 156, 192, 235–6, 283
Putnam, Robert, 250

quickening, 156, 159

"race suicide" argument, 71, 131, 134–6
Reagan, Leslie J., 163
Reagan, President Ronald, 17, 24, 229, 230–1, 299
recipes (as a sociological concept), 281–2
Reconstruction, 34
"Red Scare" (after World War I), 57
Reed, James, 26, 110, 116
Reed, Ralph, 123, 236
Reform Party, 184
Reger, Jo, 246
Religious Right. *See* Christian Right
religious pluralism in the U.S., 291–2
Republican Party, 17–18, 19–20, 24, 152, 180, 196, 229–31, 233 *See also* pro-life movement
Rhode Island, 181
Rhythm of Sterility and Fertility in Women, The, 138, 139
Robertson, Rev. Pat, 18, 19, 236
Robnet, Belinda, 246
Rockefeller family (and birth control movement), 90
Rockefeller, Nelson, 216

Roe v. Wade (1973), 3, 5, 12, 149, 191–2,
    221–8
  access to abortion after, 169, 300
  controversy over, 170, 314
  declining Supreme Court majority in
    favor of *Roe*, 231, 233, 238
  limiting (medical) frame, as a
    component of, 28, 208, 221–5
  political consequences if reversed,
    300
  privacy rights and, 169, 222–3, 232
  scholarly analysis of the significance of,
    153–4, 170, 225–7, 308–12
  state abortion policy (pre-1973) that
    resembled, 210–11, 214
  Supreme Court avoiding an explicit
    moral worldview, 223–4
Roman Catholic Church. *See also*
    Comstock laws, pro-life movement
  abortion, opposition to, 182, 183, 191,
    197–8, 202–3, 215, 235
  contraception, increased focus in early
    20th century, 132
  contraception, losing the battle over,
    132–3, 136–7, 139–41
  contraception, opposition to, 1, 23,
    31, 91, 106–7, 119–20, 129–44,
    148
  eugenics and, 131, 134–6
  immigration and, 33–5, 145
  laity diverging from hierarchy on
    contraception and abortion, 132,
    140–1
  loyalty to the U.S., suspicions about,
    145–6, 147–8
  moral veto over liberalizing
    contraception laws, 1, 23, 107,
    108–9, 129–30, 136–7, 141–2,
    146–9, 286–7
  natural law doctrine of, 132–3, 135,
    286
  Margaret Sanger, opposition to, 132
  New Deal and, 92–3, 133–4, 135–6,
    147
  political weakness, 19th and early 20th
    centuries, 1, 106–7, 144–6
  view of religious freedom and
    church–state relations, 119, 120,
    286
  rhythm method and, 120, 137–41

  use of arguments not specifically
    Catholic (to oppose contraception),
    129–30, 134–5, 136, 286–8
  the Vatican, 131, 137, 138 (*See also*
    individual popes)
Roosevelt, Eleanor, 92
Roosevelt, President Franklin Delano, 92,
    136, 147. *See also* New Deal
Roosevelt, President Theodore, 71
rubella, 166, 180, 202
Rubin, Eva R. 224
Russian Revolution, 56, 115
Ryan, Rev. John, 132, 133–4, 136, 145–6

Saleten, William, 298
Sanger, Margaret, 26, 86. *See also* birth
    control movement
  belief in radical implications of birth
    control, 127
  Comstock laws and, 43–4, 45–6, 62,
    109, 124
  eugenics and, 26, 74, 76–7, 89–103
  feminism and, 60–1, 62–3
  leader of birth control movement, 3, 4,
    52, 56, 106, 107–8, 109, 121–2, 128,
    143, 267
  mainstreaming contraception through
    medical framing, 30–1, 80–3, 125,
    137, 276
  New Deal and, 92–3, 136
  opposition to racial discrimination,
    96
  personal life of, 50, 113
  radicalism (early in birth control
    movement), 52–3, 54, 60, 61, 126,
    271
  self-promoting, 110–11
  view of Roman Catholicism, 49, 93,
    106, 120–1, 140, 143–4
Sanger, William, 43, 53
Sarch, Amy, 40
Schuetz, Alfred, 281
Selznick, Philip, 225, 307–8
Sex Side of Life, The (sex education
    pamphlet), 44, 84
sexuality (as a matter of controversy), 23,
    30, 37, 38, 47, 50, 62, 63, 89, 120,
    144, 146–7, 148, 285–7
Sinding, Steven W., 180
Slee, Noah, 90

Smith, Al, 92, 146
Snow, David, 256, 261, 264
social Darwinism, 73, 77–85, 96. *See also*
eugenics; evolution
social movements, 42. *See also* limiting
frames; moral worldviews
contribution to social change, 6,
12–13, 20–1
dominant frames dependent upon
identities within the coalition of,
78–9, 91–2
as obstacles to limiting frames, 32–3,
123–4
relationship to moral vetoes, 5, 11, 12
social movement theory
brokerage, concept of, 265
collective behavior theory, 253–4
cultural approaches, 258–62, 263–4,
266–70
frame analysis, 256–7, 260–6
network analysis, 255, 260
"new" social movements, 264–5
rational choice theory, 253, 255–6,
258–9, 260
resource mobilization and political
process theory, 253–7, 260, 262–3,
278
social order, 246–7, 304–14
socialism. *See* birth control movement;
contraception; eugenics; Margaret
Sanger; Socialist Party
Socialist Party, 29–30, 35, 41, 51–7, 60,
114. *See also* contraception
South (southern U.S.), 240. *See also*
individual states
abortion laws of, 1, 2, 5, 6, 151, 169,
171–6, 185, 191–2, 196, 219
absence of effort to repeal abortion
laws, 192, 215
racist eugenics and, 102
South Carolina, 173, 184, 185, 193–4,
195, 219
South Dakota, 240
spiritualism, 156
State and the Church, The, 145
Steinberg, Marc, 260, 263
Steinhoff, Patricia G., 217
stem cell research, 282
Stenberg v. Carhart (2000), 238
Stephens, Frank, 114

sterilization, coerced, 90, 95, 96–7, 98,
189
Stopes, Marie, 45
Storer, Horatio, 78
Souter, Justice David, 231
suffrage, women's, 35, 36, 58–9
equal rights feminism, relationship to,
59
limiting frame within the movement
for, 63–6
Margaret Sanger's view of, 116
Mary Ware Dennett's involvement in,
115–16
racial and ethnic prejudice within the
movement for, 36
Sulloway, Alvah W., 133–4, 137
Supreme Court (United States). *See*
individual case names
Sweden, 167

temperance movement, 36, 64
Tarrow, Sidney, 265
Tentler, Leslie Woodcock, 132
thalidomide, 166–7, 180
Thomas, Justice Clarence, 20, 231
*Thornburgh v. American College of
Obstetricians and Gynecologists*
(1986), 233

Valenza, Charles, 99–100
Vermont, 204
Virginia, 185, 194, 219
voluntary motherhood, 19th-century idea
of, 47
Voluntary Parenthood League, 117, 118,
121

Wallace, George, 192
Washington, D.C., 215, 229
Washington, state of, 185, 192, 214, 217,
218
"weak ties," the strength of, 251–2
Weber, Max, 267, 281, 290
Webster v. Reproductive Health Services
(1989), 232, 241, 298
Wobblies. *See* International Workers of
the World
"white slavery," early-20th-century
moral panic about, 60

Williams, Rhys, 260
Wilson, President Woodrow, 118
World War I, 54, 99, 118, 145, 147
  repression of Socialists during and
    after, 56, 57
  Socialist opposition to, 30, 42, 51

World War II, 87, 104, 105, 147, 148,
  163–8, 242
Woman Rebel, 43, 53, 54, 60
Women's Peace Party, 113

Zald, Mayer, 124, 256